Tradition and Fantasy in the Tales of Reb Nahman of Bratslav

SUNY Series in Judaica: Hermeneutics, Mysticism, and Religion
Michael Fishbane, Robert Goldenberg, and Elliot Wolfson, Editors

TRADITION AND FANTASY IN THE TALES OF REB NAHMAN OF BRATSLAV

ORA WISKIND-ELPER

STATE UNIVERSITY OF NEW YORK PRESS

Published by
State University of New York Press, Albany

Printed in the United States of America

For information, address the State University of New York Press,
State University Plaza, Albany, NY 12246

Production by Bernadine Dawes • Marketing by Patrick Durocher

Library of Congress Cataloging-in-Publication Data

Wiskind-Elper, Ora, 1960–
Tradition and fantasy in the tales of Reb Nahman of Bratslave / Ora Wiskind-Elper.
p. cm. — (SUNY series in Judaica)
Includes bibliographical references and index.
ISBN 0-7914-3813-9 (hardcover : alk. paper). — ISBN 0-7914-3814-7 (pbk. : alk. paper)
1. Naḥman of Bratslav, 1772–1811. 2. Hasidic parables—History and criticism. I. Title. II. Series.
BM532.W57 1998
296.1'9—dc21 97-39254
CIP

1 2 3 4 5 6 7 8 9 10

To my parents

CONTENTS

PREFACE

In November 1920, Rainer Maria Rilke wrote to a close friend: "Always at the commencement of work that first innocence must be re-achieved, you must return to that unsophisticated spot where the angel discovered you when he brought you the first binding message. . . ." As this work nears completion, my memory of its inception is abidingly present. Erich Heller, of blessed memory, first taught me that literature—if we are to read it authentically—must be lived, and his intense love for European culture has guided me since my undergraduate years at Northwestern University. It was Joshua Amir who opened the world of Jewish thought to me, and his inspiration and kindness led me from Heidelberg to Jerusalem. Stéphane Mosès has encouraged me in many ways to seek a synthesis between European literature and Jewish sources. This book first took form as a doctoral thesis in Hebrew written at the Hebrew University in Jerusalem. Special gratitude is owed to Jacob Elbaum for his generous guidance as my doctoral advisor there and to my dissertation committee for their invaluable criticism. I also thank my teachers, Avivah Gottlieb Zornberg, R. Daniel Epstein, and R. Avraham Smadja, whose wisdom and insight have been a vital force in my life. My gratitude to Susan Handelman for her advice and encouragement.

My appreciation to the Memorial Foundation for Jewish Culture and the Warburg Scholarship of the Hebrew University for their aid.

The unfailing support of my parents over years and continents has been a great source of strength. Thanks, finally, to my husband Eliezer and to our children.

Rilke concludes his thought: "If the angel deigns to come, it will be because you have convinced him, not with tears, but with your humble resolve to be always beginning: to be a beginner!" So many pages written, and yet the sense remains that so much is left undone, or is yet to be done. But perhaps that is the gift of awareness the blind beggar in Reb Nahman's tale really gives his listeners: the ability to be very old and yet completely young—not yet or only just becoming alive.

Introduction

The reflections that have burgeoned into the present work began with an unpremeditated encounter with the Hasidic tales of Reb Nahman of Bratslav (1772–1810). The initial sense was one of lightness, familiarity. The world in them—peopled by kings and princesses and laughing forest creatures, where journeys to golden mountains and enchanted cities shape heroes' destinies and transformations are sudden and astonishing—had been charted already in childhood fairy tales, by E. T. A. Hoffman, Guy de Maupassant, Jorge Luis Borges. As a postmodern reader and willing accomplice to all flights of an author's imagination, the anomalies and paradoxes the tales presented were compelling though abstruse. The complete lack, in the tales, of any indication their landscape was a Jewish world was, on second thought, somewhat striking as the "hero" of traditional Hasidic tales is usually the rebbe himself, and its "message" the teaching embodied in the way he lived his life. Implicit in a narrator's telling of traditional Hasidic tales is praise of the master's righteousness and sanctity, and explicit are the wonders he worked and the miracles that befell him. Here, in contrast, the zaddik and storyteller, never mentioned by name, seemed to exert an uncanny presence—not as subject but as creator. The utterly unconservative self-referentiality of Reb Nahman's tales became increasingly apparent with further reading, rereading, and exploration of his wider oeuvre and commentary on it. The "self" referred to, of course, in the tales Reb

Nahman told takes diverse forms. It is metahistorical, identifying with traditional heroes cloaked in legend; it is reflected in alter egos, characters that people the tales; it is even a surreal empathy with the very symbols, metaphors, and allegories of Jewish tradition transformed in the narrative. While it may be argued that many an author's own signature permeates his work, I believe Reb Nahman's oeuvre and his tales in particular are a rare and moving testimony this phenomenon can take place within the Hasidic world as well.

Various scholars have remarked, in one way or another, on the interrelationship between Reb Nahman's persona and his works. Most familiar to the English-speaking reader is surely Arthur Green's *Tormented Master* (1981), a psychobiography of the founder of the Bratslav Hasidic movement. Using memoirs and other material recorded for the most part by Reb Nahman's leading disciple and scribe, R. Nathan Sternharz of Nemirov, and guided by self-revelatory statements in Reb Nahman's own teaching and tales, Green formulated a "life" of the master. Central to Green's discussion are the spiritual trials he saw as besetting Reb Nahman's soul, with all their grave theological and philosophical ramifications; Green portrays Reb Nahman as a beacon for modern man, a guide and inspiration in enduring our own existential struggles.

Research published in Hebrew covers a wide variety of interests. In a collection of essays by Joseph Weiss (1972), written over a period of years and republished together posthumously, the author surveys what he isolates as the major themes in Reb Nahman's thought. Weiss's psychoanalytical insights, rooted in Reb Nahman's writings and his own sympathetic reading, exert a somewhat disputed influence on the way he portrayed his subject. The incisive theoretical and philosophical thrust of his work, though, indisputably places Reb Nahman as a seminal thinker, not only within the Hasidic world but in Western intellectual history as well.

The second important Hebrew monograph on the founder of Bratslav Hasidism is that of Mendel Piekarz (1974). Major events of Reb Nahman's life provide the structure for his discussion, which also includes a survey of the corpus of literature composed by Reb Nahman's followers. No aspect of the master's oeuvre, Piekarz contends, can be understood without attention to conditions surrounding him as he wrote and taught.

The light these scholars have shed on Reb Nahman's teaching has been invaluable in my own work, illuminating many dimensions—historical, ideological, and psychological—vital to an understanding of his thought. All of them focus on the three fundamental source texts preserved in Bratslav tradition: the teachings collected in *Likkutei Moharan*, the tales, and the records of Reb Nahman's life and times entitled *Hayyei Moharan,* penned by his preeminent disciple. The differences among these source texts in genre, in purpose, and in atmosphere do much to account for the diverse ways in which their author/subject is perceived.

The theoretical structure of Reb Nahman's worldview is set out unsystematically, with flashes of exegetical inspiration, seeming reiteration, belaborings, and, at times, labyrinthine associations, anagrams, even mathematical calculations, in the teachings Reb Nahman spoke to his *hasidim* throughout his life. Beginning with passages drawn from the Bible, the Talmud and the *Zohar*, he used the exegetical style adopted by other Hasidic masters as well to uncover new meaning concealed in their familiar words. Many of the teachings in *Likkutei Moharan* indirectly address events in Reb Nahman's public and even private life; the value of all of them, however, extends far beyond the biographical "evidence" they offer.

The tales Reb Nahman told, thirteen in all and recounted to his followers during the last four years of his life, share many of the motifs, images, and concepts developed in the teachings, but their form is wholly different. Each narrative, with its own setting, plot, and cast of characters, presents a self-contained fantasy world born of its author's imagination and received Jewish tradition. Some of the symbolic and allegorical threads woven into the tales beckon invitingly toward interpretation, while other elements remain elusive, enigmatic.

Both in the case of *Likkutei Moharan* and the tales, certain technical problems face a critical reader. First and foremost, a number of the teachings and all of the tales were not composed as written texts but rather recounted orally and only later transcribed. The textual uncertainties arising from such a process are evident and become compounded when we recall that the language of Jewish discourse in nineteenth-century Ukraine was not Hebrew but Yiddish. Whether the tales were first transcribed in Hebrew or in Yiddish remains a matter of contention; in either instance, the problem of translation shadows both *Likkutei Moharan* and the canonical tales, and is especially critical for the latter.

In the case of *Hayyei Moharan*—the chronicle of Reb Nahman's life, conversations, dreams, and aphorisms, presented wholly unchronologically—reservations take another form. The personal interest a loyal disciple could have in preserving his master's memory for generations to come must unquestionably affect, in any number of ways, the account he writes. My interest here is not to doubt the veracity of *Hayyei Moharan* or any other biographical source, but only to point out that works *about* an individual differ in nature and status from ones *by* him, even if these are received secondhand or in translation.

Reb Nahman's followers, in his own lifetime and increasingly after his death at the age of thirty-eight, devoted themselves to compiling, interpreting, and expanding their rebbe's teaching. The most extensive of such efforts is *Likkutei Halakhot* (1861–90), composed over a period of thirty years by R. Nathan Sternharz of Nemirov, with the purpose of promulgating Bratslav teaching throughout the Jewish world. His work is a series of discourses—partly kabbalistic, partly moralizing, rich in original thought—structured after the *Shulkhan ʿArukh*, the authoritative codification of Jewish law. In effect, it contains a ramified commentary both on the teachings recorded in *Likkutei Moharan* and on the thirteen canonical tales. Exegesis of the tales is interspersed throughout the numerous volumes of *Likkutei Halakhot*. A second source of commentary by Bratslav *hasidim*, different in nature and intent from the former, is *Rimzei Maʿasiyot* (1902) by R. Nahman of Tcherin. This compact work treats each of the tales individually and is included at the end of the standard Bratslav edition of the tales. A third figure instrumental in disseminating Bratslav teaching was R. Abraham Hazan of the late nineteenth century; he was the son of R. Nahman of Tulchin, assistant and disciple of R. Nathan. He comments on the tales in his works *Kokhvei Or*, *Sihot ve-Sippurim*, and *Beʾur ha-Likkutim*.

Interest in Reb Nahman's tales (outside the circle of Bratslav *hasidim*) was reawakened in the early twentieth century, partly through Martin Buber's German and romanticizing translation of the tales in 1906. Renderings of the tales into English have followed; the first translation of all thirteen canonical tales to be published is Arnold Band's *Nahman of Bratslav: The Tales* (1978). In his introduction and commentary, Band emphasizes the literary characteristics of the tales, such as plot structure, folk motifs, and basic kabbalistic allegories, and presents them as a mode of "spiritual autobiography" deliberately chosen. A second English translation, initiated and supported by modern-day Bratslav *hasidim,* is Aryeh Kaplan's *Rabbi Nahman's Tales* (1983). The volume opens with the First Introduction and Second Introduction by R. Nathan of Nemirov that preface the standard Bratslav Hebrew edition of the tales. The line-by-line commentary that accompanies each of the thirteen tales sets the Hebrew version against the Yiddish, develops numerous biblical, midrashic, and kabbalistic allusions, and refers frequently to writings by Reb Nahman and later Bratslav exegesis. A third translation of selected tales is Adin Steinsaltz's *The Tales of Rabbi Nachman of Bratslav* (1993). Previously published in 1979 under another title, each tale translated is followed by an explication of the central motifs and concepts underlying them in mystical thought, such as exile, the human form, time, the Shekhinah, and redemption. Steinsaltz stresses the literary and homiletic value of the tales by presenting the paradigms he sees at their core.

The earliest scholarly attempt to approach Reb Nahman's tales in the context of a literary analysis was made by Joseph Dan (1975) in his comprehensive Hebrew study of the Hasidic tale as a genre. Dan devotes a chapter to the Bratslav tales and discusses them in depth, with attention to kabbalistic symbolism, on one hand, and to elements drawn from traditional Bratslav commentary, on the other. Additional literary criticism of the tales includes: a structural analysis of one tale by Yoav Elstein (1984); an interpretation of symbols and folkloristic elements in a selection of the tales by Henie Haidenberg and Michal Oron (1986)—both in Hebrew; and an excursus on episodes from some of the tales by Arthur Green (1979), based on the portrait of Reb Nahman sketched in his biography. Most recently, David Roskies, in his study of the Yiddish storytelling tradition, *A Bridge of Longing* (1995), emphasizes the cultural significance of the tales and brings to the fore Reb Nahman's profound impact on later generations of Jewish writers.

An interested reader, then, can find his way relatively easily into Reb Nahman's tales themselves and gain, as well, some notion of the basic conceptual scaffolding on which they are built. But while general description of classic symbols, allegories, and paradigms from Jewish tradition does shed light on some aspects of the tales, it remains insufficient in a number of very significant ways. An artist's genius, for one, is measured not by his conformity with established forms but by his break with them: to point out allusions to pre-texts in his work is an essential first step, but leaves unexplored his transformation of them and the power that transformation wields. Caution, moreover, is needed in applying fixed schemas to a dynamic mode of creative expression, lest its unique form be contorted to fit the constructs brought to explain it. Finally, to define a work only within its most immediate cultural and literary context ignores a host of influences (conscious and subconscious), conditions, and phenomena essential to a full appreciation of it.

My attempt, in discussing Reb Nahman's tales, has been to address all three of these problems. Chapter 4 was the first to evolve. Comparison with the genre of "fantastic" literature opens up questions about mythopoeia and metamorphosis and the changeful interface between "reality" and other dimensions, and suggests a new and broader conceptual framework in which to regard—and appreciate—his oeuvre as a whole.

The other three chapters, in a sense, fill in some of the foreground, and background of the ideas of the fourth. In chapter 1, some issues useful in understanding Reb Nahman's spiritual and cultural Jewish context are raised, issues that were instrumental in forming his self-image as charismatic leader, zaddik, innovator. Questions of messianism and redemption are raised, less for their personal, biographical relevance than for their significance as narrative elements that invest the tales with great urgency.

The possibility of self-referentiality, however, exists not only on the level of characters and their destinies. Fiction itself is sanctified in Hasidic tradition and thus certain tales, when they are told, are believed to have an effect on worlds far beyond the teller's own. Chapter 2 considers the central role of narrative in Bratslav teaching and the notion of "text" as symbolic representation.

A profound spiritual renaissance within Judaism, Hasidism did not flourish in a cultural vacuum. The romantic spirit of the times reached Jewish enclaves of Eastern Europe, finding most cogent expression, perhaps, in Reb Nahman's oeuvre. In chapter 3, motifs central to the worldview of Western European romantic thinkers are traced in their diverse forms through the tales. My objective, here, is not to "prove" any kind of direct influence received, but rather to consider the phenomena themselves and their role in creating the dimension of the fantastic. In the last part of this chapter, the "romantic drama" of longing, search, and final union so pervasively present in Reb Nahman's teaching is examined from the perspective of feminist hermeneutics. Inherently female events—love relationships, pregnancy, birth, nursing, motherhood—used through the ages of Hebrew literature as paradigms of universal human experience are central in his oeuvre as well. The unique form they take there gestures toward aspects of Hasidic thought deserving of much greater attention.

Reb Nahman averred many times that his tales have the power to lead lost souls to repentance, to make barren women fertile, to heal blind eyes, and to restore, somehow, the unity of a shattered world. Such changes could take place not on the cognitive level alone but much deeper within those who hear them. One of my aims in this work has been to understand, through an intimate, associative reading of the tales, something of how they "work"—what it is about them that evokes interest, attraction, and reverence in readers of such diverse identities, from the Hasidic faithful to ordinary people who like to read stories.

One challenge has been to strike a balance between solid scholarly work, with the documentation and implicit dialogue with contemporary research it requires, and personal, honest engagement with the tales, their author, and the spiritual and religious matrix that gave birth to them. In teaching, whether of literature or of Jewish thought, my continual concern is to enable students to read texts for themselves, to point out a path they might follow rather than summarizing the journey already taken. A similar concern has guided me here: for readers attentive to and somewhat familiar with the traditional sources—the Bible, midrash, Talmud, and Kabbalah—precise references are given throughout my discussion. Readers whose curiosity or strengths are in other areas will, I hope, feel at home with the rhetorical, heuristic, literary approach that has motivated my exploration of the tales.

My citations of the tales refer to the standard Bratslav bilingual (Hebrew-Yiddish) edition (1811; reprint, Jerusalem, 1985), abbreviated in the text and notes as *SM*. Translations of passages from the tales and, unless otherwise noted, of all Hebrew texts cited—biblical, rabbinic, kabbalistic, Hasidic, and modern—are my own.

As this work has taken form, I have recalled, again and again, the visceral understanding Bratslav *hasidim* have of their rebbe, Reb Nahman. Ezekiel the prophet speaks God's word: ". . . I will take the stony heart out of their flesh and will give them a heart of flesh" (Ezek. 11:19).

It is a warning against a petrified state of being, senseless to pain as well as to joy. *LeV BaSar* is a feeling heart, introspective, vulnerable, honest about inner struggles yet no less concerned about the needs of others, to the destiny of the Jewish nation and the well-being of all of humanity. Such a heart gives life to Reb Nahman's teaching. Its letters, inverted, inform the very name BreSLaV, as Reb Nahman's followers prefer to speak of themselves. It is with such a heart that I have tried to read as well, with all the risk and all the reward such an endeavor may entail.

I • The Poet's Self and the Poem

Once there was a king whose land was conquered by a greater and stronger king. In time, though, the weaker king gained power until he was able to win his kingdom back. But even in his victory, the lesser king understood that the perfidies of fate would allow him no lasting peace. And so he built a wall against the sea, and in his fortress hid away the wealth he had amassed. (At its entrance he hung a sign describing the treasure contained in each room.) To enter the fortress was nigh impossible—at the gateway stood a machine that would behead all who did not know the labyrinthine path. But a sign hung there as well, recounting, in many languages, the wisdom needed to find the right path, to come within unharmed. Years passed, and the sea washed over the fortress. Centuries went by. Then once again a king desired to settle that long-buried island. He brought back Jews and gentiles. A poor Jew built himself a hut on the island. One Friday, as he was digging clay, he discovered the tablet that had hung in the ruined fortress. All his attempts to uncover the history of the place met with failure; it had been erased from memory. But at last a wandering Jew came in search of food and shelter for the Sabbath. The one told the other of his discovery and appealed for his advice. The humble wanderer responded, "I will read the message on it." He looked and comprehended. The two, together, went and uncovered the riches hidden so long ago.

This tale, recorded in *Hayyei Moharan*,[1] seems in some way an emblem of its creator's own history. The nameless figure who deciphers a forgotten language and leads another to treasure houses of wisdom obscured for centuries reflects the master's life, his self-imposed task as spiritual leader, linking past to present through his teachings and his stories. Essential to our understanding of Reb Nahman's oeuvre is awareness of the author's own self-image. Numerous statements, expressed in *Likkutei Moharan* and biographical sources, reveal Reb Nahman's conviction of his responsibility, both on the social and eschatological level, toward the world in which he lived. Yet they disclose, as well, the psychic tension inherent in such an awesome mission and the effect of that tension in Reb Nahman's creative life.[2]

The tales he told, then, are a transparent reflection of this composite self-image. In the chapter that follows, I would like to examine some of the myriad self-referential elements that pervade Reb Nahman's tales. My intent is by no means to present a psychological sketch of their author. Rather, I hope to propose a framework in which many in his colorful cast of characters may be seen as a face of Reb Nahman's own prismatic figure. This contention serves as the foundation stone in Joseph Weiss's discussion of Reb Nahman's thought: "In every instance that Reb Nahman speaks of the 'true zaddik' or even 'the zaddik' alone, his sole intent is toward himself."[3] Indeed, the very possibility that heroes and heroines, infants, prayer masters, beggars and prodigal sons may all be disguises of a single self is in itself a notion that beckons toward a fantastic dimension. In our endeavor to understand the dynamics of Reb Nahman's imagination, the tales he told will be considered as dramatizations of the more polemical autobiographical statements that inform the secondary sources.

Part 1 of this chapter concerns the monumental figure of the zaddik in Hasidic tradition, both as spiritual leader and as a channel connecting earthly life to higher realms of being through his life and his words. Part 2 focuses on Reb Nahman's view of his place in an historical continuum. His identification with biblical and aggadic figures becomes apparent through the tales; in various guises, his characters speak in a composite voice—messengers from the past transfigured, merging with the author's own person. In part 3 the messianic theme that informs all the tales will be discussed; the chameleon protagonist in each of them and his self-referential qualities shed much light on Reb Nahman's vision of his own potential role as a harbinger of the world's redemption.

Finally, part 4 will touch on some aspects of Reb Nahman's emotional life, on the ways in which his existential struggle finds expression in the persons and events of the tales.

The cardinal element binding these four subjects is the consciousness that disguises play a vital role in mystical thought in general; in Reb Nahman's works in particular, a fascination with alter egos serves as a motivating force in the creation of his fictions. Let us turn, then, to the first question, the author's reflexive perception of the zaddik as a historical figure, his fate bound up with the loyalty and trust of his followers, and of his own worth cast in that imposing role.

1. THE FIGURE OF THE ZADDIK

The title page of the Bratslav edition of the tales, *Sefer Sippurei Maʿasiyot*, alerts us to Reb Nahman's true aspiration as storyteller: "See and understand his wonderful and terrible way . . . to clothe and to conceal the treasures of the King in the guise of tales, in accordance with the generation and the age. . . ." In the story of the forgotten fortress above, we recognized Reb Nahman in the person of the humble Jew, master of the way leading to the hidden riches. These words, in contrast, written by Reb Nahman's followers, cast their rebbe differently—here, *he* is the master builder, intent on the castle of his creation. The metaphor of a fairy-tale structure housing precious truths reappears yet again in *Shivhei Moharan*; the wondrous process of exploring the castle is observed there from the architect's lofty perspective:

> My teachings are like a palace containing halls and chambers, exedras and mosaics—all of them beautiful, wondrous, awe-inspiring. And there are staircases upon staircases, each of them novel and terrible. The moment one enters a room and begins to look about, wondering at all the marvels it holds, in that very moment he sees that a fantastic passage has opened before him to another room, and so from room to room, from room to room. . . . [4]

The mazelike palace into which Reb Nahman entices his listeners is a compelling symbol. Yet beyond all that the enchanted edifice of his teachings holds are even more sublime truths it cannot possibly contain. The world, Reb Nahman protests, is not yet worthy of such divine wisdom. The paradoxical presence and ineffability of such knowledge is vividly described in an incident recalled by Reb Nahman's students:

> Once, when some people were with him, he drew out a piece of paper marked with his holy handwriting; grasping it, he exclaimed, "How many teachings are written on this page!" And he said, "Many, many worlds are sustained, draw life from the smoke of my teachings." And he took the paper and burned it in the candle flame. And he said, "There are many, many teachings that have not even been expressed in letters. Thus it is truly novel, a wonder, when one is permitted to bring such teachings down [into this world] and put them in the shapes of letters. . . ."[5]

In these anecdotes, the author sees himself as an emissary, an intermediary summoned to draw abstract, preexisting truths from the upper spheres, and to make them tangible and immediate to those around him. In chapter 2 we will suggest some reasons Reb Nahman chose tales in particular as the ideal genre in which to veil his esoteric vision. Here what concerns us is Reb Nahman's desire—in his oeuvre as a whole—to entice his listeners into the enchanted castle of his making and to open before them some of its endless passageways.

Two objectives may be isolated as motivating this desire. The first, and most immediate, is to engender spiritual growth in those who follow him, healing and awakening them, bringing them to repentance, that they may serve God with all their being. The idea of *tikkun*, or repair, a seminal notion guiding the Hasidic movement as a whole, is emphasized as a process occurring not only on the cosmic level but in the soul of each individual.[6] Statements throughout Reb Nahman's oeuvre attest to his consciousness that the rebbe *must* be deeply involved in the religious life of those around him. A most cogent expression of how daunting this task was is his protest, found in *Shivhei Moharan:*

> Am I not like someone who walks day and night through a desert, searching and seeking to make that wasteland into a settlement? For each of your hearts is like a barren desert, uninhabitable. The Shekhinah cannot dwell therein, and so I search and seek continually to achieve some *tikkun*, to make a place in your hearts

> where the Shekhinah may rest. Alas, what great efforts are needed to make a fruitless tree into pleasant vessels, worthy of being used by men. . . . In the same way, how indefatigably I must strive to help each and every one of you, to "repair" you in some way.[7]

Among Reb Nahman's tales, certainly the one that most directly portrays the life's work of a Hasidic spiritual leader is *The Master of Prayer*. Devoted to "drawing people to serve God," the master of prayer has the gift of knowing the way to help each and every individual "return." "If one of them needed to wear a golden cape to that end, he would provide one . . . and if, on the other hand, a rich man had to wear tattered, shameful garments, he would encourage him to."[8]

The "true zaddik"' succeeds in communicating with the masses by containing his own transcendent understanding, and speaking, instead, in the language of those he wishes to affect. Thus, the "true zaddik must talk with them of everyday things, yet clothed in those matters are words of Torah. For the people are not strangers to the words and stories the zaddik relates, and thus he raises his listeners, joining them to God."[9] Even from the filthy depths of heresy he pulls them upward, confident that their eyes may be opened.[10]

The second motivation compelling the rebbe's intercourse with those around him is, of course, the desire to perpetuate his teachings beyond his own death. Only when a person exists in both this world and the world to come, he insists, has he achieved wholeness. "Thus a man must leave some part of himself on earth, a son or a student."[11] Just as children perpetuate the memory of their parents, so students pass on their teachers' understanding to future generations. The despair of the childless man that his name will die with his death opens four of the thirteen tales: "Once there was a kaiser who had no sons" *(King and Kaiser)*; "Once there was a king who had no sons" *(The Son of Precious Stones)*; "Once there was a rabbi who had no sons" *(Rabbi and Only Son)*; "Once there was a burgher, and beneath him lived a miserably poor man. And both of them were childless" *(Burgher and Poor Man)*. Three other stories revolve around struggles of bequest and inheritance: "Once there was a wise man who, before his death, called his children and family to him and charged them to water trees" *(The Cripple)*; "Once there was a king; he had a single son and desired to transfer the kingdom to him in his own lifetime" *(The Seven Beggars)*;

and *The Two Sons Who Were Reversed* is consumed with the question of who is "the king's true son" and rightful heir.

Remarkably, the organic wholeness of Reb Nahman's thought leads him to conceive this notion of continuity in unexpectedly liberal terms. Mother as well as father wish to invest themselves in their children, and this image of parents' flowing stream of love gives birth to the following thought:

> The zaddik of the generation is called "mother," because he nourishes Israel with the light of his wisdom in Torah. . . . And the Torah is called "milk," as it is written in the Song of Songs (4:11) "Honey and milk beneath your tongue. . . ."

The mutual dependence of mother and baby, Reb Nahman continues, is evident to all of us.

> For whenever the infant is sad and dejected, as soon as he sees his mother, he awakens in a moment in anticipation of her, i.e., of the root of his being. Similarly, we see that when he is occupied with his little foolishnesses, even though he is engrossed in them, as soon as he sees his mother he casts all his passions away, and draws himself to her.

In the same way, Reb Nahman concludes, all of a person's negative attributes, all of his resemblance to petrified and vegetative life are as naught when he gazes into the face of the zaddik.[12] The pathos of a mother whose infant is missing and cannot nurse is a poignant detail in *The Master of Prayer*. The king's daughter mourns her golden baby's disappearance; her flood of tears form a sea of blood, and her useless milk a lake of sorrow (*SM*, p. 209). The image seems to suggest the plight of the zaddik bereft of heirs—his knowledge wasted, with no one to seek his abundance.

It is his followers alone who can grant the zaddik immortality. His teachings contain his essence; without students to hand them down, the master himself fades into oblivion. Whether we interpret the tales mentioned above as reflecting Reb Nahman's desire for biological or for spiritual heirs, the predominance of the theme testifies to its importance in his life. The interdependence of Hasidic rebbe and student, the existential necessity, in Reb Nahman's worldview, for their union, underlies a disquieting dream he had, recounted in *Hayyei Moharan*:

At the close of Rosh ha-Shanah, his followers surround Reb Nahman, bidding farewell as they set off on their way home. One man, whom the dreamer knew had recently died, stood among them. Reb Nahman asked him, "Why did you not come to me on Rosh ha-Shanah?" He answered, "But I am already dead." "I said to him, 'Is that why? And is a dead person forbidden to come on Rosh ha-Shanah?' And he was silent. Some people had been speaking with me of faith, and so I spoke with him of that as well. [Apparently, notes the editor, he understood that the man had lost his faith.] And I said to him, 'Am I the only one in the world? If you do not believe in me, be loyal to other zaddikim.' And he said, 'Who should I draw close to?' . . ."[13]

In the dream, Reb Nahman names one illustrious personality after another, so great is his wish to help the soul before him find a spiritual guide. The figure of the zaddik, then, is the axis of the Hasidic world, the Virgilian figure who, ideally, accompanies each individual through his religious life. Reb Nahman's teachings are filled with meditations on "the zaddik of the generation," the "true zaddik," the "hidden zaddik," the "complete zaddik," the "zaddik—pillar of the world," the "higher zaddik" and "lower zaddik." What, then, are his qualities, his countenances, appearing in the tales? And how is Reb Nahman's self-image reflected in the variegated folktale heroes that people his oeuvre?

A passage from *Likkutei Moharan*, with its description of the rare privilege of witnessing the zaddik's death, suggests a key to understanding the "fantastic" nature of his being. Reb Nahman's inspiration for the teaching comes from the drama of the prophet Elijah's parting from earthly life.[14] His pupil Elisha requests "to receive twice your spirit upon myself," and the prophet promises his reward "If you see me being taken from you" (2 Kings 2:10–12). This scene leads Reb Nahman to reflect: "The zaddik has two spirits, an upper and a lower spirit. . . . In his dying hour, that upper spirit descends to embrace and unite with the lower. For in truth, they are one. . . . Yet as soon as they reveal themselves to one another, the upper spirit must disappear once again, as it cannot suffer this world at all." It is this sudden appearance of that otherworldly spirit in the human realm that invests the zaddik's students with the power to perpetuate their master's teaching. And it is the zaddik's double state of being, his simultaneous existence in the divine and earthly realm, that makes him a central player in Reb Nahman's fantastic tales. We glimpse this duality already in the legendary zaddik hero, the Ba'al Shem Tov. Famed for his wondrous insight, that forefather could read the secrets of every heart and know and speak of distant places, transcendent realms, and past and future events.[15] In Reb Nahman's oeuvre, the hierarchy between world orders shifts continually: at times an abyss separates them; at others, they join spontaneously. The zaddik rules effortlessly and equally over both. He uses his knowledge to guide his followers, reminding them of whichever world has abandoned them.[16]

Thus the zaddik strives to create balance within the psyche of every man. Yet his essential duality enables him to conjoin valences on higher levels as well. The figure of the beggar appearing on the fourth day, for example, deftly illustrates the classic social role of the zaddik as a channel spanning between earth and heaven.

As that character explains, his crooked neck is but a metonymy, symbolizing his preeminent occupation. From his wondrous throat emerges a wondrous voice, and it is that ventriloquistic voice alone that may save the two lovesick birds, tragically estranged from one another. By directing each one's forlorn song to the other, by drawing it further in his own voice, the crooked-necked beggar can lead the birds back together again (*SM,* pp. 261–66). The allegorical identity of the two birds, and the part of the beggar between them, is set out in *Likkutei Halakhot*, with a pretext from the *Zohar* predominant in the background. The allusively crooked neck, and the air that passes through it, make the beggar himself a shofar, gathering in the windy breath of this dark world and sending it to the world to come in the voice of the ram's horn. In Jewish religious life the sounding of the shofar has bipolar meaning: as an appeal to God to have mercy on His creatures, and as a summons to the community of Israel to return to Him in repentance.[17] Beyond this cyclical, historical event, however, lies an escatological role: the shofar also alludes to the messianic era—"For on that day, a great shofar will be sounded"—and by that trumpeting voice, "They shall come who were lost in the land of Assyria, and the outcasts in the land of Egypt, and shall worship the Lord at the holy mountain in Jerusalem" (Is. 27:13). Indeed, R. Nathan avers, the long-awaited return of the Diaspora, and ultimately the Redemption itself, all depends on the union between the two birds.[18]

In other tales, a second social phenomenon centered around the figure of the zaddik provides the axis on which the plot turns. That is the quasi-ritual pilgrimage to the "true zaddik's" court, an expression of his followers' loyalty and devotion.[19] The story *Rabbi and Only Son*, for example, describes the aborted journey of the son to his spiritual mentor with its tragic and Kafkaesque consequences. In *The Humble King*, the quest of the wise servant to glimpse the face of the king evokes the *hasid*'s wish to gaze upon the face of the zaddik, as the sole way to intimate the zaddik's essence.[20] And finally, each of the omnipotent beggars, and the children's longing to speak with him and receive his blessing, recall a telling comment Reb Nahman's followers attribute to their master: "In days to come, people will say, 'Once there was such a Reb Nahman,' because they will miss me greatly. . . ."[21]

Yet Reb Nahman manifests the vital role of the zaddik as a life-sustaining force through other analogies as well. Above, we spoke of the zaddik's task as a spiritual healer. This image finds literal realization in *Likkutei Moharan*, in the tales, and in Reb Nahman's biography, where the attributes of doctor of souls are bestowed upon him. In *Likkutei Moharan*, the superior ways of the zaddik are contrasted with the dangerous reductivism of the medical expert, who sees only the body and ignores the soul. A man falls ill and is compelled to turn to a great physician. This expert councils severe measures, and the man decides to appeal to "the sage and zaddik of the generation," healer of psychic illnesses. Part of his treatment requires drugs so potent that, were the patient to receive them unadulterated, he would certainly die. Thus "he had to mix them with other substances, for there are people to whom the inwardness of the Torah, essential for their healing, cannot be revealed." This remark alerts us to Reb Nahman's true meaning: as a faith healer, this zaddik "must clothe the inwardness of his Torah . . . in stories of external things, that [his patient] may be able to receive the cure contained within them. . . ."[22]

The interaction of wise doctor and ailing patient that dramatizes the relationship of the zaddik and his *hasidim* may be traced back to a classic kabbalistic allegory, which is then transplanted as the core of the sixth beggar's story. The *Zohar* considers the verse from the Song of Songs (5:8): "I charge you, O daughters of Jerusalem, if you find my beloved, tell him that I am sick with love," and conjures this scene: The lovesick patient is surrounded by doctors striving to understand her illness. Carefully, they check her pulse. Not one of them, though, is able to grasp its meaning. For the languishing patient is the Assembly of Israel, and her heartbeat, the text declares, is the coded sounding of the shofar—it speaks of the Exile, the redemption drawing closer, and the trials of that nearly relentless pain.[23]

When we turn to *The Seven Beggars*, the identity between the faithful shepherd, the zaddik as portrayed in *Likkutei Moharan* and the handless beggar cannot be denied. The beggar's story, evocatively related in the first person, is but a filmy curtain concealing the author himself and his self-appointed role as the spiritual healer of his generation and, potentially, of the world itself. He describes the predicament of the king's daughter, helpless and mortally ill in the palace of water, in order to declare, "And I can heal her . . . by all ten kinds of music, indeed, I can heal her" (*SM*, pp. 280–81). Behind the curtain, in the backstage of *Likkutei Moharan*, the enigmatic allusions stand undisguised: On a psychological level, the king's daughter is Everyman, drawn by melancholy and sadness into the lonely, wailing prison of his mind.[24] The wise doctor, none other than Reb Nahman, prescribes his famous cure, known in Bratslav tradition as "the great *tikkun*" *[ha-tikkun ha-kelali]*. By grace of ten manners of musical playing, in the form of ten psalms,[25] souls that have estranged themselves from God in sadness may return to Him in joy.

But perhaps the most lyrical image of the zaddik in Reb Nahman's worldview is that of the shepherd/musician. Attributes of each of the traditional "Seven Shepherds of Israel"—Abraham, Isaac, Jacob, Joseph, Moses, Aaron, and David—merge with the shepherd of romantic Eastern European folklore to embody countless figures in Reb Nahman's oeuvre. Consider, for example, Reb Nahman's reflections on Moses, "the faithful shepherd," and his contemporary alter ego. In his innovative rereading of Num. 11:12, Moses' cry of frustration with his rebellious flocks—"Have I conceived all this people, have I begotten them that you should say to me, 'Carry them in your bosom, as a nursing father carries the suckling child, to the land you have sworn to their fathers?'"—becomes an affirmation. Indeed, Reb Nahman teaches, Moses—a prototype of the Hasidic zaddik—*is* responsible for bearing all the world and for engendering its blessings. At once feminine and masculine, the zaddik bears the seminal drop of all souls, in the sense of the sower who "bears the bag of seed" (Ps. 126); from his effluence, this seed passes to all of the Assembly of Israel, and she gives it to the world.[26]

The zaddik as sower of seeds, as gardener of souls, as fluting shepherd gathering his flocks, is perhaps the most romantic poetic image in Reb Nahman's oeuvre. His most detailed appearance is surely in *The Seven Beggars*, in the deaf figure who offers his story-gift on the second day. Allusively, he tells of a legendary land that once possessed a garden; there, fruits grew that contained all the tastes in the world, all the aromas, all colors and shapes that ever were. A gardener took care of that Edenic garden. But suddenly he disappeared; worse, a cruel king became ruler, and his forces ruined all the lovely blessings the garden had grown. The narrator then tells of his own resolution to try and save the kingdom. He ventures within, and discovers that the disgust, stench, and blindness plaguing it are caused by moral sins spread by the king's base servants. Emphatically, he counsels the miserable people: only when these evil ways are driven out will taste and smell, color and shape, be restored, and will their nurturing gardener be returned to them. At once they take up the task. As the kingdom becomes pure, "all of a sudden there was a tumult [and here the narrator adds sardonically]—maybe, just the same, it was that madman, proclaiming he was the gardener. Everyone thinks he is a madman; they throw stones after him to drive him away and yet, after all, maybe he truly *is* the gardener. They brought him before them, and I said, 'Certainly, in truth, he is the gardener.'" In the beggar's conclusion, the figure of madman/gardener and narrator/beggar at last converge: "Indeed, the kingdom of wealth can attest that I live a good life, for *I* restored the kingdom" (*SM*, pp. 253–54).

A hint of the autobiographic aspects of this transparent allegory is suggested in the commentary *Likkutei 'Ezot*: "Sometimes, the sins of the generation are so great that the gardener is lost, i.e., the zaddik's light disappears, is covered over. Then the world is unworthy of realizing that he is the true gardener, who can help them attain a life of goodness and truth with their garden. . . . They mistake him for a madman. . . ."[27] In part 4 we will explore the threshold between inspiration and madness that preoccupied Reb Nahman, his desire to repair, and concomitant fear of rejection. For now, let us consider the link between zaddik and gardener within the framework of kabbalistic allegory. From the verse (Ps. 97:11) "Light is sown for the righteous," the author of the *Zohar* learns that

> God sowed that primordial light in His Garden...the zaddik, who is the gardener of that garden, took the light and planted it as seeds of truth, placing it in rows. Plants are born, sprouting and growing and bearing fruit, and this fruit nourishes the world.[28]

The zaddik, then, is charged with the care and sustenance of God's creation. The world depends on his labors; in his absence, we may suppose, the garden would wither and die.

Reb Nahman expands the allegory of the garden and its divinely appointed caretaker in *Likkutei Moharan*. The idea expressed in that text sheds light on *The Seven Beggars*, and refracts, as well, Reb Nahman's understanding of the image in the *Zohar* quoted above.

> Know, that there is a field where beautiful trees and plants grow. The splendor of this field and all it holds is indescribable, happy is the eye that has glimpsed it. The trees and plants are holy souls that grow therein. Many naked souls are there as well, they wander restlessly outside the field, waiting and longing to be repaired, that they may return and regain their places within. . . . And all of them seek the master of the field, that he may further their *tikkun*.[29]

Who, then, may this field's caretaker be? Reb Nahman paints a telling portrait of him:

> He who is willing to gird his loins, to go in and be, himself, the master of the field must be a steadfast and vigorous man, a mighty hero, a wise and great zaddik.

Not every individual, Reb Nahman continues, has been able to complete the task in his lifetime; some even with their deaths did not succeed. Only a truly great man can endure, for he will suffer much pain, and many difficulties.[30] The mixture of verbal tenses, past and present, alerts us to the continuous role in history Reb Nahman conceives for the gardeners in their esoteric field of souls. The zaddik of each generation is responsible for the tender plants and trees under his aegis; it is his task to water their spirit with the Torah, and provide them space where they can flourish, and to draw those outside back to their waiting roots. As we saw earlier in this chapter, their figure is inseparable from the self-image Reb Nahman bore; to repair the separate soul of each of his followers was, in his eyes, but a fulfillment of divine intent from the first moment of Creation.

Both shepherd and gardener spend their days under the wide sky, their companions the winds, grasses and flocks. The indwelling voices of nature, an omnipresent force in the romantic imagination,[31] could not help but penetrate the shepherd's consciousness, and the song of all those speechless lives emerges, transformed, in the song of his flute. The Pan-like musician-shepherd dear to the Western European romantics and to the folklore tradition that inspired them may be recognized in the third day's mute singer of Reb Nahman's *Seven Beggars*. Hidden in the simple words of his story are ideas concerning music and its creation that stand as pillars in Reb Nahman's quintessentially romantic worldview. Let us begin with his tale, turning then to the texts linking it to powerful concepts in Jewish tradition.

As the beggar tells the child bride and groom, his apparent speechlessness is illusory; rather, the riddles and wondrous songs he can utter contain endless wisdom. The loquacity of the world, all its fragmentary blessings and praises of God—it is they, and not he, who remain forever lacking (*SM*, p. 254). A true poet, he goes on to describe the undying romance of spring and heart, and the melodies that flow from them as day fades into twilight.[32] The mute beggar's intuitive perception of these indwelling voices is explained in *Likkutei Moharan;* pointing beyond himself, our mute beggar bespeaks a dynasty of inspired shepherd-players.

The prototype of the shepherd blessed with intimate knowledge of nature's song is, for Reb Nahman, the biblical Jacob. The patriarch's sons, on their journey to Joseph in Egypt, take in their vessels "the melody of the Land" (Gen. 43:11). Indeed, the balm and honey, the almonds and ladanum, their father sent, a gift to the foreign king, sing their own song, "for every shepherd has a special melody, according to what grows in the place he grazes. . . .Each and every plant has a song it sings, and from the song of the grasses, the shepherd's melody is formed. . . ."[33]

Yet behind the poetic sensitivity of this conception lies one of the most important philosophical innovations Reb Nahman bequeathed to Bratslav Hasidism. In effect, he counters the Cartesian formula *cogito ergo sum* with the certainty that something else transcends all separate mental constructs: "Beyond the private tunes of any system of [cognitive] knowledge is the melody of faith—this song invests the light of *Ein sof* itself."[34] The unspoken conviction here is that Descartes's view inevitably leads to a destructive dualism between mind and body, to a proliferation of splintered systems that no logic can reunite. To combat all the contradictory fragments of knowledge that fill the world, Reb Nahman points to music—disembodied, entirely spiritual—as the only hope of salvation, the only means by which oneness may be restored. And then, just as his teaching threatens to recede into abstraction, Reb Nahman introduces the human element—the music master who, alone, can touch the intangible melody of faith. "Only the zaddik of the generation, in the aspect of Moses, is worthy to be on their level of faith," and that is, paradoxically, because his essence is *silence*, an entity far more supreme than speech.[35] Moses' inherent muteness, his wordless response to God's revelation of His ways (Ex. 15:1) casts him, in Reb Nahman's mind, as a sort of orchestral conductor. He raises his baton (or shepherd's staff) and, from the primordial silence of Creation calls forth the voices of his players; skillfully he combines their disparate tones to form a song of many voices. That is the symphony of faith—in God, in their ultimate redemption—the all-encompassing musical creation performed by the Jewish people. In a final thought closing this teaching, Reb Nahman merges the image of the gardener with that of the shepherd-musician in an imaginative crescendo: "Thus, by grace of the music of the zaddik, in the aspect of Moses, all the souls who have fallen into apostasy are drawn back to complete faith . . . and all the deformed melodies are annulled in that greater music. . . ."[36] Moses wields his staff and miraculously brings the dead back to life;[37] the zaddik infuses empty black notes—the forlorn, spiritually void lost ones from his flock—with breath and voice. He weaves the emerging songs of his community together, and sends that wholly new, ever new prayer and melody on high, to rejoin its source in endless Being.

Reb Nahman's intense self-awareness seems to have encouraged him to give free flight to his powers of imagination. His poetic language metamorphoses in a continuous stream of images—indeed, just as all of us bear multiple identities in our consciousness, in his eyes the zaddik is *at once* mother, doctor, musician, shepherd, artist, master builder. The multiple reflections of a single figure—Reb Nahman himself—create the fantastic effect of amusement-park mirrors that make one short and fat, tall and thin, deformed and distorted, in most convincing succession. Yet in all of them we may detect the author's concern for his (self-imposed) responsibilities as spiritual leader—more, as a legitimate zaddik of his generation.

2. INNOVATION AND INSPIRATION: LINKING PAST TO FUTURE

Reb Nahman addresses this matter directly through his highly personal understanding of classic prophetic experience in Jewish tradition. The following remarks are relayed by his followers in *Sihot HaRan*. As we know, aside from Moses, all the prophets were able to convey their revelation only indirectly, in metaphorical language, "through a mirror darkly." Moses alone envisioned all in a "luminous mirror" and his words bear the divine clarity of his insight. The same distinction exists, Reb Nahman says, in the innovations of the zaddik in the dialectics of Torah. Some scholars interweave their message with biblical verses and talmudic prooftexts, but their artfulness merely serves their own ends. Yet there are great and awesome zaddikim, after the pattern of Moses, whose innovations are pure and shining as the sun; the pre-texts they use form an organic texture with their own meaning; thus, their message is a luminous insight.[38]

Certainly, a crucial component in an individual's ability to create is his sense of the source of his vision. Reb Nahman's comments above show that a scholar's legitimacy, in the eyes of the world and in his own, is granted by his link to tradition. To prove that his understanding is not solipsistic, no imaginative invention, but rather an inherent aspect of the canonical text—this is the scholar's sole hope of winning respect, in his own eyes and in others'. Following this idea to a logical extreme, an inescapable paradox emerges: at the highest state innovation can reach, any novelty at all is utterly impossible. The moment hermeneutics objectifies itself from its source, it fissures; the commentary becomes more important than its foundation and origin. Thus, the belief that the Torah is all-encompassing and all-inclusive precludes the possibility that artistic creation may be ex nihilo. What seems to be innovation, then, can actually only be *transformation*. In Gershom Scholem's metaphor, the eternal substance of the sacred text is melted down and forged anew as it passes through the fiery stream of the mystical consciousness.[39] Or in Reb Nahman's words, the zaddik, divinely inspired, is able to clothe the true words of the Torah, welding them together in new patterns that people are able to understand.[40]

In part 1 of this chapter, we suggested some instances in which characters in the tales resemble their author's own self-image as projected in other contexts. Yet the autobiographical nature of the tales is augmented by a further degree of reflection: the polymorphous figure of the zaddik that so concerned Reb Nahman himself also embodies the attributes of many historical and biblical personages. This multiple resemblance is certainly much more than artful literary allusion; rather, it brings into play a kind of magical correspondence—between the author's own life and the history of his ancestors, and between both of them and the stories of his characters. The effect is almost self-evident: the patriarchs Moses, David, Elijah, and Elisha are called zaddikim; when a Hasidic rebbe is honored with the title of zaddik, the aura of power and of wisdom inherent in those figures' being must be transferred to him.

The ancient concept of "zaddik, pillar of the world" (Prov. 10:25), and the identification of the patriarch Joseph with the *sefirah Yesod,* or foundation,[41] determines his centrality in the Hasidic rejuvenation of that classic figure. The threefold responsibility of the contemporary zaddik, in the Hasidic conception, for his community's "spiritual lives, children, and material sustenance"[42] are directly linked to Joseph's deeds in Egypt. Reb Nahman, however, focuses on another vital characteristic of that princely figure: "Joseph, because he had total possession of the Holy Tongue, was able to interpret dreams. For the fundament of the dream is in *slumber*, i.e., *translation;* he knew how to refine out the good and the truth contained in a dream.[43] The axis on which this statement turns is the numerical equivalence *(gematria)* of the two key words, "slumber" and "translation." Here, translation is much more than a linguistic phenomenon; it symbolizes a transfiguration, a purification of essence. Joseph's uprightness enabled him to redeem the holy elements imprisoned in the impure web of the dream; by rearranging the letters of the foreign words, he reconstructed the divine order hidden in their message, and restored to them their lost and truest identity. The relationship suggested here between translation and Hebrew, between dreams and their interpretation, parallels, on one hand, the relationship between the "tales the world tells" and Reb Nahman's fantastic tales and, on the other, between his fictions and their true referent in higher worlds. Emulating his biblical master, Joseph, in narrative technique, Reb Nahman recognizes that in every retelling, the new text draws closer to its origin—the pristine words God used to create the world.[44]

A second famous zaddik and storyteller—although of a completely other order—whose influence was instrumental in Reb Nahman's self-conception is the talmudic figure of Honi ha-Maʿagel. R. Yohanan evokes his memory in B.T. *Taʿanit:* "All the days of that zaddik's life, he worried over the verse (Ps. 126:1) 'A song of ascent: Returning to Zion we were as dreamers. . . .'"[45] In his own reading of that talmudic text, Reb Nahman takes up the yarn, inserting these parenthetical comments: One day Honi encounters a man planting carob trees (that is, a storyteller who speaks of times gone by). He asks him, Do you really suppose you will live seventy years, will enjoy the fruits of these seeds you plant? (In other words, Have you not thought to awaken your students with stories of our own times, for if you tell tales concerning more sublime matters, students who are unfit may hear them.) The man responds, I found myself in a world filled with carob trees (i.e., Even if I tell stories of ancient days, I can cause unfit listeners to forget their innermost truth). Indeed, Rav Nathan comments parenthetically, God Himself protects the zaddik who has dedicated himself to arousing the world from this existential slumber by telling tales. And the planter explains, Just as my forefathers planted trees for my benefit, so I wish to plant for my sons (meaning, just as tales gave birth to me, so my stories will cause children to be born).[46] Honi's legendary interaction with the carob planter and the understanding he gains reveals, vicariously, Reb Nahman's own recognition that every zaddik bears a historical responsibility to tell stories. Inherent in them is the power to make barren women fruitful, to bring the next generation into existence, and to link past to future in the fruits of tradition.

One final element intrinsic in Reb Nahman's image of himself as an innovative heir of eternal truths is his identification with eminent mystics of history. According to the testimony in *Shivhei Moharan*, Reb Nahman spoke of the revolutionary esoteric teachings that passed directly from R. Simeon bar Yohai to R. Isaac Luria, to the Ba῾al Shem Tov, and, finally, to himself.[47] And in his biography, he represents himself as a kind of messenger from the world of the dead, charged by the illustrious talmudic mind, Rabba bar bar Hannah, to perpetuate his abstruse teaching guarded by the sage himself. The insights he revealed to him, Reb Nahman adds, are recorded in the first teachings of the book *Likkutei Moharan*.[48] The ambivalent effect of such a claim is a self-portrait at once self-aggrandizing and self-effacing. An artist's greatness is measured by his originality (as Reb Nahman is said to have said, "Never in the world has there been such a novelty as I"),[49] and yet if his creation is *true*, it must be utterly unoriginal, a veiling of the eternal body in ever-changing hues. The dialectic between innovation and perpetuation that pervades all of Reb Nahman's thought and shapes his self-conception is eloquently expressed in *Likkutei Moharan*.[50] Explaining the statement, "All my days I grew [up] among the sages,"[51] Reb Nahman says: The dissonant opinions of the sages fracture space; a void forms amidst them, and in that vacuum, the world is created.[52] To say that "all my days I grew up among the sages" means that amidst the words of the rabbis I improved myself, made my days and my character greater. And thus they are *my* days, for in their spaces I myself create the world.

A scholar gains insight only when enveloped in the teachings of the wise. Yet his understanding is, forever, uniquely his own. It comes into being in the silence between the voices.

3. THE APPROACHING REDEMPTION

We turn now to a troubling and volatile chapter in the history of Hasidism as a whole: the messianic aspirations of its leaders, and interest expressed by followers in the process of redemption.[53] Our focus, as always, is the tales Reb Nahman told; both the players and events described in them open a window upon the author's most profound beliefs concerning the theme of messianism. Exploration of this subject poses certain dangers: our intent is not to scrutinize the author's private life and records of his conversations with students in order to "prove" his personal tendencies.[54] Rather, we have, through the stories themselves, to crystallize the image Reb Nahman harbored of the Messiah in regard to the various roles and guises he adopts in the lower, material world. It is important to avoid a simplistic reading, drawing facile parallels between these messianic figures and their fabulator. More appropriate is an associative reading, in which sources from rabbinic and kabbalistic literature are introduced to shed light on Reb Nahman's unique creation. Through his theoretical teachings and comments by generations of Bratslav Hasidim, we learn of the vast sociological and spiritual task that rests on the zaddik's shoulders. The world's readiness to welcome the messianic age is inextricably bound to their awareness of its nature. And clearly, for Reb Nahman, the telling of stories plays a vital role in awakening his people to their own destiny. The recurrent protean images of the Messiah—the tragedy of his [non]-recognition, the trials he suffers as God's scorned messenger, the signs foretelling his advent—these are the testimony we seek to overhear within the texture of the tales themselves.

In B.T. *Sanhedrin*, the inherent ambivalence of the Messiah figure is weighed.[55] R. Alexanderi, in the name of R. Joshua ben Levi, points to the apparent contradiction between various biblical prophetic visions of the Messiah. Daniel, in a night vision, beheld "one like a son of man, who came with the clouds of heaven. . . . And there was given him dominion and glory and a kingdom, that all the peoples, nations and tongues should serve him . . ." (Dan. 7:13). This triumphal advent sharply contrasts with the words of Zechariah: "Behold, your king comes to you; he is just and victorious, humble and riding upon an ass . . ." (Zech. 9:9).[56] To this second image we could add the pathos of Isaiah's words: "He was despised and rejected of men; a man of pains, acquainted with sickness, and we hid our faces from him; he was despised, and we esteemed him not" (Is. 53:3).[57] Many of Reb Nahman's tales vivify the uncertainty concerning the Messiah's true identity, the tenuousness that has haunted the Jewish people throughout history. The turmoil caused by false messiahs, the anguished thought that the true one was driven away and that the search for him is unending—these experiences inform their events.

The story entitled *Burgher and Poor Man*, for example, "speaks," in the words of Reb Nahman's followers, "of the secret of the future

Redemption, and of the secret of drawing down the Messiah's soul."[58] The burgher's son, driven away from his promised bride by her ambitious father, is cast out into the world, his only link to her the map recounting their shared destiny. While he endures a long exile, paralyzed by inertia, then disaster, and finally despair, the poor man's beautiful daughter loyally resists all suitors. One by one they come to court her, singing her stolen story, each in the deceitful hope that his lie will convince her he is her promised one. All of them fail, until she falls into the clutches of the pirate. Her escape on the desert island, disguised as a sailor, leads to her unknowing reunion with the burgher's son. Then begins the true test of faith—only when each agent realizes his own destiny, when he rediscovers the *signs* on his path, can the original promise be fulfilled. For from the union of burgher's son and poor man's daughter, we learn, the Messiah is born.

The biblical prototype underlying this tale, and represented in three separate yet vitally linked narratives[59] is evoked in numerous allusions. One of the most moving among them is the "losing of the signs" in Reb Nahman's story. The map proving the lover's true identity is lost in the forest; in the midrash, it is Tamar who, as she is led to be burnt, "loses the signs," Judah's staff and signet proving her innocence. The treacherous interference of evil forces (Satan, or the storm wind) exposes the character in all his vulnerability and only a moment of grace (the angel Gabriel, the daughter's mercy) saves him from ruin.[60] Another is the idea underlying the plot that "the council of God will stand" (Prov. 18:21). The divinely appointed union (between Boaz and Ruth, Judah and Tamar, Lot and his daughters, the burgher's son and poor man's daughter) can be nullified by no power on earth, writes R. Nahman of Tcherin. Just as, according to Mishnah *Avot*, the Messiah's name was created before the world itself came into being, so the union of feminine and masculine engendering his birth is preexisting, a matter of divine will. The interference of the suitors speaks, on one hand, of the false messiahs seducing the Assembly of Israel through the ages. Yet on the other, the nightmare of the "lost signs" represents a most contemporary tragedy in the eyes of the *hasid:* "[T]he controversy and struggle over true and great zaddikim like the Baʿal Shem Tov, may his memory be for a blessing . . . and our rebbe [Reb Nahman], whose greatness the whole world did not merit recognizing. For if all of Israel had drawn close to them, the Redemption would necessarily have come to pass."[61]

The precarious search for the true Messiah, and the painful sense of wasted opportunity informs another of Reb Nahman's tales. In *King and Kaiser*, promised bride and groom strike a bond between them, but it is too early; the ring, symbolic of their union, is lost, and they wander apart. The king's son humbles himself, hiding his true identity. It is as if he must wait to appear in the world, actively to espouse the longed-for daughter. Here, too, disguises, nonrecognition, and revelation punctuate the tale.

But it is in *The Two Sons Who Were Reversed* that we find the most complete portrait of the Messiah in his struggle to fulfill his divine appointment. At issue is the protagonist's dawning recognition of his own true identity and the battle for ascendancy it compels him to wage. The striking resemblance between this tale and the biblical history of Saul, evident in many details, alerts us to the messianic valence in Reb Nahman's invention. In the biblical narrative, the young Saul sets off in pursuit of his father's escaped asses. His long search leads him, finally, to Samuel, the seer and holy man. The prophet receives him and, enlightened by God, reads his heart, tells him he may end his search for the asses, sets food before him, and at daybreak anoints him as prince over the people of Israel and sends him on his way (1 Sam. 9:1–10:1). In Reb Nahman's tale, the king's true son, reduced to driving cattle, chases the escaping beasts through the forest. At last he reaches a forest man, of supernatural and mysterious stature, who takes him up into his home, entreats him to cease his fruitless pursuit, has him eat, and sends him onward, after entrusting him with a wondrous gift, the instrument made of colors and leaves. And although in the Bible it is David, Saul's rival, who ultimately rises as God's chosen king, Saul's lineage is messianic as well. In mystical tradition, the redeemer, son of David, is drawn from the root of Leah, while the redeemer, son of Joseph, is drawn from the root of Rachel.[62] Perhaps the spiritual transformation undergone by the king's true son in Reb Nahman's tale may be perceived as a sort of composite history of the two messianic figures: the king's son first approaches his mentor as Saul did; in the course of his days he gains wisdom and understanding, until he is ready to assume his true role as Messiah, son of David.

Like so many of Reb Nahman's tales, *The Two Sons Who Were Reversed* revolves around the notion of disguises. Here, though, the protagonist's true nature is concealed—both from the world and from himself—and this double blindness, we learn, bespeaks a fundamental mystical truth that dictates the course of history. Reb Nahman, responding to the political events of his day, recognized the figure of Napoleon as driven by the same process that reigns in the destiny of the Messiah. What amazed Reb Nahman, recall his students R. Nathan and R. Naphtali, was Napoléon's unprecedented rise to power—from a simple peasant he became, overnight, an emperor. "And he said, 'Who knows what soul he has; perhaps his soul was exchanged, for in the chamber of transformations souls are sometimes exchanged.'" And he continued that once such a thing did happen, and began to tell the tale entitled *The Two Sons Who Were Reversed.*[63] Reb Nahman's allusion to the notion of the transmigration of souls offers a key to the question of mistaken identity that plays a role in each messianic tale. For if a single soul must live many lives, inhabit many bodies throughout generations, and if it is only after untold transmigrations that it may return to its original wholeness, then disguises are indeed an inseparable element of reality. The sinister quality of the "chamber of transformations" itself, moreover, mandates that disguises are the sole hope of stealing the redeemer's soul from within its depths. As Reb Nahman explains, "[F]or this reason the soul of David had to emerge first through the daughters of Lot and those terrible deeds. The same is true of Judah and Tamar. It all occurred in order to rescue his soul by snatching it from the Other Side, from the oppressor."[64]

Thus the dialectic of external circumstances and contradictory internal truth that propels the king's true son ever forward is, for Reb Nahman, a fundamental principle. In the disorder of permutations reigning before the Messiah's advent, "servants ride upon horses while princes trudge as servants upon the earth" (Eccl. 10:7). Yet the promise remains that all reversals will ultimately be righted: "And kings shall be your foster fathers and queens your nursing mothers: they shall bow down to you with their face toward the earth, and lick up the dust of your feet; and you shall know that I am the Lord: for they who wait for me shall not be ashamed" (Is. 49:23).

The servant's true son sells his birthright to his rival for a morsel of bread, and in that gesture relinquishes his claim to supremacy. That drama is, as it were, the final link in the long chain of reversals running from Isaac and Ishmael, Jacob and Esau, Ephraim and Manasseh, David and Saul. With his dawning sense of destiny, the king's true son grows ready to receive, first the inheritance of the forest man, and then the yet more precious gift of the horseman. This second gift betrays even more clearly the messianic future that awaits him. For the active, intuitive understanding he learns connects him ineluctably to the figure of David, described as *navon davar.*[65] That archetypal poet—creator through words—mastered the art of interpretation, of discovering the secret symbols and allegories manifest in the world. As the path of the king's true son leads into the enchanted garden, and enigma and mystery meet his eyes, we realize that subtle hermeneutics alone can help him go forward. Clearly, Reb Nahman suggests, the Messiah must possess this kind of understanding—it is both inherited, learned, and innovative. And as he adds in the tale's afterword, appearances (names) are deceptive.[66] To see beyond the disguises, to pierce the heart of symbols—that is the Messiah's true gift and his ultimate task. In *The Two Sons Who Were Reversed*, unique among Reb Nahman's stories, the narrative ends in resolution: the king's son recognizes his true identity and brings about the world's *tikkun*. In the emerging melody that fills the garden, the storyteller seems, vicariously, to reveal the secret of Redemption, a secret that only the Messiah himself can know.

Reb Nahman's conviction, intimated above, that his teachings are charged with eschatological power adds another nuance to our perception of his self-image. In chapter 2, in the context of Reb Nahman's perception of the art of narrative, we will explore this conviction, intimated in *The Two Sons Who Were Reversed*, in greater depth. Just as the king's true son restores the garden to its original harmony, so the rebbe, through his teachings, restores to words their primordial identity. And this messianic mission, furthered in every day of the zaddik's life, may truly be, as Reb Nahman said, "the beginning of the Redemption."[67]

As we have seen, many of the messianic figures that people Reb Nahman's tales may be recognized through the manifold attributes they share with the biblical personality of King David. Two other personages, however, demand attention as well, for both of them spring from the fertile earth of their author's imagination. More exactly, they come to be through his ability to draw together the seeds of tradition, crossing existing motifs to breed completely new forms. The first of these personages is the infant of infinite years; he appears in the guise of the blind beggar and as the golden-haired son of the mighty hero *(Master of Prayer)*. His designation in both tales as "nursling" *(yanik* or *yanuka)* betrays, like a code word, his true identity. The concept of the Messiah as a newborn baby or child embodies a logical paradox endemic to his superhuman nature. In *Likkutei Moharan*, Reb Nahman reflects on the tortuous history the Messiah will have endured as if it were the saga of a human life. But while decades of misfortune age a man, driving him ever closer to death, for the Messiah, unbelievably, the opposite is true.

> The Messiah, who has gone through all that he has gone through, and suffered all that he suffered—at the end of it all, God will say to him, "You are my son. *This day* I have begotten you" (Ps. 2:7). It seems very strange and remarkable, but it is really due to the Messiah's tremendous mental powers, to the awesome level he will have attained. . . . Thus all the time that passed over him, from the first day of Creation until that final moment—all is as naught, and it will really be as if he had been born that very day. For time itself will be annulled in his mind. . . .[68]

The figure of the blind beggar, clearly, subsumes this fantastic dual experience of incalculable age and a life ever at its most prenatal beginning—in short, existence in an eternal present, beyond time. R. Nathan points out the connection to King David, and his victory over the ravages of temporality. David "asked God for life and it was given him, length of days for ever and ever" (Ps. 21:5); and hence the declaration of immortality: "David, King of Israel, lives and endures."[69] It is an enviable mode of being; Reb Nahman himself is purported to have said, on one occasion, "I am the grandfather of grandfathers"[70] and on another, "It is forbidden to be old."[71]

The second personage who lurks, omnipresent as Fellini, in the margins of many tales is the prophet Elijah. Indeed, in Jewish tradition he is the master of disguises, appearing at weddings, completing the *minyan* in a lonely stetl, presiding over circumcisions, sitting as a sickly beggar at the gates of Rome.[72] Elijah comes to the cave where R. Simeon bar Yohai has buried himself alive, to tell him the Roman Emperor is dead, that his decree is now void, and that the time has come to emerge and live.[73] So the blind beggar enjoins his listeners to leave the remote tower to which they have fled, return to their boats, and recommence their lives. Elijah looks beyond outward appearances, penetrating the hearts of men, and perceiving their most secret deeds.[74] So the strange forest man confronts the king's true son, showing him the beasts he wildly pursues are but his own base and evil inclinations, and that he must abandon them. Elijah strives to restore faith to sinners, enlightening them to the true way. So the master of prayer relentlessly castigates the sects, condemning their idolatrous practices.[75] Elijah carries the divine message from generation to generation; at the end of time he will reconcile all the conflicting opinions and doctrines manifested in Judaism.[76] And so, all six beggars strive to teach those who listen of the divine truths with which they have been entrusted. The character of the zaddik celebrated by the Hasidic movement and most perfectly incorporated in the Baʿal Shem Tov have much in common with those attributes of Elijah.[77] Most vital, clearly, is his responsibility as a force spurring Jews to internal, spiritual development, to prepare themselves for the approaching redemption. Thus the prophet Malachi pronounces God's word: "Behold, I will send you Elijah the prophet, before the coming of the great and dreadful day of the Lord: and he shall turn the hearts of the father to their children, and the hearts of the children to their fathers . . ." (Mal. 3:23).

When we recall what is perhaps Elijah's most critical future deed, to revive the dead at the advent of the Messiah,[78] we may understand Reb Nahman's own aspirations as a reflection presaging that ultimate act. The existential dormancy (movingly described in *Likkutei Moharan*)[79] that enchains most people, paralyzing all striving toward God was, in his eyes, a death-like sleep. To be awakened is to be revived; to be inspired with divine truth is to regain the breath of life. This is Reb Nahman's strikingly literal understanding of the verse "the breath of our mouths, the anointed of the Lord" (Lam. 4:20).[80] The zaddik, through his teachings and his tales, resuscitates all who hear him. He himself restores breath to their mouths; their spirit *(neshamah)* fills and expands *(noshemet),* their soul *(nefesh)* awakens again, at last, to the source of everlasting life.

4. AUTOBIOGRAPHICAL ASPECTS

The self-referentiality of an author's work comes to the fore, perhaps most clearly, in his characters' outward actions, in their role within the fictional society he creates for them. A more subtle expression of his self-image, though, may be detected in the darker reaches of those fictional figures' minds—in their emotional reactions, unspoken (yet omnisciently narrated) thoughts, unconscious fears. This introspective aspect of Reb Nahman's tales provides moving testimony of their author's own inner life. To anyone familiar with his biography, this dimension may be self-evident;[81] my hope, in the following discussion, is to suggest some of the principles that form Reb Nahman's internal dialectics. Joseph Weiss, a foremost scholar of Bratslav Hasidism, was convinced that Reb Nahman's simultaneous identification with the protagonists of each of his tales is the most basic key to an understanding of their allegories.[82] I would suggest, in addition, that the tales may be read as a projection, not simply of their author's internal dynamics but also of seminal allegories of Jewish mystical tradition.[83] In other words, the emotional charge implicit, for example, in the concepts of "the breaking of the vessels," of "exile and redemption," of "running and returning," and of "descent for the purpose of ascending" is an inherent component of Reb Nahman's own experience. Moreover, these concepts provide a symbolic vocabulary, which the author adopts as his own, and it is this fusion of an internal and an external world that creates the mode in which this inner experience may be represented. Transmuted yet again, it emerges through the tales to be spoken, finally, in the personal, psychic language of their characters. To this extent, these figures may be understood as what Lévy-Bruhl calls "collective representations."[84] Although they never bear their original 'mythic' names—Shekhinah, God, Messiah, the Evil One, *Binah, Malkhut,* etc.—their attributes fill in the archetypical outline provided by these Urforms. We recognize Reb Nahman's characters as vital forces from Jewish tradition, yet they also bear the indelible mark of their author's hand. Thus, any interpretation of the tales through schematic comparison with preexisting sources, without regard to their author's own aural presence in them, remains necessarily abstract and incomplete. Let us turn, then, to the tales, with an eye to the presence of the storyteller in the soul of his actors.

In *The Seven Beggars*, each beggar proclaims his paradoxical dual nature: one is a blind seer, another a mute singer; there are a hunchbacked Atlas, a handless musician, a dancer without legs. In each case, external appearance belies true essence. We learn from a comment, recorded in *Shivhei Moharan*, that such duality describes Reb Nahman's own existential reality.

> He said: When am I truly alone before God [lit., "When do I have *hitbodedut*"]? When all the world is standing around him, and he sits amidst them—then is he most completely alone. For then he can cry out in a "small and silent voice," and his cry is heard to the ends of the earth. . . . Yet all those who surround him hear nothing at all. Similarly, concerning dancing, he said that when he sits in a crowd, he can dance a most wondrous dance. . . .[85]

The secret lives of the beggars, their ontological superiority to their human audience, and the naive ignorance of that audience to the beggars' true identity seems to echo ironically in this testimony. From another passage, in *Hayyei Moharan*, we learn that his self-representation in a series of *beggars* is itself very meaningful—it reflects the mixture of denigration and self-esteem that fills his biography.

> Before he went to Erez Israel . . . he said, Now I have no words. Afterwards, at home, he paced back and forth, and finally said, I am poor and destitute, more so than all the great ones—this one has possessions, that one riches, another, provinces—while I have nothing. My only solace is in remembering that in the World of Truth, everyone will need to hear my innovations, and I will speak them ceaselessly. What am I besides what my soul invents?[86]

The beggar, bereft of worldly means, his true worth hidden from all who see him, yet bearing unspeakable, even inhuman wisdom, thus seems to personify the image Reb Nahman had of his own destiny.

Were we to regard the personages of Reb Nahman's thirteen tales as a collection of psychological case studies, at least one complex seems symptomatic of nearly all of them. In each case, sadness first of all yawns like a black pit, threatening to swallow up the miserable protagonist. It is, in Reb Nahman's words, melancholy caused by lack of faith. The theological overtones of this psychic illness are unmistakable.

> The face of holiness is a luminous face, the countenance of life . . . and happiness. . . . The face of the Other Side, though, is a

> dark face, the countenance of melancholy, of idolatry. As it is written (Ex. 20:3), "Thou shalt have no other gods before My face." Those individuals who fall lusting after money, and don't believe God can provide effortlessly for all men—they chase after their livelihood with great toil, and eat their bread in sadness . . . and melancholy. . . . Yet those whose every action is done in faith—they cleave to the face of holiness.[87]

Both *The Master of Prayer* and the *Clever Son and Simple Son* dramatize this very dialectic. The sects contaminated with materialism and the clever son with his intellectual vanity worship their own egos and turn their backs to faith. The tragic end of the latter tale shows, as a warning, the fate of the apostate who refused to be cured.

In other instances, the paralyzing despair that grips the protagonist is eventually neutralized, even resolved, by hope. The king's true son *(Two Sons Who Were Reversed)* is reduced to near-suicidal thoughts and decides to live out his life as a lewd drunkard. Yet from those depths he rises to become the savior of the enchanted city. The promised groom *(Burgher and Poor Man),* also a messianic figure, likewise abandons all hope of refinding his betrothed and intends to live out his days on a desert island—but ultimately he, too, reforms and wins his beautiful bride. The king's servant *(Lost Princess),* on his endless search, battles with destructive forces in himself, stumbling from failure to failure. At last, though, he too overcomes his paralyzing misery and strides forth to free the princess. Reb Nahman saw this pattern of despair and faith as a principle taught by life itself: in the phrase made famous by Hasidism, "descent for the purpose of ascending." While *Likkutei Moharan* presents the theoretical formulation of his understanding, it is in the tales, far more, that we intimate the suffering inherent in such spiritual trials.

> The essence of Judaism is that one should live in naïveté, wholeness, and simplicity, without any undue cleverness. And a person should examine all his actions to be sure God is present in them, with no concern for his own honor. Even when he falls, heaven forbid, into doubt, and sometimes this fall may be very hard, and be fraught with skepticism and suspicion, and questions God's very existence, the ultimate purpose of this fall and his descent is to ascend.[88]

We realize, then, that each of these five tales charts a process, the dynamic in an individual's spiritual life, and points out the pitfalls that lie in his path. The transmutation of the drama of psychic development into the medium of fiction is yet another factor drawing Reb Nahman's tales into the genre of the fantastic.

Thus far, we have contemplated the question of self-referentiality in the sense of direct projection, i.e., the instances in which elements of the author's self-image reappear, embodied in his characters. Yet we must not ignore a second and highly inventive sort of self-referentiality: that is, images of the author and his world projected through the crooked, distorting mirror of parody. An inherently self-conscious genre, parody imitates reality; all its satirical effect lies in its power to reveal to the audience the truth behind the fiction. Thus the parodist himself, forcibly, must be highly aware of his intent ruthlessly to expose the follies of his times. Weiss speaks of the importance of humor in Reb Nahman's oeuvre, while pointing out that this inclination in fact emphasizes man's *tragic-comic* existential state.[89] In *Likkutei Moharan*, following the *Zohar*, Reb Nahman recognizes the champion of satire personified in the figure of the ape. He contrasts the nature of the *kelippot* with that of holiness; yet rather than declaring, as we might expect, that the *kelippot* are the antithesis and enemy of holiness, he concludes, "They oppose holiness in the same way an ape plays, imitating a man."[90] Parody, thus, is preeminently self-conscious because it is the parodist who vividly portrays the movements of the ape; the ape himself is unaware of his grotesqueness—in his eyes he *is* the man. Comical and satirical portraits abound in Reb Nahman's tales: the vice-ridden sects in *Master of Prayer*, the beleaguered lands in *The Seven Beggars* (in the stories of the second and fourth beggars), the mountain den of demons in *The Cripple*, the country of lies in *The Humble King*; and the godless philosopher of *Clever and Simple Son*. In each, Reb Nahman's Swiftian sarcasm tears away disguises. The sects, the kingdoms, the overweening sycophant—all these actors trumpet their most-cherished beliefs. Reb Nahman's parody derides their hubris and holds up their follies to ridicule: he confronts the ape with its own subhuman face.

The theater of the absurd, present in so many of Reb Nahman's tales, thus springs, in fact, from its author's radically honest scrutiny of the world. Our meeting with the tales awakens us to the haunting kinship between ape and man, between the fanatical sects and obsessive contemporary society, between the clever son and the rational ego. The power of the satire lies in its borderline existence: impossible to discount as whimsy, yet impossibly far from realism, it arouses a sense of inescapable uneasiness.

In the last pages of this chapter, I would like to consider another such borderline experience, which seems to me fundamental in Reb Nahman's creative life. That is the phenomenon of inspiration itself—and the problem of its source. The fantastic world of the tales, the flashes of insight that engender *Likkutei Moharan*, the dreams and messages that, according to his students, visited Reb Nahman throughout his life—is his genius begotten by the Creator Himself, or is he but a madman, controlled by the forces of the Other Side? A third possibility exists as well: perhaps madness is the sole escape from the grip of the intellect; perhaps irrationality is actually a higher and freer state, opening the possibility of true vision.[91] The threshold between madness and prophetic inspiration, and awareness of its tenuous nature, was clearly a dominant factor in Reb Nahman's life. The description offered by Reb Nahman's followers of their rebbe's presence and his ways vividly illustrates this dialectic:

> Before he would present a teaching he would sit with us for an hour or two, and he would labor intensely, with movements and groans. Although he sat in silence, his great efforts were betrayed by the movements he made. Finally he opened his mouth and began to speak. Once . . . when he was repeating the precious words of *Likkutei Moharan* 20 . . . he grasped the two sides of his beard in his two hands and nearly tore it out, so great was his awe and his self-abnegation. Then he said that when he relays his teachings it seems to him that as the first word leaves his mouth, his soul will leave him as well.[92]

A visionary who acts as if possessed, his whole being hanging between life and death—that is the mystic's classic, enigmatic image. Perhaps we may recognize an ironic reflection of this image in the "mad zaddikim" of the *Cripple*, the "mad gardener" in the second beggar's tale, or the "madman" in *The Master of Prayer* who alone believed in God. The poignancy of these figures cannot be ignored, for, as we learn from the tales, it is the genius's own society that judges whether he is insane or inspired. Maltreated heroes, ridiculed by those around them for their higher insight—the king's servant, in his endless search for the lost princess; the cripple, with his incomprehensible mission to water trees; the rabbi's son, hopelessly hoping to visit his zaddik—represent another aspect of the same driven personality.

The fabulator, in his ability to build worlds of words and destroy them at will, truly resembles the divine Creator. Gardens, kingdoms, and deserts spring from his imagination, and into those spaces he puts figures created in his own image, after his likeness. Certainly this is the most authentic, perhaps the only honest, kind of fiction. Reb Nahman's personal connection with the characters of his tales—male or female, simple cobblers or kings' true sons—invests them with vital force. We must regard the self-referentiality inherent in the stories he told as an essential aspect of their strength and worth.

II • Telling Tales; or, The Physics and Metaphysics of Fiction

1. THE SANCTIFICATION OF FICTION IN HASIDIC TRADITION

It is told that when the Ba'al Shem Tov was faced with the task of saving a soul, he would go to a certain place in the forest, light a fire, and meditate in prayer—and what he requested would come to be. When, a generation later, the Maggid of Mezherich was faced with the same task, he would go to the same place in the forest and say, We can no longer light the fire, but we can still utter the prayers—and what he asked became reality. Yet a generation later, R. Moses Leib of Sassov had to perform the same task. He, though, went to the forest and said: Now, we cannot light the fire, and we do not know the secret prayers and meditations, but we know the place in the forest to which it all belongs, and that must be enough—and it was enough. But when another generation had passed and R. Israel of Ryzhin was called upon to perform the task, he sat down on his golden chair in his castle and said: We cannot light the fire, we do not know the prayer, we do not know the place, but we can tell the story of how it was done. And, the storyteller adds, the effect of his tale was no less than the actions of the first three.[1]

This emblematic description of the evolution of the Hasidic movement—despite its end a century after Reb Nahman's death—intimates the theme of our chapter: the status of the narrative in Bratslav tradition, the role played by "fiction" both in the human and divine realms. Essential to our discussion is an unconservative, associative utilization of the lexicon of literary analysis. This approach guides us throughout. In the first part, our concern is the sanctification of the tale, as a literary form, in Reb Nahman's worldview. Its inherent mirroring of historical as well as cosmic events, its mystical function in linking lower to upper worlds, and its importance as a didactic tool—all three aspects of the tale as genre justify its centrality in Reb Nahman's oeuvre. In part 2, we will consider the nature of other narrative models that seem to have inspired our author in his creation. Among them: folktales of non-Jewish tradition, allegories and midrashim preserved in rabbinic lore, biblical prophecy. The influence of sources such as these in stylistic, thematic, and interpretative terms will be explored. Part 3 seeks to compare the Jewish mystical perception of the Torah itself as the ultimate text—polysemous, inherently symbolic, ontologically potent—to Reb Nahman's conception of his own tales. From this phenomenology of the Text we turn in part 4 to an investigation of the nonverbal "texts" that appear in myriad forms in Reb Nahman's oeuvre. Some of these symbolic microcosms include hands, maps, portraits, instruments—each of them telling its own wordless story. The unprecedented uniqueness of Reb Nahman's thirteen tales in Hasidic narrative tradition will, I hope, come to the fore in the course of our discussion. Yet before focusing our attention on them alone, it is important to place Reb Nahman within the context of Hasidic literary tradition. What were contemporaneous narrative forms? How were teachings (narrative as well as theoretical) transmitted and recorded? And can the authenticity of the texts engendered be verified, the author's and redactor's hands distinguished? The historical problematics of this subject are beyond the scope of our discussion; nonetheless, some brief mention of them is necessary in order to place Reb Nahman's oeuvre in proper perspective.

Initially, I. Tishby and J. Dan explain, Hasidic literature consisted almost entirely of *drushim,* collected in books interpreting the Torah, specifically biblical texts that accompany the Jewish yearly cycle. Hasidic masters in the first and second generations used this form almost exclusively in the dissemination of their ideas. The literary value of such works, these scholars add, is negligible; they serve, though, as the first and sometimes the only source of early Hasidic teachings.[2] As for Hasidic stories, Tishby and Dan recognize three categories: stories told by the zaddik; stories told by his followers about the zaddik; and *sihot,* with predominantly ideological and moralistic content. *Shivhei ha-Ba'al Shem Tov,* the first published collection of stories, is composed largely of the second type, and represents, in the eyes of the authors, the first propaganda document of the rejuvenated Hasidic movement. In other works attributed to the Ba'al Shem Tov, his teachings have been compressed to epigrams and sayings, many of them enigmatic. Reb Nahman's thirteen tales were the second collection of stories to be published; *Hayyei Moharan* contains all three narrative types, as does *Sihot Moharan,* the first collection of *sihot* to appear in print.[3]

According to S. A. Horodezki, an early-twentieth-century scholar of Hasidism, Reb Nahman told his tales in Yiddish and R. Nathan Sternharz translated them into Hebrew. As the latter testifies in his First Introduction to the tales, it was Reb Nahman's own wish to publish the *Sippurei Ma'asiyot* in a bilingual edition: "the upper 'text' in the Holy Tongue [i.e., Hebrew] and the lower in the 'foreign tongue' [*lashon la'az,* i.e., Yiddish]."[4] However, the question of the correspondence between two versions, Hebrew and Yiddish, remains unresolved. Chone Shmeruk suggests that the Yiddish version of the original stories differs from the text printed in modern editions, and his view is confirmed by Piekarz.[5] Moreover, in the Second Introduction to Reb Nahman's *Sippurei Ma'asiyot,* R. Nathan Sternharz contends that in his Hebrew redaction, he "lowered himself intentionally to simple language when he transferred the stories, recounted in 'the language of Ashkenaz,' into 'the Holy Tongue.'" This was "So that the meaning [was] not altered, for those who read them in Hebrew, from the way [Reb Nahman] told them originally."[6] The dubious correspondence between the two versions poses clear difficulties for any critical reader. The Yiddish, more detailed, colorful, and lively, is, at the same time, more verbose and diffuse. The Hebrew, erudite by its very nature and directly allusive, is also awkward and at times impossibly recondite.

Moreover, as Jacob Elbaum writes, we do not yet have tools fine enough to distinguish the elements, carefully transmitted, of Reb Nahman's own formulation and those added by R. Nathan Sternharz of Nemirov as he poured them from one vessel to another.[7] Nonetheless, Reb Nahman himself is said to have warned his followers that each word of his tales contained tremendous and precise mystical intention; to change even a single word of the stories as he himself uttered them would severely cripple them. The text on which my discussion, throughout this work, is based is the Hebrew part of the traditional Bratslav bilingual edition, published by Aguddat Meshekh ha-Nahal, Jerusalem, 5745 (1985). The Yiddish version serves, at times, as a supplement, an aid in understanding obscurities in the Hebrew text, but the latter dominates by far.

The polyphony of causes leading to the narration of Reb Nahman's tales is loyally recorded by his students: "As a rule, each story he told developed from some conversation he had with us about events in the world. He would begin a tale because an aspect of some event was connected to an event in his heart. It was a matter of 'awakening in the lower realm,' drawing down a divine conception clothed in that event. . . ."[8]

How, then, did Reb Nahman perceive himself, as an individual and as a storyteller, within this narrative continuum? In his eyes, a vital distinction exists between "tales of ancient days" and "tales in the midst of the years" (also called "tales of seventy faces" or "of seventy years"). The former are timeless, immortal tales, reflected in primordial, divine thought, before the world's creation. The latter, inextricably bound up in temporality, speak of earthly reality; in this second category are the tales about the life and times of zaddikim. Reb Nahman recognized these tales as his literary heritage: his forefathers' occupation with tales "gave birth" to him, and he saw it as his responsibility to emulate them, bearing his own children, as well, through the telling of tales.[9]

My contention is that the art of creating narrative forms is an essential cognitive tool; Reb Nahman's recognition of his entire heritage as a complex of "stories" engendered his choice of the same genre to perpetuate that heritage. Underlying our theme is the implicit dialectic between the occurrence of objective, factual events and the account of those events spoken in a second voice. This recounting of history seeks, ideally, to record and preserve the sequence of seminal events, but each representation of those events is, unavoidably, interpretation as well; in the *relating,* the teller cannot help but relate cause to effect, searching for the inner direction hidden in the events of which he speaks. The etymological kinship between *zählen* and *Erzählung, conter* and *conte, sofer* and *sippur,* etc., is clearly no accident; the clever narrator forever orders his material. Like a rich man who counts and recounts his money, so a storyteller recounts his tale to keep alive the memory it tells. This act of verbalization serves a vital role: what happens in the world can make no sense to us until we make it into an account; only by telling about reality may we hope to grasp it. This vicarious reliving of events through narrative holds tremendous psychological power: in effect, it taps the same mechanism that activates psychoanalysis.[10] The storyteller relates his tale to himself and to his audience, communicating to all who hear him their personal connection with his message. The first biblical narrator-figure is Abraham's servant, sent in search of a wife for Isaac. The future that master and servant imagine together (Gen. 24:2–9), Eliezer's prayer at the well foreseeing imminent events (Gen. 24:12–15), the events themselves (Gen. 24:15–34), and his retelling of them to Rebecca's family (Gen. 24:35–50) and later to Isaac (Gen. 24:66) suggest the multiple guises of fact and fiction. Each of these units is indeed an independent *fiction* in the most literal sense. Over and over, Eliezer fabricates reality: he suggests hypothetical, alternate endings to his mission; ostensibly he "tells" God of his predicament; then he experiences what he himself foretold; in the subsequent narration the story is canonized, and finally, back home, it becomes but an abstract gesture—"And the servant told Isaac all the things he had done." "Fiction," therefore, must not be understood as a mere arbitrary invention, an imitation of reality, but rather a process of interpretation inextricable from life itself. In this sense, fiction actually strives to preserve fact, to immortalize truth as it has been experienced.[11] What Reb Nahman calls "tales of ancient days" are, then, a history of primordial, cosmic events—though unexplainable, their order has been preserved in that abstruse form. It is this ineffable history that is retold in "tales in the midst of the years"; there, as in a mirror, divine truth may be recounted in human terms, related to human experience, communicated to the human heart. Thus, in his eyes, all of tradition exists on two planes: from the story of Creation to the story of the Jewish nation's birth, from the lives of the patriarchs to the legends of great mystics and zaddikim—all these accounts are both physical and metaphysical. Though bound up in time, they are, as well, a sort of divine mythology, a cryptic theosophy naively disguised.

The thirteen canonical tales in the collection of Reb Nahman's *Sippurei Maʿasiyot* must be seen as an organic part of this genealogy.

Charged with biblical allusions, with esoteric symbolism, with Hasidic ideas, they retell the same undying mythology. The paradigms of Lurianic Kabbalah—the Breaking of the Vessels and their restitution, the saga of exile and redemption—are vital components of this mythology. Their formative presence in nearly all of Reb Nahman's tales testifies to their status, in his mind, as archetypes, that any tale "in the midst of the years" must unavoidably re-present. But what is essential in this re-presentation is not merely to recombine the dry bones of their plot but rather to convey the drama of those "tales of ancient days," somehow to relive the pathos inherent in the original events themselves. Perhaps the most clear illustration of this point is in the tale entitled *The Master of Prayer*. The parallels I will draw in the following discussion between this tale and the Lurianic paradigm are founded on commentaries in which schematic analysis is prominent.[12] The story is set in a world of brokenness and confusion; in the middle, the cataclysmic disaster (the storm and the chaos it wreaked) is recounted a posteriori, but primarily in order to set the narrative present in its proper context. It is the reckless search for a king in the absence of the True King that motivates all the actions of this tale. The essence of each sect is rooted in some villainous reversal of the divine attributes informing the system of the *sefirot*. All the world's false beliefs, all idolatries, R. Nathan says, come from the Breaking of the Vessels; it is the *kelippot,* the shards of those shattered containers, that cause this fundamental distortion.[13] Thus each character in the king's original court—the master of prayer, the mighty warrior, the treasurer, the wise man, the bard, the faithful friend, the infant—corresponds with one of the seven lower *sefirot,* while the antithesis of each figure's dominant attribute is reflected in the immorality of each of the sects.[14] The upper three *sefirot,* according to the Lurianic paradigm, remained intact, though damaged through the influx of divine light. Thus the king, queen, and queen's daughter of the tale cast themselves into voluntary exile—for a king who has no kingdom, no court, and no throne is but a caricature; he sits in a lonely field, his crown askew on his head. The master of prayer finds himself in this world where the *kelippot* seem to reign, and he sets out to lead it to its restitution. Thus the tale ranges from a legendary cataclysm *(shevirah)* to the realization of a prophetic vision (Is. 31)—idols of gold and silver are cast away, sinners repent, and the throne, king, and kingdom are restored.

The cipher nature of these paradigms, so prominent in *The Master of Prayer,* becomes apparent when we consider other tales Reb Nahman told. *The Humble King* concerns, as well, a land in need of *tikkun*. The protagonist ventures through a country of lies, seemingly abandoned by the king who hides his face; his aspiration to restore the kingdom is linked, once again, to a revelation of that king's true being. In *The Lost Princess,* it is the act of *zimzum* that becomes the focal event.[15] The mention of the king's six sons serves to verify the identity of his only daughter (the seventh, feminine *sefirah* of *Malkhut*); the father's unexplained anger at this beloved daughter leads to her imprisonment by evil forces and creates the necessity of her rescue. In contrast to these tales, with their focus on dissolution and their summary resolution, *The Two Sons Who Were Reversed* dramatizes the process of *tikkun* in rich detail. The tale itself is an Odyssean search for "the foolish land and its clever king"—a quest that culminates in the heroic trial of restoring the garden. The true son's first insight, to find refuge by the statue-king and thus avoid the invisible terrors that would block his entrance, signals the first act of *tikkun*. It is the mirror image of Adam's appeal, upon his expulsion from the Garden, to the Sabbath to grant him peace on his lonely path.[16] He approaches, one by one, the monumental symbols of the bed, table, chair, and lamp; he discovers the subtle flaw that has imprisoned each one in silence (the misplaced rose, the forgotten animal), and wordlessly returns the artistry of each object to its former wholeness. And in reward for his new-won intuition, the garden itself breaks into song; it begins to play—a fantasy music box of *tikkun*. The *Zohar* reveals the mystical valence of that humble quartet of bed and table, chair and lamp. Together, they are four components of the Shekhinah; by grace of human prayers her damaged form may be restored.[17] Though this esoteric dimension is not explicit in the tale, the garden's Ninth Symphony rings with its truth, the miracle of ultimate restoration.

Turning to the second paradigm, that of exile and redemption, we see that it, too, provides a skeletal frame on which the tissue of many tales is woven. The protagonists of *The Cripple, The Two Sons Who Were Reversed, The Lost Princess, King and Kaiser, The Seven Beggars,* and *Clever and Simple Son* are all estranged in some way—driven from their land, from their family, from themselves. All of them suffer the pain of separation and yearn to return, to regain or to win what has been lost to them. Indeed, one may argue that all folk and fairy tales are about exile, about battles with evil, and about escape to freedom. Yet, far from robbing the Lurianic paradigm of its validity, this argument only strengthens it. Truly, the tragedy of the holy sparks imprisoned in matter is an omnipresent aspect of reality. Whether played out in the history of the Jewish nation or in the human soul, regardless of the actors' names, all stories must, inevitably, tell that single, undying, and primordial drama.[18]

"In former generations, when kabbalistic matters were discussed, they were spoken of in such language," Reb Nahman adds after concluding *The Two Sons Who Were Reversed.* "For until R. Simeon bar Yohai, Kabbalah was not discussed openly . . . before him, when people spoke of mystical matters, they spoke in such a way." Thus like the Torah, this tale of the sons of kings and slaves, the forest, the journey, and the garden is yet another phrasing of something that cannot be told directly. It is like the Soma juice in the ancient Vedic sacrifice: if unfiltered, the ambrosia is dangerous for mortals to drink, but when filtered it gives a taste of immortality.[19] So the divine truths that the Torah contains are drugs of life as well as of death;[20] they must pass through the sieve of narration, be clad in the guise of dreams, of fantasy, or translated into a foreign tongue, that their essence may be internalized by human beings. At issue, in fact, is an irreducible dichotomy between "fiction" and "reality." The lament that "we have spent our years like a tale that is told" (Ps. 90:9) implies that perhaps there really is no difference between our lives and the story of our lives—both are equally fictitious, both are equally a mirror reflection compared to the reality of realms beyond our own. "For all the events that occur in the world, all of them surely allude to sublime matters, because nothing is senseless/solely in the world; the world never rests, even for a moment . . . certainly everything alludes to what it alludes, yet all is but mere hints compared to infinity without end."[21]

In chapter 1 we spoke of the influence of the author's self-image in the formulation of his works. Inspired by the image of the Baʿal Shem Tov, Reb Nahman recognizes yet another responsibility upon the zaddik's shoulders: he is a storyteller who, through his tales, has the power to effect changes both on the cosmic and the human level. In Reb Nahman's words, "[T]he Baʿal Shem Tov, may his holy memory be for a blessing, was able, through stories, to unite disparate entities. When he saw that channels on high had been blocked, and they could not be repaired through prayer, he would make them whole by a tale."[22] The implication, as Joseph Dan explains, is that not only prayer but stories as well are invested with theurgic power. Their narration may cause the reunion of *sefirot* such as *Tiferet* and *Malkhut,* which had grown distant from one another, preventing the influx of divine mercy from emanating outward and downward into the lower world.[23] Yet the need for reunion exists not solely on that esoteric level; through his tales, the zaddik restores his listeners' souls; he draws them from their path of error and returns them to the will of the Creator. In the image of the crooked-necked beggar, who "throws his own voice" through the dark night to draw together the two lost birds, so the zaddik "clothes the Torah in tales, i.e., sends the voice of God to the Assembly of Israel" in simple, human tones they can understand. "And the opposite is true as well—he must convey the praying voice of the Assembly of Israel to God. Thus the zaddik clothes prayer in the tales he tells. For the advocates *[ha-mekatregim]* are mighty, so much so that prayer cannot rise simply; it must be disguised in tales."[24] These antithetical effects of the zaddik's stories, then, illustrate the celebrated Hasidic principle of *it'aruta diletata*—action awakened in the nether realms opens blocked channels linking heaven to earth and catalyzes change above, and this change, in turn, reverberates sensibly in the human spirit.

The notion of the theurgic power inherent in the zaddik's stories helps us understand why some of Reb Nahman's stories end in a strange state of incompleteness, and others with an accelerated denouement disproportionate to the rest of the tale. In *The Lost Princess,* for example, the servant's anguished search for the captured princess trails off, "And how he saved her is not told, and in the end he saved her." Even more obscurely, in *The Seven Beggars* the last, legless beggar never even appears at the wedding, and the frame story of the king and his son with which the story opened is abandoned. *Burgher and Poor Man* ends in three short sentences with a speedy spiral of events: the heroine reveals her true identity, honor is restored to her father, the couple weds, and "happiness was complete." *The Cripple,* similarly, draws to an abrupt conclusion—war breaks out, the earth quakes, the world collapses, evil is destroyed, and the vital tree is watered at last. Both unresolved endings and summary endings point to some sort of disparity in conception between the tale's development and denouement. Certainly the experience of exile, of distance, and of longing and search is much more palpable than the unreal hope of redemption in the promised future. It can be told with greater sympathy and insight, and that telling, in fact, helps all who listen become conscious of their own existential state and of their people's destiny. But how the longed-for messianic age will come about has not yet been experienced; it belongs—for us—wholly in the realm of fantasy. When we consider what many scholars recognize as Reb Nahman's impetus in turning to stories in the last four years of his life, we find a key to understanding the intent behind these enigmatic pseudoendings. The death of Reb Nahman's son in 1806, dashing the messianic hopes the infant had borne, combined with Reb Nahman's failure in disseminating his esoteric works beyond the circle of his intimate followers are thought to have radically altered his expectations. "Reb Nahman felt that redemption, which had been imminent, had been delayed, and that was because the nation was not ready. Thus he understood that the harbinger of redemption must be brought them in a different way, little by little, concealed in the veil of tales."[25] The zaddik's stories may be seen, then, as "awakening the lower worlds" in the most literal sense. He prepares the world, spiritually and viscerally, for the Messiah's advent; yet until all is ready, the end cannot fully be told. For as soon as it is narrated—if the zaddik's intent is pure—it must come to pass.

2. ADOPTION OF NARRATIVE ELEMENTS FROM OTHER GENRES

Folktales

Reb Nahman's celebrated aesthetic pluralism, the regard he inherited from the Baʿal Shem Tov for multifarious media of human expression, is most visible in the influence folktales exerted in creating the dynamics of his own narratives. Holiness, he insisted, is inherent in such tales as well, for "God's glory shouts from everything—'the whole earth is full of His glory' (Is. 6:7)—even from the stories of non-Jews, His glory shouts forth."[26] The idea of divine immanence permeating the material world, all languages, and all melodies is conceived, in fact, as an ontological necessity: "for without His holiness, they cannot exist at all—'You preserve them all' (Neh. 9:6)—only, in them, divine vitality is greatly contracted and minimal, just enough to keep them alive but no more."[27] Hence the responsibility of the zaddik to redeem those holy sparks imprisoned in all manner of forms—by retelling the tales the world tells, and thus restoring their original order before the Vessels shattered and the endless light they held was scattered. In the following pages, I would like to consider some of the generic elements characteristic of folktales that Reb Nahman adopted—plot functions, motifs, narrative style. The tools developed by modern literary criticism aid us, on one hand, in perceiving the kinship between these two narrative traditions. Yet they also enable us to penetrate beyond their schematic similarity toward the secret working of the tales Reb Nahman told. It is important to remember, as well, that Reb Nahman's own narrative tradition, from biblical and talmudic to kabbalistic sources, is similarly informed with folk motifs. The difference lies in the allegorical dimension omnipresent beyond these motifs. In his integration of such thematic elements, the flesh and blood of folktales, Reb Nahman deftly draws on their hermeneutics as well, on the implicit referential level that is his inheritance, bound to the pre-texts he has assimilated.

Consider, for example, the motif of the path, or way *(derekh)*. A universal metaphor, it speaks of destiny, of movement through time and space—away from and toward. The path, in literature, is the archetypal meeting place; every inch of it presents a potential intersection, perhaps a juncture, a crisis, a turning point. Bakhtin speaks of the "chronotopos [space-time], the fusion of spacial and temporal attributes of road":

> Here the spacial and temporal series of human fates and lives form peculiar combinations, complicated and concretized by the social distances which are overcome. Here time . . . pours into space and flows through it (forming roads), hence the rich metaphorization of the path-road: "the path of life"; "take a new path"; "a historic path" . . . the metaphorization of the road is varied and has many planes but its basic center is the flow of time.[28]

In the opening verses of the *Divine Comedy* Dante writes, "In the middle of the journey of our life, I found myself in a dark wood, where the straight way was lost." The entire story *Burgher and Poor Man* speaks in this metaphor—the danger-wrought escape of the burgher and poor man's wife from pit to *mikveh,* to ponds and springs, streams, rivers, and seas recurs as a leitmotif throughout the lives of their children, the hero and heroine. It is the secret text binding their betrothal; it is the song of desire the true bridegroom must sing to his bride; it is the path the beloved herself must pass by to enable her reunion with her lover. *Rabbi and Only Son,* similarly, tells of a journey—begun again and again yet stymied, the destination never reached. In *The Cripple* all the protagonist's adventures occur on the highway—he sets off to make his fortune, falls victim to robbers, and finally waits by the wayside to watch as the wicked and the holy tread their own paths to redemption or damnation. Both the king's true son and the servant's true son *(The Two Sons Who Were Reversed)* spend most of their tale on the road; whether in pursuit or in flight or in search of a legendary kingdom, their movement through space symbolizes their gradual self-realization. Alone in the wide world, far from home, each must discover the path meant for him. Finally, in *The Master of Prayer,* the pathos of the ruined kingdom is portrayed by the trail littered with the iconography of its exiled court (the lakes of blood and milk, the scattered golden hairs, the abandoned crown, the shield, and so forth). What is remarkable in all these tales is their fantastic geography. The whole world is faceless and nameless; only the critical points of meeting that penetrate each character's life stand out in relief, like black points on an unlabeled map. There is only *one* desert island where hero and heroine must inevitably land *(Burgher and Poor Man);* there is only *one* forest, and in it *one* tree where the two rival sons encounter each other. All the randomness of human life is contracted; the essential, abstract meeting points alone remain.[29]

In *Likkutei Moharan,* Reb Nahman rereads the following talmudic parable as the account of a Hasidic spiritual quest.

> It is like the man who was walking on a road in the dead of night and darkness, in fear of brambles and holes, wild animals and bandits. And he does not know which way to go. Then he comes upon a torch and is saved from the brambles and the holes and the briars, yet he is still afraid of wild animals and bandits. And still he does not know the way. When dawn comes, he is delivered from both animals and bandits, but still he does not know

> the way. Until he comes to a junction, and is saved from every danger.[30]

R. Hisda, expanded by Rashi, explains the allegory: the torch is the commandments; the dawn is the Torah; the junction, the meeting with a learned man and/or the day of death. Both of these encounters, with oral teaching and with one's own mortality, aid the individual in understanding the course of his life. Reb Nahman adds his own perception of the dangers along that uncertain way. There are destructive qualities, he writes, each of them drawn from one of the four evolutionary levels of existence: sadness, embodied in stony, inanimate bodies; negative desires, personified in thorny plant form; idle words, represented in phlegmatic animality; and pride, incorporated in the grossly verbal highway robbers. In one way or another, the protagonists of all the tales struggle with these four adversaries, both in their metaphorical and literal forms. The pirates and highway bandits, the pits and traps and malicious beasts, are stock enemies of every hero. The trials to overcome them, whether as symbols of moral flaws or as reality—such are the adventures informing Reb Nahman's and folktales alike.

Formally and functionally, narratives in both corpora speak of a fated course of events. The oaths of loyalty that cannot be broken *(King and Kaiser; Burgher and Poor Man),* the unalterable royalty of the king's true heir *(The Two Sons Who Were Reversed),* the mandatory rescue of the lost princess—superficially, all these seem to suggest that the outcome of the story, like that in all folktales, is predestined and the actors are will-less puppets. But in Reb Nahman's worldview, the pagan notion of fate is transformed. The hidden force guiding events, far from blind, is in his tales divine providence. It is a theological necessity that such providence remain secret, unrevealed, for only then is free human choice possible. Paradoxically, the dynamics of these simplistic tales inform our own world as well; to understand that all the twisting paths of history, all the tortuous choices people are forced to make, are secretly guided by God's hand—this is the challenge and the ultimate message Reb Nahman, through his tales, conveys.[31]

Complementing the "unrealistic" notion of space that characterizes folk tales is the strange unreality of time. Figures in Reb Nahman's tales journey "for years and years"; they wait for one another, search, and wander for immeasurable periods; kingdoms pass away and wars are fought; and yet those vast temporal spaces may be passed over in a moment. Years, days, minutes compress and expand in complete freedom. Italo Calvino evokes a fascinating model to describe what we call "plot" in literature. He remarks that our verbal imitation of the clock's "tick-tock" implies a fundamental humanization of time we cannot live without. "Tick" he suggests, signifies a beginning, Genesis, while "tock" is the end, Apocalypse, the expectation of closure. "The fact that we call the second sound 'tock' is evidence we use fictions to enable the end to confer organization and form on the temporal structure. The interval between the two sounds (tick-tock) is now charged with significant duration." Calvino calls the time of the novelist *kairos,* as opposed to the simple chronicity *(chronos),* or "passing time" we normally associate with reality. *Kairos,* in contrast, must be "a significant season," an instance of "temporal integration" on which perception of the present, memory of the past, and expectation of the future are bundled together in a common organization.[32] The eschatological paradigm on which Reb Nahman's tales are built mandates that their temporality be *kairos.* What begins in exile will end in redemption; what begins in ruin will end in harmony. Thus ages of waiting are subsumed in a handful of words; moment is linked to pregnant moment like pearls on a string. The time between is as naught, as faceless as the uncharted roads linking one fateful meeting to the next.

Reb Nahman's tales also seem to be narrated in typical folktale style. There is dramatic use of direct speech ("And they asked each other, 'Who are you, son of man?' 'Who are you, son of man?' 'Whence did you come here?'" [*SM*, p. 145]); there are superlatives in every manner of description (maidens of unsurpassed beauty who know all languages; brilliant children whose hair shines with all colors; problems with one sole solution; illnesses with one sole cure); there are stereotypical characters and actions (beautiful princess, clever son, evil king, loyal servant; rebellion, estrangement, search, reunion). Yet as we have suggested, the naive facade of the tales actually betrays their true referential valence.[33] Could the Messiah, the true zaddik, the Shekhinah, or the King of Kings be portrayed in anything but superlatives? How could there be more than one supreme love song, more than one ultimate redemption? In other words, although Reb Nahman's tales wear the same guise as the tales the world tells, their style is but another disguise. The similarity between the two is no accident. Indeed, such simplicity, such stark oppositions of good and evil, and such dialogues exert tremendous appeal. But we must look beyond them as well, realizing they are but another means the storyteller chose to reach his listeners' hearts.

Rabbinic Literature

Thus far, we have considered the presence of elements of folk literature in the world of Reb Nahman's imagination. It would be shortsighted, however, to overlook the dominance of elements endemic to folk or fantastic literature in the pre-texts of Jewish tradition. Reb Nahman's interest, for example, in the "tall tales" told by Rabba bar bar Hannah[34] is apparent in the teachings concentrated in *Likkutei Moharan* based on them.[35] Serious study of those talmudic parables is, of course, beyond the scope of our discussion.[36] Yet the attention in them to the natural world, the romantic aspiration to penetrate the mysteries of Creation, the sense of the uncanny inherent in the world's wonders—all these qualities reverberate in Reb Nahman's own oeuvre. Moreover, as R. Samuel ben Meir, or Rashbam (whose interpretation accompanies citations of the talmudic text in *Likkutei Moharan*), reminds us, tales such as these are told to illustrate the recognition "How great are your works, O God" (Ps. 104:24) or to explain biblical texts, such as those in the book of Job which speak of giant birds, beasts, or fish.[37] Thus when Reb Nahman evokes an atmosphere resembling that of Rabba bar bar Hana's tales—when he tells of sea voyages, giants in deserts, human beings made of precious gems—the astute reader detects the subtexts beneath that imaginative conception. The stock characters that people his tales have wandered over from the hundreds of parables *(mashalim)* of kings, queens, princes, old men, children, and merchants that fill talmudic and mystical tradition: "A king of flesh and blood had a fine orchard, and he appointed two watchmen, a cripple and a blind man," etc.[38] Finally, the catharsis, whether immanent or explicit, concluding many of Reb Nahman's stories and substories (especially in *The Seven Beggars*) reconjures biblical prophecies envisaging the end of days. Isaiah's vision of everlasting harmony in the animal kingdom—"the wolf shall dwell with the lamb, and the leopard shall lie down with the kid . . ." (Is. 11:6–10)—prefigures the scene evoked by the hunchbacked beggar in which beasts and birds rest at peace in the shade of the wondrous tree (*SM,* p. 271). The benevolent flood of waters described by Ezekiel (47:9) as issuing from Jerusalem and healing all ills appears in the last scene of *The Cripple,* in which waters flow forth to save the vital tree. Indeed, even the simple coda of each of the seven beggars' tales, "And there was great happiness and very much joy," reflects the prophet's moving expression of the ultimate redemption: "And the ransomed of the Lord shall return, and come to Zion with songs and everlasting joy upon their heads: they shall obtain joy and gladness, and sorrow and sighing shall flee away" (Is. 35:10, 51:11).[39] The emotional charge of these visions, truly the catharsis of ages of suffering the prophets knew so intimately, is transplanted to the tales that incorporate them.

We must, therefore, widen our definition of "folklore" in considering the influence of related genres on Reb Nahman's narrative works. The motifs, plot functions, and style characteristic of Western folktales play a significant role in his tales as well. Yet many of the same elements are also an essential component in other sources in Jewish tradition. Perhaps this fact only reinforces the conviction that the tales the world tells must be redeemed. For their events and motifs are no alien invention by impure hands; rather, they are strikingly familiar, rooted in centuries of Jewish "folk" tradition.[40]

3. THE TORAH AS TEXT AND ARCHETYPE

In the first part of this chapter, we spoke of the phenomenology of the tale in the Hasidic conception, in its evolution from the Ba'al Shem Tov to Reb Nahman. The inherent holiness imprisoned in folk tales, the need to reorder their erroneous construction, and the theurgic power contained in the proper narration—these ideas are seminal in the conception of the tales Reb Nahman told. Yet this revolutionary discovery of the ontological nature of stories is no innovation plucked from the air. On the contrary, the radical notion of "fiction" developed by Hasidism is modeled on the ancient mystical perception of the Torah itself. The metaphysics of the ultimate Text (recorded by Moses, divinely inspired) provides a source of fascination throughout Jewish history. I would like to present some of the many thoughts on this subject, in the hope of demonstrating their effect on the Hasidic conception of the tale (a narrated text) described above.

Job asks (28:13): "But where shall wisdom be found? And where is the place of understanding? Man cannot know its *order;* nor is it found in the land of the living." R. Eliezer ben Pedat understands his words as speaking of the Torah's internal structure. He comments that the various sections of the Torah were not given in their correct order; had they been, anyone who read them would be able to raise the dead and perform miracles. For that reason the correct order and arrangement of the Torah were hidden. R. Eliezer ben Pedat cites Is. 44:7, "Who is like me? let him proclaim it, let him declare it and set it in order for me."[41] The schism between a whole spiritual Torah and the partial, disordered revelation in the Torah we know originates, in mystical thought, in the two sets of tablets given to Moses before, and again after, the sin of the Golden Calf. The first tablets, traced by the finger of God and read by Moses alone, were, the *Zohar* teaches, from the Tree of Life. "Truly spiritual, they represent the revelation of the Torah for man in his original pure state, to be bestowed on a world in which revelation and redemption coincided. They were completely holy, contained no mention of impurity or death. When they were shattered, this pure spiritual element receded, remaining visible only to mystics. The tablets given in their place, written by the hand of man at the word of God, are from the Tree of Knowledge."[42] It is this revealed Torah, therefore, that tells our own human story; as Reb Nahman teaches, the history of all the nations—Ashkenaz, the Saxons, Hungary—is alluded to in that text.[43] This statement, of course, reminds us once again that in his eyes, historical events and the story of those events are at the same existential level. Both stories and the events themselves speak secretly of divine occurrences alone; that sublime referent, however, is as far beyond the conception of readers as it is hidden from those physically present at the events as they occur.[44]

By definition, a text of divine provenance must encompass all of time: it must speak simultaneously of the historical past, present, and future; moreover, it must bear meaning in both a national and personal sense. The atemporality of the Torah is suggested in the expression *Torah kedumah,* which springs from the notion that "the Torah was pre-existent before the world's creation."[45] Yoav Elstein points out the semantic connection between this idea and Reb Nahman's concept of *sippurim me-shanim kadmoniot* (tales of ancient years)—the stories of the Torah are timeless, their message transcending all limitations posed by human temporality.[46] An example, offered in *Likkutim Yekarim:* "In explanation of the verse, 'And Jacob left Beʾer Sheva and went toward Haran': the Torah, as we know, is primordial, and is not in time; all that this story concerns is eternally present. Even man—who is called 'a world'—contains this story as well."[47] Jacob's life, the text explains, is an allegory of the soul, which leaves its heavenly place to wander in the exile of this lower world; its only hope is to act with integrity and be granted the chance to return and reunite with the divine source of truth. The conviction that the narrative recounting events in the lives of biblical figures must be seen as an encoded message is voiced repeatedly in the *Zohar;* R. Moshe Hayyim of Sudilkov emphasizes the personal significance to every listener's own life of the adventures of the patriarchs he reads:

> "And [Abraham] removed from there to a mountain on the east of Beth-El, and pitched his tent, having Beth-El on the west and ʿAy on the east . . ." [Gen. 12:8]. As it is written in the holy *Zohar,* there is not a word or letter of the Torah that does not allude to holy and sublime matters; certainly this story of Abraham our father's journeys contains mysteries of the Torah relevant to every individual in every age.[48]

The "doctrine of ecstatic identification" recognized by Gershom Scholem in the teaching of R. Abraham Abulafia refers to the same essential phenomenon in kabbalistic terms. In the supreme state of *devekut,* or ecstasy, man and the Torah become one; Abulafia supplements the injunction of Mishnah *Avot,* "Turn [the Torah] over and over, for it contains all," adding, "And all of it is in you and all of you is in it."[49] In chapter 1, we discussed Reb Nahman's striving by means of the tales he told to shake his listeners to spiritual wakefulness, to engender each one's personal *tikkun* by joining him, emotionally and intellectually, to the contents of the narrative. His preface to the first tale he told, *The Lost Princess,* contains an emblem of this hope: "On the way I told a tale, and everyone who heard it began to have stirrings of repentance. And this is the tale. . . ." The resemblance between Reb Nahman's concept of personal engagement between listener and narrative and the traditional, unquestioned recognition of engagement vis-à-vis biblical narrative seems more than coincidental. As we shall see, this is but one of the ways in which Reb Nahman's phenomenology of tales perpetuates the traditional Jewish view of the Torah as a metaphysical text.

Praise for Rabbi Akiva's exegetical precision rings through rabbinic literature; from the most unassuming grammatical article ("and," "but," "*et,*" "also") he would unearth heaps of halakhic teaching concealed in the text. Legend has it that even the *tagim,* the crownlets upon some letters, were affixed there by God Himself with R. Akiva in mind, as storehouses of divine intent.[50] This intense respect for the finest details of the biblical text serves as a model for Reb Nahman's followers regarding their master's oeuvre. He is quoted as saying, "My teaching [lit., Torah] is profound. Consider its language—one must be as precise as with the Bible." His scribe adds: "For he repeats things, sometimes seemingly superfluously. But his intent is sublime. . . ."[51] In a holy text, no "repetition," whether of words, phrases, or accounts of events can be brushed aside as oversight; on the contrary, the fundamental assumption is that such details are in fact planted in the reader's path as hints that no matter is so simple, that here he must dig deeper to discover the text's true meaning. Apparent repetition conceives a subtext—it opens up the underground labyrinth that is Oral Law.[52]

The constant protests of Reb Nahman's disciples that their rebbe's tales are deceptively simple[53] recalls the severe remonstration voiced in the *Zohar:*

> Rabbi Simeon said: Woe to the man who says that the Torah intended simply to relate stories and the words of commoners, for, if this were the case, we ourselves at the present time could make a Torah from the words of commoners and do even better. If the intention was to deal with the affairs of [this] world, then the [profane] books in the world contain better things. Shall we then follow them, and make a Torah out of them? But all the words of the Torah are exalted and are supernal mysteries.[54]

In the teaching of the Baʿal Shem Tov, we find a renaissance of this view, and with it a newborn awareness that biblical stories, more than any other genre within that Text, are the medium chosen by God Himself to relate His truth to the world's elite:

> "And God saw the light, that it was good; and God divided the light from the darkness" (Gen. 1:3). The Holy One, blessed be He, saw that the world was not worthy of this primeval light, and He hid it away for the zaddikim in future days. . . . How could it be hidden away? . . . "Light" *[orah]* is "Torah"; at first He intended to give the revealed light of the Torah and its secrets to the world. Then he hid it away. Where? In the stories *[sippurei ma'asiyot]* of the Torah.[55]

The Hasidic zaddik's choice to share his own illuminated vision through stories *(sippurei ma'asiyot)* thus becomes a highly provocative act. For although the biblical tales predate his own narrative chronologically, the implicit belief is that both the "original" text and his "copy" share the same metaphysical status. Both of them, equally, are deliberately fashioned to clothe a single teaching, which belongs exclusively to higher realms.[56]

This implicit suggestion of kinship between Reb Nahman's tales and those of the Torah is reinforced by certain stylistic details, which seem to be employed in deliberate imitation of the biblical narrative. One of the most unassuming yet powerful among them is the constant use of the word "and." Quite often it appears as the simple conjunctive *vav,* yet at times as the distinctively biblical conversive *vav,* which turns a future verb to the past tense, and past verb to the future tense.[57] A second is the interjection of the portentous phrase "Now there was a day" *[va-yehi ha-yom].* In the midrash R. Ishmael recognizes this phrase as the signal of impending misfortune.[58] In biblical narrative, these words open the tale of the tragic downfall of King Saul's son, Jonathan (1 Sam. 14:1); they intersperse the trials of faith endured by the Shunammite woman with the prophet Elisha (2 Kg. 4:8, 11,18); memorably, they begin the accounts of Job's dreadful woes (Job 1:6, 1:13, 2:1, etc.). In Reb Nahman's tales, the phrase prefaces the account of the burgher's wife's disastrous carriage jaunt *(Burgher and Poor Man)*; it introduces the scene in which shocking injustice committed against the king's true son is divulged *(The Two Sons Who Were Reversed);* it appears like a storm cloud, bursting into the tornado that nearly destroyed the world *(Master of Prayer).*

I would like to turn, for a time, from this question of the metaphysical nature of stories to consider the even more fundamental issue that lies beneath it: the phenomenology of language itself. The mystical semantics that guide the rabbis and kabbalistic masters in their exegetical forays are a vital part of Reb Nahman's heritage; in both his teachings and his tales, this unique linguistic theory serves as the vehicle for his own creativity. In chapter 1 we spoke of innovation in the context of the author's self-image. The subject must be broached again, this time in a wider sense: Reb Nahman teaches that innovation is an existential necessity; the very nature of the revealed Written Torah mandates a continually new reading. For that text, passed from generation to generation by self-effacing scribes, penned on parchment according to strict rules preserving its graphic integrity, is composed solely of consonants. Missing are all signs of punctuation and all vowels. The configurations of mute black bodies on white background are somehow arrested in time; bereft of a soul within them, they remain inanimate. It is the *nekudot* that breathe a living soul into these letters—those vowel points are the domain of the vital Oral Law, responsible both for the conservative vocalization and for all alternate understandings based on permutations of that order.[59] A paradigmatic example: Moses, in his first descent from Mount Sinai, bears the work of God's own hand: the Bible says the letters of the Law were "engraved *[harut]* upon the tablets" (Ex. 32:15). "R. Abba bar Ya'akov declared, Do not read *harut*—engraved—but *herut*—freedom—that the Children of Israel may be free human beings."[60] And R. Joshua ben Levi goes one step further: "Do not read *harut* but *herut,* for the only person who is truly free is one who learns Torah."[61] To fill in the vowels that link the immutable consonants is thus the scholar's inviolable right, granted simultaneously with the reception of the Holy Scripture itself. Moreover, this possibility of infinite variations, of endless rereadings, is a necessary condition qualifying the Text as divine. Because the Torah can have no single vocalization, every interpretation reveals yet another aspect of divine intent—many a talmudic conflict is resolved with the reminder: "Both this [view] and that are the words of the living God." Reb Nahman integrates this axiom of hermeneutics in his own teaching, and applies it in a most romantic and personal way. He speaks of the need "to draw the vowel points to the letters" as an essential gesture of actualization, of bringing silent words to audible speech. This act of resuscitation is possible, though, only if one truly "longs and desires" to invest the mute text of his own thoughts (about Torah, or his prayers) with a vital spirit, to speak them and thus make them move and live.[62] The parallel between this notion of the animating power of verbalization on the human level and the role of divine speech in bringing the world into being is instrumental in Reb Nahman's conception of innovation. As we shall see, this conception entails a highly inventive internalization and humanization of mystical teaching and, in the end, serves as a sort of justification for its creator's raison d'être. In *Likkutei Moharan* he explains:

> Creation was through speech, as it is written, "By the word of the Lord were the heavens made, and all the hosts of them by the breath of His mouth" (Ps. 33:6). In speech is wisdom *[hokhmah]*, for all of speech is subsumed in the five oral openings; these brought everything of Creation into being, i.e. "In wisdom You have made them all" (Ps. 104:24). And speech is the boundary of every thing, for God enclosed His wisdom within the letters; these letters are the boundary of this, those letters the boundary of that. But in the *hallal panui* [empty space] that surrounds all the worlds, in that space completely void, so to speak, of all—there no speech exists, not even intellect without letters.[63]

In this novel retelling of the Lurianic doctrine of *zimzum,* the words uttered by God ("Let there be light," etc.) metonymically replace the entities they signify. Creation, in this description is a universe of signifiers. Ironically, though, each of them speaks most eloquently of what it is not; each is a symbol of limitation rather than of plenitude. This description recalls the strikingly modern yet ancient mystical belief that the true text of the Torah will ultimately be read not in the story told by the black letters, but rather in the white spaces that surround these letters on all sides.[64]

In this paragraph, Reb Nahman's intent seems to be that, in divine terms, any constriction of infinite being into discrete and separated verbal form is indeed an act of limitation. A literal reading of the biblical text yields a single, prosaic, one-dimensional message—meaningful, to be sure, yet finite. For this reason, Reb Nahman advocates a process of radical designification, emulating the talmudic and mystical approach to Scripture: the original power of the words may be unleashed by their deconstruction, by breaking them into nuclear elements—syllables, consonants, vowels, even the graphic form of the letters themselves. As his students testify:

> He said, My teaching is very sublime—every instance in which I use the technique of combining letters (i.e., the initial letters of words, the final letters of words, and awe-inspiring combinations he reveals in his holy writings) is very great. And he said, I would like to go beyond the permutations of letters, yet I remain with that technique, and am even content with it. For some matters are so enigmatic and hidden that the only way to discover them is through the recombination of letters. . . .[65]

This approach, of course, permeates Reb Nahman's teachings; hardly a page of *Likkutei Moharan* lacks some insight gleaned from the rearrangement of elements from biblical verses and words. It is a child's game: taking the building blocks of that original text and constructing from them an entirely new edifice—entirely new, to be sure, in human experience, yet preexisting in divine intent.

A second sign of this process of designification appears in the continual recognition of *behinot*—"*x* is an aspect *[behinah]* of *y*"—on which Reb Nahman's teachings stand.[66] It is designification, because underlying such statements is the conviction that unseen metaphysical ties bind together the most seemingly disparate elements in the world. Thus, for example, "'Speech' is the breath of the mouth of the Holy One, blessed be He, which means *[behinat]* the kingship of mouth, which means *[behinat]* the sea, for all rivers flow to the sea. And that is an aspect *[behinat]* of 'Adonai.' . . ."[67] Perplexing free associations such as these must be reexamined; what seem, at first sight, to be wild impossibilities are revealed as a more penetratingly true reading. "Aspects," then, become the pillars of Reb Nahman's mystical teachings.[68]

But the paradigm of *zimzum* presented in *Likkutei Moharan* is used to illustrate not only the divine act of creation but the human art of re-creation as well. In Reb Nahman's words:

> [Exegetical] dispute is an aspect of the world's Creation. For essential in Creation is the *hallal panui* [void]: without it, *Ein sof* [God's boundless presence] would have filled all, and there would have been no space in which to create the world. Thus He contracted His light to the sides, creating a vacuum, and in that space made all of Creation, time and measure, through speech. . . . The same thing occurs through *mahloket* [exegetical dispute]; were all scholars of the same opinion, there would be no room in which to create the world. Only when they disagree, each of them is

> drawn to one side or another, and a vacuum space is created in their midst. . . . The sole purpose of all their words is to create the world, accomplished in the *hallal panui* among them. For Torah scholars create everything through their speech, as it is written (Is. 51:16), "'Say to Zion, You are my people'—Do not read 'my people' *[ʿammi]* but 'with me' *[ʿimmi]*; just as I have made heaven and earth through speech so do you."[69]

The daring suggestion here, with its inception in the *Zohar*,[70] is that human beings are actually charged to participate in the continual re-creation of the world. Through verbal intercourse, including conflict and innovation, man himself *in imitatio Dei* renews and perpetuates the original divine creative act. Yet Reb Nahman makes clear that this miraculous event does not occur in the hidden recesses of the *beit midrash*. "For the true zaddik 'builds worlds and destroys them,' raises lower wisdom and joins it to upper wisdom by means of his discourse and the stories he tells to the masses."[71] Here, then, is perhaps the most extreme expression of the belief in the metaphysical power of narrative as one manner in which re-creation occurs.

In chapter 1 we emphasized the author's declaration of independence, his decision to build, in that space seemingly emptied specifically for him, a brave new world of his own. Now let us consider the paradoxical nature of innovation in greater depth—as both a rupture and a continuation of tradition.[72] We note that in Reb Nahman's scenario, the empty space for his own creation is engendered, in fact, by the positive *absence* of other scholars; it is their views, contracted to the margins, that serve to define the limits of the *hallal panui*. Tzvetan Todorov, in his discussion of Bakhtin, speaks of human re-creation as a continued dialogue with preexisting texts. He describes it as a fundamentally dynamic interchange, since "even past meanings, that is those that have risen in the dialogue of past centuries, can never be stable . . . they will always change (renewing themselves) in the course of the dialogue's subsequent development. . . . At every moment of the dialogue, there are immense and unlimited masses of forgotten meanings but, in some subsequent moments, as the dialogue moves forward, they will return to memory and live in renewed form. . . ."[73] The unending metamorphosis of previous works is, in this theory, an irremediable aspect of innovation. This image of the immortal soul of ancient texts, reincarnated from age to age in subsequent literary works, corresponds perfectly to the Hasidic conception of intertextuality. All the "texts" in question in the Hasidic worldview, of course, are incorporated either in the Written Law or in the Oral Law (i.e., the Bible or rabbinic and kabbalistic literature); their divine origin is self-evident, and hence their infinitely polysemous nature. Reb Nahman's followers record the following conversation:

> R. Simhah, the son-in-law of R. Samuel Isaac, of blessed memory, once asked about the practice of the zaddikim of clothing their insights in biblical verses and the words of the sages, sometimes interpreting a single statement in many ways, and each time alluding, through it, to a different perception. He asked our teacher, Reb Nahman, of blessed memory, if the Tanna or Amora [rabbi from the period of the Mishnah or Talmud] himself, who had spoken those words, had intended that meaning or not. And he answered, No. Only because of their good deeds, they were granted divine inspiration, awesome and great, drawn from God Himself whose knowledge is endless. Thus all their words, uttered with the holy spirit, are invested with such inestimably awesome perception that even they themselves knew not of it.[74]

It is this quality planted in the texts that ensures the undying dialogical relationship. As in some modern literary criticism, the notion of "author's intent" is rejected out of hand. The fullness of this spoken text, unrevealed even to the speaker, must be discovered by later generations. New reader/listeners respond to yet unheard meanings and the dialogue with infinity resumes. Reb Nahman stresses that the experience of reader-responsiveness is open to everyone in study of the Torah, the inherently self-deconstructing Text:

> Even a simple person, if he sits down to read, and regards the letters of the Torah, is able to see novelty and wonders. As he closely watches the letters, they become luminous and join together, like the letters [of the names of the tribes inscribed on Aaron the Priest's breastplate (Ex. 28:21)] that stood out in relief and combined [as the rabbis taught in B.T. *Yoma* 73b, enacting a verbal transmission of divine will]. Then he will glimpse miraculous new permutations, and be able to perceive, in the book, what even the author/redactor himself did not intend. . . .[75]

This comparison between each individual's modest attempt to understand the Text and the High Priest's interpretation of the fantastically animated breastplate of judgment makes evident that, for Reb Nahman, every moment of reading must be accompanied with awareness of God's presence in the text. Any innovative rereading that discovers hidden truth is as much a gift of inspiration as was the original impetus of composition. It follows that if such a reader then forms his new insights, conceived from the seeds of the text he learns, into a new creation, the holiness of those texts flows onward through the channel of his own works. As Kohelet says, "All rivers return to the sea"—the thinker who breathes new life into words already spoken, who invests them with utterly novel significance implants their eternal soul in his own oeuvre. And just as the full divine intent contained in those great texts is not to be revealed in this world, so Reb Nahman knew his tales and his teachings would become transparent only in time to come.[76]

4. MULTIFARIOUS "TEXTS" AND THEIR SYMBOLIC VALUE

Moses, in despair at his people's infidelity, turns from the travesty of the Golden Calf to beseech atonement from God. At a nadir of hopelessness, he speaks this fractured sentence: "Yet now, if You will forgive their sin—; and if not, blot me, I pray You, out of Your book which You have written" (Ex. 32:32). In a reversal of Pirandello's *Six Characters in Search of an Author,* Moses begs his own Author, if He will not forgive, to delete him from the Holy Text. This interchange between weary character, overcome by the part set out for him, and his truly omniscient Inventor (which foreshadows the artifices of modern literature of the absurd) underlines the enigmatic nature of "reality" as *sujet* suggested throughout our discussion. We shall return to this disquieting problem in the conclusion of this chapter. For now, let it serve as an introduction to our present concern. As we have seen, mystical conceptions of the Torah, of its internal narratives, of the configurations of its letters, and even of each one's graphic form may all be viewed as excurses on the theme of symbolic representation. This perception of worlds within worlds certainly seems to be a fundamental element in esoteric thought. In addition to the concentric circles of signification enciphered in the written text, and to the phenomenology of language itself as a map of reality, the notion of *microcosm* finds expression in many ways: the Tabernacle symbolically reenacts the drama of creation; man himself is described as a "universe in miniature" *[ʿolam katan];*[77] his physical form is a reflection of the universe's supernal structure;[78] his internal anatomy is recognized as a manifestation of the Torah's positive and negative injunctions;[79] his countenance is an anthropomorphization of the lower *sefirot;*[80] engraved in his hand is a revelation of God's divine plan, for his own life and the order of all the cosmos.[81] The complexities of these ideas lie far beyond the scope of our discussion; I mention them here to designate a point of departure as we embark on the final subject of this chapter. For microcosms in myriad forms pervade Reb Nahman's oeuvre as well. The present discussion is concentrated on the tales, yet even in that limited corpus the recurrence of this unique symbolic form is striking.[82] In essence, it restates Reb Nahman's awareness, suggested above, that in the generation of his own works he, as storyteller, imitates the divine artist. Reb Nahman evokes the image of broken worlds whose true story is compressed in a shard: it is a hand, a map, a portrait, a musical instrument, a garden, a dream. The "imitative" aspect of these elements will soon become evident; all of them reflect that essential construct of microcosm so central in mystical tradition.

Let us begin with the hand, perhaps the most widely recognized metaphorical "text." The invincible protagonist of *The Master of Prayer* tells of the king and the legendary image of a hand he possessed; it had "five fingers . . . and all the lines of that hand formed a *Landkarte,* a map of all the universes, and of all that had been from the creation of heaven and earth until the End, and what would be afterward—all was drawn on that hand." No mere picture, "those lines formed a manner of letters," naming places as a map is labeled, "in order to make known the essence of each place, the details of the countries, towns, rivers, bridges, and mountains—all was written in those lines." Yet not only a topography and archive, the hand also recorded the biography "of every person in the land, all the events of their lives." Finally, "the roads leading from country to country, and from place to place" were drawn there, "and even the paths of ascent from one world to the next," those inconceivable journeys taken by Moses, Elijah, and Hanoch (*SM*, pp. 190–92). Truly monumental, the king's treasured hand embraced three dimensions: *time,* in its chronicle of personal and universal history; *space,* in its illustration of the world's physical face; and *spirit,* in its metaphysical representation of that earthly terrain and the heavens above it.[83] Transparently, the treasured 'hand' can be nothing but the Torah. Such an interpretation is implicit in the last words of the Pentateuch, in the "strong hand" presented by Moses before all the Children of Israel (Deut. 34:12). Its five books parallel the five fingers;[84] each of them speaks of crucial events in the past and future history of the Chosen People. That is the teaching in *Pirkei de Rabbi Eliezer:*

> "The five fingers of the right hand of the Holy One, blessed be He, all of them appertain to the mystery of the Redemption—the smallest finger He showed to Noah [pointing out how to make the ark]. . . . With the second finger, which is next to the little one, He smote the firstborn of the Egyptians . . . with the third finger . . . He wrote the tablets. With the fourth, which is next to the thumb, the Holy One, blessed be He, showed Moses what the children of Israel should give for the redemption of their souls. With the thumb and all the hand the Holy One, blessed be He, will smite in the future all the children of Esau, for they are His foes . . . and likewise the children of Ishmael, for they are His enemies.[85]

The idea expressed in Genesis Rabbah and the *Zohar*[86] that God used the primordial Torah as a blueprint in the act of Creation suggests not only that His omniscience is contained in that supernatural text, but that the "work of His hands," the universe itself is, in turn, but a magnification or actualization of the infinite lines and signs marked on that all-encompassing map. Only naturally, the knowledge that man is created in God's likeness leads, in the *Zohar,* to the astonishing supposition that human fingers and palms also contain those sublime mysteries; by gazing at his own inscrutable hand, man is somehow able to conceive a notion of the map of all Creation that is, so to speak, drawn on the divine hand.[87] Reb Nahman's students, in a chain of associations, link the series of psalms that open the morning prayers *(pesukei dezimra)* with the hand in *The Master of Prayer*. Sung by King David to the melody of his hands upon the harp, those poems tell of the wonders of Creation. When a Jew echoes his inspired words to praise and acclaim the Creator, he himself "discovers and illuminates the paths and ways [of emanation] of all the worlds." In fact, through the reiteration of the saga of emanation from the first down to the tenth *sefirah*, i.e., "the connection and union among all aspects of Creation, . . . divine effluence may be drawn from one place down to another . . . and all may be joined and returned to their source as One.[88]

Such was the wisdom, the prayer master recalls, enciphered in the king's treasured hand image. But when his greedy listeners demand the hand, to read in it the path to fortune, he recounts the disaster of the storm wind: in the chaos it wreaked, the hand was lost. The face of reality reflects the tragedy: "The world is utterly confused. What was sea is now land. . . ." The roads each member of the king's court could once ascend to restore his strength are gone, and all the names the places had are changed (*SM*, p. 197). Later, in his travels through this ruined landscape, the prayer master comes upon the traces of the expatriated court, though the members of the court themselves are nowhere to be found. "And I saw a standing stone engraved with the image of a hand . . ." (*SM*, p. 209). This copy twice removed from the world it signifies, a picture of a map, is the work of the king's wise man. In the absence of his master, this wise man later explains, he could not bring himself to read the original hand image at all, and so he carved its form in stone, compelled to use that reproduction in place of the original (*SM*, p. 220). Returning to the understanding of that five-fingered metaphor as the Torah, we realize that its fate reenacts the stages of loss that mark the history of the Jewish people. The first tablets, written by the finger of God to be given to a more pure world, must shatter; the nation distorted by the sin of the Golden Calf is given a second set in their place, a lower, prosaic version fashioned by human hands. Centuries later, the ark holding both the second tablets and the fragments of the first is stolen from the ruined Temple. The paths of ascent to Jerusalem are obliterated. The scent of the holy sacrifices rising from earth to heaven is no more. In the wake of national destruction, new paths must be found, new spiritual pilgrimages and symbolic sufferings.

The motif of an intricate text of ontological significance appears, as well, in *Burgher and Poor Man* in the *Landkarte* drawn by the promised bride. This document maps the "seven places of water" that sealed the bond between her mother and the father of her betrothed. Entrusted to the bridegroom as a pledge, he carefully hides the map in a tree, intuitively knowing it will one day serve as sole proof of his identity.

Thus the storm wind that rips through the forest truly spells disaster. The signs he made to distinguish the tree are defaced and the map is lost, and with it his hope for reunion with his betrothed. From that day his life is consumed in search: the map recounts both prehistory and his present trials, and only when it is refound will his future be realized. Thus this symbol, though less complex than the hand in *The Master of Prayer,* is three-dimensional as well. The heroine herself rejects false suitors with the words "The waters have not passed over you," and we realize this map charts a terrestrial path and a genealogical history, in addition to a spiritual journey of personal *tikkun.*

A third microcosm woven into a number of Reb Nahman's tales is the *portrait.* This form of symbolic representation is so evident that it needs no explanation; when the king *(Spider and Fly)* dreams that his portrait is beheaded, even the bewildered dreamer divines the implications toward his person. The quest for the king whose portrait cannot be seen or possessed informs the tale *Humble King.*[89] In *King and Kaiser,* the "beingness" that imbues the human face (in Max Picard's phrase) is transmitted to the portrait as well, with crucial results. The heroine in male guise returns to her home, having eluded a league of potential husbands—base kings, greedy merchants, wicked pirates. Set on bringing justice to these predators, she places her own portrait (in her disguise as newly crowned king) before all the fountains in the town, with this plan: people will come to drink, and "if anyone comes and stares at the portrait, and his face contorts, he will be seized" by the guards standing there (*SM,* p. 27). For that unspoken dialogue between countenances is a sign that her essence has been recognized; each false suitor's face betrays his depraved past. Reb Nahman ironically suggests, in the last words of the tale, that the portrait is an even more transparent likeness than the living original—brought before the king, she knows the prisoners but they cannot see beyond her outward guise, impersonating a man.

The motif of microcosm appears in *The Two Sons Who Were Reversed* in the magical "instrument made of leaves and colors," which is the forest man's inheritance from his forefathers. Its power far exceeds its modest proportions: "When it is placed on any beast or bird, it immediately begins to play that melody"—the wondrous music of the dawn that has enchanted the two sons. The interconnection between the strange music box and the animals that bear it is oblique but undeniable. In the biblical story, as the holy ark was rescued from the Philistines and returned to Beit Shemesh, the very cows who pulled it sang with joy and praise (1 Sam. 6:12) The *Zohar* extends the double entendre suggested in the midrash (*yisharna*—"they sang," lit., "they walked straight ahead"): their triumphant bearing of the holy ark corresponds, in esoteric teaching, to the four beasts of the prophet Ezekiel's vision who, singing praises, bear the royal throne.[90] Thus the forest man's unassuming instrument not only awakens the eternally "new song" of earthly Creation, but makes audible that other, utterly otherworldly melody.

As we conclude our discussion of the metaphysics of narrative, we return, with the concept of microcosm in hand, to Reb Nahman's notion of "tales of ancient days" and their reformulation in "tales in the heart of the years." We recall the teaching, reiterated throughout Jewish tradition, that the inconceivable play of cosmic events is translated into human language in the stories of the Bible, and recounted, clothed again in yet more familiar guise, by the zaddik in the tales he tells to simple people. This continual act of (re-)creation in the artifice of fictions, undertaken first by the Creator, is imitated by every storyteller in his own "tales in the heart of the years." To be sure, on one hand, a certain reassuring inevitability invests such tales of modern times, in their ineluctable recounting of the divine prototype from Genesis to Apocalypse. Yet the sense that the story, and thus indeed every subsequent story, has already been written, and cannot be rewritten, may engender sinister foreboding: perhaps the narrator truly is as helpless as his own characters in determining their fate. The elusive distinction between fiction and reality that characterizes works of fantastic literature seems to underlie this shared sense of impotence—the sense that neither author nor character is a free agent, that all choices and errors are illusory, that all apparent causality is but a fabrication. Did the biblical Moses really have the awesome responsibility of living his own life, of withstanding the trials besetting him, or was he but a player upon a stage, whose end had already been determined? In the midrash *Tanhuma*, the idea of omniscient narrator takes on clearly malign ontological implications. Commenting on Joseph's troubled life, the verse is cited, "Come and see the works of God: terrible are His stratagems to the children of man" (Ps. 66:5). What follows is a chilling argument investigating the nature of these divine "plots" in which man is "set up" to feel guilty for what are in fact predetermined events. In a prime example, death is seen as implicit in the "darkness on the face of the deep" (Gen. 1:2) in the first verses of Genesis, yet Adam is blamed for bringing mortality into the world by eating from the Tree of Knowledge. Moses is forbidden entrance into the Land of Israel—not for his sins (as the Torah suggests on the literal level) but, in truth, for larger, metahistorical reasons. And Joseph—although actually a victim, taken down to Egypt in order to guide his family and nation toward their destiny—is "framed" as an agent in that terrible story.[91] Though the prooftexts are drawn from biblical "stories," the introductory verse from Psalms implies that these examples are but symptoms of a much more far-reaching phenomenon. Indeed, the midrash implies, we human beings function under the delusion that our lives are our own. We overlook the "plot" in which we are implicated; we, the "nonfictional," choose to remain blind to our role as characters in God's novel.

If we apply the contention voiced in the *Tanhuma* to our own subject, we see that, here, the experience of identification between audience and story, so central for Reb Nahman in the tales he told, reaches its most radical endpoint. If every servant of the King must search for the lost princess, if every individual must recognize the clever apostate and simple son in himself, if every orphaned child must open himself to receive the beggars' gifts, then what is it that distinguishes listeners from the figures in the tale? Where does their story end and our own begin? To his generation and his people, entrenched in the long night of exile, Reb Nahman chose to speak from within that darkness and to tell of the journey into the dawn. In the blackness of the night, feelings of helplessness overcome the wanderer; unknown forces seem to guide his footsteps. Perhaps this is the foreboding consciousness of being implicated in a "plot" that troubles the author of the midrash *Tanhuma*. The moral imperative to assume responsibility for one's deeds seems outrageously to contradict the axiom that the eschatological end has been predetermined. In Reb Nahman's worldview, all manner of confusion and uncertainty germinate in the shadowy obscurity of this world; nameless necessity alone battles with doubt to drive one forward. The king's true and miserable son "is forced to act out his dream"; the unbearable longing of the rabbi's only heir compels him again and again to set off for the true zaddik; the clever advisor's consuming curiosity spurs on his relentless search for the king's portrait. These tales begin in darkness. Some of them end in darkness as well. Yet, in others, Reb Nahman allowed himself to tell not only of journey, search, and faltering but of the promised light of day as well. The story continues beyond this world. And although the last scenes seem an unreal fantasy, impossibly distant from our own experience, they too may be our story. Fiction is forever on the threshold of becoming reality—"Today, if only you will listen" to the inwardness of the tale.[92] Redemption, then, depends solely on man's ability to become a willing actor in the divine comedy.

III • The Romantic Drama

"And God created mankind in His own image, in the image of God He created him, male and female He created them" (Gen. 1:27). R. Joseph ben Shalom Ashkenazi (Ravad) recalls these words of the Talmud, reiterating the fantastic notion that this original human being was double, Janus-faced, the two countenances of Eve and Adam joined back to back. Divine intent, in his eyes, was "that intimacy and fraternity and peace may be forever between them; that they may never part, and their home be imbued with tranquility.[1] But this primordial wholeness, alas, was too perfect to endure; the author of the *Zohar,* in his own time, recounts the preface and afterword of this story:

> All the souls in the world . . . all of them are complete in the mystery of union. Come, and see: the longing of the female for the male engenders a soul. And the will of the male's longing for the female, and his cleaving to her draws out a soul—this soul contains the first soul, born of the female's longing. Desire is joined to desire, lower to upper; the two souls fuse in a single will, with no separation.[2] . . . Afterwards, upon the souls' descent into the world, [male and female halves] part from one another, each goes its separate way. The Holy One, blessed be He, alone rejoins them in the end, for no one but He knows their true combination.[3]

Reb Nahman takes this crucible of mystical and aggadic heritage, places it over the blue-yellow flame of imagination, and forges this fantastic scene:

> The letters of the Torah conjoin and unite by grace of the yearning of the vowel points. For the conjunction and union of the letters is through the vowels, which are engendered by longing and desire; through them, souls come into being. . . . And the souls conjoin, and conceive and give birth. . . .[4]

This cycle, without end or beginning, of separateness and longing, union and separation, this dynamic that transfixes realms from the sublime to the orthographic is, beyond all doubt, an essential concept throughout Reb Nahman's oeuvre. The forlorn birds, each pining for its lost lover; the spring and the heart of the world singing their love songs into the dusk *(The Seven Beggars);* the promised, unreachable bride awaiting her expatriated betrothed *(Burgher and Poor Man);* the faithful servant in his search for the exiled princess *(Lost Princess)*—each of these tales, and others, as well as vignettes throughout *Likkutei Moharan,* are hypostases of a single, primordial, and incontestably *romantic* drama at the core of Jewish tradition.[5]

1. ROMANTICISM: A GENERAL DEFINITION

The title of this chapter, a bit tongue-in-cheek, signals a (perhaps unconservative) intuition that Reb Nahman's oeuvre, and the tales in particular, truly encompass all the manifold senses borne by the concept "romantic." In the following pages, I would like to sketch the literary history of that enticing term and its liberal application in literary criticism to a wide variety of artistic works, and briefly to characterize those works. My hope is to gain a view of Reb Nahman's teaching as an integral part of that newly appropriated generic context; such a comparison may well lead to a recognition of the romantic elements inherent in many classical texts—whether biblical, talmudic, kabbalistic, or Hasidic. The second section of this chapter concerns the stages of the "romantic drama"—separation, loneliness, search, reunion—acted out in the course of Reb Nahman's tales and their links to earlier sources. In the third section, the romantic conviction that the natural world is inhabited with a living soul is discussed, again through a comparative consideration of the tales and classic biblical and aggadic pre-texts. The medium of music, championed by the European romantics as the ultimate spiritual art, is also explored in the context of Bratslav tradition. The final section of chapter 3 focuses on the perspective of one half of the interactive dynamic treated throughout. It is a topic informing much current interest in traditional texts: images of women—particularly in the Bible and midrash. My tenuous conviction is that Reb Nahman's oeuvre in particular, and Hasidic teaching in general, contain certain notable elements of central importance in feminist hermeneutics. But let us turn, first of all, to a general definition of terms.

Despite the seemingly revolutionary character of European romantic theory (which sprouted as a distinct movement, broadly speaking, in the third quarter of the eighteenth century and blossomed to overripe decadence by the mid nineteenth century),[6] numerous scholars stress that romantic aesthetics are actually an instance of continuity in intellectual history. Jean Paul Richter, for example, in response to Novalis, interpreted (in 1804) *die Romantik* not as a discipline but as a poetic quality. To writers of all ages—Sophocles, Petrarch, Ariosto, Cervantes, Shakespeare, Herder, and Tieck—he attributed a *verschiedene Romantik,* a peculiarly romantic style distinguishing them from all others.[7] In Friedrich Schlegel's understanding of *die Romantik* as a cultural phenomenon, the historic era spanning from the fall of Rome to his own time was a romantic age; he found romantic elements in such ancient writers as Homer, Aeschylus, Plato, Horace, and Virgil. In Schlegel's eyes, "every object or phenomenon in the world, every image and symbol in art or poetry, is also on the one hand unique and individual and at the same time a microcosmic 'hieroglyph' of the universal macrocosm." Those writers, he believed, made a synthesis of the fantastic and the sentimental; their works were imbued with primacy of feeling, a sense of "the spirit of Divine love hovering over the whole."[8] More recently, M. H. Abrams states that "ancient rhetorical theory incorporated a number of elements which can be traced, in a straight line of descent, to central components of romantic theory."[9]

Interestingly, just as the Hasidic movement has been widely recognized as an intellectual and emotional countering of the scientific rationalism posed by the Haskalah, the romantic movement is also seen as a reaction against the reason-dominated values of the eighteenth century.[10] Turning to powers beyond the reach of reason, thinkers such as Novalis channeled their strength into "the act of romanticizing" *[romantisieren].* "By giving a higher meaning to what is ordinary, a mysterious aspect to what is commonplace, the dignity of the unknown to the familiar, a semblance of infinity to the finite, I romanticize it."[11] One of the primary tools of the poet's craft, of course, is the use of tropic language; indeed, "symbolism, animism and mythopoeia, in richly diverse forms, explicit or submerged, were so pervasive in this age as to constitute the most pertinent single attribute for defining 'romantic' poetry.'"[12] August Wilhelm Schlegel, rejecting Aristotle's definition of art as imitation, called the composition of poetry "an eternal mode of symbolizing: we either seek an outer covering for something spiritual, or we draw something external over the invisibly inner."[13] Through this double-vectored process of "involution," says Northrop Frye, the locus of the beyond comes to be perceived as hidden in the depths of human consciousness, and the natural world becomes a mirror of the romantic poet's inner reality.[14] In the wake of medieval writers such as Aquinas and Dante (in his *Letter to Can Grande della Scala*), who maintained that secular works of literature may, like the Scriptures, be made "polysemous" or significant both of literal and of allegorical truths, Schlegel proposed a notion of romantic polysemism. Thus, he held, a romantic work may be multiple in meaning, but in the particular sense of having, like God's creation, bidirectional reference—both outward and inward, objective and subjective.[15] With the growing conviction that, in Schleiermacher's words, "the introspection of the spirit into itself" was the "divine source of all plastic art and poetry," the dominant mode of reading in the early nineteenth century increasingly became what Herder had termed (as early as 1778) a "living reading, this divination into the soul of the author."[16] In his concern with the relationship of the romantic to the sublime, Schiller obliquely suggested that romantic experience is a spontaneous psychological phenomenon that must be transformed into the sublime through intellectual and ethical discipline.[17] Later writers probed the darkness of the artistic mind more deeply. Richter, for example, spoke of the unconscious as an abyss; in the coolness of its shadowy night, dreams and prophecy bloom.[18]

The belief of the romantic poets that the supernatural lives in the midst of reality, their abiding sense of the "mystery of existence," and the ideal of transcending the tangible world in the quest for "the eternal, the infinite and the one," in Shelley's words, led to the emergence of a new genre, the *Kunstmärchen*. These artistic tales, inspired by (more naive) folktales and fairy tales, sought to evoke a world in which appearances are deceptive, in which reality speaks a subtle language of signs and the "world within us all" is suggestively evoked.[19]

The romantic shrugging-off of the responsibility to imitate the empirical world through art suddenly won the poet new status: "By the magic of his presentation," in A. Schlegel's words, he "knows how to transport us into a strange world, in which he can rule according to his own laws."[20] The literary work becomes a "heterocosm" or microcosm, a "self-contained universe of discourse" true to itself alone, a "second nature" created by the poet in an act analogous to God's creation of the world.[21] This revolutionary esteem of the poetic ego as creator was accompanied, not unexpectedly, by great interest in the workings of the creative process. Adopting the ancient view that artists are inspired by a divinity, Schelling says that every human creator "seems to be under the influence of a power that sunders him from all other men and forces him to express or represent things that he himself does not entirely fathom, and whose significance is infinite."[22] But perhaps the most striking testimony of the *Zeitgeist* of the romantic age is in the recurrence of certain poetic motifs. Among them is the image of the wind harp, used as a construct for the mind in perception, as well as for the poetic mind in composition. Shelley affirms, "[T]here is a Power by which we are surrounded, like the atmosphere in which some motionless lyre is suspended, which visits with its breath our silent chords at will. . . . This power is God. . . ." and those who have "been harmonized by their own will . . . give forth divinest melody, when the breath of universal being sweeps over their frame."[23]

The experience of the human spirit aroused to song finds its partner in the never silent voices of nature; the "overflow of feeling," as Wordsworth called poetry, brings the artist to regard all he sees, hears, and feels as "but a stream That flowed into a kindred stream; a gale Confederate with the current of the soul."[24] A testimony to the romantic self-absorption is the prevalent theme of the heroic search (for truth, for beauty, for the poet's calling). A golden age is envisioned at its rainbow end, as in Heinrich von Ofterdingen's *Atlantis:*

> Ein Herz voll Einklang ist berufen
> Zur Glorie um einen Thron;
> Der Dichter steigt auf rauhen Stufen
> Hiran und wird des Königs Sohn.[25]

In sum, an awareness of the romantic *Weltanschauung* seems to be essential in understanding Reb Nahman's oeuvre. A mythopoetic interpretation of nature and human sensibilities is common to both, and the innovative, often fantastic conception that interpretation yields is perceived as an intrinsic, preordained aspect of divine Creation. Both read the world in its inwardness, drawing out truths inherent in it. Moreover, both integrate the experience of romantic love as a rich metaphor in which to portray creative experience. Recognition of the correspondence between these two parallel movements will accompany us through the course of our discussion.

2. THE ROMANTIC QUEST

The metaphors of the Bible (particularly in the prophetic and wisdom books evoking the profoundly human bond between God and His chosen people—"as the bridegroom rejoices over the bride, so shall thy God rejoice over thee" [Is. 62:5; Zech. 9:9]) expand in midrashic literature into the hundreds of parables about kings and queens, fathers and daughters/sons, husbands and wives. These personages, often translated into mystical figures, are understood as speaking of dynamics between the Holy One, blessed be He, and His Shekhinah, and of interrelationships within the realm of the *sefirot*.[26] The history of the Jewish people as well, bearing some resemblance to a stormy Gothic novel, is recounted as a saga of promises, betrayal, loneliness, spiritual searches, a first marriage, unfaithfulness, repentance, and longed-for, far-off reunion.

In all postbiblical, inherently hermeneutic literature, these three realms—intimate human experience, the historical, and the metaphysical—are inextricably intertwined; though ontologically distinct, they form a single thread, share a common destiny. Perhaps the most transparent reflection of this multiplicity is in interpretations of the Song of Songs. The languishing beloved, who lies upon her bed at night and searches for "him whom my heart loves," searches for him yet finds him not (Song of Songs 3:1)—"She is the Assembly of Israel, who pleads before the Holy One, blessed be He, concerning the Exile. For she sits among the gentile nations, lying destitute with her sons in the dust of a foreign, impure land."[27] But when did this exile begin? In what temporal context did this tragic estrangement occur? We learn from the *Zohar* that wholeness became brokenness at the dawn of human history. The Tree of Knowledge of Good and Evil, in that text a reification of the Shekhinah, contained the promise of union with powers of holiness *(Tiferet)*. Adam's eating of the forbidden fruit severed that potential tryst, and cast the Shekhinah into the arms of "the Other Side," the powers of evil that pull her ever deeper into a nether world.[28] The pathos of this rupture is conveyed in the *Zohar* through the figure of the abandoned woman, helplessly entwined in a stranger's embrace, or as a mute cry—her words inaudible, she is robbed of a voice.[29] In the second scene of the drama, the setting changes from the Garden of Eden to desert wastes: "I am asleep but my heart wakes; the voice of my beloved knocks . . ." (Song of Songs 5:2). Here the allegory expands. In R. Yehudah's understanding, the Assembly of Israel laments her dormancy, her unconsciousness of God's commandments as the Jewish nation trudged through the wilderness. Yet her heart is alert; from afar she hears the voice of the lover—senses his longing and knows that he waits for her as she prepares herself to enter the Land; or, on the cosmic level, as the Shekhinah prepares for her redemption.[30]

Romantic *Sehnsucht* penetrates these scenes; at times, feelings of isolation and despair well into nearly unbearable *Weltschmerz*.[31] For Reb Nahman, the experience of exile has not paled in urgency through the centuries—the princess's voiceless sobbing continues unabated. She appears, in perfect correspondence to the aggadic prototype, in the first and last tales Reb Nahman told: the king's lost daughter *(Lost Princess)*, stolen away by malign invisible forces, leaving silent messages written in tears for those who falteringly seek her; and the princess of the handless narrator's tale *(The Seven Beggars)* who pines imprisoned in the watery palace, her life threatened by her evil and envious royal lover. The betrothed in *King and Kaiser* comes to gaze secretly at his bride through a crack in the wall. In other tales, though the characters change and sex roles are reversed or adapted, the same essential emotional principle is perpetuated. Thus in *Burgher and Poor Man* it is the hero who loses the signs of his bond with the heroine—filled with emptiness he returns to his island, resigned to waste away his poor and meager days (*SM*, pp. 227, 239). In *Rabbi and Only Son*, the young protagonist is portrayed as an ardent student longing to join his master and rebbe, his path blocked by demonic and rationalistic persons. His desire unrequited, the lonely student dies.

Yet this *Sehnsucht* is not a static existential reality. Rather, it serves as an impetus for the vital process of searching, and that process, in Reb Nahman's eyes, is the vector of personal as well as historical and metahistorical development. Indeed, the search is infinitely more important (in the course of the tales) than the finding:

> Because [the heart of the world] longs for the spring, for that reason it does not reach it. When it comes too close to the mountain [where the spring emerges], it sees the slope no longer, and cannot gaze upon the spring. And if it cannot gaze upon the spring, it will perish, for the spring is the source of its strength. And were the heart of the world to die, heaven forbid, the entire world would cease to exist.[32]

Similarly, the two lovesick birds—their voices wander the night like the interweaving themes of a fugue, unable to meet yet linked together in the inseparable association of their search (*Seven Beggars,* fourth tale). In *Likkutei Moharan,* and later in commentary, Reb Nahman and his students recognize the psychological, even theological, necessity of this arduous experience of distance, longing, and search.

> The intensity of desire is created by its purposeful unfulfillment [lit. *meniʾah,* that which is set up to prevent its fulfillment] . . . for when a person is held back from something, his desire greatly increases. . . . Indeed, the more distant and concealed the object is from him, the greater is his desire to attain it. . . .

From these observations, Reb Nahman reaches the conclusion that "Everything that stands in one's way—all is placed there only for the sake of desire, that one's longing may be very great.[33] Most literally, this teaching speaks of the *hasid*'s journey to the zaddik of the generation, yet ultimately it tells of the endless journey toward the One who has hidden His face. In another passage, Reb Nahman evokes the question, sighed by angels and men—"Where is the place of His glory?"—to foreshadow the mute beggar's tale of the spring and heart of the world. That source of life is concealed in the highest unknown realm. Yet humble mortals dare "to search and seek—'where is His glorious place?' And that is the essence of repentance—for when man seeks Him, may He be blessed, and sees how very far he is from His glory—

when he longs, and asks and regrets his own distance from that Place—that itself is his answer/repentance *[teshuvah]* and his spiritual healing."[34]

The lost princess longs to return to her father, who in a moment of anger has abandoned her to the powers of evil. Yet the focus of the tale is less on her trials than on the king's servant, an intermediary sent to save her and restore her to his master. And though his search begins as a duty, he, too, is charged to become a romantic soul—"You must choose a place," the princess tells him, "and remain there one year, and all that year you must long for me, long to rescue me; every chance you have you must long and seek and await the time when you will rescue me . . ." (*SM,* p. 5). Clearly, what Reb Nahman describes is the responsibility of every Jew to concentrate his religious energy, in prayer and in ritual acts, on "the union of the Holy One, blessed be He, and His Shekhinah."[35] The search for God, portrayed in *Likkutei Moharan* in purely emotional terms (with no sexual valences),[36] is re-presented here as a romantic lovers' quest. In the same way, thc hcrocs of *King and Kaiser* and of *Burgher and Poor Man* are consumed in looking for their beloved. A telling comment by R. Nahman of Tcherin suggests these tales actually reveal the nature of Divine Providence. Her identity and their shared destiny must be hidden from him, "that free choice may be possible."[37] The elusive beloved is made so by her Author—unbeknownst to the hero, his heroism is being tested. The obstacles in his path—the rivers of wine, ruining his vow of abstinence; the tempests obscuring his crucial documents—these caprices of nature are no accident. Outrageous fortune bares its slings and arrows; the struggle seems endless. Yet, paradoxically, these trials themselves are a merciful gift, for it is they that help the searcher gain the privilege of finding, and the joy of reaching, the object of his quest.

We spoke in chapter 2 of the striking disparity, apparent in all Reb Nahman's tales, between the serpentine account of spiritual trials and their facile resolution in the eclipsed gesture of denouement. There, we attributed the relative simplicity of such endings to the storyteller's conviction of the theurgic power inherent in narration. Yet the escatological vision they suggest—however imprecise and "unrealistic" (compared, of course, to the all-too-human suffering that fills the tales)—deserves our attention as well. Though inspired by classic mystical conceptions, the ideal of ultimate oneness is also a thoroughly romantic conception in the spirit of Novalis, Brentano, Eichendorff, or Moerike. The allegory of the Song of Songs, so influential in German medieval poetry, found expression in romantic verse in the notion of "earthly love and religious faith blended into one by a mystical union with God, a union mediated by their beloved."[38]

In Reb Nahman's tales, the union toward which all hearts yearn is signaled in the "marriage" and "complete happiness" spoken of in their last words. When we consider the fundamental allegory underlying this ideal marriage, we catch sight of the code implicit in each of them. In *Likkutei Moharan,*[39] Reb Nahman declares that oneness is the most cogent quality of the world to come: the prophetic vision that "On that day the Lord shall be one and His Name shall be one" (Zech. 14:9) speaks, most profoundly, of the union between the *sefirah* of *Tiferet* (i.e., mercy, signified in the ineffable Tetragrammaton) and that of *Din* (severe judgment, signified in God's effable Name, Elohim)—in other, words, the manifestation of the divine visible in the natural world. By remarking that the word "one" *(ehad)* is numerically equivalent to "love" *(ahavah)* (= 13), Reb Nahman suggests that the sexual valences (masculine/feminine) implicit in these attributes are the impetus behind his conception.[40] Paradoxically, in their ultimate harmonization, these two discordant tendencies lose their separate identity. The coda of happiness and joy that is repeated in the tale each beggar offers during the seven days of the orphan children's wedding is thus a premonition of that final catharsis that belongs entirely to the future. "The world to come," in the words of the *Zohar Hadash,* is "wholly happiness"; the human experience that gives some slight intuition of that unimaginable plenitude is the joy of bride and groom as they join in marriage.[41]

3. THE INDWELLING LIFE OF NATURE

In light of the conviction, voiced above by prime movers of the European romantic movement, that romanticism is a poetic quality found in works of every age, we begin our consideration of nature in Reb Nahman's worldview with a passage from the *Zohar*. The enigmatic opening verses of Psalm 22—"On the hind of the dawn, a Song of David—'My God, my God, why have you forsaken me?'" are read as the lamenting end of a lovers' tryst, witnessed by two journeying sages.

R. Eleazar and R. Yose rise early to walk by the first light of day. Upon seeing two shooting stars, R. Eleazar recounts the secret rendezvous:

> When the East begins to grow light, and the darkness of night fades away, a certain emissary is appointed from the East, and he draws a ray of light from the South. Soon the sun rises, opening the windows of the firmament and illuminating the whole world. That ray marks the boundary of the night's darkness, and then the hind of the dawn comes at once. A black light comes in its darkness in order to unite itself with the day, and the day shines forth, and the light of the day envelops the hind. . . .

Yet in another moment she deserts the day, and then, realizing her loneliness, exclaims, "My God, my God, why have You forsaken me?"[42]

The belief that elements of the natural world are imbued with a feeling soul, that that soul suffers pangs of love and longing, and that natural phenomena conceal a symbolic dimension—all these are characteristic components of a romantic *Weltanschauung*. Herder, for example, recognized the unavoidable sympathy between the poet's inner world and external reality; nature, he held, "is an organism, and man, inextricably a part of that living whole, is in himself an organic and indissoluble unity of thought, feeling and will, exhibiting in his own life the same powers and functions as the nature without."[43] Indeed, it is a pillar of kabbalistic thought that all of creation bears, as a single organism, the signature of God's four-letter Name—*yod, heh, vav, heh*. The author of the *Zohar* demonstrates the ubiquity of His literal sovereignty through the orders of nature: "First, the human figure: the *yod* is manifest in his head; the two letters *heh* are his hands [with ten fingers, 5 + 5, the numerical value of the letter *heh*]; the *vav* is his body. The same holds for the eagle—head, wings and body—and for every animal and for every angel. There isn't a hair on the head where the four letters do not abide, and not a plant in which the Name does not dwell. . . ."[44] We shall return presently to Reb Nahman's idea, issuing from this principle, that the divine handwriting must be read aloud; the individual is thus led to join his own voice with it in creative dialogue.

The correspondence between the "world spirit" and the human spirit that entranced nineteenth-century romanticism stimulated a new genre of landscape description: language is displaced, and the outer world becomes but a mirror of the human soul. Thus Tieck portrays a heroine's sorrow and anxiety by her path through a day "gray and sad," in which a few bushes, "lone and dejected," mark the countryside and the trees murmur a melancholy melody; Brentano uses the desolate desert wilderness to speak of the heart's thirst and its wide isolation as a symbol of dreams and hope.[45] Reb Nahman, in the spirit of his times, subtly borrows this "pathetic fallacy" (with these words Walter Pater castigated the romantic merging of souls). Inhuman wastelands, power struggles fought on stormy seas, flight through a labyrinthine forest—such are the settings of many tales. In chapter 4, Reb Nahman's use of mythopoetic archetypes (kept alive in fairy tales and rediscovered by the romantics) in conjuring the atmosphere of his tales is considered in detail. For now, let us remark that this romantic awareness of nature as animated being is necessarily discovered in a moment of enlightenment. Even as he senses that nonhuman presence, the romantic poet knows that he is being granted but a glimpse of the natural world's secret inner vitality.[46] Nostalgia—for the lost Edenic world in which creation was yet unviolated, in which man intuitively knew the animals' names as God brought them before him[47]—thus marks the romantic soul. For this reason, every moment of intuitive communication with the natural world carries with it inconsolable sorrow, for the moment cannot last. R. Abba, recalls the author of the *Zohar,* would lament: "If human beings only realized what all this enciphered, they would tear their garments to their navels [in mourning] for the wisdom lost to them."[48] Emblems in Reb Nahman's works—of the map nowhere to be found, of broken tablets, of forgotten rings and shifting letters—echo this feeling of hiatus and disconnection. Shelly wrote that the romantic "looks before and after, and pines for what is not"; indeed, he is the burgher's son, estranged from his beloved, who builds musical instruments to sing his melancholy memories and muse upon what is no more.[49]

The Garden

But perhaps the most thoroughly romantic motif of Reb Nahman's oeuvre, in which nostalgia, animism, nature symbolism, and trials of the soul combine, is the "field" or "garden" evoked both in *Likkutei*

Moharan and in many of the tales. Fecund with metaphors of growth and nurturing, of blossoming and ripening, these botanical enclaves are blessed with an aura of peace; within their borders a precious, primordial order somehow remains, either in potential or actual form. In *Likkutei Moharan,* for example, inspired by the pastoral love story of Boaz and Ruth, Reb Nahman presents the following lyrical allegory:

> Know that there is a field, and in it grow beautiful trees and plants. The splendor of that field and all therein is indescribable—happy is the eye that has glimpsed it. Well, the trees and the plants are holy souls that grow there. Many, many naked souls also wander outside the field, waiting and longing to be repaired, that they may enter once again and regain their places within. . . . And all of them seek the caretaker of the field and pin their eyes on him, that he may aid in their restitution.[50]

As the scene unfolds, it becomes clear that the caretaker represents the zaddik of the generation and the trees he prunes and waters are Jews faithful to him. The mutual dependence between them in a sociological sense is expressed through the horticultural parallel:

> The caretaker is attentive and always takes care to water the trees and raise them, as well as tending to all the needs of the field. . . . And know, when the souls bear fruit—when they do the will of God—the eyes of the caretaker are illuminated, and he can see every place where something is needed. . . . But when, heaven forbid, they do not do His will, the caretaker's eyes are dimmed. . . .[51]

His whole being devoted to the plants entrusted to him, the caretaker's/zaddik's vision must be bright with his responsibility "to observe each and every one, and lead him to his ultimate purpose."[52] As we saw in chapter 1, this personal involvement in the spiritual lives of his followers—from their efforts to make a livelihood to the words of their silent prayers—is the zaddik's highest mission. But those leafy souls, in turn, are a vital source of support for their gardener himself; Reb Nahman's students extend the allegory to emphasize the caretaker's link to his field:

> From all the trees and plants and from everything in the world—from all, messengers set forth, traveling from one to the next and

> to the next, until they reach the ears of the true zaddik, and he understands, from them, how he should serve God.[53]

Beyond his private nurturing of each green life in his care, the zaddik is the representative of his entire community in his divine service; the plants' tiny voices join with his, raising his human words on high. Yet in Bratslav tradition, the zaddik is by no means the only one privileged to experience this wonderful chorus of voices surging in himself. Every individual is urged to distance himself from the city whenever he is able, to "wander solitary in fields where plants grow from the earth, and to pour out his thoughts before God." His heart is awakened by the plants themselves, for if he is worthy, "he will hear the songs and praises of the grasses, how each and every plant sings for God, with no distractions or vagrant thoughts."[54] The unself-conscious devotion of nature, intuited by the Thoreauvian *hasid* as he walks through fields and woods, engenders a continual sense of renewal; in the words of Reb Nahman's followers, "in every step he takes, he has the taste of Paradise, and when he returns, the world seems different to him, utterly new'."[55]

The comparison is far from poetic idiom. On the contrary, Reb Nahman's romantic awareness of the "world spirit" leads him to a profound and unique interpretation of the archetypal garden of Creation. Every word of the biblical description holds seeds of countless tropes, which sprout in unforetold forms throughout his writings. In one passage of *Likkutei Moharan,* Reb Nahman encodes his message in traditional and straightforward Garden of Eden metaphors:

> As it says in *Tikkunei Zohar,* Tikkun 12, the Garden is the Torah. And the souls of Jews who learn and gain understanding of the Torah—they are plants and grasses that grow in the garden. And how are they watered? From the fountain of wisdom, as it is written, "A fountain of gardens, a well of living waters . . ." (Song of Songs 4:15). Whence do they receive the wisdom and intellect contained in the fountain? From *prayer,* as it is written, "On that day . . . a fountain shall issue from the house of the Lord . . ." (Joel 4:18), "For my house is a house of prayer" (Is. 66:7). Indeed, prayer brings what is potential to actualization; prayer is an aspect of the world's renewal.[56]

Here the intermediary role of the zaddik is replaced with the metaphysical spring itself, spontaneously flowing forth to water the souls planted in the garden. Reb Nahman sends the figurative language immortalized in Jewish tradition ("fountain of wisdom"; "outpouring of prayer," etc.) back to its most literal roots in his description of this spiritual ecosystem. Interestingly, the scene truly portrays an organic, natural dynamic: the plants themselves must merit the living waters that are their sustenance; human devotion alone wins the outpouring of wisdom *(hokhmah)* whose source is divine.[57]

Turning to the tale entitled *The Cripple,* we see just how fruitful this kabbalistic concept of emanation, expressed through nature metaphors, is in Reb Nahman's imagination. The story is framed by the opening words ("The tale of a wise man who, before his death, summoned his sons and family and adjured them to water trees") and the closing ("The world collapsed and the tree was watered"). Although the plot of the story spirals down through many and infernal circles, the constancy of the theme, the tree in need of water, points to its extratextual origins. In another passage of the *Zohar,* the same garden metaphors we have considered are associated, as well, with the most basic aspect of human life:

> Whoever concerns himself with the commandment to "be fruitful and multiply" *[peri'ah u-revi'ah]* causes that stream [originating in the *sefirah* of Yesod] to be forever flowing, its waters never ceasing, and the sea [the Shekhinah] grows full; new souls are born and emerge from the Tree, and power increases above along with those souls.[58]

In this mystical conception, the flow of divine effulgence into the human realm is engendered as a response mirroring the cycle of human life itself. *The Cripple* speaks of this interconnection as self-understood; the father's veiled injunction to his sons to perpetuate his seed is woven into the texture of the tale in a fantastically literal alter image.

The tale, though, in which the "indwelling soul of nature" swells into the most thunderous chorus is incontestably the story called *The Two Sons Who Were Reversed.* In the darkness before the dawn, the two adversaries listen, terrified, to the cacophony of the forest animals. "They roared and cried in strange voices, all the beasts and birds joined in—the lions roared and the tigers growled, the birds twittered and chirped. . . ." But when, encouraged by the forest man, they listen more closely, they discover that that chaos is, in fact, "a most wondrous and melodious singing voice, a wonderful and tremendous pleasure to hear; in contrast to that song all the pleasures in the world are as naught." (*SM*, p. 158). The forest song subsequently becomes a portable leitmotif: magically contained in the "music box" built of leaves and colors, the song reemerges at the will of the king's true son (*SM*, pp. 159–60). With that gift from the forest man, the two sons make their way to the kingdom, and find themselves, at last, at the gate of its walled garden. The baroque eerieness of this petrified world—the cold plants of gold and silver, the statue of its former king, the great chair flanked by wooden creatures, obscured by serpentine paths—has driven out all souls who seek to penetrate it (*SM*, p. 166). Undaunted, the king's true son studies the silent scene and perceives its cleverly concealed order. He restores the rose to its rightful place, adjusts the position of a lion, a bird, a lamp, and a table. And the moment the subtle corrections are completed, "All began to play a wondrous melody." Like a glockenspiel on the hour, the garden bursts into song; it is the same melody of the forest and of the music box—and as a reward for his insight, the true son and heir "was awarded the kingship" (*SM*, pp. 169–70).[59] In this tale, the hero's dawning perception of the melody composed by the divine *Konzertmeister* Himself and implanted in Creation serves as a metaphor of spiritualization; only when he himself awakens to the silent symphony of the garden can the king's true son ascend the throne.

Music

In quintessentially romantic terms, E. T. A. Hoffmann speaks of the same notion of music that "lies enshrined at the heart of nature, like a profound mystery which only a higher intelligence can fathom." In his words, music brings its listeners "into the presence of the highest and holiest things, of the spiritual power that kindles the spark of life in the whole of nature."[60] Although in Reb Nahman's tale *The Two Sons Who Were Reversed* the drama of enlightenment is told in less flowery language, its kinship to the romantic ideal is undeniable. Meditations on the theme pervade his writings. Examples: the third beggar's tale of the spring and the heart of the world; the fourth beggar's tale of the two birds; the sixth beggar's tale of the captive princess; the images of shepherd-musicians and prophet-bards that people *Likkutei Moharan;*

the innovations on King David's harp, Moses' song, and the music of heresy and its roots in the highest music of supreme faith. And although the word "music" (of Greek/Latin origin) is never used in his texts, the prevalence of Hebrew cognates such as *niggun* (melody), *neginah* (playing), and *shirah* and *zimrah* (song), and even the mention of *lider,* clearly indicate that his subject is that "most romantic of the arts."[61] We have discussed many of Reb Nahman's texts concerning music elsewhere in this work;[62] my intent here is in pointing out the bonds linking his conception of the metaphysics of music to that of the German romantics.

Recalling that it was Orpheus's lyre that opened the gates of Orcus, E. T. A. Hoffmann writes that "music unfolds before man a new kingdom, a world which has nothing in common with the world of sensuous reality around us, and in which we leave behind all precise emotions in order to surrender ourselves to an ineffable yearning. . . ."[63] This "longing for the Eternal," which he describes as the essence of romanticism, is aroused by melody—held to be the most pure expression of the spirit precisely because it is nonrepresentative, unaltered by its physical medium. Wackenroder evokes the image (familiar from the mute beggar's tale) of living waters and heart to describe this play of feeling in time: "So it is with the mysterious stream in the depths of the human spirit—speech reckons and names and describes its changes in a foreign matter; music streams it out before us as it is in itself. . . . In the mirror of tones the human heart learns to know itself.[64] And finally, the notion of the supremacy of music is set forth by Schopenhauer in his unique philosophical terms:

> In that it by-passes ideas, Music is independent of the physical world—in fact, is completely ignorant of the physical world and could exist in a sense even if there were no world. . . . Music is as direct an objectification and reflection of the entire Will as is the World itself, and as are the ideas whose manifold forms make up the world of individual objects. Thus, far from being, like the other arts, the reflection of these ideas, Music is a reflection of the Will itself, with the same objectivity as that possessed by ideas. This is the reason why the effect of Music is so much more powerful and penetrating than that of the other arts. For while these latter deal only with the shadow, Music deals with the substance.[65]

A precise expression of the romantic conception that the cosmos is ordered by and thus conceivable through music alone, Schopenhauer's idea has a striking correlative in Reb Nahman's thought. Ascending to the pinnacle of the sefirotic system, "even to the primordial point of Creation, the source of emanation *[azilut]*, beyond which there is nothing . . . but Endless Light *[or ein sof]*," Reb Nahman declares that the wisdom of that all-encompassing sphere is utterly unattainable by the intellect. *Faith* alone is possible—"and faith has melody and music all its own . . . more sublime than all the melodies and songs in the world, belonging to every separate manner of knowledge and belief." Moreover, he adds, the "music of faith in the light of Endlessness *[Ein sof]* Himself" is the source and container from which all the lower ideas and objects flow to fill the world.[66]

The power of music to awaken man's innermost spirit is not only a romantic conviction. The experience of the biblical Elisha, inspired by the minstrel's melody to prophesy (2 Kg. 3:15), becomes an emblem of divine inspiration through the medium of music that transects generations of Hebrew literature.[67] It resonates in Reb Nahman's teaching in the conviction that "the spirit of prophecy, of divine inspiration, comes only with happiness, i.e., by playing upon an instrument."[68] Elsewhere, the act itself of making music is explained in mystical-phenomenological terms: "By searching for and gathering together the points of goodness [within each individual's own psyche and in the members of a community], melodies are formed—just as one plays a musical instrument, winnowing the good wind/breath from the base winds of sadness."[69] Strangely enough, the most gifted musician, in Reb Nahman's view, is personified by Moses. The Talmud tells his tale.[70] Teetering on the edge of a theological abyss, Moses dangerously questions—for a moment—the justice of God's acts. Yet he is thrown at once back into silence, a silence more deafening than any response. Moses' muteness, for Reb Nahman, is the supreme quietness of faith, superior to speech itself.[71] Paradoxically, though, it is this experience that wins Moses the title of zaddik and the mission of descending into those very depths of heresy to save the souls of apostates lucklessly imprisoned within. And truly like Orpheus, whose marvelous music charmed the Shades of Hell, Moses, by grace of his *niggun* of faith, is able not only to enter but to raise those sorry souls fallen into the Nothingness of unbelief.[72]

Thus, in Reb Nahman's eyes, music is not only an inspirational but a redemptive force as well. Evil, here, is embodied by "apostates" and conquered by "the melody of faith"; in numerous other contexts Reb

Nahman speaks of this battle against the malign shadowing human life using the classic kabbalistic term "the sweetening of harsh judgments" *[hamtakat ha-dinim]*—and there as well, music is the secret weapon.[73]

In the teachings collected in *Likkutei Moharan,* we glimpse the many metaphysical faces of music; borrowing themes from traditional texts, Reb Nahman transposes them to a new, uniquely Hasidic mode. In his oeuvre, as in those pre-texts, music serves as a complex vehicle: most basically, it is a precious component of human creative experience; yet it serves, as well, as a metaphor to speak of the most esoteric truths. These two functions, of course, are inseparable; the effectiveness of music as metaphor is founded on its pervasiveness in our lives. Of all Reb Nahman's narrative compositions, the most fantastic merging of musical concepts with mystical thought is found in the tale *The Two Sons Who Were Reversed.* A few pages earlier, we considered the romantic overtones of the "forest song" described in it, the *Pastorale* that climaxes in the joyous chorus of the restituted Garden. Yet the impressionistic remarks made there must be amplified, for the naive words of that story conceal a brilliant kabbalistic superstructure. Indeed, Reb Nahman's description of that surrealistic concert, the bewildering *Nachtmusik* overheard by the sons who were reversed, contains the key to an understanding of the tale as a whole. Let us return, then, to the treetop where prince and slave begin to discover their destiny, and consider the measures of that music in greater detail.

United in misery, their first night's vigil ended at last; as the forest grew light, the terrifying roar of the animals became "a tremendous laughing voice that spread through the forest, laughter so huge that their tree trembled and swayed from its great sound" (*SM,* p. 153). In the following day's adventures, the king's true son finds the sack of bread (which the servant's true and ravenous son will buy in exchange for his usurped throne) and encounters the forest man. By evening, safe in the latter's "house that floats in the air," the two sons sleep peacefully. Once again, the thundering laughter of the dawn awakens them; this time, though, the slave's son prods his new master to find out its meaning from their host. This is his enigmatic answer: 'That laughter—it is the day laughing at the night, for the night asks the day, 'Why is it, when you come, that I have no name?' And then the day laughs a great laugh, and afterwards daylight comes" (*SM,* p. 158). The king's son is as dumbfounded by this answer as the reader. The next night, as the two sons gradually overcome their fear, the dissonant roaring of the beasts reveals the "wondrous melody" at its heart. Once again, the king's son questions the wise forest man about its meaning.

> And he responded, "That is how the sun makes a garment for the moon. And all the animals of the forest say that since the moon does them a great favor (for their reign is largely at night, and sometimes they need to enter some inhabited place—in daylight they cannot, only in darkness—and the moon kindly lights their way) thus they agree to make a new song in honor of the moon. And that is the sound of music you hear." (*SM,* p. 159)

These deceptively whimsical exchanges cast the tale over an invisible threshold, from a familiar story of prince and pauper into a new genre paved with allusions. The elusive singing of the creatures, the seeming power struggle between night and day, between moon and sun, the laughter, the garment—these motifs are no mere flights of fancy. Rather, their threads are most skillfully interwoven; like Helen's masterful tapestry, the texture they form tells the odyssey—past, present and future—of the Jewish nation, and thus of the world.

My aspiration, in the following discussion, is not to unravel the fantastic fabric Reb Nahman has made and scrutinize each of its separate threads. Such a task would be enormous; a complete reading of their origins lies far beyond the scope of this work. Rather, I would like to probe the inner logic that entwines one allusion with another in the hope of glimpsing the secret story within the veil.

To begin with, certain stereotypes must be exorcised. The audience is warned, just after the telling, of the semantic dangers lurking in the interpretation of his tale: "Everything must be placed in its proper order, for sometimes a matter is called in one way and sometimes in another..." *(SM,* p. 171). Indeed, the deceptive nature of names is at the heart of this story—struck, most visibly, by the false titles of "servant's son" and "king's son" and spreading, like concentric ripples in a still pond, to the opposition between night and day, moon and sun, darkness and light, evil and good, obscurity and revelation. This fundamental principle is traced, in *Likkutei Halakhot,* back to its primary sources, where R. Nathan points, from afar, to the enigma of the ultimate divine Name and its myriad lower permutations. The transience of the signifiers nearly obliterates all memory of the unchanging signified. As R. Nathan says, "It is as if God deliberately changes His name, clothing Himself in ever-shifting disguises, and concealing Himself in those names we invoke. They are His garments, but the essence is invisible, wholly hidden. For His name is not complete, nor is His throne complete."[74] Later in this section, we will see just how intricately this notion of the single Name, temporarily splintered, is bound to the kabbalistic symbolism that informs Reb Nahman's tale.

The typology I am about to present is destined to self-contradiction—not (of course) because it is faulty, but rather because the tale *The Two Sons Who Were Reversed* is a game of duality and reversal, in which entities are named for the very purpose of revealing their negating, other identity. Just as a dynamic process is mapped by a curving line of immobile points, so, here, separate scenes—the gleaming crescent moon, the triumph of a crimson dawn, the feeble candle blinded in daylight—combine like movie frames to depict a story of transformation. Contradiction—and paradox—therefore play a vital role, for they announce the advent of radical, nonrational, futuristic change: the moon will *become* the sun; day subsumes the shadows once and forever, the supreme Entity is reunited with its Name.

Consider, first of all, the ambivalence of the night in the collective consciousness of the Jewish people, reflected in *The Two Sons Who Were Reversed.* On one hand, evil spirits roam the lugubrious forest (*SM,* p. 153); the malicious Other Side grasps the upper hand;[75] mankind stumbles in the long darkness of exile.[76] Yet at the same time, the moon and stars gently reign over the nocturnal kingdom. By grace of their borrowed brightness, herbs and trees and all that grows draw strength to flourish.[77] The fragile light of the moon is compared to a candle flame, to a vessel glowing with the sun's refracted rays; in its mutable ever presence it is the Shekhinah, the Assembly of Israel, the *sefirah* of *Malkhut,* the Redeemer, son of King David.[78] How, then, may this favorable identification of the moon with the Jewish nation be explained in the face of her fading to anonymity in the daylight, and of the laughter (derisive? benevolent?) of the Sun King as his chariot crosses the sky?

As we shall see, the stereotype of dualistic opposition implied in that question is consciously replaced, in Reb Nahman's conception, with a more mystical and integrative notion. The talmudic image[79] of the disappointed flame that pales as darkness brightens is imbued with new and clearly positive significance in the *Zohar:* there the candle light that reigns at night is not conquered but enveloped, not obviated but stored away like a sacred treasure within the light of day.[80] In *The Two Sons Who Were Reversed,* this subtle merging of the night into the emerging day is announced by the forest music—"the sun makes a garment for the moon." The intent implied is that she not be left naked (i.e., nameless) and vulnerable at sunrise. In these few words, a truly fantastic and rather incomprehensible image is created. We turn first of all to *Likkutei Moharan* in search of the paths that could have led Reb Nahman to it.

A battery of esoteric associations concerning this strange "garment," *Likkutei Moharan* 42 opens with the affirmation of a vital dialogical bond. Citing Ps. 106:44, "Nevertheless, He regarded their affliction, when he heard their cry: and He remembered for them His covenant," the hermeneutical dance begins.

> For through music, harsh judgment is sweetened. As it is written in the *Zohar,* the [rain]bow is the Shekhinah, and its three hues are the patriarchs, and they are the garments of the Shekhinah. When she clothes herself in luminous garments, then "I will look upon her, that I may remember the everlasting covenant" (Gen. 9:16), and "the king's wrath is assuaged" (Esther 7:10).

The allegory Reb Nahman recalls has its roots in *Zohar* 3.230b: the king, angered by his son, is pacified at the sight of the queen, dressed in lambent garments—her beauty arouses his mercy toward their child. But with no apparent comment on the parable's referent, Reb Nahman proceeds to entwine his themes yet further.

> Now, the letters of prayer are the Shekhinah, as it is written, "O Lord, open my lips . . ." (Ps. 51:17), for speech is the name Adonai [Lord]. And [words of prayer] are called bow *[keshet],* as Rashi comments on the verse "With my sword and bow" (Gen. 48:27)—i.e., "by prayer." And the melodious voice contains the three hues of the bow. For voice holds fire, water and wind, and they are the three patriarchs. These patriarchs are the three luminous colors that God saw [in the rainbow] and was reminded of His covenant.

At first reading, this path seems impossibly circuitous. Reb Naman claims that "the [rain]bow is the Shekhinah"; "the three hues are the patriarchs"; "the patriarchs are the garments"; "words of prayer are the Shekhinah." Yet at the heart of this teaching, reiterated on ascending planes, is the dialogical principle nascent in the biblical tale of the Deluge. Divine wrath at mankind's moral degradation turns at last to pity; God responds to the appeal for mercy voiced by His creatures' repentance and vows never again to destroy His Creation. The *Zohar,* in an innovative twist, suggests that it is the rainbow that embodies that appeal, as well as God's response. There, R. Yose affirms, "The rainbow appears in order to protect the world."[81] Inherent in the allegory, however, is the belief that this prismatic protectress is no autonomous agent, but rather a shimmering messenger. For it is the merits and acts of humbly righteous human beings—personified, ultimately, in the figures of Abraham, Isaac, and Jacob—that adorn her in her brilliant colors. Her presence as graceful queen, the *Zohar*'s author explains, is actualized through prayers canonized by Jewish tradition—prayers founded on the composite history of those three patriarchs.[82] The *Zohar*'s exegesis of the rainbow is recalled, in effect, to lay the ground for Reb Nahman's own thoroughly practical, universalizing message. In his Hasidic conception, not only the rare and precious zaddikim of each generation have the power magically to "dress" the divine queen. Rather, "When any individual plays the letters of his prayer, and the voice of his melody emerges in merit and great clarity, he himself clothes the Shekhinah, i.e., the letters, in brilliant garments. . . ."[83] Reb Nahman bases his thesis on Rashi's remark (re. Ps. 106:44, above): "God heard their cry"—"Because they invoked the patriarchs' memory." Rashi's apparently simple editorial comment (suggesting the text of their appeal) is cited, though, because it alludes, in Reb Nahman's eyes, to one of the most fundamental kabbalistic axioms. The paradigmatic triad personified in the patriarchs resonates, a tonic chord, throughout mystical thought. According to the chromatology of the *Zohar,* the "rainbow" is formed of three primary colors—white, red, and green. Each signifies a separate metaphysical mode: white is the attribute of mercy, the *sefirah* of *Hokhmah,* in the person of Abraham; red is the attribute of harsh judgment, the *sefirah* of *Binah,* in the figure of Isaac; green, the hue of synthesis, is the *sefirah* of *Tiferet,* embodied in Jacob.[84] No flight of fancy, then, is needed to recognize the organic connection between the "bright garments of the Shekhinah," 'the colors of the rainbow," and classic mystical personology. In the course of his teaching, Reb Nahman evokes two fantastic instances of chromaesthesia, two eras in the history of the Jewish people in which God "hears" the nation's plea for salvation through the colors of the "rainbow." The first era was the days of Noah (Gen. 9:16), and the second was the metahistorical days of distress described in Ps. 106:44.

Returning to the tale *The Two Sons Who Were Reversed,* we find that the events of that story relate, in the playful guise of fiction, the same essential message as *Likkutei Moharan* 42. The chromatic song rising from the throats of birds and beasts and filling the forest dramatizes the pure melody that should, ideally, animate man's own words of prayer each morning. It is a dramatization, in fact, much less original than one might think, and may be read, rather, as a gesture transplanting a transparent and mystical second allegory. In *Tikkunei Zohar*, the *sefirah* of *Malkhut* is characterized as the unified chorus of "the angels, the heavenly beasts, the serafim and ofanim, the utterances of all the upper and lower worlds . . . voice, speech and though—she contains them all." In the next lines, the focus drops from heaven to earth.

> The twittering of all the birds—they are the holy souls that twitter in prayer. The conversation of the animals—they are Torah scholars. And of [the Shekhinah] it is said, "Isaac went out to meditate *[lasu'ah]* in the field (Gen. 24:63)—'meditation' can be nothing but prayer."[85]

What we find in Reb Nahman's tale, then, is a fantastic realization of this second allegory as well: the responsibility of human worshippers, specifically in their morning prayers, to "draw mercy *[hasadim]* to *malkhut*" is portrayed in the tale in the "new song" offered by the birds and beasts of the forest to the moon. The remarkable effect of the scene stems from its fusion of simile and metaphor: the forest creatures act *like* man, sending praises and thanks on high; man aspires to *imitate* the naive honesty of their awakening. Yet at the same time, the creatures *are* human beings; their song, in the surreal "reality," *has* the ultimate effect of human prayer.[86]

But clearly, Reb Nahman's tale is more than a romantic soliloquy on the anthropomorphic "nature spirit," and his aim lies beyond inspiring his listeners in their personal religious life. It concerns the fugitive and enigmatic moment when "night" will turn to dawn, the fateful instant in which the name of the "servant's son" becomes "king's true son." The commentary offered by R. Nathan in *Likkutei Halakhot* brings an important observation to the fore. He remarks that the crow of the rooster *(tarnegol)* in the dead of night serves, in fact, to mark the beginning of the *end* of night, to announce in the blackness that dawn is approaching. This phenomenon, in his eyes, speaks of the need to perceive "in the tenacious darkness of exile" the impending daylight of messianic days.[87] Indeed, in Jewish historiography, the momentous "first redemption" experienced by the Jewish people—the exodus from Egypt—is seen as a prototype of the "final redemption" of messianic days. "And it came to pass, that at midnight the Lord smote all the firstborn in Egypt" (Ex. 12:29), and the children of Israel went out from the land of their affliction. This is the signal, the rooster's crow, announcing that the escape to freedom has begun. In mystical tradition, however, subsequent events in the story of the Exodus are even more portentous. Pharaoh and his horsemen pursue the fugitives to the edge of the Red Sea. In that last terrible night before all would be lost,

> the angel of God, who went before the camp of Israel, removed and went behind them, and the pillar of the cloud went from before their face, and stood behind them: and it came between the camp of Egypt and the camp of Israel; and it was a cloud and darkness to them, but it gave light by night to these, so that the one came not near the other all the night. (Ex. 14:19–21)

The *Zohar* makes this astonishing proclamation: "At that moment the moon became complete in every aspect once again. Seventy-two holy names surrounded her from three sides. . . ." In telling imagery, these three aspects are described. The moon (a reification of *Malkhut*) was clothed in the glory of supernal *Hesed,* in the compassion of *Gevurah,* and in the royal crimson garments of *Tiferet.*[88] Here is the omnipresent triad, evoked, once again, to speak of the restitution of the moon, the return to her original brilliance prefigured in the "first redemption." The prophet Isaiah foretold her ultimate transformation in most moving terms: "The light of the moon shall be as the light of the sun, and the light of the sun shall be sevenfold, as the light of the seven days . . ." (Is. 30:26); and R. Hisda, the talmudic sage, declares that such a miracle will be the sign that the messianic era has come.[89] Paradoxically, in such a metamorphosis, the state of "having no name" thus becomes thoroughly positive. No longer the "lesser luminary," the "moon" gains a radically new identity. In the words of the *Zohar,* "[W]hat is on the highest plane cannot be named. The light of a candle is invisible in the day, in the light of the sun."[90] R. Nathan, referring to his master's tale, yet doubtless aware of this text as well, explains that the candle is analogous to a name; the "name" labels the entity, but most often only facetiously. Authentic identity is first realized when things can struggle free of their lying titles. To be nameless, then, would be an emblematic victory, a liberation from falsehood; namelessness sets the stage for the revelation of essence, concealed no longer by deceptive names, in the bright light of truth.[91]

If this is so, the question in *The Two Sons Who Were Reversed* that the moon asks the sun—"Why, when you come, do I have no name?"—must be reconsidered. If the "moon" undergoes an ontological change at the final dawn, it would follow (especially in light of the prophet Isaiah's vision cited above) that the "sun" undergoes a corresponding transformation, that "daylight," too, all at once signifies something utterly different. Audible in the sages' description of their world order—"Israel's calendar is measured by the moon, while non-Jews measure time by the sun"[92] is the implication that the "sun" represents the alien, inimical reign of pagan and Christian empires. Israel, as in the midrashic image of the diminished moon, endures centuries of humiliation under the hand of the heliotyrant. Excessive light, R. Nathan reminds us, is forever an infamous destructive force, whose effects are only too tangible in this, our shattered world.[93] This is the notorious, second metaphorical face of the Apollonian "sun": the sterile neon brightness of "Enlightenment," in which human intellect ascends as the supreme monarch, in which microscopes and telescopes penetrate the secrets of the universe and promise true vision. In this celebrated *age de lumières,* belief in Divine Providence is ridiculed as obsolete. It is the epoch of Science, in which the "laws of nature" rule. The only way this brilliant and terrible regime can be overthrown, R. Nathan continues, is through a "strengthening of faith"—naive faith that germinates like ferns and moss in the cool darkness of the night. And though computers shamelessly scan the planets' orbits, and their programmers seem as gods, this injustice will not endure. "Natural law" will be annulled; God will reveal His supremacy through awesome wonders, reversing the "laws of nature" in defiance of all man's proud calculations.[94] For Reb Nahman, the proclamation of Psalm 98, "Sing to the Lord a new song, for He has done miracles," thus bears witness to the dawn of a new age, in which the "melody of Divine Providence alone" will fill the world.[95] This new age was prefigured, in mystical tradition, in a historical event documented in 1 Sam. 6:7–15. The holy ark and the covenant, recaptured at last from the hands of the enemy Philistines, was triumphantly brought back to its rightful owners. A joyous pair of milch cows pulled the cart that bore it, lowing God's praises as they went up to Beit Shemesh. The text of their song, the midrash tells us, was Psalm 98. The military victory was but a symptom of a greater miracle: according to the *Zohar,* the ark (a symbol of *Malkhut,* the moon, the throne of royalty) was returned to "the house of the Sun" (the literal meaning of "Beit Shemesh") and the song of ascent ushered in a monumental *tikkun* in that reunion.[96] Reb Nahman's tale *The Two Sons Who Were Reversed* reenacts this event three times over. The strange box/instrument *(tevah)* the forest man bestows on the king's true son, like the ark *(tevah)* of the Covenant, arouses the beasts who bear it to sing the "new song" of the forest creatures. (*SM,* pp. 160–61). And in the enchanted garden, the restitution of the throne elicits that wondrous melody once again and for always, as the prince (and redeemer) wins his true name.

As we have seen, the rich array of sources integrated into Reb Nahman's oeuvre form a chimerical topology, in which every element (moon, sun, light, darkness, etc.) is a veritable Hydra of countenances. Emphasis, thus far, has been placed on their multicolored comparison as dialectical pairs, as thesis and antithesis. Our discussion of the dialectic, however, still remains incomplete, for in Reb Nahman's inherited tradition, its culminating point is necessarily a Hegelian synthesis. The prophet's vision mentioned above that "the light of the moon shall be as the light of the sun, and the light of the sun shall be sevenfold, as the light of the seven days" (Is. 30:26) may certainly be read as a premonition that these two concurring luminaries will one day merge into some higher comprehensive truth. The profound significance of that astronomical synthesis, though, can only be grasped when we perceive the dynamic—in such opposing pairs as moon and sun, day and night—of feminine/ masculine sexual valences. And although the tale *The Two*

Sons Who Were Reversed never betrays such a romantic union, the mysterious dialogue in the forest dawn whispers just such an intimate secret.

The "greater luminary," or the sun, the *Zohar* teaches, is an inherently male entity—he is master of the day, providing for all the material needs of the diurnal world. The "lesser luminary," in contrast, is the female moon, who "rises while it is yet night and gives food to her household" (Prov. 31:15). (We remember the words of gratitude, in Reb Nahman's tale, spoken by the animals indebted to the moon for giving them nourishment.) The author of the *Zohar,* however, sees this division of roles as a schism, a sign that some primordial union that once existed between them has been ruined. "And it was evening and it was morning, one day" (Gen. 1:5)—it was a continuous day, unpolarized by its "evening" and "morning."[97] Incongruously, though the schism came about at the dawn of cosmic history, "days" and light years before human beings inhabited the earth, it is, in Jewish tradition, *humankind's* unique responsibility to repair the disunion between these most esoteric entities. This sense of responsibility is reaffirmed in the performance of every religious act; it is a fundament of mystical teaching, vitally adopted in Hasidism.[98] In the following teaching from the *Zohar,* for example, this process is conceived in surprisingly vivid detail.

> There are two stages of prayer—first seated and then standing, yet they are one. There are also two phylacteries, the arm-tefillin and the head-tefillin, corresponding to day and night, and these, too, are one. The sitting prayer corresponds to the arm-tefillin, and makes it complete—as we make the bride complete by adorning her, preparing her to enter the *huppah,* so the *nukba* is adorned. . . .

As the prayer following the Shem'a is completed, the adorned bride enters the presence of the king, her groom; the meeting is embodied in the *'amidah,* the core of nineteen blessings. "He comes forth to receive her, and then we stand before the supreme King, for in that moment male *[dekhura]* conjoins with female *[nukba]*. . . ."[99] The scene reveals, for the author of the *Zohar,* the true meaning of the important halakhic precept that there must be no pause between these two vital sections of prayer, called respectively *ge'ulah* and *tefillah.* The romantic union engendered by the prayer of every Jew must never be interrupted in that ultimate moment of consummation. And indeed, it is in a talmudic discussion of this very halakhic precept that we discover the meaning of the "laughter" that fills the forest of *The Two Sons Who Were Reversed* at dawn. The betraying clue is the rare Aramaic word *huka* (laughter) used in the tale, rather than the more common *zhok*. It appears but a single time in the Babylonian Talmud:

> R. El'a said to 'Ulla: When you go up [to the Land of Israel] give my greetings to my brother, R. Berona, in the presence of the whole college, for he is a great man and rejoices to perform a precept [in the correct manner]. Once, he succeeded in joining *ge'ulah* to *tefillah* and laughter did not leave his lips the entire day. . . .[100]

The apparent pleasure of that sage at his successful performance of a rabbinic injunction seems to be transported, amplified to gargantuan proportions, in Reb Nahman's fantastic tale. After our discussion in the previous pages, we may now recognize that immortal dawn as an awesome reconciliation, a dramatization of the mystical union between cosmic masculine and feminine valences. The laughter bears witness to the union. It appears in *The Two Sons Who Were Reversed* with the Mona Lisa smile that forever graces the face of literary allusions.

In sum, that tale speaks of many things—of the mysterious and romantic effect of "music," of the tension between entities and their names, of the "indwelling soul of nature" as an evocative kabbalistic metaphor. All these themes, in turn, are vehicles for presenting the notion at the heart of Reb Nahman's conception that romantic love is an ultimately cosmic force—reflected, a faint glimmer, in the cycle of human life.

4. IN GOD'S IMAGE HE CREATED HER

In general terms, we could indeed say that Reb Nahman (like many thinkers before him) fashions his often esoteric teachings in the image of Man.[101] Yet I would like to suggest, in the final section of this chapter, that the predominant image in his thought is more often that of Woman. Whether this image is paternalistic, stereotypical, sexist, or "gynofocused"—I wish to argue none of these possibilities.[102] Rather, extensive study of his works leads me to conclude that in them, "woman" is not "the Other"[103] but that, on the contrary, an intuitive sense of female being informs them. Interest in experiences unique to women is, of course, intrinsic in Jewish mystical thought as a whole and should certainly not be considered Reb Nahman's invention.[104] That interest, though, comes to fruition in a variety of metaphors in *Likkutei Moharan* and in fictional figures in the tales. The connection to the subject of this chapter— the romantic drama—is more than tangential; Reb Nahman's attention to inherently feminine modes and consciousness allows him to portray that drama in a most compelling form. Let us begin with a consideration of the many classic symbols whose valence, in kabbalistic thought, is female, and trace some of their transformations in Reb Nahman's imaginative retelling of those essential teachings.

R. Simeon bar Yohai asked R. Eleazar ben R. Yose if his father had revealed to him the esoteric significance of the "crown with which [King Solomon's] mother crowned him on his wedding day" (Song of Songs 3:11). His answer was this parable:

> Once there was a king who had only one daughter and he loved her dearly. His affection led him to call her "my daughter," as it is written, "Listen, O daughter, and consider . . ." (Ps. 45:11); his affection did not cease, and he called her "my sister," as it is written, "Open to me, my sister, my love, my dove, my undefiled" (Song of Songs 5:2); still it endured, until he called her "my mother," as it is written, "Hearken to me, my people, and give ear to me, O my mother *[immi]*/my nation *[ʿammi]*" (Is. 51:4).[105]

Indeed, the allegorical king, the Holy One blessed be He, is joined to his people with a tangle of sentimental bonds that succeed one another endlessly through the ages. The protean female entity, called the Shekhinah or the Assembly of Israel, reflects, in her metamorphoses, the nature of their bond at any given moment. As princess, her being is defined by fatherly indulgence, protection, unbridled affection; as sister, she is platonically chaste, though liminally, even euphemistically, also a beloved bride; as mother she is the source of life, of knowledge; she is the symbolic field or vessel open to receive the sky's abundance, the earth in which seed grows, the pale moon, illuminated by the light of her Sun.[106] Cast in many of Reb Nahman's tales is the long-awaited daughter, her parents' only child *(Burgher and Poor Man, King and Kaiser, The Seven Beggars)* or a single daughter among (seven) sons *(Lost Princess, Prince of Precious Stones)*. Invariably, her ethereal beauty is superhuman, nearly unbearable; she is a gifted musician, a graceful polyglot—in short, the *sefirah* of *Malkhut* personified in the *Zohar*.[107] An even more compelling female image in Reb Nahman's oeuvre is surely that of motherhood, with its inherent metaphors of conception and pregnancy, birth and nursing, raising children and creating a family. Many feminist critics would doubtless reject Reb Nahman's writings outright as a chauvinistic and repressive presentation of women, their identity subsumed in the capacity of reproduction. Yet it seems to me that, in Reb Nahman's eyes, these inherently female events serve as a paradigm of universal human experience. Physiological and biological processes that take place in women's bodies become, for him, an intimate metaphor of the most metaphysical phenomenon—from the creation of the world to the miraculous re-creation of human life.[108]

Metaphors of Motherhood

Standing on the bank of a stream, the prophet Ezekiel is told of the wondrous trees nourished by its living waters: "Their leaf shall not wither, neither shall their fruit fail; they shall bring forth new fruit every month, because their waters have issued out of the sanctuary, and the fruit shall be for food, and the leaves for medicine" (Ezek. 47:12). The sages interpret this homeopathic power through a *notarikon:* the letters of "medicine" *(TeRuFAh)* reseparate to form other words—"to free the mouth" *(le-haTiR-Fe)*. But what (or whose) mouth is to be freed? Well, "mouth," as R. Isaac bar Abudini and R. Hisda teach, politely refers to two openings in the human body: one upper and one lower. And thus when muteness is healed, words are born; when barrenness is healed, new life is conceived and finally emerges.[109] The constriction of these two vital openings—unmoving lips and sealed womb—characterize, for Reb Nahman, the state of physical as well as spiritual slumber. The inability to procreate, in turn, signifies an inability to create; it is a petrified internal wasteland—no plants can take root in the dormant earth and no fruit can blossom. The focus of the teaching concerning the subject in *Likkutei Moharan*[110] is the power of the tales the zaddik tells to arouse his listeners from their state of existential sleepiness. The charge to listen and internalize the message of the Hasidic narrator reminds Reb Nahman of the ultimate awakening in Jewish life: the blast of the shofar on Rosh ha-Shanah shakes the people to recall their sins and return in repentance. Indeed, the New Year marks an eternal return to the cosmic Genesis as well as the day on which each of the matriarchs was delivered from her long barrenness.[111]

Yet the notion of "birth" is, for Reb Nahman, far from a tranquil, schematic metaphor. In another context, he speaks of the process of birthing in all its stages as a paradigm of beginnings.

> To do the commandments and good deeds, and all manner of serving God—that is, in a sense, to bear. What groans and pain, what contractions precede a birth. Especially the first time, a woman undergoes great trials. . . . For an opening must be made . . . and widened, stretching more and more.[112]

This opening *(nekev)* in the female *(nekevah)* body is thus a changeful passage: it is the narrow doorway to her womb, the symbolic storehouse of unborn souls as well as the channel through which newborn life enters the world.[113] Not accidentally, these motifs of metaphorical openness and closedness that inform kabbalistic thought serve to explain the metaphysics of the Hebrew alphabet itself. The fifth letter, *heh,* is recognized as archetypically feminine: on two sides, its graphic form is open "in order to receive an abundance of blessings," i.e., of seed and, later, to nourish the rest of the letters from within herself as a mother nurses her infant.[114] Only when Abram becomes Abraham, and Sarai Sarah, only with the addition of the letter *heh* to their names, could the first patriarch become "father of many generations" and the first matriarch bear Isaac (Gen. 17:5); this fact, reinforced by the cryptic verse that "God engendered the world with the letter *heh*" (Gen. 2:4) leads to the ancient conviction that that letter must be the primordial symbol of (pro)creation.[115] Reb Nahman takes up this nearly mythic theme, augmenting it to emphasize the psychological aspects of the human acts of conception, birth, and nursing. Returning to the biblical words, "And Adam knew Eve his wife" (Gen. 4:1), he declares: "The essence of birthing is through knowledge." Just as minors, who lack knowledge, are unready to have children,[116] so an individual who has no cognitive bond with God can actualize nothing of himself; his creative powers remain passive, in potentiality.[117]

The zaddikim of each generation, then, play a critical role: "They exhaust themselves, pursuing other people in the effort to bring them nearer to serving God." Hence their power "to make barren women fertile"—by helping others grow in their "knowledge" of divine will, the zaddik helps them both to be born and to bear.[118] Through the tales he tells, through the Torah he teaches, the zaddik is indeed a mystical midwife. In Reb Nahman's view, the very process of revealing the mysteries concealed in the Torah—as unknown "as the bones growing in the womb of her that is with child" (Eccl. 11:5)—is an act of birth.[119] Yet that is not all. For as he brings these truths from darkness to light, he himself draws new souls to life, investing them in the consciousness of his listeners.[120]

Turning, now, to one of the most pathetic scenes in all of Reb Nahman's tales, we may find some clue to its meaning. In *The Master of Prayer,* the most terrible tragedy for the princess, as her father's kingdom is thrown into chaos, is the loss of her golden infant son. Her sorrow, and the pressure from within her, becomes unbearable; rivers of milk flow from her, forming a lake—the testimony of her despair (*SM*, p. 209). That cataclysm, of course, speaks of other ages of destruction and exile, in which no one remains to receive divine revelation, in which the Jewish people feels estranged from His indwelling presence, manifest in the maternal Shekhinah.[121] The emotional as well as physical interdependence of mother and son underlying the scene bespeaks a fundamental historical relationship. In the ages after the Temple's destruction, the Israelite nation is banished from the Land, yet realizes again and again that this alienation is not total: "See, how beloved Israel is to God—wherever they were exiled, the Shekhinah went with them. . . . And when they will be redeemed, she will return with them as well."[122] Thus, although the figure of Rachel haunts the lonely hills, weeping for her lost sons (Jer. 31:14), the author of the *Zohar* insists that is was not she who was exiled; rather, willingly she has gone after them to protect her sons from harm.[123] Though the golden son is hurled into the cruel world, his mother the princess nowhere to be found, he sits down in the midst of the lake of her milk and there he stays and drinks until he is taken and made king (*SM,* p. 224). The lake is an oblique sign of her omnipresence; she could never abandon him completely.[124]

The Shekhinah as loving mother who commiserates with her exiled sons, however, constitutes but one scenario used to explain the history of the Jewish people. In a second, alternative scenario suggested as well, evil powers gained force as the Temple met destruction; the Shekhinah herself was kidnapped and spirited away by them.[125] In many texts in the *Zohar,* demonic forces become atemporal and their motives "romantic": the *sitra ahra* [Other Side] is portrayed as a jealous suitor who lies in wait for the chance to abduct the Shekhinah, stealing her away from her true lover, the Holy One, blessed be He.[126] In Reb Nahman's tale *Burgher and Poor Man,* this paradigm guides the narrative; the pious poor man's wife is "snatched" by a passing general (*SM,* p. 110), and his daughter years later is captured by the impotent murderer-pirate out of sheer spite. (*SM,* p. 131) It is a dominant motif in *King and Kaiser* as well, in which a series of false suitors attempt to possess the chaste heroine by force.[127] In this situation, the Shekhinah, in the words of Scholem, takes on a "terrible aspect," or becomes "filled with sacred fury," in Tishby's expression.[128] The attribute of mercy is superseded by that of stern judgment, which invades the Shekhinah "from without." Embattled with the "evil husks" that threaten to envelop her, to suck her holiness from her, she may strike out vengefully, furiously, wreaking destruction.[129] This *belle dame sans merci* is the incarnation of the divine attribute of *din,* or harsh judgment, recognized throughout mystical literature as archetypically feminine.[130] In some instances, she is the agent charged to punish evildoers and make justice reign. The armies that surround her, flaming swords, coals of glowing fire—all of these are emblems of her dangerous force.[131] This frightening alter ego of the Shekhinah seems to be the model for the heroine of Reb Nahman's *King and Kaiser.* Sailing over the seas with her retinue of eleven musical maidens, she cruelly attacks the bald prince who deceitfully sought her hand: as he flaunts his prowess high on the mast of his ship, she focuses a lens against the rays of the sun, relenting only when she has "burned his brain" and he falls dead into the sea (*SM,* p. 24). The kaiser's daughter's cleverness subsequently leads her to take on disguises—she appears as a sagacious doctor and quickly rises to kingship; her final self-revelation as a woman rather than a man occurs only when her true beloved is found. Only then does this liberated woman set down her armor before all her male predators. (*SM,* p. 27). In fact, her plan to distinguish her true and long-awaited betrothed from the slew of lying suitors is a brilliant manipulation of a trope wielded by many feminist writers. "The metaphor of the 'mirror'—its reverse side and edges, its splintering and doubling effect—is now commonly used to describe female self-awareness controlled by the male gaze."[132] Reb Nahman's heroine erects fountains around the city, and next to each fountain places a portrait of herself (disguised as king). Watchmen guard each post, searching the faces of those who come and drink. Each false lover recognizes her image; his countenance reflects his treacherous past with her, and he is seized. The face of the promised groom, of course, changes as well, though many years have passed: his recognition proves their tryst.[133] In the kaiser's daughter's scheme, "male self-awareness" becomes the victim of the woman who gazes from her portrait. His reaction betrays his own failure to dominate her, and her ultimate victory over him.

The Shekhinah: From Mourning to Joy

The Shekhinah, recognized in the *Zohar* as the symbol of "eternal womanhood,"[134] thus takes on, in midrashic and kabbalistic literature, all of the roles—daughter, bride, beloved, wife, mother—assumed by many women in the course of their lives. Far from denigrating the experiences that define those roles, Reb Nahman champions them; women's ways in the world become symbolic of intrinsic qualities of God Himself and are portrayed, moreover, as attributes to be emulated by all of humankind. Many of the characteristics attributed to the Shekhinah in classic sources—passivity, weakness, muteness, loneliness, dependence—would be decried by feminists as the inventions of male authors striving to prove their "superiority." Yet I would suggest that here, as well, the opposite is true. In Reb Nahman's oeuvre, we witness the evolution of centuries of Jewish thought on the supremacy of femaleness. Again and again, those "negative" characteristics relative to maleness are evoked to speak of a temporary state, a lamentable condition that must be rectified. The restoration of equality between male and female, apparently even the ascendancy of femaleness, is emphasized many times as a harbinger of the messianic age. Let us consider some instances in his writings in which these revolutionary ideas come to the fore.

The sixth beggar *(Seven Beggars)* tells of a princess desperately fleeing the clutches of an envious king and her attempt to find refuge in a fortress of water. Restlessly, wordlessly, she walks around its threatening exterior; as the evil lover approaches she decides to run through its walls, "for she prefers to drown than to be seized and taken as the king's own, and maybe, just maybe she would succeed" (*SM,* p. 279). The whole scene is evoked in the third person; an omniscient narrator projects the heroine's thoughts, and she remains throughout her struggle as speechless as she is helpless. The desperation of this wholly internal drama seems most acute because it is frozen in silence; the princess's pain is so terrible *because* she cannot cry out. The muteness of the female, her violent silencing at the hand of male authors, is indeed, in the eyes of feminist writers, the primary ill of all literature not written by women, and can be righted by women alone. Yet, in mystical thought, the imprisonment of words in silence, estranged from the voice that could speak them—is a fundamental condition of Exile itself. The voice of prophecy is taken from the Jewish people when they are driven from the Land: this loss is an emblem of schism, both physical and metaphysical, between the Creator and His servants.[135] Analogous metaphors of oppression—the moon that has no light of its own, reduced to anonymity, waxing and waning as the months pass, wavering between hope and despair—are portrayed, similarly, as lamentable states. Paradoxically, it is the pathos of *women's* pain that most eloquently represents the existential pain of a quite patriarchal nation. Not surprisingly, then, that nation's anticipation of its redemption is imagined as a romantic reconciliation, a timeless moment in which the moon's own light is restored; she regains her independent identity, her beauty and full form, and is reunited at last with her lover.[136] Reb Nahman suggests the escatological vector of this romantic tryst in his commentary on the biblical book of Ruth. Boaz, the heroine's protector and future husband, "is the intellect . . . while Ruth is an aspect of the soul *[nefesh],* the source of speech, speaking prayer and song and praises to God."[137] The seeds of thought have their inception in the mind, while the soul is the matrix of their growth and development. Remembering that King

David, traditional author of the book of Psalms, is the great-grandchild born of the union between Boaz and Ruth, we find a striking association: King David, "the anointed of the Lord," is the Messiah in a figurative sense as well—his name, *meshi'ah,* signifies, at the same time, to invest with speech *(me-si'ah).* The means to draw words from the narrow straits of the throat, to allow one's nascent soul to struggle forth in words—that is the great gift King David gave to his people through his own lifelong dialogue with God.[138] The outpouring of emotion in myriad forms, for which King David is famous, truly is stereotypically unmasculine.

It is interesting that of all of Reb Nahman's tales, the one in which direct speech (rather than an omniscient narrator's voice) is most prevalent is dominated, in fact, by a woman's voice. In *The Lost Princess,* the heroine, stolen away from her father's home by the mysterious Not Good, speaks to the king's messenger with profound inward understanding of what has become of her. The messenger, in contrast, is wholly external, a man of action; he comprehends nothing of her womanly suffering, and yet realizes that she alone knows how he must save her. And truly her demand is a stereotypically feminine task. The questing hero must undergo a trial of the heart—"every moment you must long and seek, and hope to release me. . . ." His mightiest opponent is his own body; "And you must fast, and on the last day of the year of waiting you must not sleep . . ." (*SM,* p. 5). The part of crusading knight is exchanged with that of fair lady; only after the servant is consumed in "passive" longing does his victory become conceivable.[139]

A reversal of gender stereotypes, similarly, marks *King and Kaiser.* In this case, though, Reb Nahman's innovation is far more revolutionary: directly after the secret betrothal between king's son and kaiser's daughter, the ring is lost, the lovers are lost to one another, and the king's son disappears from the story, to return only at its denouement. The tale itself concerns her adventures, her loyalty to the promised one, her ingenuity in diverting all manner of romantic foes, from doddering kings to their plotting merchant sons, pirates, and courtiers. Here the male "savior" is absent; the maiden saves herself. The contrast between her furious activity and his passivity, though understated, is unmistakable; the heroine clearly runs circles around each and every one of the male characters. Her dominance, throughout the tale, seems to me no accident. Rather it suggests, more explicitly than any other tale of Reb Nahman's, an essential view in Jewish tradition regarding "women's liberation." In the words of the midrash:

> R. Samuel said in the name of R. Nahmani: In this world, man surrounds [courts] woman, but in time to come, woman will court man, as it is written, 'Woman will surround *[tesovav]* man" (Jer. 31:21).[140]

The idea is further developed in Lurianic teaching: this experience of female dominance, envisioned by the biblical prophet, is seen as a harbinger of the messianic age, an age in which women succeed in righting the ills of patriarchal society.[141] The kaiser's daughter in Reb Nahman's tale, in her disguise as foreign king, stages a scene in which she recognizes her betrothed and her suitors but is not recognized by them. Perhaps the court of eleven lost maidens who accompanied her encourages a hidden iconography—our heroine resembles the biblical Joseph. Thus she, though a woman, seems to be a messianic figure, taking on the role usually played in Reb Nahman's tales, as in Jewish tradition as a whole, by men.

As this chapter draws to a close, let us consider one final element in Reb Nahman's teaching that demonstrates his conscious choice of metaphors of femininity to speak of supreme metaphysical convictions. The traditional description of a woman's body (metonymically, of women) as a vessel *[keli]*[142] evokes the following innovation on the Lurianic doctrine of the prenatal cosmos:

> God, in His compassion, created the world in order to reveal His compassion, for if there were no world, to whom would He show His compassion? . . . But when He desired to create, there was no place in which to put the world, for all was full of His endless presence. Thus He contracted His light to the sides, making a void space. And in that emptiness He created . . . the world.[143]

We cannot ignore the etymological association between Reb Nahman's term *rahmanut* (compassion) and the word *ReHeM* (womb). In his reiteration of R. Isaac Luria's teaching, Reb Nahman speaks of that phenomenon when space is found in the fullness of a woman's body to engender and house new life. Compassion *(rahmanut),* in the words of

S. Trigano, "is essentially the capacity to conceive the Other in oneself."[144] This vivid image, then, describes a primordial divine act as a choice, on the part of the Creator, to bear His world from within Himself as an expression of the inherently feminine attribute of compassion.

But it is in his excursus on an historically later and continuous process of revelation that the motif of femininity in Reb Nahman's thinking finds most striking expression. In *Likkutei Moharan,* interpreting the divine promise voiced by the prophet Isaiah to the people He has formed and called by name—"When you pass through the waters I will be with you . . ." (Is. 43:3)—Reb Nahman says:

> The Torah is hidden and revealed, and the Holy One blessed be He is also hidden and revealed. That is, what is revealed to us is the garment, the external, and what is hidden from us is the internal.[145]

How, though, he asks, can man grasp this inwardness? Through prayer, in which he binds his thoughts to the words he speaks.

> For God desires the prayers of the righteous (B.T. *Hullin* 60b); He is forever ready and willing to send down an abundance of blessings. Yet that abundance can only descend if there is a vessel, an "I" *[ani]* . . . that vessel is made by each and every Jew who, through his prayer, connects thought to speech.

Each letter of the word "I" *(ani),* he continues, signifies a component of this idea: the *aleph* designates the righteous; the *nun* embodies speech; and the *yod* thought. These esoteric allusions, though, bring him to propose a clear and astonishing meaning:

> It is well known that one who receives pleasure from another is called female *[nukba]*. . . . We find that God, may He be praised, receives pleasure from [His people] Israel, from their prayers, and thus becomes the female, as it were, relative to Israel. As it is written, "A burnt offering *[isheh]* of a sweet savor to the Lord." For by the sweet savor God receives from the prayers of Israel, He mystically becomes woman *[ishah]*.

This audacious play on words introduces the final step in the total reversal of roles he calmly presents:

> "Woman will surround man" (Jer. 31:21)—Thus, what was inward becomes outward. . . . And that is what the verse means, "When you pass through the waters"—"pass through" in the sense of revelation, [as when God passed over Egypt, inflicting the final plague]. . . . And there is no "water" aside from "Torah" (B.T. *Baba Kamma* 17a). In other words, when He wishes, God will reveal to you the secrets hidden in the Torah. ". . . I will be with you," i.e., see to it that you become the vessel that is called "I."

For Reb Nahman, then, the notion that "woman will surround man" speaks of much more than a new world order in the human realm. His definition of femininity as hiddenness, inwardness, and mystery and masculinity as overt, external, revealed, cognitive understanding enables him to draw much more far-reaching conclusions. In his vision of the future, our basic ontological truths are turned inside out, upside down. In a world transformed by revelation, the "feminine" assumes a new and diametrically opposed identity—"What was inward becomes outward": God Himself, receiving the shower of blessings from his People, becomes God "Herself."[146]

In sum, the leitmotif in our discussion of the romantic drama seems to be the notion of harmonious union, expressed in countless forms throughout our sources. The players change (sun and moon; heart and spring; prince and princess; God and His creation) yet the play remains the same. Lovers' trials of longing, search, despair, and hope become paradigms, in Reb Nahman's oeuvre, of the purest spiritual quest. Yet despite this tropic movement of abstraction, inspired by a rich array of pretexts, Reb Nahman takes great care to present the most honest and intimate human content of the experiences he utilizes. While his view of nature is imbued with the *Weltanschauung* of nineteenth-century romanticism, the attention to femininity that permeates his teaching seems to mark the awakening to a new consciousness of a universal woman's voice.

IV • The Dimension of the Fantastic

Abraham and his son Isaac set off on their foreboding journey to the Land of Moriah, bearing wood for the nameless altar; for three days they walk, watching and waiting for the promised sign showing them the place God has chosen to test their faith. The midrash names the two servants who accompany them—Eliezer and Ishmael—and at the portentous moment when the site of the ʿAkedah is revealed, the profound spiritual differences separating the figures becomes clear. Abraham is transfixed; the rabbis understand his vision of *ha-makom* literally, as a theophany, while the servants, more akin to beasts than men, remain blankly indifferent. They must, then, be left behind while Abraham and his chosen son ascend alone.[1] All four characters journey in the same landscape, yet the enlightenment of the patriarchs is set in sharp contrast to the blind ignorance of the two outsiders, symbols of the non-Jewish world. The experience of divine revelation, an instinctive, almost innate gift for the figures of the biblical narrative, becomes a polemical weapon in the hands of the rabbis. The question in both texts, though, remains the same: Who is worthy of communication with God, and how does that dialogue take place, how may one glimpse God's will through sudden lacunae in the texture of reality?

Revelation, in the widest sense, can be understood as an instance of that dialogue; in a moment, a person is translated, removed from the ordinary, simple, and human context of being. It is as if the true face of the world had been veiled until, for a moment, the mask is drawn away, and one contemplates the features of reality in a entirely new and unexpected way. Moses gazes at the unsilvered, luminous mirror *(aspaklaria me'ira)* and, through that transformed looking glass, sees what no other man has seen and lived. Other, lesser mystics detect God's presence in the thin small voice of silence, through the opaque cloak of dreams, remote behind the curtain *(me-ahorei ha-paragod)*. This concept of revelation, which has its conception in the Bible and threads through the generations of Jewish thought, is founded on a conviction that "truly, you are a hidden God" (Is. 45:15), that God is invisible yet omnipresent in His created world, that the world is thus clothed in an endless variety of guises, all of them equally illusory, all of them in fact disguises, concealing the single, too awesome countenance.[2] My concern here, of course, is the mystical worldview embraced by Reb Nahman and the imaginative expression it takes in his teachings. The fabric of the fantasy world inhabited by his tales' characters is, as it were, full of holes. Moments of revelation lived by Elijah, King David, and Isaiah, in which God's presence is suddenly and unexpectedly made manifest, expand into dramatic scenes. Natural phenomena, human actions, and entire events that prophets and figures of rabbinic invention may have understood and interpreted only in flashes of intuition, engulfed in a broader expanse of unawareness, become in the tales a nearly continual experience, transparently and naively symbolic. Yet though the curtain is pulled away many times to reveal the face of the King, it always falls back in place, and He is hidden once again. This dialectic between concealment and revelation, between symbol and the symbolized, between the natural and the supernatural, is an intrinsic element of mystical experience as a whole. It is central in the corpus of Jewish sources—the Bible, midrash, Kabbalah—and Reb Nahman, heir to this multicolored tradition, makes it the cornerstone of his own worldview. His characters, as they listen in the darkly shrouded forest, discover the majestic tree in a singing field, or suffer a labyrinthine search over years and seas for a lost beloved, live, for us, in two superimposed realms of reality. The nature of the dialectic between these two realms, its creation, purpose, and effects will be the subject of this chapter.

My fundamental contention throughout this work is that Reb Nahman's oeuvre may be considered literature of the fantastic. A definition of terms, then, is essential; although the stories are often considered as symbolic, allegorical, metaphysical, or even obscure, the genre of the fantastic is invoked, for the most part, in speaking of late-nineteenth- and twentieth-century works and has not, to the best of my knowledge, been used extensively in speaking of Reb Nahman's stories.[3] Yet as I hope to show, the profile of "fantastic" literature sketched by modern theory, most prominently by Tzvetan Todorov,[4] is strikingly applicable to Reb Nahman's tales as well, and the implications of such a comparison are far-reaching.

Most basically, the world described by "fantastic" literature resembles the reality familiar to the reader from his or her own life. Its order is compared, throughout the story, and either overtly or covertly, to the laws of the rational world, of "objective" reality. Within this essentially recognizable context, though, an event occurs that neither the reader nor the character (who shares the same ontological assumptions) can explain by the logic of that world. Both are posed with the problem of interpretation: Is this departure from the standards of rationality essentially an unknown yet true aspect of reality? Or is it only an illusion, the result of faulty perception, with no connection to outside reality at all? The hesitating uncertainty (primarily of the reader, but also of the character) between belief and disbelief is at the very heart of the fantastic.[5] A story of this genre flirts with things metarealistic, but it is no simple tale of enchantment, of passive participation in a magical world accepted unquestioningly. (If it were, it would be a fairy tale or some other genre bordering but distinct from the fantastic.)[6] Rather, it mandates a very human, very troubled confrontation that must continually be experienced between the realm of the rational and that of the transcendent.

In completing his definition of the fantastic, Todorov adds a final condition concerning the reader's attitude toward the text: he or she will reject allegorical as well as "poetic" interpretations.[7] This rejection is an essential first step in the encounter with and appreciation of fantastic literature. By calling an image "poetic" (or symbolic), one denies its representational power; rather than describing, the image is reduced to an aesthetic, rhetorical existence, "a combination of words, not of things."[8] The branding of a story's events as exclusively allegorical is similarly emasculating. Allegory, in Todorov's view, implies the existence of at least two meanings for the same words, and this double meaning is indicated *explicitly* in the work. If what we read describes a supernatural event, yet we refuse to understand that event literally, insisting on some other, nonsupernatural explanation, we have eliminated all space in which the fantastic can exist.[9] In another view, voiced for example by Ortsion Bartana,[10] a much broader definition is possible: any description of the supernatural appearing in the story is enough to make it fantastic; the supernatural element serves to draw the reader's attention to the metaphorical nature of the work and its comment on the reality that exists beyond the bounds of the fiction.

While these definitions certainly guide us in the right direction, they lack one element that is vital in understanding the dimension of the fantastic as it is expressed in Reb Nahman's tales. At issue is the ontological status, in the author's eyes, of the two superimposed realms. Todorov's interest in the psychological effect of the encounter with the supernatural, whether by the character or the reader, is indeed relevant in the case of Reb Nahman as well, for as we have seen (chapter 2), the Hasidic storyteller/author does strive to engage his listener/reader emotionally in the tale as it is being told. But his aim, in contrast to nearly all authors of the fantastic (E. T. A. Hoffmann, Maupassant, Poe, Borges, to name only a few) goes far beyond exhibiting his own creativity, manipulating his audience, or even "questioning the existence of an irreducible opposition between real and unreal."[11] To admit that the unreal may get tangled up in the furniture of the rational, logical world by no means implies that one's entire house really floats suspended in the air. The author and reader of most fantastic works continue resolutely to inhabit their familiar, positivist, desanctified world. One trips over the supernatural from time to time; the reader may be astonished, perplexed, even amused, but, after all, "the fantastic, even the enchanted, is commonplace in contemporary literature,"[12] and so its appearance can be relegated to the safe confines of narrative technique. As Todorov himself admits, his view of the function of the fantastic in a literary work remains somewhat tautological; as he says, "the fantastic . . . permits the description of a fantastic universe, one that has no reality outside language; the description and what is described are not of a different nature."[13]

Indeed, in the corpus of fantastic literature available for Todorov's analysis, the realm beyond the physical world is completely ephemeral, conceived and sustained artificially through words. In those works, the supernatural is a means and not an end. The only role this realm beyond the "real" plays is as a mirror: an amalgam of the author's invention, inspired, perhaps, by notions gathered from his cultural milieu, the supernatural is set up to portray, by ironic reflection, the true nature of the reality shared by author, character, and reader. In all secular literature of the fantastic, the supernatural has no existence as an independent entity. It depends completely on the artistry of the author, and only, as Coleridge says, with a "willing suspension of disbelief"—the stigma that marks our too-rational lives in a demystified world—may we think about it at all.

As one can see, the comparison of Reb Nahman's tales to other works of fantastic literature leads us down a bifurcating path: on the one hand, the Bratslav stories have much in common, in morphology and function, with modern, secular "fantastic" works. On the semantic level, however, the difference between the Hasidic tales and their Western counterparts is marked.

To illustrate this difference, I would like to return to an image suggested at the beginning of this chapter. It is the image of a glass surface, silvered or transparent, set at the interface between man and the meta-physical world. Silvered, the glass surface is a mirror; transparent, a window. The magically changeful nature of this interface makes it an ideal metaphor of man's relationship to realms beyond his own materiality: when his awareness is muted, he turns to the glass and is confronted with his own face, his own imaginings, his own limitations. But as his consciousness is heightened, the mirror may suddenly, without warning, give way, become luminous, revealing another world unlike anything of his own creation. In Jewish tradition, the metaphor of the variously dark or luminous mirror describes the various levels of prophetic vision. It is no coincidence, however, that one of the most prominent figures of twentieth-century literary criticism, Northrop Frye, evokes the same metaphor to speak of his subject, human contemplation of the world as embodied in art. In his book *Creation and Recreation*, Frye speaks of the element of narcissism inherent in the way we see the world, and recalls a haunting childhood impression. It is the sight of a lit-up railway carriage at night. The window of the carriage is the "cultural insulation" that separates us from the world we strive to understand. While most works and acts of human creativity feign to speak of "objective" reality, in truth they only reflect our own concerns.

As a mirror, the cultural aura around us "fills us with the sense that the world is something which exists primarily in reference to us: it was created for us; we are the center of it and the whole part of its existence."[14] Can we ever actually see outside the carriage, out into the darkness through which we travel? Yes, says Frye; in rare moments the mirror may turn into a real window. But the vision revealed through it is terrifying: we glimpse "an indifferent nature that got along for untold aeons of time without us, seems to have produced us only by accident and, if it were conscious, would only regret having done so." In this gloomy image of man propelled blindly through a godless universe, the landscape outside the voyager's carriage is profoundly unsettling, and to human perception it remains forever fragmentary as well. The Creator, for Frye, has receded to the dusty pages of mythology, and the void left by His absence is haunted only by dark, immutable cosmic forces. While for the Jewish mystic the mirror becomes a window in a moment of divine revelation, twentieth-century man is unbearably ill at ease with such a transformation. He would gladly avert his gaze from that sinister and empty universe, turning back with relief to the bright confines of his constructed world. The impervious window of the carriage is a hiatus; the voyager's self-reflection alone protects him from the threatening incomprehensibility of the night.

Both Todorov and Frye are concerned with the meeting between the physical and the metaphysical that takes place in literature. In the genre of the fantastic as Todorov describes it, the author contrives to represent that encounter playfully, imaginatively. He is cognizant of the inhabited darkness, yet even he never really leaves the lighted carriage, never ventures out into the unknown. Rather he tells a *story* about the night as if he knew it intimately. Through his fiction, the forces of the cosmos are named and tamed—they become his harmless own. The story of an encounter with the "supernatural" realm fashioned by artifice may indeed grant profound insight into the true nature of human reality. But with all its fascination, such a tale is forever solipsistic. No secular literary work can truly explore the realm of the supernatural, because it does not authentically conceive of the beyond as an autonomous, metarealistic realm. In Frye's conception, there is something pitiful about the whole phenomenon of human creativity: the secure carriage sounds suspiciously like a prison, carrying its passengers hostage through a dark world they can never understand. Both critic and author are really trapped in a tight, small space between life and literature.

I believe the fantastic as a genre can be regarded as a paradigm of modern literary endeavor as a whole. Its distinctive characteristic is self-consciousness; implicit in the tale (on the semantic level) is the voice of Narcissus himself. Gazing into the pool of water, he wonders and wonders whether it is another who gazes out at him, or whether it is the reflection of his own enamored countenance.

We run a certain unavoidable risk by adopting the terms of literary and philosophical discourse ("objective," "supernatural," "metaphysical," "realistic") to talk about Reb Nahman's stories. Implicit in these ideas is a certain dialectic, and the very juxtaposition of two counterparts—natural/supernatural; realistic/fantastic—suggests they are two halves of a whole, mutually exclusive, each defined through the other. The genre of fantastic literature does indeed seek to undermine that impression, founded as it is on the blurring of boundaries between two such opposed realms. But what I would like to emphasize now is the meaning of the obscured line of demarcation when we speak of Reb Nahman's tales. His comment on the world and human understanding of it, though self-reflective as well, contains a dimension completely absent in Western secular literary works. The mystical worldview that imbues his thought causes him to envisage the realm of the supernatural in a way radically different from the authors of profane literature of the fantastic.

In his tales, the supernatural is not invoked as a literary ploy to speak either of the writer's own art or of the hall of mirrors leading, perhaps (for one is never sure), from the text to "reality." Rather, in his conception, the "supernatural" takes on another name and another identity: it is the higher, divine world, ontologically truer and eternal compared to the transience of the lower world familiar to human quotidian experience.

Before analyzing this essential difference, however, we must consider the basic phenomenon central both to Reb Nahman's tales and other modern works of "fantastic" literature—the dynamic between two super-imposed domains of reality. In the first part of the chapter I would like to trace this dynamic back to its most naive origins, marking along the way the stages of its literary and cultural development. Insight into the nature of the animistic universe conceived in pagan mythology, and the later reincarnation of the primitive mythic world in the form of folktales will lead us to a deeper understanding of the supernatural, which undergoes a final evolution to appear in works of fantastic literature in completely secularized form. Through this comparison, in turn, the unique nature of Reb Nahman's created "fantastic" world will become more transparent. Ultimately, the idea that Reb Nahman's tales may be considered literature of the fantastic bears profound theological significance; the implications of this thesis will be suggested throughout our discussion.

The second part of this chapter is devoted to an examination of the transmutations of reality within all of Reb Nahman's stories. At issue are instances of that primary encounter with the supernatural, and the uncertainty such confrontations evoke both in the characters and, obliquely, in the reader. In the third part we will consider the bivalent problem of interpretation: How can the figurative language that is the lifeblood of the stories be understood as referential as well as poetic imagery? And how must we, Reb Nahman's audience, recognize their allegorical aspect without robbing them of all enchantment, without annulling their nature as purely fantastic literature?

1. A CHARACTERIZATION OF THE FANTASTIC WORLD

The tremendous interest in myth aroused in modern times, generating such monumental studies as those of James George Frazer, Mircea Eliade, Ernst Cassirer, Rudolf Otto, and Claude Lévi-Strauss, testifies to the conviction that primitive worldviews have played a vital role in the formation of human culture.[15] It is not the naked anthropological aspect of these works that concerns us here; rather, the *mythos* itself, the narrative of primordial events and the projection of that story as a model of human experience, is the phenomenon relevant to our discussion. It stands as an archetypal, naively pure literary form: myth begins in a time when concepts and abstractions are not yet a part of language, when metaphor is still unborn. The undifferentiated energy of the primitive world, the continuous and inescapable presence of an original creative force—these infuse the archaic mythic narrative. All subsequent literary endeavor strives, in some sense, to recreate that immediate awareness, to recall the animistic vitality of that lost world.

The anatomy of primitive religious belief is vast; my intention in the following comments is to present but one nuclear mythic concept that evolved into a universal folktale motif. In the third part of this chapter I hope to show to what extent the figurative language of Reb Nahman, inspired by that of the Bible, is inextricably linked to this mythic concept. But throughout, the crucial matter is this: in its original form, mythic description of the world is literal, and serves as an intimate and direct expression of reality as man perceived it. His awe for natural phenomena causes him to imagine the sun, moon, mountains, the sea, and the wind as animate, as possessed of will and emotions; man himself implants the presence of the divine within elements of his surroundings in his striving to create a dialogue with the world and to understand his place in natural history. It is the very inhumanness of natural phenomena that gives primitive man the sense of something beyond his own powers. Rudolf Otto, in his seminal study, *The Idea of the Holy*, describes the primitive fascination with some aspect of mystery, awesomeness, majesty, or "energy" in the natural world as the experience of the numinous. This fascination, in Otto's view, informs the legends and mythology of most primitive peoples, and is what drives the imagination again and again back to the original experience of *mysterium tremendum*.[16] This encounter is a moment of intense self-consciousness, a sudden realization that one is not alone, that a higher power has made the world and caused certain events to occur. In folktales, this vivid primitive experience of the numinous is often expressed in another dimmed and suppressed form as the magical.[17] In the fantastic tale, as opposed to the more simple and conventional folktale, the meeting with the numinous or the dimension of magic in everyday reality becomes a central event. It is, in fact, this encounter that occasions psychological development in the characters of the story.

Although my concern in this work is the stories of Reb Nahman in particular, and not the genre of fantastic literature as a whole, I would like to isolate one historical tendency that seems to have induced the evolution from folktale to literature of the fantastic. The mythic core that endures in both genres, of course, is what serves as the link between them. Just as the dimension of the fantastic in these non-Jewish works is related to a transmutation of the pagan inhabited cosmos, so

Reb Nahman founds the fantastic dimension of his stories on the worldview expressed in ancient Jewish sources, with their inherent, polemical deification of contemporary pagan beliefs.[18]

Folk tales have been widely recognized as an organic and immediate outgrowth of myth and legend,[19] as a narrative form incorporating the vestiges of lower stages of human culture. Even a summary of that research is beyond the scope of the present discussion. What interests us in the subsequent stage: Why did folktales and fairy tales capture the attention of prominent, sophisticated writers? When did such traditional tales begin to nourish a burgeoning trend of literature of the fantastic?

Although fantastic literature is bound to no single historical period (Ovid's *Metamorphoses*, Dante's *Divina Commedia*, and Voltaire's *Candide* share many defining characteristics with the works of Lewis Carroll or Jorge Luis Borges), the flourishing of the *Kunstmärchen* in the romantic period bears witness to the discovery of that genre as an expression of modern European historical sensibility. Engendered, in part, by an awakening sense of national identity, folk traditions became a subject of scholarly interest—anthropological, philosophical, and religious. Some fruits of this research were the collections of folktales and fairy tales published for the first time in the late eighteenth and nineteenth centuries. Many of the tales presented in Perrault's *Contes du temps passé* (1696), Musäus's *Neue Folksmärchen der Deutschen* (1789–92), or B. Naubert's *Neue Volksmärchen der Deutschen* (1789), for example, were markedly altered by their editor in his desire to suit the material to contemporary taste. Still, these collections, and perhaps most importantly the *Kinder- und Hausmärchen* (1812) and *Deutsche Mythologie* (1835) published by the Grimm brothers, brought the narrative traditions of the peasant classes to the eyes of the more cultured literary public for the first time.[20]

Thus the literary history of the late eighteenth and early nineteenth centuries shows the simultaneous reworking and editing of preexisting folktales as well as the production of a wholly innovative species of tales, that is, the *Kunstmärchen* or artistic tale. The difference between the two genres is as follows: while the folktale is orally and collectively transmitted, and recorded in writing only by a later, external agent, the *Kunstmärchen* is the invention of a known author, published, preserved, and read. It may be composed of both artificial narratives and original naive works; it may be closely modeled after the folktale schema or may be freely given to the supernatural and marvelous (as is E. T. A. Hoffmann's *Der goldene Topf*, 1827) and may be used as a metaphor for philosophical-existential declarations (such as Ludwig Tieck's *Der blonde Eckbert*, 1795). Alternatively, the folktalelike may itself become the theme of the story, as in Goethe's *Märchen* (1795).[21]

The Mythical World and its Evolution

The simplicity and authenticity of "the folk," their seemingly idyllic life in harmony with nature, and the ardent, nearly pantheistic faith expressed in their tales impressed the romantic poets. Impressed them, yet left them feeling shunned, for the intimate world of the folk seemed irretrievably distant from their own too-enlightened existence. This nostalgia for a childlike wholeness forever lost, though focused on folktales, actually penetrated to the most inward essence of the genre. Wilhelm Grimm gave a name to this awareness in his observation: "Common to all folk tales are the remnants of a belief that reigned in earliest times, expressing itself in a figurative conception of supernatural things. The mythical is like the shards of a shattered precious stone—they lie on the ground, overgrown with grass and flowers . . . their meaning is long forgotten, but they may yet be found."[22] Though no longer whole, these fragments have not lost their primitive potency; in folktales, he believed, they are gathered up, and those immortal mythic elements woven into the texture of the folk narrative. Hence the abiding authenticity the romantics discovered in such tales, on the one hand, and the impetus they found, on the other, to transmute those elements, which stood in radical conflict with their own rationalistic worldview.

As we saw in chapter 1, a parallel renaissance of interest in folk traditions took place in the Jewish world. From its very inception in the teachings of the Baʿal Shem Tov, Hasidism held the "tales the world told" and melodies of shepherds' flutes in high regard, both in their formal aspect and as entities of great metaphysical significance. Those creative traditions continued to exert a seminal influence in the development of Bratslav Hasidic thought. The transition from anonymous folktale to conscious literary creation can be distinguished in both traditions: in the *Kunstmärchen*, an archetype of the modern fantastic tale, on one hand, and in Reb Nahman's stories, on the other. To illustrate the striking kinship between these two outwardly disparate traditions (romantic *Kunstmärchen* and Hasidic tale), I would like briefly to compare a masterful artistic tale by Ludwig Tieck with Reb Nahman's tale *The Two Sons Who Were Reversed.*

Tieck, articulating the ideology of his time, held that the old folk books were unacceptable to modern consciousness and must be reformed, "uralte Geschichte in ein anderes Gewand gekleidete."[23] The setting of his tales is the landscape of rural Europe, the villages, forests, and mountains familiar in folktales. In *Der blonde Eckbert* and *Der Runenberg*, nature initially represents a place of refuge, a haven where loneliness is palpable, where voices are silently waiting to be heard and where the marvelous is revealed. Yet this refuge is ambivalent in its essence, for it is also at the mercy of a pessimistic consciousness, and in a moment may become disembodied and threatening. It is a place to be reached only with difficulty, temporarily, and remains dreamlike and unstable. As a utopia, the natural world is a golden image, compelling but forever unattainable. The heroes of both stories are young people who yearn to escape the confines of their parental homes and journey out into the wider world. The setting serves, ironically, to emphasize the truth of man's incommensurate distance from nature, an eternal condition of exile from the Garden, from the home one can never find again. Both heroes long to penetrate the veil of unintelligibility estranging them from nature, and their stories tell of such attempts to initiate communication, with dire consequences.

Tieck's *Der Runenberg* serves in this context as the axis of our discussion. The story is indeed a classic example of a romantic *Kunstmärchen*, with its deliberate reformulation of numerous folktale elements. If we were to adopt Propp's terminology and numbering, some of the many functions present in the action include: (1) Absentation—the solitary hero ventures out into the world; (2) an interdiction is violated—the youth disturbs the harmony of nature; (5) the villain—here a stranger, conspicuously otherworldly—appears inexplicably; (6) he attempts to deceive his victim, who (7) submits, descending with him into the bowels of the earth, etc.[24] These functions, as well as the central motif of discerning the language nature speaks, show Tieck's interest in the folktale model.

Secondly, *Der Runenberg* has all the features of an artful fantastic tale, with its vivid description of the hidden life of nature and the hero's emotional trials, his wonder, horror, disbelief, and final surrender to the seductions of the unworldly realm. In counterpoint to his acceptance of the fantastic is his wife's incomprehension; she witnesses his growing madness, yet remains solidly planted in her rational, Christian world.

Third, and most important in our present discussion, is the field of comparison the story provides with *The Two Sons Who Were Reversed,* one of Reb Nahman's most representative stories. It must be emphasized that this comparison is by no means accidental, nor is it obscure. Reb Nahman's writings as a whole are suffused with a *Zeitgeist* strikingly similar to that of the German romantic poets. In its postmedieval form, the narrative as a genre flowered in Eastern European Hasidism in the same decades as the *Märchen* enjoyed a renaissance in the Enlightenment period.[25] Although I make no attempt to prove there was any direct influence from Western European belles lettres on Reb Nahman's creative tendencies, the similarity between the spirit of the two movements—Hasidism and romanticism—is undeniable. Like Tieck's story, *The Two Sons Who Were Reversed* opens with the hero's journey from his father's home, his wandering through the world, and his eventual lonely vigil in a dark wood. The crux of this episode turns on identical phenomena: the king's true son's changing perception of the voices of nature, and the accompanying experience of revelation described as a psychological process. This development itself proves to be emblematic of the hero's evolving existential situation.[26]

The conflict of ascendancy between the king's son and the servant's son, switched at birth by a diabolical midwife, is what initially drives both figures out into the world. Each of the two sons must in the end discover his true identity, and this is the inner meaning of the "revelation" that takes place for both of them in the forest. The king's true son, desperately confused, pursues the beasts he was hired to herd into a thick forest. He loses their trail, and as night falls the roaring of the unseen forest creatures fills the blackness. For two nights in the forest, the haunting voices, coupled with his loneliness and guilt, arouse in him a feeling of terror. On the third day, he climbs a tree, seeking refuge, and comes upon the servant's true son, his contester, lost like himself far from home. Together they wait out the night and at dawn, to the king's true son's amazement, the moaning roar of the wild animals turns to a voice of laughter, penetrating the forest. The servant's son, ironically, is the one who reassures the king's true son; he has heard the laughter before in the nights he spent alone in the forest. Unlike the king's son, the servant's son had already intimated his real identity, and has admitted his willingness to cede the throne to its rightful heir. Yet the king's true son, still filled with doubt, is not yet aware he must overcome his lusts, must become master of his destiny. The separate and dissimilar perceptions by the two characters of the identical sound surrounding them symbolize, then, each one's awakening realization of who he truly is. The uncanny laughter, unknown to human ears, makes them understand that the forest is *makom ha-yeduʿim*: the spirits that haunt this place seem to know and will make known the vital difference between them. And the following day, in a fateful moment of weakness, the servant's son sells himself to the king's true son as a slave for life. Thus the natural order between them is at last restored.

The subservience of the false prince and the new dominion of the king's true son set the stage, then, for the great discovery of the inward forest music. Clearly, it is not the sounds of the forest that have changed, but the characters' perception of that chorus of voices. Estranged from themselves, ignoring their mission, they were helpless and what they heard only made them tremble. But as they become more circumspect, guided by the wise forest man, they listen more closely and discern something completely different (*SM,* p. 158). The all-consuming pleasure aroused by this secret song is described with Edenic sensuality, and in fact serves as a leitmotif throughout the rest of the story. The melody first heard in the forest signifies the advent of the messianic age. In the last scene of the story, the forest music reaches a crescendo; emerging from its shadowy recesses, it becomes a symphony played by the garden itself, pervading the entire world.

The crucial revelation in *The Two Sons Who Were Reversed* and in *Der Runenberg* occurs, by necessity, in an uninhabited place, remote from the shielding certainty of town and family; the hero is painfully alone, in direct confrontation with the dark forces of nature. We could say that in the forest, both Tieck's hunter and the king's true son encounter something numinous; the rustling trees, the roaring animals, the stream, and the wind seem suddenly animated; they speak to the hero, and he is drawn to action. Both protagonists react in the spirit of fantastic tales: they vacillate between feelings of terror and the desire to abandon themselves to the strange events that overtake them. After the forest scene, Reb Nahman's story gives way entirely to the fantasy mode; in Tieck's story, on the other hand, the tension between reason and madness, the dark side of fantasy, is preserved until the end.

Freud was convinced the sensation of the numinous was not a phenomenon that began and ended with primitive cultures. In modern life and literature, our encounters with divine or supernatural forces in the world takes an altered, more secular form; although we lack the naïveté authentically to experience the numinous itself, the sensation of something 'uncanny' is still possible, either in our personal lives or vicariously through literature. In his important essay, "Das Unheimliche" (1919)[27] Freud exposes "the uncanny" in all its semantic ambivalence. The German designates at once the sense of closeness, familiarity, recalling *Heim*—home—and, on the other hand, something strange, foreign, threatening. The *Unheimliche* is, then, in Freud's view, something that is secretly familiar—i.e., is part of a primitive, animistic worldview—that has undergone repression in human consciousness and suddenly reappears, threatening by its very unexpected familiarity. Hence the hesitation of both the king's son and the hunter, and the polysemous forest voices. Initially, the two characters are caught up in the rationality of the world whence they came. Yet, little by little, both come to understand the potential of communication inchoate in the forest itself. And ultimately, it is the excitement of that dialogue that propels them—to ruin or to redemption.

Interestingly, a number of Reb Nahman's stories contain a secondary figure, unmistakably inhuman, who serves as a sort of psychopomp, guiding the protagonist into the realm of the fantastic.[28] They await him at a critical juncture, and their intercession in his life marks a turning point in the story by changing his perception of reality. One such figure is the forest man. When the true prince, already haunted by the primeval forest noises, meets the forest man in that place he thought devoid of human beings, he is convulsed with terror. But after a time, despite that figure's awesome presence, the true prince confesses how he has happened into the forest: chasing after the beasts he could not control. The forest man's response is a flash of hermeneutic insight: "Stop chasing after sins, for they are not beasts at all; it is only your own sins that goad you on. Enough" (*SM*, p.154). It is as if his life had been a dream, a dream in which the dreamer thought himself awake. In that moment, the king's true son is freed from the tormenting elusiveness of the beasts: they fade away to symbols and obsess him no more. This meeting conducts the protagonist from his former life of debauchery and helpless envy to a higher plane of reality. Once there, he is granted the implements of a fairy-tale prince and rides off to restore the world.

In *The Seven Beggars* we find a similar mercurial figure who interrupts the action of the story and redirects the characters by interpreting their words allegorically. It is the "great eagle" (*SM*, p. 245) who pounds on the door of the tower, exhorting the shipwrecked souls who have gathered there: "Stop being poor; return to your treasures. . . ." The clever explanation that follows shows the eagle's omniscience: he reveals the symbolic essence of each one's earliest memory, and breaks up their meeting by concluding that the ships are the bodies those souls have abandoned.[29] The eagle then takes the infant *(yanik)* (alias the blind beggar and narrator of this episode) under his wing, so to speak, and proclaims him winner of the contest; he is, paradoxically, the youngest and oldest of all. As the eagle's protégé, the blind beggar is invested with his mentor's inconceivable longevity and metaphysical vision. It is this meeting that renders his blindness not literal but metaphorical. This is the gift of symbolic blindness, representing profound insight, that he awards to the children. The eagle's governance serves to transmute the blind beggar—his outwardly miserable state loses all importance, and he acquires the attributes of a superhuman figure by grace of his contact with the eagle.

A third story, *The Lost Princess*, demonstrates just how instrumental such guards of the threshold are in Reb Nahman's tales. Here, the figure in question (who appears as three brothers, but has a single function), instead of aiding the protagonist in traversing the boundary between two planes of reality, tries to impede him, to convince him the fantastic realm does not exist. In *The Lost Princess*, the king's vassal, sent to rescue the beloved daughter captured by evil forces, searches many years for her. At times she is palpably close, but again and again he is frustrated by his own impotence to withstand the trials he must in order to save her. At last she is spirited away to a remote fortress of pearls, high on a golden mountain. With unwavering determination he trudges on, into the trackless wilderness far from any town, resolved to find her. Finally he meets a giant, carrying a tree as a staff, and appeals for his help in finding a mountain of gold and a pearly fortress. The giant's nihilistic response threatens to undermine the vassal's entire quest: "He said, Surely there is no such thing, and he pushed him away and said he had been duped, that it was all nonsense, for no such thing exists . . ." (*SM,* p.8). The existential doubt he seeks to instill in the vassal is potentially lethal: the princess has already passed into a transcendent realm of unreality while the vassal, his feet unbearably heavy, seems to sink deeper by the minute into the sand of his humanness and limitation. He turns to the giant's brothers, respectively master of the birds and master of the winds, but the identical dialogue is only repeated. You cannot bridge the gap, they tell him; there is no magic mountain, it's all a figment of your gullible imagination. Worst of all, their words threaten to rob the vassal of the future itself as an existential possibility. "Go back," they urge him—the only time that is real is the past. To rescue the princess is but a dream that can never come true. In the end, the vassal does overcome their skepticism, and the passageway they had tried to bar before him is opened. The tactic used by the three giants is thus the mirror image of that used by the forest man and the eagle. While the latter two urge the protagonist to loosen his grip on literalness, to interpret his reality figuratively, thus winning access to a fantastic realm, the giants mock the very notion that such a transcendent world exists. The effect, of course, is but to inflame the vassal's desire even more. When he finally is taken there, it is in fact by the third giant's own agent.

In conclusion, we may note a curious iconographic coincidence. Jung cites three identifying elements related to the mythic figure of Hermes, the classical psychopomp, who transports souls from the land of the living to the underworld. Each of these elements corresponds with one of the figures of the three stories presented above: a bird form, Hermes has wings and flies, like the eagle *(The Seven Beggars);* he bears a staff, like the desert giants *(The Lost Princess),* and his chthonic nature recalls the earthy mystery of the forest man *(The Two Sons).*[30] In any case, these intermediaries prove to be essential in the creation of the fantastic tale. His encounter with them is what allows the protagonist to meet his fortune, to cross the abyss, wide as the eye of a needle, between reason and fantasy.

The eagle and the forest man play the role of the folktale "helper"; they show the hero how to be *tropically*, show him there is an alternative to playing out a literal existence. But symbols may be used as a weapon as well; in the hands of a villain they can destroy the trusting soul who too willingly believes. Such is the disaster that befalls the beautiful heroine of *The Burger and the Poor Man.* A murderer plots to kidnap her, and to lure her into his clutches constructs a supremely clever trap. Of the finest wires and glittering gold, he fashions an odious imitation of nature: lifelike birds roost weightlessly on fragile sheaves of wheat and as one gazes upon them, they seem to twitter and sing. The woman is entranced with this baroque vision, so deceptively natural, forgets herself, and is stolen away (*SM,* pp.127–30). The enticing realm of unreality is a perilous ploy; there is no true fantasy, no ethereal magical realm but only the artifice of an evil eunuch, hoping to induce the woman to take the symbol literally.

All these secondary figures, then, stand at a conceptual crossroads. The protagonist's encounter with them is a crucial moment in his life's story, for it is they who willfully alter the course he would have chosen alone. Notably, all the intercessors we have profiled belong, themselves, to a plane of reality inaccessible to the hero on his own. Whether the intermediary takes animate or inanimate form (Agnon's goat, Aladdin's lamp), it remains a ubiquitous element in the tale of the fantastic. Someone or something must mark the threshold, because the existence of that frontier, crossed and recrossed by every hero, is endemic to a story of the genre. In another tale told by Reb Nahman, *The Cripple,* we find an object, rather than a talking character, that transports the hero from the largely reasonable framework in which the story opens to a surreal land of demons and cloud kings. The crippled orphan son, fresh victim of highway bandits, throws himself from the ravaged wagon he was traveling in. He lies alone and helpless in the fields, and stays alive only by eating the plants he gathers by crawling along the ground. Then one day he comes upon a weed unlike any he has ever seen before, uproots it, and discovers beneath it a pyramidal diamond, inscribed on each face with a different message. The hero grasps the jewel as it instructs, and in a moment indeed finds himself "in the place where day and night, sun and moon are brought together" (*SM,* p.32). In this story, although the hero is spirited to a fantasy world, no one guides him; he remains an outsider, as if invisible in that world. Throughout the action, he is but a silent, wide-eyed witness, inactive in the weird drama that unfolds before him. Perhaps for this reason *The Cripple* is one of Reb Nahman's most opaque stories: no dialogue between the protagonist and an omniscient character helps make events more transparent to the reader. The figure of the cripple, wandering through demons' lairs, among the spirits of the dead and the unborn, recalls a talmudic aggadah that speaks, similarly, of a threshold between two planes of reality.[31] The anonymous subject, "a *hasid*," driven from home by his furious wife, goes to a graveyard where he would pass the night. There he overhears the conversation of two dead women and gains their precious knowledge of what goes on "behind the curtain." This information proves, in the course of the story, to be forbidden to the living, and the *hasid*'s eavesdropping in the world of the dead is effectively chastised. Although the talmudic source is not a fantastic tale, and one may even be supposed to doubt its veracity, it does suggest a naive recognition (perhaps in the guise of superstition) that certain locations in the rational world are held to be passageways to a transreality. Burial sites embrace mortality and immortality; both in religion and in cult, they represent the intersection between two possibilities of existence, and are thus sites of pilgrimages, rites, and mystical experiences.[32]

Mythopoetic Archetypes

Returning to Reb Nahman's tales, we must now consider the setting in which marvelous events are possible, those places where one may pass freely into another, supernatural realm.[33] From folktales as from myth, from fantastic stories and Reb Nahman's tales, we learn that the surface of the world is by no means metaphysically flat or uniform. Magnetic concentrations of intensity mark its features, surrounded by plains of placid reason. If, as Rudolf Otto suggests, the numinous is most tangible in elements of nature, we may suppose that the further one draws from the natural world, the more isolated one becomes from any potential sense of indwelling energy, of the divine. Cain the murderer, driven from God's countenance, flees eastward *(kidmat ʿeden)* and builds a city, the first city, to shield himself from the furious hatred of all creatures. Walled with stones, lit up to deny the night, the city represents security *(yishuv ha-daʿat)* and confidence, a place where a community can defy the monstrousness of what it does not understand.[34] Yet, such a place built by human hands ultimately alienates its inhabitants from the world, dulls their senses, stifles their individuality. Abraham's destiny is forged with the words *Lekh lekha* (Gen. 12:1); his story can begin only when he leaves all that is familiar, his home and his country, and casts himself into uncertainty. Such metaphorical voyages have drawn the contours of the world's literature. Metaphorical, because on the personal level they speak of self-actualization, of a quest for enlightenment. Dante's wondrous path of descent into the Inferno and spiraling ascent to Paradise begins when the pilgrim inexplicably finds himself lost in a dark wood. Odysseus's journey, peopled with mythic players, is acted out upon the wide green seas. And Moses must lead the Children of Israel through the howling desert to the foot of a lonely mountain in order to meet God face to face. These uninhabited landscapes, pervaded with mystery, are the natural setting for the epic events of the narrative. In them, man's arbitrary control over his world is weakened; suddenly, he is rendered powerless, insignificant, conscious of and influenced by cosmic forces incalculably greater than himself.

It is no accident that the backdrop of nearly all Reb Nahman's stories is one of those three basic settings—forests, deserts, and oceans and that the distance of these places from cities and towns is emphasized. This division of space, in effect, is a fundamental principle in Bratslav teaching.

In a classically idiosyncratic reinterpretation of a statement in the Mishnah, Reb Nahman learns that spiritual intimacy with God must be sought, and promises to be found, in just such transitory places. "R. Hanina ben Hakhinai says, He who remains awake at night, and walks alone, and makes room in his heart for that which is futile, incurs guilt expiable by his life."[35] On the most simple level, R. Hanina's statement is clearly a warning, a reinforcement of societal norms and caution against unholy thoughts lurking in abandoned places. Reb Nahman, though, reverses it completely, and sets it as the foundation of the Hasidic concept of *hitbodedut*,[36] the necessary first step in achieving the supreme mystical goal: to be drawn into the unity of God Himself, so reaching the state of *bitul* (negation of selfhood). Only through *hitbodedut*, says Reb Nahman, only when one struggles free from those very conventions set out in the Mishnah, can such an aspiration be realized. The mishnaic text itself, he explains, gives the conditions:

> *Hitbodedut* must be done in a certain place and time, that he not be distracted by forces that would impede him. The time is at night, i.e., when everyone is asleep. And the place is on a solitary path, that wayfarers not interrupt him; it should be a road untraveled by many, and there he must go to be alone *[lehitboded]*. Then he can turn his heart from all other concerns, then all of his being becomes as naught. And when his selfhood is negated completely, he becomes part of God's oneness.[37]

No longer merely partial, subjective, the individual is joined with God and His being is absolute. By passing from the state of possibility to becoming part of divine *necessity* of existence, the individual validates his very life *(mithayev benafsho)*. Reb Nahman's interpretation turns on the root *het-vav-bet,* which implies both guilt and necessity; in rabbinic usage, the phrase may be translated as "deserves death"; figuratively, in allusion to Maimonides' philosophical principle of God's being, it is translated as "makes his soul become absolute."

The contrast between the literal interpretation of R. Hanina ben Hakhinai and Reb Nahman's reinterpretation emphasizes the inherently dual nature of lonely places, represented in the stories by forests, deserts, and the ocean. Myriad forces seem to dwell in them, and the solitary person feels himself infinitely vulnerable, open both to revelation and to alienation or destruction. If his faith is strong, his solitude is inspiring—something evident, for example, in the life of the master of prayer. But if he himself has embraced evil, dark forces, they will overcome him, as in the story *King and Kaiser*, which describes in gory detail the deaths of pirates and luckless suitors on the high seas.

The suggestion of this intrinsic duality brings us to a charged theosophical problem, whose shadow has darkened the paths of mystics and philosophers alike. Is evil an autonomous entity, irreconcilably opposed to good, i.e., to God? Or is the polarity between good and evil but transitory, an illusion? It is important to note that in Hasidic ideology, the ontic existence of good and evil in the kabbalistic conception is transformed; it becomes symbolic of the psychological struggle constantly waged in the human soul. Many accomplished scholars of Jewish thought have presented the intricacies of these arguments;[38] my discussion in the following pages is not meant to summarize or to analyze those positions. Rather, I would like to explore the manifestations in Reb Nahman's stories of doctrines of evil developed in the *Zohar* and in Lurianic mysticism. My comments are necessarily schematic; what interests me are the basic models Reb Nahman adopts and their part in his creation of some supernatural realm. As we shall see, Reb Nahman's references to his sources of inspiration, while often direct and explicit in his theoretical teachings, become more abstract in the narrative works.

I would suggest that, in Reb Nahman's view, our very perception of evil in the world is the stigma of our existential state. In other words, in the most primeval cosmic time before Creation, God's world knew no evil; all was utterly good, harmonious, whole. Yet we can only intimate that unimaginable state through negative comparison. The sages as well as the Kabbalists felt empowered to describe the earthly realm as the obscured world *(ʿalma deʾetkasia),* the world of falsehood *(ʿalma deshikra),* and the world of disunion *(ʿalma depiruda)* because of their sustaining vision of its polar opposite—a world of light, of truth, of unity. I would like to consider two fundamental allegories that recount how that cataclysmic change came to be: how harmony engendered disharmony, unmitigated good gave birth to "evil," and wholeness became brokenness.

One model, of course, is the Lurianic myth of *zimzum* (divine contraction) and *shevirat ha-kelim* (breaking of the vessels). Let us consider a passage from *Likkutei Moharan*, in which a reexamination of this seminal paradigm lays the groundwork for Reb Nahman's own innovative conception. His concern there is the nature of heresy *(apikorsut)* and the psychology of the unbeliever, drawn to the antithesis of faith. Clearly, for Reb Nahman's religious soul, heresy must be based on a tragic mistake, a misperception of the cosmic order. Through retelling the allegory presented in the opening pages of *ʿEz Hayyim*, he dramatizes the fallacious logical process that led the unbeliever astray. Thus:

> When God wanted to create the world, there was no place for it, because all was *Ein sof* [filled with His infinite presence]. Hence He contracted the light to the sides, and by that contraction an empty space [*hallal ha-panui*] was formed. Within the void, time

> and space came into being; the world was created. The empty space was essential in the world's creation, for without it there would have been no place for the world to be. That, then, is the *zimzum* of *hallal ha-panui*; only in the world to come will it be understood.[39]

Here is the core of the irremediable paradox, or *kushiya,* that haunted Reb Nahman from the beginning of his life to the end.[40] Compelled to accept the Lurianic idea of *zimzum*, he confronts the impossible truth that that act created two opposites: *yesh* and *ayin*—Would we be wrong to translate them as "being" and "nothingness"? The dangerously problematic aspect of this opposition is signaled in the expressions of reservation that leap into the next sentences: "as if" *[kiveyekhol],* "but in truth" *[aval be'emet],* "just the same" *[af-al-pi-khen]*. For how can one speak of nothingness when God, by definition, is omnipresent, when according to the ancient dogma, "no place is devoid of Him"?[41] It is there, in the frightening *possibility* of the *hallal panui* that evil lurks: there, in a place that *seems* devoid of God, from which God Himself is said to have intentionally withdrawn His presence—there, in that vacuum, evil becomes manifest. When an unbeliever voices this argument of God's absence, Reb Nahman says, there is no way to answer him. He has fallen into the black hole of *hallal ha-panui*, imprisoned in a Kierkegaardian sort of radical doubt. The very notion of *zimzum* puts the man of faith on a theological tightrope; the abyss yawns wide beneath him, and he rushes to the only conclusion possible: "Israel alone [can be saved], by passing over all sorts of [earthly] wisdom, even that blasphemy that comes from the void. For they believe in God without any sleuthing or cleverness, but only with total faith."[42] Beyond knowledge, beyond inquiry, a kind of postcritical belief is man's sole refuge from that unbearable contingency, the bitter harvest of *hallal ha-panui.*

The second stage of the Lurianic paradigm, that of emanation and its tragic consequences, corresponds in Reb Nahman's conception with a second, and answerable, type of blasphemy. In this case, the unbeliever is at the mercy of a vortex of forces. Evil seems to whirl around the good, and though he yearns to grasp the fruit, his hands touch only the shell, the peel, the skin. Here Reb Nahman's allusion to the original myth is more graphic: "The light was too great and the vessels shattered, and so the *kelippot* came into being. . . ." The husks, shards of the splintered vessels too frail to contain the abundance of divine brightness, scatter throughout the material world. Although the original "bowls" themselves were necessary in the genesis of the world, they represent boundedness, harsh judgment. Their purpose was to differentiate, to contain the endless sea of tender mercy symbolized in the light of *Ein sof.*[43] And although the task was nigh impossible, all the world suffers from their failure. Forces of impurity hold earthly existence in their grip. The *kelippot* envelop the sparks of light; leechlike, they ruthlessly suck vitality from every remaining source of holiness.

As we see in the idea of *tikkun*, the third, redeeming stage in the cosmic process, the situation is far from unmitigated, but rather dynamic and charged with potential. For the moment, however, I would like to remain with this earlier aspect, the metaphor of the broken vessels. Reb Nahman assimilates it freely, and it serves as a vital component in his conception of the realm of the fantastic. Perhaps most remarkable are the many personifications of the *kelippot* in the stories: the demons of *The Cripple* and their notorious parasitism, the mocker of the *Rabbi and Only Son*, the suitors of the kaiser's daughter in *King and Kaiser*.

But it is Reb Nahman's comment in *Likkutei Moharan* later in the same teaching discussed above[44] that bares the entire problem of the *kelippot* and our perception of the world. He evokes God's charge to Moses that generations to come should know "What I have done *[asher hitʿalalti]* to Egypt, and the signs I made there, and you will know that I am the Lord" (Ex. 10:2). These words conceal a subtle dialectic, a double interpretation of the whole situation that summoned the plagues, the defeat of Pharaoh, and the Exodus. Egypt, with its intransigent heart, drove all thought of the divine from its midst. In the spiritual wasteland that remained, Pharaoh and his kingdom made themselves oblivious to God's continual signs of providence, to His mastery over the world. What Egypt experiences as disorder *(hitʿolelut)*, as incomprehensible events, is, in Rashi's words, God's mockery. Their obstinate disbelief made the world, for them, absurd. Throughout the plot of their story (the *ʿalilah*), miraculous signs, manifestations of God's omnipotence, were discernible. Yet they experienced the surreal drama unfolding in Egypt act by act as *a plot*, a sinister act of *hitʿolelut* against them.[45] It is the *kelippot*, Reb Nahman avers, that create this blindness: "The *kelippot* are opposed to holiness: they are like someone who dissimulates and playacts and twists himself before another; they are a mere ape, imitating and pretending to be a human being."[46]

The Egyptians are thus victims of a grotesque kind of distortion. Their natural world is turned on its head: rivers run bloody, darkness invades. Yet it is only *their* internal space that is blighted; for "all the Children of Israel had light in their dwellings" (Ex. 10:23). In the biblical Exodus story, what appears to the Egyptians as macabre and senseless accident is, for Israel, a transparent experience of divine will. This ambiance, in which confrontation between God and His Creation is preceded by dialogue, in which the world's events transparently reflect divine will, marks a unique era of human history. The virtues of the patriarchs, Moses, the kings, and the prophets granted them understanding and the chance to lead the world toward actualization. Yet, again and again, their shortcomings and those of mankind impede that pure desire. In such moments it is the *kelippot* that gain the upper hand and havoc, rather than divine will, seems to have dominion. Reb Nahman concludes this teaching by exhorting his listeners to recognize the presence of God, paradoxically, in the satirical play of the *kelippot*, at the heart of the absurd, fantastic world they conjure: "'For I put my signs in your midst, that you may know I am the Lord' (Ex. 10:1)—even there you must find the signs, draw out the sparks of holiness, and restore them."[47]

The cataclysm of the Breaking of the Vessels *(shevirat ha-kelim)* thus had a profound effect on human ability to interpret and occasion events, to discern the divine manifest in the lower world of deeds *(ʿolam ha-ʿasiyah)*. That crucial drama is, in fact, the frame on which nearly all Reb Nahman's stories are woven. Perhaps the clearest instance is in the tale *The Master of Prayer*. The secret wisdom of the protagonist concerns an idyllic lost kingdom, which harbored within it treasures of strength, beauty, unique knowledge. His description of the king and his loyal court, the queen, and their wondrous son prefaces the account of the disaster that, without warning, befell all of reality: "And the day came, and there was a great storm wind in the world, and that wind disrupted the entire world, turning seas to land and land to seas, turning deserts to towns and towns to desert" (*SM*, p. 196).

The storm wind not only wreaked havoc in the natural world but struck to the innermost heart of the kingdom, stealing away their very hopes for the future—the infant heir and successor to the king: "And the storm wind came into the king's palace . . . and snatched the queen's baby." The people whom the master of prayer strives to enlighten, with their delusions, fanaticism, and iniquity, know only this ruined, upside-down world left in the wake of the storm. Ignorant of any higher order, their internal confusion and unfocused desires drive them from one idol to another—wealth, fame, beauty, power. This moral deformation, clearly, is the effect of the *kelippot* set loose in the world like evil spirits from Pandora's box. The vices that capture each people are not inherently evil, but rather a distortion, an exaggeration *ad absurdum* of positive tendencies. The master of prayer, then, devotes his life to reordering the chaos, striving to find and teach a new reading of the map, to lead each person out of the dusty wind that still stings his eyes.

The second paradigm I would like to discuss originates in the biblical creation story. Elements of this narrative play a vital role in the whole of Reb Nahman's oeuvre as well. One theme in particular returns again and again, with variations, in nearly every story Reb Nahman told. It is the idea of unity and subsequent division, embodied in the image of the Garden of Eden and the fatal fall from grace. Of all the implications of the primal sin, the most profound and tragic in Reb Nahman's eyes is the change it engendered in man on the cognitive level. A passage from the *Zohar* clearly illustrates how fine human perceptions became hopelessly crippled:

> When God created man He instilled in him divine splendor, and told man to cleave to Him, that he be whole [*yahid*], with a single heart, and that he adhere to one sole and unchanging source. . . .

That single, unanimous truth is symbolized in the Tree of Life, which stands majestic at the center of the Garden. The prelapsarian harmony of Adam and Eve's world, of course, soon turns to polyphonic discord:

> They strayed from the path of faith and abandoned the Tree, more sublime than all the others, and cleaved to the place of transformations, with its changes from one color to another, from good to evil and from evil to good.[48]

The moment Adam and Eve violate the primordial oneness of the Tree of Life, their world becomes amorphous, relative, uncertain. All human tools of perception prove to be incapable of grasping the new, slippery inconsistency of reality. The countenance of the world is thus utterly altered after the Fall. And man, because he must face a lifetime of grappling with shifting images, is possessed with longing for that constancy lost forever, for that time when appearance and reality were one. Two angels bar the path back to the Tree of Life (Gen. 3:24). And the flaming Sword of Changes *(herev ha-mithapakhat),* brandished there, nearly obviates its very memory.

In the paradigm of the biblical creation myth, evil personified in the snake has visited the world with the curse of distortion. Just as the *kelippot* whirl in a demon dance around divine sparks of light, so in this model the world is possessed by some unseen force causing endless mutation. The element both paradigms have in common—the Lurianic myth of *zimzum* and *shevirah*, and the Zoharic picture of the Fall—is their concern with the tension between perception and "reality," that discrepancy which, as we have seen, is so central to the genre of the fantastic. Both describe this duality as an existential situation, the outcome of a luckless fall or process of descent and deterioration. And both hold the shining image of some elementary state yet unmarred by distortion or limitation. That realm of changelessness is held as the higher world of Truth, while the realm of human perceptions is a shadowy world of appearances.

Let us recall, in conclusion, the views expressed by critics of literature of the fantastic and the essential difference between Reb Nahman's conception and that of other authors of the genre. As we said, in fantastic tales of Western literature, no model of what existed before the beginning of time still casts its shadow upon the author's own world. Rather, a new myth must be invented, recreated by the author himself. It must be a syncretic blend of myth and fantasy, and be invoked primarily to portray some existential discomfort, often the phenomenological doubt of the modern age.[49] For Reb Nahman, in contrast, the metaphysical realm is a vitally real, fundamentally holy dimension, and is made sacred by the most revered mystical texts of Jewish tradition. All the mutations, the changes, the illusions that may occur in the world are but symptoms of incompleteness. Thus the play between natural and supernatural, between perception and deception, that informs his stories simply takes up and continues the dialectic of the two paradigms presented above. Each of the stories, in its own way, incorporates the metaphysical realm of those paradigms and contrasts it with the broken world, our world, described in them. Finally, each is essentially a saga of how the sparks of holiness may be rescued from among the husks, how the shattered vessels may be restored, how the Sword of Changes may be overcome, and how the Tree of Life may be regained.

Between Past and Future: Nostalgia and Expectation

The involuted journey that takes place in each of Reb Nahman's stories is, in effect, a "return to the future." As we have seen, two principal creation myths, his inheritance from Jewish mystical tradition, are at the very core of his worldview. We recall Lévi-Strauss's contention that myth in general belongs to both Saussurean categories, *langue* and *parole*: as a historical account of the past, myth is diachronic; yet it is synchronic as well, serving as an instrument to interpret the present and future.[50] When we remember the experiential aspect of Hasidic tales, both in narration and message, we realize the tremendous relevance of this contention to Reb Nahman's oeuvre. By telling of that time *in illo tempore* (whether in the form of a perfect garden or blessed kingdom), the path leading from—and back to—that Beginning is rediscovered. Anamnesis is an essential element of psychic wholeness: through recollection of a cosmic, mythic past, the storyteller brings his listeners to an understanding of their own lives and, further, to a vision of the distant horizon toward which he, as they, gaze.[51] We may even say that this narration resembles the psychoanalytic process: it is only through understanding the earliest, primordial moments of being that the way may be revealed leading to the eschatological end.

In addition, and most important in the context of our present discussion, the temporal texture of the narrative is a vital element in the creation of the fantastic dimension. For if perception and measurement of time and its passage is one of our most fundamental gauges of reality, then "time warp" would be a clear signal of the dominion of some different, sur-realistic set of laws replacing the normal order. Here, again, the criteria set out by Todorov are intrinsic: the characters, or the reader, must be *struck* by an unanticipated upset in the continuum of time. Only then does the instance of distortion become enigmatic, only then do accepted, normative structures of the linear progression of past, present, and future come into question. That impression of linearity, we could say, is created by the basic progression of human life: birth, maturity, death (and all that people write novels about crowded in between). We remember the past, live the present, anticipate the future. Yet when these prosaic verbs and tenses are rearranged—when we remember the future, live the past, transform the present—we are reinterpreting, infusing our reality with new and more complex meaning. While a conception of time as linear is the mark of a rationalistic worldview, time as circular belongs to a mythic, or mystical, conception. Implicit in such an understanding is the consciousness that human temporal perception is subjective: the true nature of time is hidden from human experience; intimations of that true nature strike us as contradiction, as paradox.

Gaps, fits, and starts in the temporality of the narrative—this is a phenomenon that informs all of Reb Nahman's tales and bears great ontological significance. Let us consider *The Seven Beggars*, the story in which the ever-present theme of time and relativity is perhaps most apparent. Contemplated explicitly by the first and third beggars, time, in fact, is the scaffolding on which all six internal stories are built and connected to the superstructure, the external story. Each beggar begins by anchoring his story in the vague, unreal past with the words "once upon a time" [*ki paʿam ehad*]. Yet in the events of that "fictional" kingdom, garden, or faraway land, the storyteller himself, indisputably real and alive before his audience, is the hero. Here, then, is the first anomaly: the simultaneous presence of legendary past and the narrator's present. Yet his story, we discover, concerns not only the past; what each beggar recounts is a saga of *shevirah* and *tikkun*, of primal sin, repentance, and ultimate redemption—in short, a drama inspired by one of the mythic paradigms discussed above.

While this drama has its inception in obscure moments of some distant age, it progresses into the present (of the fictional audience and, certainly, of the reader as well) and continues to unfold until its denouement in the unimaginable future. We discussed the kabbalistic symbolism of these events in detail in chapter 2. What concerns us now is the perplexing disparity between this allegorical tale, with its eschatological end (as wholeness, happiness, restored harmony) and the stubbornly present, fragmented reality of all who hear it.

The abrupt shift between the captivating events of the story and the comparatively static time frame of the external story occurs in the final sentence reiterated by each storyteller: "And now . . . I give it to you as a gift." This parting gesture is the third bewildering element in the substructure of *The Seven Beggars*: each presents the children, his silent audience, with the story he has just told as a wedding gift. Or, more precisely, through it he symbolically grants them his own most essential quality. His story itself, though a fiction (or by grace of its fictionality) is the vital tool that empowers them to actualize his wisdom in their own world.

We turn to the blind beggar's tale: What understanding did the storyteller himself gain, through the biographical events he recounts, concerning the ontology of time? And how does Reb Nahman make that knowledge relevant to his own listener?[52]

In the first words of his story, the blind beggar sets the scene: "Once upon a time, people set sail in many ships upon the sea. A storm wind came and wrecked all the boats. The people escaped and made their way to a tower, and they climbed up into it . . ." (*SM,* p. 243). Alert to the allegorical level such an internal story might conceal, we are reminded of the *Zohar*'s reading of Jonah the prophet's story, and its very similar use of motifs: "Jonah went down into a boat: that is man's soul, which descends into this world to be in a human body . . . a person goes through the world like a ship upon the wide seas. But man sins in this world, and thinks he can escape his master. Thus God sends a mighty storm wind—He invokes His stern judgment—and it rocks the ship, reminding man of his sin. . . ."[53] We realize that the beggar's tale is but a thinly-veiled allusion to this classic source. Reb Nahman's playful imagination, though, makes the ancient aggadah come alive. In his story, as if to while away the time, each survivor, each disembodied soul—from hoary elder to innocent babe—is challenged to recall his earliest memory. And while the first honored sage proudly remembers the very moment of his birth, each subsequent competitor delves deeper into the mysterious reaches of his beginnings, from fetal existence back even to before conception.[54] As the memories they evoke pass from the corporeal to the spiritual realm, from the body of the fruit to its metaphysical essence, they grow more and more abstract. Finally, with the words of the youngest, our hero, and his recollection of *lo klum*, "*gor nisht,*" of Nothingness, memory disappears into the inner chambers of esoteric teaching.[55] The paradoxical truth that comes to light from this strange competition is, of course, that "The younger a person seemed, the older he really was. . . . And the oldest among them was the youngest of them all" (*SM,* p. 245). Any former notion of "age" must therefore be abandoned: the criterion, the blind beggar teaches, is not years of earthly life but rather conscious memory. For days and weary years dull the mind, and all the moments from birth to death are only gradual forgetting. Thus the infant is immeasurably older than the grayest grandfather; so new, he still bears the impression of infinity, the cosmic time that envelops his own existence. What he actually describes is the process of divine emanation itself, mirrored in the creation of a human being. In R. Nathan's words, the parable speaks of "the descent *[hamshakhah]* of man's soul from the initial emanation to the final point, the beginning of *zimzum* . . . until it starts to *materialize* in vessels, just as [God created] light, water, land . . . until [the infant] emerges from his mother's womb into the physical world." The whole process in which an individual comes to be, then, reflects in a microcosm the Lurianic vision of cosmic genesis.

The reversal of all preconceptions concerning youth, age, and memory is clearly recounted to create a sense of wonder—both for Reb Nahman's audience and in the narrative. Hence the ironic procession in reverse chronological order out of the tower: the oldest, i.e., the babe, leads and last to hobble out is the infant bearded sage. Yet the blind beggar's story not only presents this theme of temporal consciousness and the bounds of human life; in the scene that follows, it illuminates the nature of time itself. The astonishment that grips all the competitors with the infant's evocation of Nothingness is interpreted by a new character, who breaks in on the seance of souls to dissolve the allegory. He sends the people back to continue their seafaring journey and, left alone with the winner, the narrator, his true identity comes to light.

Although Reb Nahman designates him only as "the great eagle," for the circumspect student he is not a winged creature as in just any tale. His deceptively simple name, and the blatant contradiction of his life's years, leads us to seek his ancestors among other figures in Jewish sources. We discover that the *nesher*, in midrash and medieval commentary, is attributed extraordinary powers. Based on a verse in Isaiah (40:31), "They who hope in the Lord shall renew their strength; they shall mount up with wings as eagles; they shall run and not be weary; they shall walk and not faint," the eagle is a symbol of endless vitality.

R. David Kimhi, in the name of R. Sa'adia Gaon, comments on "they shall mount up with wings": "they shall return to their younger days."[56] This suggestion, not only of innate strength but of past force continually regained, echoes the metaphor of Ps. 103:5, "[He] satisfies your old age with good, so that your youth is renewed like the eagle's." But this extraordinary gesture of divine kindness, it turns out, is no mere metaphor. Our aquiline figure is, in fact, an alter ego of the phoenix, the wondrous bird of Greek mythology. In aggadah, the phoenix is given a Jewish name *'of ha-hol* or *milham* (sandbird) after the verse in Job (29:18), "Then I said, I shall die in my nest, and I shall multiply my days like the sand." His destiny is entwined with the biblical story of the Garden of Eden: the midrash tells that Eve gave the forbidden fruit of the Tree of Knowledge not only to Adam but to the birds and the beasts as well. One faithful bird, *'of ha-hol*, refused to eat it; in reward for his obedience to God's injunction, he was granted immortality.

Thus, in the words of the midrash, "He lives a thousand years. And then his body perishes, his feathers fall away and only a bit of him remains [lit., "he is left as an egg"]; then his wings begin to grow again." In another midrashic source, the element of fire is added (or preserved): "And after a thousand years flames burst from his nest and consume him. Then once again he grows wings, and lives."[57] Rising from the ashes of the past, robed in glory, the phoenix is a potent symbol of hope after destruction, both in Western literature and in Jewish tradition. This, then, is the immortality of the "eagle" or *nesher*, typographically linked to the same legendary bird: in the cyclical continuity of his life, he is both subject to time and timeless.

This merging of myths—from the ancient Near East, Hellenistic culture, and rabbinic literature, to Reb Nahman—is interesting in and of itself. Yet how did the great eagle, the blind beggar's mentor, gain the wisdom enabling him to interpret the competition of memories that took place in the tower? Undeniably, his personality is complex: he has observed the ways of the world, and yet that experience has not aged him in spirit.

The counterpoint between youth and age that reverberates throughout the story seems to lead us to another biblical verse, which provides the key to the great eagle's full identity. It is Ps. 37:25. "I have been young, and now am old; yet I have not seen a just man forsaken, and his seed begging bread." That omniscient speaker, who testifies with such self-assurance to God's providence in the world, has been an object of tremendous interest in rabbinic literature. In talmudic sources he is identified as *sar ha-ʿolam*, and in the *Zohar* he is, indisputably, described as Metatron.[58] When we recall that Metatron is the angel charged with the resurrection of souls, our search comes full circle. In a characteristic gesture, Reb Nahman takes hold of an abstract, far-from-human figure in mystical tradition, draws him down into his own tale, and softens him with an aura of intimacy. The great eagle, who so kindly confers his knowledge to the blind beggar and, by extension, to the children themselves is truly not of this world. Concealed in his beneficence is the authority of the angel: when he orders all those in the tower to return to their bodies, he is directing them to repent *(lashuv)*, symbolically to be born again—to return to this world, or to transmigrate after the tempest that shipwrecked them, i.e., after their ruinous sins.[59]

The blind beggar, then, wishes to teach something about the structure of reality itself. The Kabbalists call this ontological truth *razo veshov* (running and returning); anthropologists, "the myth of the eternal return" (Eliade); philosophers, "the eternal recurrence" (Nietzsche)—yet at the core of all these concepts is a single conviction:

> What we call the beginning is often the end
> And to make an end is to make a beginning
> The end is where we start from.[60]

The blind beggar inhabits a realm beyond time; like the great eagle, like the angel who soars high above the earth, he is free of the subjectivity inherent in human temporal awareness.[61] His very presence in *The Seven Beggars* creates a sensation of the uncanny on at least three levels: within the framework story, the children, lost in the woods, look into his blind eyes with amazement—"It was a marvel for them: he was blind, then how did he know his way?" (*SM*, p. 239);[62] in his internal narrative, his supernatural memory arouses wonder among the other souls (*SM*, p. 245); and for the reader/listener, whose locus is outside the fiction altogether, his confluent literary ancestry is awe-inspiring. His essence is truly uncanny in the Freudian sense: the figure of the blind beggar is both familiar and wholly bewildering, incongruous in the new context of the tale. As a messenger from another, unworldly place, more divine than human, the tale he tells is fantastic in its wide embrace of both realms.

A Definition of the Fantastic as a Literary Genre

In concluding our preliminary exploration of the fantastic as a literary genre, I would like to highlight some of the concepts that have been and will be vital to our discussion throughout this chapter. Earlier, we compared examples from world literature to the corpus of Reb Nahman's stories in the attempt to sustain our view of his narrative works as literature of the fantastic. The very vocabulary used to speak of the genre, however, is confusing, even misleading. Fundamental words are invoked with no consistency between one critic and another, and without a definition of terms, our entire discussion risks becoming but dubious acrobatics. Let us begin, then, with "fantasy" and its relative, "the fantastic." Consultation with the *Oxford English Dictionary* and Alex Preminger's *Encyclopaedia of Poetry and Poetics* reveals the ambivalence inherent in fantasy/phantasy even from its inception. In early Greek, *phantastikos* connotes "representing, or making visible"; in late Greek, the meaning becomes "to imagine, or have visions." Here, then, the crucial question already rears its head: Does fantasy fetch its images from what is *real*, objective, and present—merely re-presenting them in other form—or are those images drawn from some other realm of mental concepts (called "imagination") devoid of correspondence to the reality of things? Continuing down the etymological path, we find that the Greek term was first transliterated and later replaced in Latin with the word *imaginatio*. The plot thickens. After the philosophical definition of 'imagination' paraphrased above, the OED offers a second meaning: imagination is "the creative faculty of mind in its highest aspect; the power of framing new and striking intellectual conceptions." But is imagination a process superior or inferior to fantasy? We remark that creativity is the human faculty *imitatio Dei* par excellence: to create is to "bring into being, to cause to exist, form out of nothing." Imagination, it would seem, bears witness to "poetic genius," to acute creative fancy, while fantasy speaks of "illusory appearance" (definition 5), of fabulous, eccentric, even grotesque devising (definition 6).

But such a distinction is naive. First of all, with the renewed interest in Greek culture during the Renaissance, the original Greek spelling crept back into the English language. "Fantasy" and "phantasy" came to be apprehended as separate words: the former most frequently denoted "caprice, whim, fanciful invention," while the latter designated "imagination, visionary notions." And to complicate matters further, the hierarchy of (inferior) *fantasy* and (superior) *imagination* present in English is reversed in medieval Latin, Italian and German, according to Preminger. In these languages, *imaginatio, immaginazione, Einbildungskraft* connote a repository of mental images or conceptions, while fantasy (in its Greek root form) describes the higher artistic power that operates upon and *synthesizes* those conceptions.[63] Finally, we must not forget the sinister innuendos that cling to "fantasy" (back to the *OED*)—in a psychological sense, such ideas whisper of "alleged reasons, fears previously or irrationally imagined" (definition 3). The suggestion is of illness, or demonic possession (definition 2).

Admittedly, this morass does little to inspire a drive for consistency. The countless mutations undergone by "fantasy," "phantasy," and "imagination" perhaps render hopeless any attempt to discern some exclusive meaning for each, or to invoke them in loyalty to sharp distinctions. If asked to analyze my own intuitive understanding of these terms, I would say it tends to reflect the European hierarchy, and ignores the archaic form "phantasy." In sum, regarding Reb Nahman, I would suggest that the specific figures, images, and details of plot are the fruit of imagination, i.e., the conjurings of a unique, creative mind. In and of themselves, they do not build a novel world; each belongs to thoroughly human experience. Imagination empowers Reb Nahman to transform concepts from Jewish literary tradition and invent new ones; by expanding into the dimension of fantasy, he combines these basic elements to create a wholly other world and, through it, to speak, at once, of the most human and most esoteric reality.

In conclusion, an observation by one modern critic concerning fantasy as a literary genre illuminates this relationship between means and end in the construction of the story. Diana Waggoner writes that fantasy "is not primarily about the material it uses—the symbols and dreamstuff, myths and images, which are the flesh and blood on its skeleton of rationality. Fantasy deals with mythopoetic archetypes of great antiquity and power—enchanters, princesses, quests, dark towers, hidden cities, haunted forests, walled gardens. . . ." This use, of course, is not confined to fantasy (it also occurs in fairy tales, folktales, etc.), but the decisive factor is how the material is treated. "Fantasy places mythopoetic material in a fictional framework, within which it is treated as empirical data, the common stuff of ordinary reality."[64] As we saw earlier in this chapter, Reb Nahman's stories integrate archetypes from two realms—those primitive, universal elements common to all folktales, and the classic motifs of Jewish biblical, aggadic, and mystical sources. This confident evocation of "ordinary reality" brings us back to the sensitive issue of artistic representation and interpretation of reality that so fascinates modern thinkers. We recall Northrop Frye's contentions (among many others) of the intractable subjectivity, even falsehood, in all attempts to speak of the "real" world. Oscar Wilde, in his essay "The Decay of Lying," protests that what everyone calls realism is not founded on nature and reality at all. We never see these things directly, he claims, "but only through a prism of conventionalized commonplaces, outworn formulas within the art itself, the fossilized forms of earlier attempts to escape from nature and reality." The only true creativity in the human sense of the word, he concludes, is "a distorted imagination that breaks away from all this and sees reality as a strange, wonderful, terrible, fantastic world. . . ."[65] Paradoxically, then, "realism" becomes alienating, turning against those who use it to bring reality closer; distortion is direct vision, and the iconoclastic, fearless romantic the true artist. In the next section we will examine the ways this paradox is embodied in Reb Nahman's thought and finds expression in his tales.

2. PERCEPTION AND DECEPTION: TRANSMUTATIONS OF REALITY WITHIN THE TALE

The Talmud describes a telling experience, in which R. Joseph became ill and fell into a trance. When he recovered, his father, R. Joshua ben Levi, asked him, "What did you see?" He answered, "I saw an upside-down world; the high were brought low, and the low raised up." And his father affirmed, "My son, the world you saw was clear."[66] The implication, of course, is that the world R. Joseph envisioned in his delirium is the ultimate and just one, while the social order father and son share in their conscious reality is a misleading reversal of that true human order to be actualized in the world to come. In part 1 we spoke of thresholds, loci of mystery such as forests, graveyards, and night that mark places of meeting between the real and some "metareal" or more absolute realm of being. Now I would like to consider another category of such thresholds: these are located not in a natural, external setting but within man's own psychic life. R. Joseph's story points to the febrile vision granted by illness; in his faint, R. Joseph was "spirited away," that is, his mind was somehow disconnected from his body, left behind on the sickbed, and rose unhindered to a higher world. Even more common than such visionary swoons, though, is a second, altered state of consciousness, most universally recognized as a window onto other worlds—that of dreaming. Understanding the dream paradigm is indeed vital in our appreciation of Reb Nahman's stories, for the tension he creates there between illusion and reality mirrors the duality inherent in the dream experience itself. Our discussion begins with the nature of dreams, both on the cognitive level and in Hebrew literary sources. We will then expose two characteristic elements of dreams—the blurring of boundaries between symbol and symbolized, and transformations of human identity—as fundamental components in the creation of the fantastic dimension. Finally, the implications emerging from this dialectic of perception and deception, which informs Bratslav teaching as a whole, and the suggestion of some supreme truth beyond appearances will be explored.

The Dream Paradigm

The lives of the patriarchs, of kings, wise men, and the commonest of servants are guided, even changed utterly, by the dreams that visit them in the night. No heir to Jewish tradition can ignore the many and colorful appearances of the dream motif that sparkle, jewel-like, throughout the sources. It is a motif uniquely suited to Reb Nahman's vivid imaginative affinities, and his tales are thus studded with allusions to dreams and their interpretations presented in the classic texts. In the biblical narrative and prophetic books, dreams are incorporated as a real component of human life. Abraham, still childless, begs God for some assurance of the future; he performs the strange threefold sacrifice he is commanded

(Gen. 15:10) and, as the sun sets, he falls into a deep sleep. While he is pressed beneath that "horror of darkness," God speaks to him and recounts the years of suffering and salvation awaiting his seed. The midrash interprets the immobility that overtakes Abraham as the state of exile itself—the words of the verse are a premonition of the four periods of oppression in Jewish history by the empires of Babylon, Persia, Greece, and Rome. "And when the sun was going down, a *deep sleep* fell upon Abram; and lo, a *horror* of great *darkness fell* upon him" (Gen. 15:12).[67] Jacob, beset with worry like his grandfather about a future that seems precarious and foreboding, is also suddenly overcome with sleep[68] and plunged into a prophetic vision. "And he dreamed, and behold a ladder set up on the earth, and the top of it reached to heaven: and behold the angels of God ascending and descending on it" (Gen. 28:12). In this instance, the ladder may be understood as a metaphorical image of the dream itself; the dreamer lays upon the ground, yet angels rise to upper realms as his human soul does, transported in his dreams. In the lives of Abraham and Jacob, the dream is a portentous event that shapes their destiny; the divine message it contains is indisputable, and no man resists or questions its meaning. In the story of Joseph—the notorious dreamer—however, dreams and their interpretation become a matter of contention: the subservient sheaves and the sun, moon, and stars that bow down before him are harbingers of Joseph's illustrious future, yet his dreams strike jealousy in the hearts of his brothers and bring all of them to sorrow. From the dungeon of his exile in Egypt, Joseph slowly gains renown for his insight and inspiration; he untangles the dreams of the butler and baker and finally of Pharaoh himself. The intricacies of the solution of these dreams become a model for the rabbis. The sages of the Talmud and the *Zohar* base their own judgments concerning the value of dreams on these biblical accounts; they were influenced, conversely, by the beliefs and superstitions of their own cultural milieu as well. Some, such as Rav Hisda, hold dreams to be a potential wealth of information sent to the sleeper, as if from a distant, autonomous realm: "An uninterpreted dream is like an unread letter."[69] The providence of such a communication may be ambivalent: Samuel suggests good dreams come from angels but bad dreams from demons.[70] Yet another, more rationalistic tendency is prominent as well. In the debate whether meaning is borne by the dream itself or whether dream images are fluid and undetermined, and their significance infused only when the dream becomes external, reflected in the mind of an interpreter, R. Eleazar declares: "All dreams follow the mouth."[71] R. Jonathan's stance goes even further; it is psychological and antivisionary in the extreme: "A man dreams only about his own thoughts and preoccupations."[72]

But it is the compromising view expressed by Rabba bar bar Hannah that addresses our own problem most directly; he evokes the image of the biblical prophet-dreamer Jeremiah, and thus binds together those two phenomena, dream and prophecy, as turning on a single axis. Both can be conceived solely in figurative language, and both are consequently open to interpretation. "The prophet who has a dream, let him tell a dream; and he that has my word, let him speak my word faithfully. What is the chaff to the wheat, says the Lord" (Jer. 23:28). The sages understand the metaphor of chaff and wheat as a comment on the verbal formulation of the prophet's vision. In the words of R. Yohanan, citing R. Simeon bar Yohai, just as there is no wheat without chaff, so there is no dream without superfluous elements.[73]

Rabba bar bar Hannah's statement is much more than a condonation, a posteriori, of figurative language as a legitimate medium in communicating the divine word. What God says to the prophet in sleep, through dreams, cannot be transmitted in a conscious, wakeful state. The prophet is a fragile vessel; only when cloaked in sleep can he contain the influx of divine light. Thus, the words the visionary utters when he awakens are *inherently* metaphorical; God's ineffable truth must be phrased in human concepts—the pure kernel can grow but encased in the husk. In his famous discussion of biblical metaphor, in response specifically to the theological problem posed by anthropomorphism, Maimonides expands the talmudic notion of hyperbole and figurative language. In his view, symbolic expression is an unassailable component of the Torah, manifest most trenchantly in the prophetic books, dreams, and prophetic visions. There, he asserts, such media are a uniquely literary device. They are the antithesis of realism; indeed, their hyperbolic images are invoked purposefully to instill wonder and capture listeners in rapt attention.[74]

In mystical thought, the dream is made a vivid image of nighttime ascent and spiritual enlightenment; in contrast to the reductionist explanation offered by R. Jonathan, the *Zohar* describes the dream as a fundamental mystical experience. "Every night, the souls of zaddikim rise to the Garden of Eden," and at midnight God comes there to delight with them.[75] The souls of both the living and the dead are gathered there in paradise, and by grace of their ardor day by day in Torah study, they are granted vision of divine secrets. When the night ends, and the living return below, the words they utter in wakefulness unconsciously express that wisdom revealed to them in the night.[76] The kabbalistic view models the nightly experience of the righteous man after the biblical accounts of the patriarchs. The dreamer's merits as a devoted Jew and scholar win him understanding of God's ways and even knowledge of His plans to be realized on earth.

As we will see presently, this image in the *Zohar* of secret knowledge revealed to zaddikim during dream visits to the world to come reappears in a fascinating conception in *Likkutei Moharan*.[77] There, Reb Nahman portrays the zaddik of the generation and the infinite potential understanding that surrounds him like an aura. The entire teaching speaks of the bounds of the human mind; the term for not yet realized conceptions (adopted from Lurianic teaching) is *mekifim*—which Reb Nahman describes as "the delight of the world to come." The key word linking the two images is *sha'ashu'a*—God's amusement, His pleasure, as it were, in imparting divine wisdom to those faithful to Him. I would suggest it is this *mishak*, this sense of a game without end ("and I was daily his delight"—Prov. 8:30), played by the blessed all their life (in their continual study, assimilation, and transmission of Torah), that gives birth to the dimension of the fantastic in Reb Nahman's tales as a whole. But we will consider this idea of playfulness later in our discussion. Let us return, for now, to our overview of the dream phenomenon in its varied manifestations in Jewish tradition.

Naturally, our comments have direct bearing on Reb Nahman's integration of the dream paradigm in his worldview and the expression of that conception in his narrative works. It seems that in all the sources, interest in dreams is bound to the question of epistemology. We can distinguish three basic positions concerning this question; in the first and the second, dreams are indeed relevatory of something, while in the third they point to the problem of phenomenology itself. Thus, in one view, dreams are prophetic, transferring some aspect of divine knowledge to the dreamer, who carries his newly received understanding into his waking life. In the second view, dreams grant insight, but only in the Freudian sense, as a window onto the individual's unconscious world.[78] And in the third, dreams are an emblem of human cognition in general, a metaphor of relativity, of the illusory existence in which man is imprisoned.[79] The implicit contrast here is thus between the imaginings of a dream and the absolute reality of the divine realm. In the Kabbalah, though, this third view never reaches the radical negation of man's cognitive powers.

The positive valence dreams have in the *Zohar* is balanced by an opposing, negative valence.[80] While dreams transport the righteous to a higher world of playful union in the Garden of Eden with God, less innocent people may be spirited away on sinister, even demonic, nighttime voyages. The author of the *Zohar* teaches that though all souls seek to leave their sleeping bodies and rise to heavenly worlds, the night is fraught with obstacles. Forces of impurity and evil roam through the world; many souls are captured by them, seduced away from the paths of truth. Thus, while the dreams of the righteous contain jewels of secret wisdom, the dreams of evildoers are bitter as dust; they come not from God but from the Other Side.[81]

In sum, whether dreams are held to be real experiences of disembodied souls or inspired by God, whether they are prophetic, demonic, or merely irrational, whether their meaning speaks of some transcendent realm or of the dreamer's own psyche—all these views share the conviction that dreams indeed contain some message. Inherent to the account of a dream is some sense of enigma, for the dream experience itself intimates the dual nature of human consciousness. Erich Fromm opposes the preconceptions that would make this duality hierarchic: he contends that the relationship is, rather, relative: consciousness and unconsciousness are states of mind referring, respectively, to two different states of existence.[82] The dream may point inward or upward, it may be sinister or felicitous, but in every case a dream narrative exerts tremendous fascinating power: it is recognized as symbolic, yet the object of which it speaks, the symbolized, remains both invisible and at the same time manifestly present. It is thus the symbolic language of dreams and the desire, aroused by such language, to interpret that makes them an ideal model for Reb Nahman's fantastic tales. In the following pages, I would like to examine the phenomenology of dream logic and symbolism outlined both in Jewish sources and in modern psychological methods, and consider Reb Nahman's conception in the light of those theories. In addition to the tales themselves, my comments are based on two other sources: accounts of Reb Nahman's own nocturnal dreams recorded in *Hayyei Moharan* and his teachings collected in *Likkutei Moharan.* I hope to show that the stories he told truly are "dreams that wander in the daylight";[83] helplessly they cross the barrier into our rational world, yet remain wrapped in the shadowy mystery of the night.

The Tale Entitled The King's Evil Decree

This tale is perhaps the best example illustrating the ubiquity of the dream paradigm in Reb Nahman's fiction. Let us begin our discussion with the question of symbolic language and the incumbent phenomenon of literary allusion. We recall that Maimonides links the fruits of the prophetic imagination with the dream state; the images the prophet evokes are his conscious formulation of knowledge infused in him during a visionary trance. These images—such as Zechariah's golden candelabra, colored horses, and mountains of brass (Zech. 4:2, 6:1–7), Ezekiel's scroll (Ezek. 2:9), Amos's wall (Amos 7:7) in Maimonides' eyes can be understood only as metaphors, representative of some abstract idea beyond their literal meaning.[84] The figure of the inspired prophet is replaced in Reb Nahman's story by an anonymous narrator, yet the unfolding of the plot similarly quickens by a series of undisputed symbols whose meaning is left hermetically sealed, not even hinted at in the following pages. The story tells of a merciless king and the oppression of his Jewish subjects. Plagued by the knowledge (revealed through occult magic) that he will be ruined by mysterious forces, symbolized by a bull and a ram, the king's lust for power nonetheless drives him from conquest to conquest. He seems to be invincible; and here Reb Nahman inserts a cryptic chain of associations, ostensibly to reveal the source of the despot's dominion: "For all the world is divided into seven parts. And there are seven planets, each planet shining on one part of the world, and on one of seven kinds of metal" (*SM,* p. 49). The king orders these seven metals to be gathered, along with the golden icons of all the world's kings. And from these materials he fashions a metal idol and places it on a high mountain (*SM,* p. 50). Although these lines may appear completely incomprehensible to an unlearned audience, the triple repetition of the magic numeral 7, in and of itself, evokes an atmosphere of mystery; the elemental potency suggested by primal metals and astrological energy adds mythic dimensions to the king's realm. For a more erudite listener, aware of the kabbalistic meaning underlying Reb Nahman's thought, the evocative power of these images becomes unspeakably more intense. The seven planets, identified explicitly in the midrash *Pirkei de Rabbi Eliezer*, parallel the seven days of Creation, the seven days of the week, and further, are linked to the twelve signs of the zodiac.[85] The seven metals are mentioned in Lurianic teaching and identified with the seven lower *sefirot* manifest in material existence and the metaphorical "vessels" used by God in the world's creation. "For there are seven kinds of metal: silver and gold are *Hesed* and *Gevurah*; copper is *Tiferet*; tin is *Nezah*; lead is *Hod*; mercury *Yesod;* and iron is *Malkut.*"[86]

Yet Reb Nahman not only implants these two sets of symbols, heavy with their esoteric burden, in the text of his story; they are integrated in a larger context. That framework is composed of elements borrowed from three separate biblical prophecies, welded together and altered, yet unmistakable. From these and other elements, the story comes to life. On the moral level, Reb Nahman's tale is most basically about the triumph of simple religious faith and the downfall of an evil king, ruined by his animosity to the Jewish people.

This course of events is the very promise and reassurance described in Psalm 2 and cited by R. Nathan as one of Reb Nahman's primary sources. The second of these sources is an eschatological presaging voiced by Zephaniah (3:8–9). The third is the dream of King Nebuchadnezzar, unlocked by the prophet Daniel (Daniel 2). The story Reb Nahman tells employs these biblical texts in two basic ways: they are dramatized, and, moreover, are somehow actualized. In that way, the events foretold in the Bible are verified in a pseudohistorical sense. Thus, he adopts the characters and props of these three texts—the foreign kings, their scorn, their dreams, the anointed king on his high mountain, the iron rod, the destroying flames, and the incongruous *tallit* (prayer shawl) and *tefillin* (phylacteries)—and rearranges them in a strange, new permutation. At first reading, the tale may well seem disconnected, illogical, a collection of bare and incongruent statements. But the cumulative presence of these disparate elements effectively creates a dreamlike atmosphere of free association.

By considering Reb Nahman's sources, we may be able to trace that process of free association: the key is in the king's dream and its interpretation by the anonymous "wise man." The dream itself, the king's psychological reaction, his subsequent acts, and the mystery of its symbols, disclosed in the tale's final words, are largely borrowed from preexisting sources in which dreams are central. The clandestine Jew, fallen out of favor with the latest, capricious king, becomes victim of the latter's megalomania and is forced to conceal his true identity. The vicissitudes of fortune endured by this Marrano, who has nonetheless reached a position of status in the king's court, reminds us, of course, of Joseph's story. In demoting the loyal Jew, the king commits a fatal error; the injustice of the situation is made intolerable, and then one night the king has a dream. Gazing into the clear, starry sky, he sees two constellations, Taurus and Aries, laughing at him. Unaware of the astrologers' prediction, made a generation earlier, concerning his fate, the dream inexplicably terrifies him. He awakens and summons his servants to bring the annals of the kingdom *(sefer ha-zikhronot)* in the hope that digging into the past might reveal the workings of his collective unconscious. This inquest into the "book of memories" to penetrate the significance of waking events echoes the decision of yet another monarch. King Ahashverosh, resolved to hang Mordechai, the Jewish hero, on the morrow, tosses and turns, unable to sleep, and finally calls for the annals of his kingdom as well. This recourse to a written, preexisting text in the attempt to understand the present and alter one's actions accordingly links this biblical story (Esther 6:1) to Reb Nahman's tale of a nameless despot. Returning to the framework of the Joseph story (Gen. 41ff.), the king learns of the forgotten prophecy (that his seed is destined to be wiped out). Reb Nahman describes his anxiety with the phrase used in the tale of Pharaoh (Gen. 41:8) and of Nebuchadnezzar (Dan. 2:2)—"and his spirit was troubled." His pounding heart compels the ruler to consult his magicians. The test of interpretation then begins. The analyst able to unlock the ruler's secret thoughts, hidden even from himself, will win personal honor and recognition for the religious tradition on which he draws. In all three stories, the wisdom of the Jewish hero is set against the solipsism of the king's men. Nebuchadnezzar accuses his perplexed conjurers of stalling. Pharaoh is unconvinced by the solution they offer; as the midrash says (*Genesis Rabbah* 88.5), "their voice did not enter his ears." Reb Nahman transplants that phrase untouched into his tale (*SM*, p. 51). The stage is thus set for the protagonist's entrance as true interpreter. His minimal title—"a wise man"—actually points to both figures in our biblical parallel texts: Joseph is praised as discrete and wise (Gen. 41:39), and Daniel's wisdom *(hokhmah)* is remarked over and over (1:17, 2:20, 2:21, 2:23, 2:30, etc.), particularly in the chapter on his interpretation of Nebuchadnezzar's dream. All three insist with humility that their knowledge is not their own (Gen. 41:10; Dan. 29:31; *SM*, p. 52). Components of Nebuchadnezzar's dream itself are strewn throughout Reb Nahman's tale. Let us consider two allusions that are most substantially present.

The mighty and terrible figure the king beheld in his night vision is reconjured, telegraphically, in Reb Nahman's tale. "This image's head was of fine gold, its breast and its arms of silver, its belly and its thighs of brass, its legs of iron, its feet partly of iron and partly of clay" (Dan. 2:31–33). The statue built by Reb Nahman's evil king, likewise composed of gold, silver, and other metals, becomes an object of idolatrous worship and a symbol of the ruler's tyranny. Nebuchadnezzar actually constructs the image of his dream, and the golden god becomes a nexus of religious coercion. By the king's decree, all who do not bow down to it will be cast into a fiery furnace. Daniel and his compatriots proclaim their faith in God alone, and the king's mighty men throw them to their death by burning. Yet—in this text and Reb Nahman's story—the righteous miraculously pass unscathed through the flames: "Lo, I see four men unbound, walking in the midst of the fire, and they have no hurt" (Dan. 3:25); "And he saw that kings and Jews were walking through the fire wrapped in *tallit* and *tefillin*" (*SM*, p.52). The wicked are annihilated by them: "the flame of the fire slew those men . . ." (Dan. 3:22), "and the flames overcame them, and [the king] and his seed were wiped out utterly" (*SM*, p. 53). Reb Nahman links these two elements from the book of Daniel with brilliant legerdemain: the infernal test of faith in God becomes, in Reb Nahman's story, the interpretation, *acted out* by the dreamer himself—singed in his flesh—of his portentous dream. Ignoring the wise man's warnings, he walks, entranced, into the flames. It is the king's insistence he is invincible, his inability to recognize the significance of the dream message in his waking life, that leads him to destruction.

The constellations of Taurus and Aries laugh mockingly from the heavens. These two animals are, naturally, a code, repeated in the *tallit* and *tefillin*; they symbolically shield those who pass through the fire. It is only in the last words of the story that the astrologers' prediction is finally resolved: "For *tefillin* are made from the hide of the bull, and from the wool of the ram, *zizit* and *tallit* are woven" (*SM*, p. 53).[87] The hellish journey through the landscape of pits and traps, mire and flames, ends and the wise man returns alone. It is as if he has emerged from a nightmare back into the waking world. The wise man meets the astonishment of the king's subjects with a simple observation: both the king and his magicians had made the fatal error of literalness. In their blindness, they had failed to recognize the bull and ram as symbols pointing beyond the beasts themselves.

It seems to me that one of the distinctive qualities of Reb Nahman's stories is the dreamlike, unreal atmosphere that pervades them. Two causes that engender this quality demand our attention. First, the incorporation of dreams and prophetic visions from biblical sources reproduces, through association, the sense of wonder and terror inherent in those encounters with the divine. And second, the use of a prooftext, mentioned explicitly by Reb Nahman's commentators, links the elements of the narrative together according to the peculiar logic of allegory. It is peculiar because the sole claim to any rational order the narrative can make is in its loyalty to the source text. Let us illustrate with the tale under discussion. The immutable truths narrated in Psalm 2 contain, schematically, the following elements: the kings of the earth take council together against God and His anointed; yet God laughs at their vanity, and soon His anger will burn against them; God promises to set His own king in Zion and have His people inherit the earth; His sole demand—awe, purity, and trust in His dominion. The parallel with Reb Nahman's tale is clear. We have pointed out the presence of all but one of these motifs, and that is the provocative scene of God's derision (v. 4). I would suggest that in Reb Nahman's story, God's scorn or ridicule *(la'ag)* of the malevolent kings is planted in the figures of the derisive bull and ram—initially in the astrologers' prediction and repeated in the king's dream. Thus "He who sits in heaven laughs"; God sends enigmatic dreams to evil people, voiceless threats that shake them to the root of their being. The midrash binds together the experience of the two potential destroyers of Israel, Pharaoh and Nebuchadnezzar, to that of the king in Reb Nahman's tale. Why, the midrash asks, does

God speak to the wicked in night visions? The response is a two-edged sword: "In order to make a mockery of them."[88] While the dreams of zaddikim, the midrash explains, guide them in their path, the wicked live in a world of darkness, blind to divine providence, believing their will is stronger than God's. Interestingly, the prooftext the midrash cites suggests that the dreams of the wicked actually serve to nullify them existentially: "As a dream when one awakens, so, O Lord, on awakening You shall despise their image" (Ps. 73:20). Just as a dream image fades in the light of dawn, so the wicked themselves will become as substanceless, powerless in the reign of divine justice. The verse suggests, in addition, that the dreams of the wicked confuse them profoundly: on one hand, the king does awaken from his dream, leave it and return to reality. Yet, on the other hand, he is plagued with the fear that the dream will come true—that its events will leave the night and invade his waking life. This uncertainty, the unbearable convergence of dream and conscious reality, is the brand of God's derision. And in fact, the king's life ends in a macabre scene, irrational and closer to a nightmare than to realism.

The Dream of the Circle in Hayyei Moharan

But what are the elements in dreams and prophetic visions that actually create their uniquely unreal, oneiric atmosphere? What subtle mechanics does Reb Nahman incorporate in his tales to reproduce the emotional effects engendered in the psyche of the dreamer? The accounts of Reb Nahman's own dreams related in his biography, *Hayyei Moharan*, offer a glimpse of the creative process by which the stories were conceived. My intent in this context is not to probe the personal, autobiographic meaning of those dream fragments themselves, but rather to compare their form and content to his overtly narrative works.[89] Perhaps the most salient characteristic common to the dreams in *Hayyei Moharan* and the tales is the disconnectedness of the plot. Events succeed each other, linked by association rather than logic; figures appear, cloaked in allusions, and suddenly vanish, leaving in their wake only a shimmering hint of their true identity. Consider, for example, Reb Nahman's summer night's dream of 1804 (5564): in brief, the dreamer sees a crowd surrounding, in concentric circles, a mutely speaking figure. He looks again, and the man is gone; the people begin to run, he follows them. They reach two palaces, confront two strong men, are sent to a candle suspended in midair. The people "throw their good deeds" into the candle; these turn to sparks and fall down into their mouths. The candle becomes a river from which they all drink. And then creatures, neither human nor animal, begin to grow inside them, emerging through their mouths as they speak. The people wish to return from whence they came, but their path is blocked by a monstrous figure whose many-edged sword touches the sky. They plead for a merciful death, and all at once find themselves back at the opening scene, in circles around a central figure.[90] The drama seems cyclical but the subtle moral development of the people gradually becomes apparent to the dreamer, at which point he leaves them. Remarkable in this dream account is its detached, wondering tone—the dreamer is like a passive observer, drawn from scene to scene after the other characters, exerting no willful control over his movements. The sole transition between events is the phrase "and I saw," echoing the visions described by the biblical prophets.[91]

The dream is composed on two levels: a drama, related by a figure who is personally unembroiled in the events themselves, and his subsequent attempt to understand that drama. The dream's enigmatic nature troubles the narrator within the framework of the dream itself. In search of an explanation for what he has witnessed, he comes upon a solitary old man, who grasps his beard in his hand and declares (with veiled absurdity), "My beard is the meaning of it all." The dreamer protests his incomprehension; the old man directs him to a room of infinite expanse, filled with texts: "And whatever I opened, I found a meaning of those events." So Reb Nahman's dream ends.[92]

A cryptic account, even more graphic and bizarre than the most abstruse of Reb Nahman's narratives. The Borgesian library, a clever symbol of the intertextuality of the dream, does not actually extend any explicit information to the perplexed reader; rather, it suggests only that the meaning of the dream is concealed in preexisting writings. In essence, each hieroglyphic image of the dream to be deciphered—candle, sparks, creatures—entails some kind of transformation, which occurs in flagrant disregard of natural law or logic. The invisible suspended candle suddenly becomes a river; words describing deeds turn into sparks; the sparks are ingested, and reemerge as quicksilver fleeting beings. Each transformation signals the presence of a textual allusion: what appears in the Bible as a metaphor—"as for the likeness of the living creatures, their appearance was like coals of fire . . ." (Ezek. 1:13)—is, in the drama, a concrete literal image. Similarly, the candle/river points to Dan. 7:9; the dynamic creatures are as magical as those glimpsed by Ezekiel. Part 3 of this chapter will be devoted to an exploration of Reb Nahman's metamorphosis of biblical metaphor in the tales; here, I would like merely to point out that the very fabric of this and many dreams recounted in *Hayyei Moharan* are woven of such linguistic transformations.

The Tale Entitled The Lost Princess *and the Song of Songs*

If we may consider the accounts recorded in *Hayyei Moharan* as an authentic record of his own dreams, they indeed point to some elements Reb Nahman employed in his tales as well to conjure a dreamlike atmosphere. Yet a second source, and certainly a vital influence on many of Reb Nahman's stories, is a specific biblical text, which I would like to discuss as two extended "dream sequences": the Song of Songs, 3:1–6 and 5:2–9.[93] In the first passage, the heroine prefaces her story with the ambiguous words, "On my bed at night" rather than something more definitive such as "As I slept," evoking unresolved uncertainty concerning the dimension of reality in which her imaginative/dream experiences take place. To illustrate the pervasive influence of these passages in the stories, let us consider them parallel to Reb Nahman's first story, the tale *The Lost Princess*. My contention is that the internal, subconscious experience of dreams is an integral component evoked in both texts. Further, the dream sequences of the Song of Songs and the tale *The Lost Princess* describe an archetypical search, and the dynamic of this search is rooted in the fantastic, essentially surreal, logic unique to dreams.

We begin, then, with the biblical text. The alternate reality of sleep and imagination in the Song of Songs is intimated in the first and last words of each passage: both in chapters 3 and 5, the initial setting is a bedroom at night. In both passages, the transition from that intimate, enclosed space to the flight of the female protagonist through the open streets of the city is blurred and imprecise. One scene follows another in rapid succession, connected by no discernible logic. The obscurity of events is emphasized by the darkness permeating the scene: her lover is there, and gone; he eludes her like a shadow, concealed in the night. Hope alternates with despair and her helplessness robs her of all control. The very style of both passages reflects their dreamlike nature. The words *levakesh* (to search for) and *limzo* (to find) are repeated almost compulsively in chapter 3, as if the traumatic search is endlessly lived and relived in the woman's consciousness. The syntax of that passage is vitally unstable as well. Past turns to future and back to past, as volatile as her thoughts, as insubstantial as her actions. Does the woman's desire really draw her outside, does she really run desperately through the city, is her lover at last in her arms, or does she only imagine what would happen were she to live out her fantasy?

The passage in chapter 5 is likewise charged with ambivalence. Chastely she resists his impassioned entreaty to open the door, but is clearly torn by desire and restraint. The passage is filled with expressions of boundaries—a door separates her from him, inside from outside—yet everything that seems impermeable ultimately reveals an opening. Eventually she yields, but it is too late. As closed as she was before, she is now infinitely open, vulnerable, without defense. Numerous hints in the two passages suggest neither describes a unique, isolated scenario but rather one basically identical, *recurring* dream. In the first she successfully eludes the city guards, miraculously finding her fleeting lover. Freud would describe it as a happy, wish-fulfilling dream. In the second she is caught, stripped, beaten—certainly an anxiety dream, even a nightmare. It is as if the sleep-ego of the dreamer causes her to be punished for her forbidden desires, for relenting, even in fantasy, to her lover's beseeching. The very blatant contradiction between the happy and unhappy ending of the two passages annuls any remaining notion that either refers to objective, external reality. And despite the frustrated conclusion of the second search, the subsequent verses (vv. 11ff.) describe the beloved vividly, as if he were there before her, as indeed he is *in her mind*. Now we can understand the refrain that echoes throughout the Song of Songs: "I charge you, O daughters of Jerusalem, that you stir not up, nor awake my love till it please." The love that must not be awakened is a metonymy for the beloved herself; consumed by her love, the identity of person and attribute become fused. That is her averment and her plea to the daughters of Jerusalem: I am caught up in a dream of love, I know I am asleep, but I wish that dream to continue. Do not rob me of my fantasy, do not awaken me until I am ready to return to reality, and to my loneliness.

The mystical commentary on the Song of Songs expounded in the *Zohar Hadash* supports the thesis that chapter 3 describes a wish rather than its actual fulfillment. The words in those verses are spoken by the Shekhinah, or Assembly of Israel, who sits abjectly in the dust, among strangers in a land that is not her own, and pleads with her faraway King. She knows He will come to her only when they are together in His palace, and she longs for Him to bring her there, to return her from her exile. The same allegorical interpretation naturally extends to chapter 5: in the view of the *Zohar Hadash*, that scene is a transparent description of the torture inflicted on the Jewish people at the hands of the gentile nations. When we draw this symbolism to its logical conclusion, no doubt remains why both searches portrayed in the Song of Songs are equally unreal, why they belong equally to the realm of fantasy. The historical reality is that the exile goes on—the King and His bride remain tragically separate, the world is yet unredeemed.

We return now to Reb Nahman's tale *The Lost Princess*. Nighttime, darkness, and sleep, vast undefined spaces, powerlessness, and ambivalence pervade the story. The princess is mysteriously stolen away at night; the servant travels, directionless, "for a long time" and the places where he finally discovers her hang abstractly in nowhere. The giants he meets in the desert serve the identical function as the city guards in the Song of Songs—both are the same classic folktale figure. They test the hero, attempting to discourage him from his mission, and by overcoming them he proves the strength and devotion of his character. Like the heroine of the Song, the king's servant wrestles with his own will, and his loss of control leads to his own downfall. These two scenes, in which the servant forgets the princess's warning and, on the crucial day, eats or drinks what was forbidden to him—evoke in the reader a strange sense of déjà-vu. The garden, the warning, the apple—the allusion to the primal sin described in Genesis is unmistakable: the servant eats the apple, seduced by the sight of it just as Eve was seduced in the Garden of Eden. And the sleep that overtakes him then and there—it corresponds with the first exile of human history, the estrangement of Adam and Eve from the idyllic paradise. The power of the biblical allusion casts a fatalistic shadow over the entire event. The servant is held fast in the grip of his humanness; helpless as a dreamer, he can act no differently. He is a symbol and yet he also cries, painfully aware of his inescapable destiny, to repeat the tragic acts of Adam. Other aspects of his adventure seem dreamlike as well. Time and space have no substance, and barriers that first seem unbreachable—the palace guards, the pearly fortress—are overcome in a moment.

In this comparison, the Freudian notion of repressed thoughts emerging to become overt, motivating forces in the dream is particularly relevant. Each of the two texts speaks of the longing and search for a lover/beloved who is distant or even lost, and of the trials, dismay, and hopes of the figure in search of him/her. The subconscious struggles silently waged during the searcher's waking life are acted out upon a stage within the innocent sleeper. The emotional charge of the tale, and of the biblical text, can thus be traced to that universal experience Freud describes.

The Tale Entitled Fly and Spider

In the tale *The Lost Princess*, the dream atmosphere is implicit, indirectly evoked through the landscape, unrealistic temporality, the awareness of intangible evil forces and the abrupt ending like an uncanny awakening. These same basic elements inform all of Reb Nahman's stories: in a number of them, though, the dream motif becomes overt. The narration of a character's dream is incorporated in the story itself, adding yet another dimension of metareality. Perhaps the clearest example is the tale *Fly and Spider*. In that tale, the conscience of the protagonist, soon to become dreamer, is portrayed in classic psychoanalytic terms. A powerful king holds an annual feast in commemoration of his most glorious victory. One year, amidst the raucous gaiety, the conqueror becomes entranced with a tiny drama taking place on the pages of a book open before him. A spider creeps cunningly toward its prey, but again and again the fly is protected by a page of the book eerily lifted as if by a breeze, which stymies the spider's advance. The relentless audacity of the spider at last tempts it to its own death, entrapped and crushed between the pages. This sight strikes at the king's very heart; he recognizes the spider's frustrated hunt and the fly's blessed escape as a sign, a message meant for him. In his musing, the king drowses; the story line slips smoothly into his dream. The subsequent events are, transparently, instances of displacement, in which the dreamer's inner experiences are externalized in symbolic acts.[94] In his dream, he holds a precious stone. As he stares into it, innumerable people begin to emerge and in horror he flings the jewel away. Now, kings have a portrait of themselves, and over the portrait hangs their crown. The people who issue from the stone grab the portrait and behead the *picture* of the king, then cast his crown into the mud. After this symbolic revolt and assassination, they turn to pursue the man portrayed. But the king, while still himself, is also the fly; he lies upon an open book, one of the pages of which inexplicably rises to cut off the advance of his enemies. This coincidence between the original sight of spider and fly and the king's own predicament reminds the dreamer of his waking perplexity: What is written on the page that so mercifully shields the king/fly? Of what nation does it speak? The king is afraid to look, and in his uncertainty and terror shouts "Gewald!" For a moment, the narrative shifts back to the framework story—in a humorous scene, the king's ministers watch their ruler writhe upon his chair, trapped in his dream; they try to awaken him by beating about him, but he does not hear. Then the narrative returns to the consciousness of the sleeper. The subsequent phases of the king's dream aptly illustrate basic ideas in Jungian and Freudian theory concerning symbolic thinking. The crux of that conception is the process of displacement, in which abstract, verbal thoughts are exchanged for their concrete, pictoral expression.[95] In the instance of *Fly and Spider*, the genesis of the dream images can clearly be traced from the story backwards through the metaphorical prooftext of Psalm 3, and further to their inception in the feelings of persecution, vulnerability, and, ultimately, faith in God from which the psalm is born. King David the speaker/poet, taunted and demeaned, turns to God: "I cried to the Lord with my voice, and He heard me out of His holy mountain" (Ps. 3:5). The king of the tale, pursued by assassins, also cries out "Gewald" and is answered in his dream by that mountain itself, a personification of the biblical metaphor. The biblical speaker's helpless withdrawal from his life's turmoil—"I lie me down and sleep"—mirrors the king's own dormant escape from all that threatens him subconsciously. And the most bewildering of Reb Nahman's images, the heaps of teeth, actualize the verse "Arise,

O Lord, save me, O my God; for You have smitten all my enemies upon the cheek, You have broken the teeth of the wicked" (Ps. 3:8); the pathetically useless teeth are a playful metonymic representation of those enemies rendered impotent. These images—the decapitated portrait, later rehabilitated; the beleaguered mountain; the troubled sleeper; the abandoned teeth; the mysterious page—exemplify the phenomenon of displacement and "condensation" of abstract thought in symbolic form that Freud recognized as so intrinsic to dreams. The process of concretization itself possesses what Freud calls "a predestined ambiguity": in the tale *Fly and Spider*, these phantasmagoric pictures compel the dreamer himself to seek the meaning he senses is disguised in them.

We spoke of the juxtaposition of planes of reality that characterizes literature of the fantastic; *Fly and Spider* provides perhaps the most indisputable instance of such a juxtaposition. As his dream draws to a close, the king thankfully witnesses the restoration of his honor, and immediately awakens. The emotional intensity of the drama generated by his unconscious bursts the natural barrier between sleep and wakefulness; the dreamer's relief at his salvation causes his immediate repentance. Its impression, moreover, inspires him to seek a wise man who can decipher his dream. This act, indeed, is the next stage in the psychotherapeutic process itself: the symbols evoked by the unconscious must be *interpreted*, traced by an objective listener from their graphic manifestation back to their inchoate origins. Thus the king sets off, in search of his analyst.[96] The subsequent oracular scene, obscured in clouds of incense, adds yet a fourth plane of reality to this thoroughly fantastic tale. The humble wise man leads his "patient" through a truly Freudian "regression," back even to the time before the king's birth. Together, the two watch the king's soul struggle to be born. The vision of that struggle points darkly to the king's messianic identity. But although his life's story is spread before him, the king is returned, in the end, to his own present; his destiny (as potential redeemer?) has not yet been realized. Thus, Reb Nahman's tale trails off, inconclusive—it is as unfinished, indeed, as the psychotherapeutic process itself must be. Despite all the understanding of himself the subject may gain, his life waits to be lived.[97]

We see, then, that the device of dreams performs three essential functions in the story: first, it provides the landscape in which symbols may run wild, blithely oblivious of the constraints imposed by rational thought. Second, the dream, like a wavering reflection on the still lake of consciousness, directs our gaze always upwards, toward *interpretation*, to its solid form in the world of substance. And finally, just as R. Joseph comes to realize that the "upside-down world" he envisioned is really the world of truth, so dreams intimate an ineluctable uncertainty. Which realm is more vitally "real"; where is the dreamer more truly alive; when does he truly awaken? An incident relayed by Reb Nahman himself illustrates to what extent this fundamental sense of ambivalence permeated the master's consciousness. He tells of being on a journey on the day preceding the Sabbath. As nightfall approaches, Reb Nahman is gripped with a growing sense of urgency. He wishes the horses would run more swiftly—they must reach their destination before the Sabbath begins. Yet, perversely, the horses seem to gallop more and more slowly, "And it was like a dream—one has to escape and he absolutely cannot"; everyone has had this nightmare of paralysis. "And as he traveled, he felt like one must as he is being led to Gehenna, that same boundless terror—such was his fear of desecrating the Sabbath, God forbid."[98] In this brief experience, dream and reality merge, are reversed, and become indistinguishable.

3. BLURRING OF BOUNDARIES, SHIFTING IDENTITIES

"Our rebbe answered, 'Everyone says there is "this world" and "the world to come." Indeed, we believe the "world to come" does exist. Maybe "this world" also exists somewhere, in some world. Here, it seems like Gehenna, for people are always filled with great suffering.' And he said, 'There really is no "this world" at all.'"[99]

The above passage seems to utter a Kafkaesque cry of despair, an admission of impotence—only the fragile belief in that distant higher realm can save one from the abyss of suffering; only the thin hope of "seeming," that the "hell on earth" is not really so, can give strength to continue. All, the master fears, may be illusion. The passage expresses Reb Nahman's grappling with the irreconcilable dialectic of human existence: on the one hand, awareness and yearning for the bright "world of forms," for completeness and resolution; on the other, the dim cave where captives lie chained, taunted by flitting shadows. In many other contexts in Reb Nahman's teaching, however, the same idea is expressed less tortuously. Although the concern remains that all we perceive is illusion, the faulty nature of human perception is recognized as temporary and, moreover, as a failing that can and ultimately must be overcome. In this section we will address the question of perception and deception, of human encounters with a world of disguises, as a fundamental element in all of Reb Nahman's tales. What I would like to suggest is that the intimation of hidden identity, and the process of unveiling, is a dynamic intrinsic in literature of the fantastic as a whole.

In such works, the sense of the supernatural as an active force is created through accounts of metamorphoses, of transformations in the identity of figures, and of the fluid nature of spacial and temporal dimensions. These events impress the character and the reader with the amorphous nature of reality, on one hand, and on the other, they shake his confidence in the accuracy of his own perceptions. Yet, in Reb Nahman's view, sustained by Hasidic and mystical teaching, this overwhelming uncertainty is a necessary first step in attaining true understanding of the world; only when one begins to search beyond appearances can one see the glimmering of the divine—indeed, among the shadowy forms of one's own world. The tales describe manifold instances of this process of encountering deceptive appearances and of penetrating beyond such outward disguises. In the following pages, I would like to examine some of those encounters, and demonstrate the intimate connection between the idea of metamorphoses of human personality in its literary form and a seminal concept in Hasidic and kabbalistic teaching, that of *levushim* (garments, disguises).

The dank and clammy cave, famed by Plato's allegory, recalls a kindred, similarly miserable pit, in which Reb Nahman's masterful story *The Seven Beggars* is set. This tale, like the laver of the Tabernacle inlaid with women's mirrors (Ex. 38:8), is composed of autonomous vignettes, all of them about appearances, about perception and deception and true understanding. Each beggar, designated by his crippling flaw—blind, deaf, mute, handless—tells a story in which he reveals the illusory nature of his deformity: his vision is transcendent; his hearing superhuman; he is a master of song, a life-restoring doctor.[100]

The marriage feast of the orphaned children, at which each beggar arrives as an unexpected guest, takes place in the most degraded place imaginable, a hole roofed with planks, dirt, and rubbish. Yet it is precisely in that humble pit that bride and groom, guests and reader, realize *their own* blindness, deafness, etc., relative to him, and precisely there that they are permitted to glimpse the wholeness informing the beggars' essence. Each in his own way shows that, through his unique attribute, he is capable of restoring the constricted, fragmentary world to its original state, and it is this potential that gives each story its eschatological valence. Further, in his parting gesture of offering his story as a wedding present, each beggar bequeathes the secret of his perfection, truly an element of the world to come, to his human audience. The very setting of *The Seven Beggars*, then, epitomizes a central theme in Reb Nahman's thought: the incongruous coexistence of the two realms, this world and the transcendent one, in human consciousness. True identity can be revealed only when appearances have been acknowledged as a disguise.

The process of struggling away from what seems to be true is at the heart of *The Two Sons Who Were Reversed*. As we saw earlier in this chapter, the characters themselves are forced, little by little, to abandon all their preconceptions concerning their own identities. The subjective and then objective transformation of both characters, catalyzed by the famished servant's son selling his birthright for a hunk of bread, reenacts the fateful biblical scene between Jacob and Esau—there, similarly, a mess of potage makes Jacob the rightful heir to his father's inheritance. As a result, both sons begin to assume their new roles—the king's true son discovers his royal dignity and the servant's true son his humility. Reb Nahman's students attribute these cases of reversed identity between the two sons to an infamous cosmic phenomenon that, in turn, accounts for the deceptive nature of all of reality. In an enigmatic place called the "chamber of exchanges" *[heikhal ha-temurot]*, essences are disguised; justice is turned on its head, fools reign, and true kings are exiled.[101]

The distortions of identity fabricated in the "chamber of exchanges" reflect, in the material world, the cosmic phenomenon of divine concealment the Kabbalists call *levushim*. In the *Zohar*, the primordial light that filled the universe is described as unbearably brilliant; when God created the world, He *clothed* that divine brightness in the earthly light. The heavenly bodies thus contain some glimmer of the original, true light. Yet more important, they point beyond themselves: the essence of the divine is embodied in that most intangible symbol of endless light, *or ein sof*.[102] The concept of *levushim* as the only possible manifestation of a transcendent God in the material world permeates both the *Zohar* and Lurianic teaching in *'Ez Hayyim*. Every object of human perception conceals the divine, and it is, paradoxically, only clothed in those material "garments" that God becomes immanent at all. This is the meaning of the verse, "The whole earth is filled with His glory" (Is. 6:3), the phrase recalled again and again in Hasidic teaching to describe the sense of urgency in recognizing the constant revelation of God's presence. In the end, all the transience of human reality, the capricious twists of fortune, and the humors of the stars are revealed as no more than an illusion, the disguises of the Infinite.[103]

We find the same motif of concealed, transcendent being transferred to human figures as well. The image of God "clothing" Himself in earthly forms reappears in the classic concepts of the hidden zaddik and the disguised Messiah.[104] Reb Nahman's tale *The Master of Prayer* contains perhaps the most telling example of the author's fascination with disguises and with assumed identity. The story opens with a description of the master's psychological technique: he draws people away from their misguided lives to his forest retreat and begins their spiritual rehabilitation by giving each the *costume* he must have to help him turn and repent. "If one of them needed to wear a golden cape to serve God, he would provide one . . . and if, on the other hand, a rich man needed to wear tattered, shameful garments, he would have them, too" (*SM*, p. 175) Yet the master of prayer's tremendous sensitivity to people's innermost desires extends much further. So responsive is he to his listeners that he can adapt his very self to their unspoken souls. Thus, he continually infiltrates the country of riches, eluding all captors: "It was impossible to recognize and nab him, for he would change himself before each and every person: to one he would appear as a merchant and to another a poor man, etc., and then quickly escape" (*SM*, p. 184). By grace of his chameleon nature, the master of prayer is also a master of disguises; he helps his followers to find themselves through their costumes (*lehithapes* in both senses), to play the most honest role they can in the human comedy of their lives. As for himself, the "true" identity of the master of prayer is somehow irrelevant. The multiple appearances of this transparently autobiographical figure are in fact an emblem of all the masks Reb Nahman assumes throughout his oeuvre. The madman, the prince, the prophet, musician, and sage—each alter ego is but another face of a single crystal, the omnipresent author.[105]

If we may consider *The Master of Prayer* as an improvisation on the theme of the hidden zaddik, we find in another of Reb Nahman's tales a drama of the disguised Messiah. We recall the question posed by R. Joshua ben Levi to Elijah the Prophet: "Where is the Messiah to be found?" and the answer, that he sits among the lepers at the gates of Rome, binding and unbinding his bandages.[106] The suggestion that this figure so urgently sought may be in our very midst, his true identity obscured in distorted human form, provides the material for a powerful drama. Reb Nahman's tale *The Burgher and the Poor Man* is constructed around an extended scene in which the heroine, disguised as a man, puts her beloved through trials testing his love and devotion before she finally reveals her true identity in the last words of the story. Rav Nathan's commentary intimates the messianic character of the heroine. In the following discussion, I would like to compare this tale with the biblical Joseph story, for central to both is the intense dynamic of concealment and recognition—in both, dramatic tension is created by the disparity between the reader's awareness and the characters' ignorance of who the pivotal figure really is.[107] Shipwrecked along with the treacherous kidnapper on a desert island, the kaiser's (alias poor man's) daughter, disguised as a sailor, escapes her captor and flees. His search for her fruitless, the villain finally gives up, concluding, "She was doubtless eaten by wild beasts" (*SM*, p. 134). We recall the nearly identical fate of Joseph, bound and sold by his brothers; at the ghastly sight of his son's bloody cloak, Jacob cries, "He was eaten by wild beasts; they tore Joseph to bits" (Gen. 37:34). As the story unfolds, the kaiser's daughter encounters her true beloved, but her disguise as a man guards her true identity from him. Even her father, coincidentally shipwrecked on the same island, does not recognize her.

Reaching Egypt, Joseph's brothers were received in the court: Joseph saw his brothers "and recognized them, and he was a stranger to them. . . . And he recognized them but they did not recognize him" (Gen. 42:7–8). The brothers must endure a long time of uncertainty, completely unaware of the import of their actions. Joseph reveals himself to his brothers only after they have proven their submission to his will. Similarly, in *The Burgher and the Poor Man*, only after the crucial letter, proof of their lovers' bond, has been found does the heroine decide to return home, reveal herself to her promised one, and restore justice to the world.

In both narratives, time and circumstance have changed the protagonist, and he initially exudes an aura of strangeness. Catharsis occurs when his familiar mien becomes visible to all. This unexpected shifting between what is alien and what is recognizable evokes, once again, Freud's description of the uncanny. To be blind to the presence of the Messiah, the disguised savior who could right all wrongs, is a profoundly unsettling possibility. In the story *Burgher and Poor Man*, this figure is doubly disguised: from the eye of the characters as a male sailor, and from the eyes of the traditionalist reader as a woman. We might say, then, that disguises in this and many of Reb Nahman's stories serve to heighten awareness that appearances may conceal precious truths. In her essence, the kaiser's daughter is messianic; the most agile dancer has no legs; even the bizarre forest man may be a hidden zaddik.[108] Clearly, although all human actors must necessarily wear costumes, although *levushim* are an inseparable part of reality, the concealing veils are really meant to be drawn away. Reb Nahman describes the attempt to come closer to God as a gradual removal of those disguises: "And the higher one goes, the more flimsy the garments, and the less severe the *zimzum*; then one can love God with ever greater love." God's apparent silence, His hidden face, will not be so forever. The day will come, Reb Nahman continues, "when He will strip away all the masks [*levushim*]. 'For the earth shall be full of the knowledge of the Lord, as the waters cover the sea'" (Is. 11:9).[109]

Theological Implications: The Kushiya

Our interest in this chapter has been to examine the dialectic of perception and deception that penetrates Reb Nahman's teaching. One technique he uses to expose the unreliability of human cognition, as we have seen, is the integration in the stories of dream symbolism, logic, and atmosphere, and of dreams themselves. Another device, used to the same end, is the appearance of disguised entities combined with the ensuing challenge to discover their true identity. Yet as the reader of Reb Nahman's tales well knows, the denouement of all of them is deceptively simple; in effect, any sense of resolution at the close of these fantastic stories is absolutely false. A surrealist land of demons is destroyed by an earthquake; a bereft father bewails his son's senseless death; crippled beggars give intangible gifts to bride and groom; the ailing princess is left in suspended animation, imprisoned in the watery palace. In confronting these tales, rationality can cling to nothing: both characters and plot are stubbornly opaque, and paradox is granted unbounded legitimacy. There are questions, Reb Nahman avers, that can be answered only by silence: "And how the princess was rescued he did not tell, and in the end she was rescued" *(The Lost Princess)*. Certain explanations belong not to this world; they will be revealed only in the future, in messianic times, or in the world to come.[110] We meet this silence again and again in Reb Nahman's stories, this speechlessness before some truth the author himself experiences as ineffable.

The centrality of paradox in Reb Nahman's worldview has been extensively examined in modern research. Mordechai Rotenberg, for example, writes that "in Bratslav theosophy, the paradox of living in contradiction and in the 'questioning hypothesis' or *kushiya* state [literally, "difficulty" or "challenge" in Hebrew dialectics] characterizes the relationship both between man and God (father and son) and rational empiricism and irrational intuition."[111] Marc-Alain Ouaknin emphasizes the modernity of Bratslav theory: "The 'there is' and 'there is not', *yesh ve-ayin*, at the same time, is the foundation of the whole of R. Nahman's thought. It is not a philosophy of the option that chooses either *one or the other* (disjunction); nor is it a thought of *neither one nor the other* (negative conjunction) such as one encounters in the dialectics of antinomies. . . . Nor is it a question of the Hegelian synthesis, which offers us a *both one and the other* (positive conjunction). . . . But with Rabbi Nahman—somewhat in the same way as for Kierkegaard—it is the scandal of the antithesis without the synthesis that the commentators have called a 'paradox', and that Rabbi Nahman calls *Kushiah*. . . ."[112] Joseph Weiss devotes a weighty and incisive chapter of his study of Bratslav Hasidism to the problem of "'contradiction in thought' and 'ontological antinomies.'"[113] Arthur Green describes Reb Nahman as "a *zaddik* for modern man" because of his "willingness to live at the edge of the void." He concludes his excursus on faith, doubt, and reason in Reb Nahman's thought: "The moment of doubt or of God's absence has to be confronted on its own terms, without the comforting thought that it was but a passing phase. Only by seeking faith *within* doubt, and by the paradoxical assertion that in God's very absence is He to be known, may the doubter be transformed once again into a seeker after Him, and the need for religion be maintained."[114] The primary source used by these scholars is the collection of teachings presented in *Likkutei Moharan*, in which Reb Nahman wrestles with the most intractable philosophical problems of religious thought. It is the questions for which no rational answers may be found, Rotenberg concludes, that compel Reb Nahman to construct "his systematic dialectic-dialogue theory of the paradox, which puts the hypothesis, or the question, in the center of the world."[115] But it is precisely there, caught between the devil and the deep blue sea—in that unanswerable, irrational uncertainty and doubt—that faith is born, the paradoxical faith that is the lifeblood of Reb Nahman's conception. Weiss expresses this idea in all its radicality: "Without the *kushiya*, faith cannot exist; its flame is fueled by the paradox alone."[116] These studies are illuminating, and invaluable in gaining understanding of Reb Nahman's oeuvre. They concentrate, however, on the theoretical rather than the narrative works.[117] In the following pages, I would like to consider how the omnipresent force of paradox outlined above is manifest in the stories Reb Nahman told. I believe it exists on two levels, which may be referred to as the theological and the phenomenological; the second, terrestrial dimension is a result, or an outgrowth, of the first.

Three tales—*The Master of Prayer*, *Clever Son and Simple Son*, and *The Humble King*—explore the dilemma (psychological as well as social) of accepting the sovereignty of a transcendent, unknowable God. Here, the tortured, impossible search for truth, so movingly expressed in *Likkutei Moharan*, is undertaken with striking single-mindedness. In *The Master of Prayer*, the ridiculous distortions fostered by the idolatrous sects are a parody of modern-day vices in the guise of polytheism. Each sect chooses a king who embodies its highest value: the blind and crooked Gypsy with his crowd of bastard children for the worshippers of honor; the schizophrenic and verbose Frenchman for the worshippers of speech; the lascivious queen for the worshippers of fertility. The senseless beliefs of all of them are contested by the master of prayer, who tirelessly and with utmost simplicity offers the way of truth: "Prayer and praise of the Holy One, blessed be He." In this story, the difficulty of adopting a religion with an invisible king is mitigated by the figure of the prayer master himself; this prototype of a Hasidic rebbe purifies each one, helps him repent, and makes these disciples into a community of God's faithful.

The tale *Clever Son and Simple Son*, in contrast, dramatizes the tormented struggle between apostasy and faith in all its pathos. While the simple man becomes a simple cobbler, the clever one's intellect gives him no peace; a born philosopher, his wanderings through the world lead him to take up and master one art after another: silversmithing, stonecutting, medicine. But all this enlightenment only drives him into the darkness of nihilism: "Afterwards, the world began to be worthless in his eyes" (*SM*, p. 82). He suffers endlessly—from loneliness, from a gnawing sense of imperfection, from frustrated honor. The bitter dissatisfaction of the clever son is contrasted with the quietism of the simple one; unsoiled by the clamoring of the world around him, every aspect of life fills him with joy. The test comes when each man is summoned to appear before the king. The simple man's willing trust soon wins him love and acclaim; the clever man, meanwhile, is paralyzed in a fierce storm of internal argument. Self-denigration alternates with overweening pride in his mind, until he decides: "There is no king at all, and the whole world errs in the ridiculous supposition there is" (*SM*, p. 96). To all who contest him, he counters, "Have *you* ever seen the King?" The absurdity he perceives in their tenuous faith only deepens his scorn. Scandalously denying the existence of the king and the sanity of his servants, the clever son drives himself to ruin, finally sinking to an ignominious torture at the hand of the devil himself. Yet the message of this story is not so superficial as it may appear. The philosopher's error was not gross apostasy (i.e., declaring God is dead); tragically, though, he mistook paradoxical faith for absurd delusion. All the unholy knowledge one can reap, Reb Nahman avers, is weighted with unbearable heaviness. God cannot be found in that howling wilderness, for He Himself removed His presence from it to enable the world to come into being.[118] The only way to overcome the threat of a senseless universe, to continue beyond that terrifying empty space *(hallal ha-panui)* is, as Kierkegaard says, a leap of faith. Such a leap requires lightness of being, a casting off of "the heart of stone" and gaining "a heart of flesh" (cf. Ezek. 11:19).

But it is certainly in the third story, *The Humble King*, that theosophical paradox is most skillfully interwoven, with the ironic result that even the "wise" protagonist does not notice it. The tale opens with a description of a remote kingdom in the midst of the sea, ruled by the renowned "true and humble man" whose portrait no one owns, and whose face has never been seen. When the "wise servant" appears before this hidden monarch, he is astonished to discover that the king is utterly removed from the web of lies that entangle his kingdom. He begins to praise the presence behind the royal curtain. "But the king, because he was so humble—'and His greatness was in his humility'—the more he was praised and aggrandized, the smaller and more humble he became . . ." (*SM,* p. 63). The king begins to shrink by the minute, like Alice in Wonderland. And just before he disappears "into nothingness, he couldn't resist, and flung away the curtain to see who that wise man was who knew and understood so much. His face was revealed. . . . He saw him, and brought his portrait to his king." Is it a prophetic vision, an encounter with infinity? Or the vain imaginings of a too-clever fool, a servant who vaunts his success in outwitting the king? I believe the joke is on the protagonist. Unaware of the paradoxicality of his own discovery (that the king truly is both great and humble), he impetuously grabs some supposed likeness and scurries away, convinced he has captured the hidden king's essence. What he does not realize is that this, too, is merely a partial image, a static picture; like the faces of all the other, earthly kings, it is but one aspect of the true king's will, an utterly false portrait because of its very materiality. The servant watches as the king seems to vanish; he sees the *ayin* (nothingness) but never knows that *Ein sof* is there as well, infinity on the other side of the looking glass.[119]

In all three stories cited, then, theosophical paradoxes—the incomprehensibility of a transcendent God whose immanence fills the world—are potent ingredients in conjuring their fantastic nature.

Let us turn now to the second dimension of paradox as it appears in Reb Nahman's tales: oxymora in the phenomenological realm. We began this chapter with a mention of the enigmatic place *(ha-makom)* Abraham sees from afar—the site or the presence before which he will bind his son Isaac. It is enigmatic because, as we learn from the midrash, "the Place" is but a code name for God Himself; as R. Yose ben Halafta remarks, "The Lord is the place of the world, but the world is not His place."[120] The logical contradiction in any human notion of the divine thus comes to the fore in the appellation *ha-makom*, for God Himself, "the Place," is, finally, bounded by no material constraints. The only space in the universe that *does* have concrete manifestation is our own phenomenological world, and this world, we know, was created from *zimzum*, by God's act of withdrawing, of removing Himself from some part of being. Hence the only *makom* human perception can grasp is, paradoxically, the very space He cleared of His presence.[121] We search this place, our natural world, for signs, messages, remnants of His presence, hoping for some understanding to lead us toward Him, toward truth. Underlying Reb Nahman's entire worldview is the belief that no aspect of creation should be disregarded or considered meaningless; rather, the face of the natural world and all its events are signs and symbols of a truth beyond earthly limitations. "All that occurs in the world, all is a certain sign of divine things, 'for nothing is empty/only in the world.'"[122] The double meaning of the unvowelled word *rek/rak* (empty/only) contains the essential message: no element of existence is devoid of meaning and, on the contrary, each one has another existence beyond its earthly manifestation. Thus all phenomena both speak of themselves and point beyond themselves; their physical presence itself is symbolic of something higher, non-material. Further, in Reb Nahman's world, this allusion to higher planes of existence is not only perceived subjectively, but objectively occurs: the elements of nature *themselves* take up the task of hinting God's influence in the natural world. "Everything shouts of His glory, for 'the whole earth is full of His glory' (Is. 6:3)."[123]

While the way of science is to discover the order and logic of phenomena, and describe them in rational terms, in the eyes of the mystic those phenomena draw their vitality from another, transcendent realm. The tool of both is language, a collection of human words drawn only from the senses. But while the philosopher combines those building blocks systematically, reasonably, constructing a stable edifice, the mystic, in flagrant disregard for logic, fashions a castle in the air. D. T. Suzuki, characterizing religious expression as a whole, wrote: "When language is forced to be used for things of this ['transcendental'] world it becomes warped and assumes all kind of crookedness: oxymora, paradoxes, contradictions, absurdities, oddities, ambiguities and irrationalities."[124] The appearance of mystical paradox, then, is no mere literary device, but is rather a flash of insight, born of, yet forever incommensurable with, the sense experiences of the space-time world. Instances of such linguistic or conceptual "crookedness" abound in Reb Nahman's tales, culminating perhaps in *The Seven Beggars*, which speaks most transparently of sense perceptions: the blind beggar who sees to the ends of the earth; the handless doctor whose music heals the ailing princess; and, notably, the crooked-necked beggar whose speech is most eloquent and pure. The narrator presents these paradoxes in full awareness of their blatantly antilogical nature, yet his own naive acceptance of them as pure truth hints at their legitimacy. The bizarre events, the strange juxtapositions, and the unlikely characters of the tales may initially leave us at a loss. Yet when we realize how deeply Reb Nahman is rooted in Jewish mystical tradition, we understand why the fantastic dimension is so necessary. Our inability to accept and integrate the oxymora we confront is a cognitive problem related to our spiritual level.

Thus, in Reb Nahman's hands paradox and logical contradiction become didactic tools, modeled on the principle of surprise. An impression is made only to be exploded: "You think I am deaf, but I'm not at all; it's just that the world means nothing to me—all their voices shout only of what they lack . . ." (*SM,* p. 248); "You think I am dumb, but I'm not at all; rather, all the words of the world—they are not praises of God—it is those words that have no fullness . . ." (*SM,* p. 255); "You think I am blind, but I'm not at all," etc. This dialectic tactic is epitomized in the talmudic exclamation, *addrabba—ipkḥa mistabra* (on the contrary, the very opposite stands to reason!). It is the signal that the student must awaken to a logical reversal, that he must reconsider everything, distinguish anew between truth and falsehood.[125]

Who, then, is responsible for ministering this dialectical shock treatment, in Reb Nahman's view? None other than the zaddik—he diagnoses the existential state of each of his students, and counters them with the paradox they must overcome for their own spiritual growth. In effect, there is but one sole paradox—the unbearable contradiction of immanence and transcendence. It stands before each individual and affects his vision like a prism according to his position relative to it. The zaddik, through his teaching, initiates a radical shift in that position, and the student's world is turned upside-down. Specifically, for those who feel mired in materiality, hopelessly distant from God, he shows them it is not so—God is with them, even "the whole earth is full of His glory." Those, on the other hand, complacently sure of their intimacy with God, he humbles, showing them they are unutterably distant and can know nothing at all of His essence—"Where is the place of His glory?"[126] Each confrontation with paradox is calculated to alter the listener, to shatter his illusions, to present him with the undeniable verity of the mirror image of his life.

Let us return for a moment to the story of the deaf beggar *(Seven Beggars)* to see just how this didactic principle, described in *Likkutei Moharan,*[127] works within Reb Nahman's tales. In his explanation of the true nature of his flaw, the deaf beggar offers an aural parallel to the Platonic cave allegory. He begins by exposing the futility of the voices that fill the world: no one speaks of fullness, of happiness, of positive value, but only of emptiness, of what they lack and, at best, of what they once lacked and have finally attained. This preoccupation with absence and its elimination is, for the deaf beggar, the nadir of vanity. In the same way the prisoners, chained in their cave, imagine the shadows that flit across the walls are true forms, so the inmates of this hermetic chamber believe the echoes that fill it are true voices. R. Nathan makes explicit the parallel between the two allegories: just as shadow is created when a stream of light is obstructed by matter, so echo is created when a pure voice hits some obstacle—as in a forest, for example, or between mountains, when voices issue and return.[128] And just as shadow occupies the place where light has been blocked out, so echoes invade an enclosed space, driving away the sound of the original voice. Thus the beggar's deafness to the world's clamoring, to the confusing, distorted echoes that pervade it, releases him from that maddening echo chamber, enabling him to hear the Voice that brought the world into being and ordered it through speech, the only voice of true wholeness. The deaf beggar's hearing, the blind beggar's vision, the dumb beggar's speech, the crippled beggar's dance—each figure draws our attention to a higher realm of truth arching, like a promise, over our world of incompleteness, yet reminding us how distant we are from it.

Finally, we understand that paradox, in Reb Nahman's teaching, is a two-edged sword: it arouses, even enlightens, but in the end it drives home, ever more painfully, the troubling limitations of human understanding. The fantastic, irrational world opened up before us in the tales remains impenetrable. We recall Reb Nahman's contention that some enigmas can summon no response other than silence. But why? Because were these logical impossibilities to be completely unraveled, explained, that would lead not to the longed-for resolution, but only to yet more difficult epistemological challenges, before which we may falter hopelessly. In *Likkutei Moharan,* Reb Nahman speaks of the ineluctable presence of *mekkifin*, of the boundless knowledge that encompasses us as we drift like boats in the midst of the sea.[129] It is this presence that both urges us on and remains tantalizingly beyond our grasp. In an emotional twist that captures his worldview, Reb Nahman declares that the very dynamic of attaining some drop of knowledge, only to realize the utter inaccessibility of the endless ocean—this continual trial is in fact "the highest *delight* of the world to come" [*sha'ashu'a 'olam ha-ba*]. An astonishing suggestion, that striving without respite could be more pleasurable than putting an end to all questions and, gratified, sitting down to rest. Of his Sisyphus Camus says "We must imagine him happy." This is the dynamic of the Song of Songs, the breathless pursuit through deserted streets, moments of union, the haunting pleas, "If you see my beloved, O daughters of Jerusalem. . . ." It is the very essence of the philosopher's being as well, that lover of wisdom. Is love most alive in its consummation or in the search? Clearly, rational and synthetic answers connote finality, stalemate; they are tinged, somehow, with death. Questions, on the other hand, enable a continuous dialogue—they arouse, to be sure, uncertainty, but at the same time they open the possibility of creativity. This dialogical relationship, which exists not only between individuals but between man and God is not only God's will but His greatest delight.[130] We find the same term, *sha'ashu'im* (the delight of the Holy One, blessed be He) invoked to speak of His amusement, like a benevolent father, with His child's smallest accomplishments. I believe this notion of delight or amusement, with all its emotional valence, is of central importance in Reb Nahman's worldview: the tales, much more than the teachings in *Likkutei Moharan*, are charged with humor, audacity, tongue-in-cheek exaggeration, fantastic associations. They carry in them an unspoken request for indulgence (from the reader, but more from God Himself) and their author's innate sense of encouragement, of confidence that God approves, even enjoys, the stories he spins.[131] In his teaching on *mekkifin*,[132] Reb Nahman quotes a verse from Psalms (31:20) that combines the central ideas suggested above: "How great is Your goodness that You have hidden away for those who fear you." It is the question *ma?* ("how, what great goodness!"; in gematria, *ma* equals 45, and points to the forty-five-letter name of God)—the paradoxes with no answer that remain concealed. God's true face, as well as the inconceivable blessing of the world to come are secreted beyond our human gaze. And yet we are drawn into an unending game of hide-and-seek, hoping to glimpse the countenance beyond the masks. And we are caught up in an eternal treasure hunt, tirelessly looking for the traces leading to that promised store of goodness. It take two to play these games—the seeker, exhilarated in his search, and the hider, delighting in revealing and concealing, watching as His creatures draw ever closer to Him.

4. METAMORPHOSIS OF IMAGERY

On the fifth day of the orphan children's wedding feast, the hunchbacked beggar appears to offer his gift, and a strange gift it is. He tells the story of how his distinguishing attribute of "the little that contains a lot" enabled him to bring people access to the wondrous tree they so desired to reach, the abstract, unearthly tree with its mysterious shade, "beyond space." Yet before he describes his own triumph, the hunchbacked beggar recounts the competition with other pretenders to his ability: each in turn offers an instance of the principle from his own experience. This preface psychologically prepares the narrator's audience, skillfully guiding them to a more complete understanding of the philosophical concept he embodies. From the crudest example of the diminutive human being who produces a mountain of rubbish and excrement, to the moving image of the man who meets his roving oppressors with a silence charged to bursting—each account points to some truth that contradicts appearances. The hunchbacked beggar tops all these testimonies: he not only presents an example of "the little that contains a lot"—i.e., the legendary tree whose shade provides an individual, unique place where each beast and bird of creation can dwell in peace—but teaches the "intellectuals" impatiently searching for that tree how they, too, may reach it. In other words, the beggar *in his very person* represents an aspect of "the little that contains a lot" as well, for he is able to carry them, on the broad shoulders of his own intuition, to that undeniably symbolic entity. The hunchbacked beggar, in essence, is a master of trope. His whole being, and the parable he tells, speaks of the mode of figurative language, of the hidden path leading from the signs to the objects they represent. This mode is, of course, an integral component of Reb Nahman's oeuvre. The images that inhabit his stories—the languishing rivers, intangible portraits, storm winds—

clearly are not born with him, nor do they live solely in him. Rather, they hearken back to the poetic tradition underlying him, the symbols, metaphors, and allegories that people the Bible and are reincarnated in rabbinic and kabbalistic literature. Figurative language is inherent and instrumental in all these sources, for all of them speak, ultimately, of a sublime realm that exceeds the grasp of human cognition. The only way to speak of this divine world, to allude, in a tangible way, to what is fundamentally intangible, is thus through trope. Maimonides' famous statement (voicing a conviction already expressed by the sages)[133] that "the Torah speaks in human terms" addresses the problem, particularly troubling for rationalist philosophers, of biblical poetics. Maimonides refers to numerous descriptions of the "hand of God," of pleas that "enter His ears," of "His voice . . . like the sound of many waters." This visionary mode, to which the prophets innately turn, is euphemistically described in *Midrash Tehillim* as "comparing the creation to its creator"; the actual intent, as Solomon Buber points out, being just the opposite: the Creator Himself is compared, unavoidably, to His creation. Such audacity can be excused only because, the midrash continues, "the ear is presented with what it can hear, and the eye is shown what it can see."[134] For tropes and, most basically, symbols, as Tishby says, always take the place of what is invisible; were these transcendent things completely revealed to human comprehension, we would not need to represent them.[135]

In this part, I would like to explore the role of figurative language in the tales, considering both Reb Nahman's metamorphosis of preexisting imagery in conceiving his own tropes and the effect these tropes create in the dimension of the fantastic. The scope of this subject—in effect, of symbolic representation in mystical thought—is daunting; in the following pages I hope only to highlight the vast body of research that speaks of it. My discussion is ordered, perhaps arbitrarily, according to three distinct forms of figurative language. First of all, I would like to consider the presence of *symbols* in Reb Nahman's sources and his reworking of them to his own ends; second, his transformation, on the linguistic level, of *metaphors*; and third, the integration of familiar *allegory* as a dramatic element in the tales.

As Reb Nahman himself teaches again and again, words, in their very anatomy, contain the secret of their essence. The Kabbalists focus on the Hebrew language and the inherent holiness that imbues it; yet perhaps even the Hellenic counterpart of the Holy Tongue can be contemplated to a similar end. Let us begin, then, with a deconstruction of the three central terms of our discussion: symbol, metaphor, and allegory. All three send us back to the hunchbacked beggar, to that *animal symbolicum* par excellence.[136] The Greek word *symbolon*, from *symbalein*, means "to put together" two halves or corresponding pieces of an object. R. H. Hook offers the image of a potsherd, broken into two fragments that could be rejoined and, eventually, recognized.[137] We see the symbol and through it we can envision the true form of its other part. This implies not only an organic relationship between the symbol and the symbolized but some sort of ontological equality between them. The symbol, therefore, is a full and legitimate part of the symbolized; it is not merely the latter's reflection but part of its essence. (We recall, in light of this understanding, Todorov's protest that sterile symbolic interpretation vitiates the power of a fantastic work—see the opening pages of this chapter.) Because the symbol is accessible to human cognition, while its referent is infinitely beyond man's grasp, it epitomizes the concept of "the little that contains a lot." We recognize the tree the beggar describes as the mythic Tree of Life in Daniel's vision—"the beasts of the field have shade under it and the birds of the sky dwell in its boughs, and all flesh is fed from it" (Dan. 4:17–19). It is the cosmic tree of *Sefer ha-Bahir*, which grows downward, its roots above, created in a primordial aeon, toward which all souls yearn. And it is the unifying tree central in medieval Kabbalah to be regained in the end of days, the spiritual origin of the First Man.[138] The hunchbacked beggar understands the fundamental nature of symbols. His wisdom wins him the role of interpreting reality by pointing, with the precise words of his story, from the symbolic tree to its transcendent other half.

We turn, now, to the original, etymological sense of metaphor. Like "symbol," "metaphor" speaks of the way in which separate entities are joined. But here, simultaneity *(sym)* is replaced with vector: to metaphorize is to transfer, or carry, meaning from one element to another. The initial recognition, in the case of metaphor, is one of distance: it is not an instance of A *is* B (symbol); rather A is *like* B. This removal of the signifier from its source, the signified, may seem, at first, to weaken the evocative power of the image. But the alternate perspective distance gives engenders a new, enlightened view of the metaphor's object. As we see in moments of revelation described in the Bible, distance is a necessary precondition—"And he saw the place from afar off" (Gen. 22:4); "the Lord appeared to me from far away" (Jer. 31:2). Thus the beggar initially emphasizes the distance that separates his audience from the object of their quest: "For not every man can reach that tree, only he who shares the attributes of the tree . . ." (*SM*, p. 272). Eventually, though, his teaching urges all his listeners toward moral wholeness. In the end, the hunchbacked beggar does much more than evoke the symbol of that tree; as a Hasidic zaddik, he helps people ascend spiritually, beyond space and time, to the place of the Tree itself. The gift he gives the bridal pair, then, is his intuitive metaphorical understanding, his ability to arrive from a verbally evoked image to the ontological source of that image beyond the material world.

Both symbol and metaphor are explicitly present in the tale of the hunchbacked beggar. In the case of allegory, though, we must turn to secondary sources. *Allos* (other) and *goria* (speaking) suggest that allegory is "speaking otherwise than one seems to speak." In other words, recognition of allegory belongs entirely to the realm of interpretation; in the hunchbacked beggar's story, the narrator's implicit autocommentary stops short of explaining the relevance of this cosmic tree, or Tree of Life, to his listeners' religious existence. Allegorical meaning, though, is discovered simply by pursuing the metaphors of the tale, by extending them into some more manageable, comprehensible shape. Such interpretations are manifold; the seeds of all of them are planted in the narrative, yet they grow to full flower only outside its confines. Allegorical exegesis is the backbone of the commentary offered by Reb Nahman's students. Throughout traditional Bratslav literature we find expansions in this mode. Thus, on a moral level the Torah is "a tree of life to those who hold fast to it" (Prov. 3:18)—the truths it communicates sustain, protect, and preserve all who embrace it. On the metaphysical level, "the little that contains a lot" speaks of the Torah as well: the letters on the parchment and the myriad worlds they hold.[139]

The self-consciousness of allegorical interpretation serves to estrange it from the work of fantastic literature. For unlike symbol and metaphor, which shift ambiguously between identity and seeming, allegory, when made explicit, demands a divorce between signifier and signified.

Its effect, within the narrative, is preserved only when it remains implicit.

Symbol

Perhaps more clearly than any other of the thirteen tales, the axis on which *The Seven Beggars* turns is the fundamental composite symbol of kabbalistic cosmology, indeed its very backbone. The system of the *sefirot*, i.e., the emanation and manifestation of the Godhead in the lower worlds, is conceived extensively, especially in the *Zohar* and with fascinating implications, on the model of the human figure, the Adam Kadmon.[140] This correspondence clearly serves as an inspiration for Reb Nahman's tale, in which each beggar's essence is subsumed by one particular physical part—his mouth, his eyes, his legs, his hands. Reb Nahman's students emphasized, through a mirror image, their master's interest in the power of this kabbalistic anthropomorphism: "There is no human limb that he failed to speak of; indeed, he gave a teaching about each and every member of man's body, for the human form, as is well known, alludes to what it alludes, etc."[141] This veiled assertion suggests a radical innovation initiated by Reb Nahman. The traditional mystical code is diametrically reversed: rather than retracing the trajectory of the process of creation from its highest, divine origin down into the physical world, Reb Nahman points first of all to our own image, to the body we know so intimately, and from there toward what is beyond. The ancient idea, echoed by earlier Hasidic masters, is that "man is called a microcosm [i.e., miniature world]; he is the picture, sign, and symbol of sublime matters, higher than high."[142] This conviction reflects the centuries-old teaching expounded in the *Zohar* that the lower form of man *(Adam tahton)* was created, in body and spirit, in the image of his higher form—the lower manifestation being but a faint copy of the true, original divine Man. As a result, "man's soul can be known only through the organs of the body, which are the levels that perform the work of the soul. Consequently, it is both known and unknown. In the same way, the Holy One, blessed be He, is both known and unknown, because He is the souls' soul, the spirit's spirit, hidden and concealed from all."[143] Man himself, then, has but to gaze into a looking glass to recognize himself, to understand that his whole being is but a kind of portrait, a symbolic representation whose physicality enciphers his spiritual essence. The dualism of body and soul so central to Jewish thought leads us back to the primary dynamic of symbolization itself: the tangible counterpart, the symbol (here, the human body) is in effect a vessel holding another, abstract and wholly intangible entity—the soul, in the divine image of Man.

The tale *The Seven Beggars*, I would suggest, is emblematic of the intertextuality that pervades Reb Nahman's oeuvre. As we become aware of the nature of this intertextuality, we may begin to appreciate its full effect in creating the dimension of the fantastic. The superimposition of layers and associations, so acute in Reb Nahman's works, is in fact present, according to Russian structuralist literary theory, in every text. Mikhail Bakhtin speaks of the dialogical relations that exist, on the most molecular level, between an utterance and those that precede it. "For the poet, language is actually totally saturated with living intonations. . . . The artist receives no word in linguistically virginal form. The word is already impregnated by the practical situations and the poetic contexts in which he has encountered it. As a result, every text unavoidably presupposes a system of signs everyone can understand—conventional, reiterative, and reproducible."[144] Every text, then, every combination of words is engaged in implicit discourse with innumerable works that came before it. When we adopt this notion to contemplate the primordial text embodied, in the kabbalistic world view, in the book of Genesis, we discover that therein are contained the pure tones, the creative language of God Himself. All that lives is an expression of that sublime language. Man appropriates this originating speech, adding his own resonances, to give his own names to the elements of his world. And thus dialogue is born, engaging every subsequent human composer of words. Each one gathers up the echoing remains of those first utterances, joining them in new, unexpected chords, to form a melody that is his alone.[145]

Yet every text, Bakhtin continues, has an opposite pole as well: it is also individual, unique, nonreiterative, and *therein* lies all its meaning. It is this delicate balance between the echo and the new song that I would like to focus on in the following pages. The words and the images of Reb Nahman's tales indeed reverberate with associations. Yet within that crowd of sounds a still, small voice may be heard, speaking of something that has never been said before. It is that voice that compels us not to be deceived by familiar figures. What is imperative, as Todorov says, is to take each image literally.[146] And, moreover, that double game of reflection and innovation leads us, unfailingly, back to the dimension of the fantastic.

Let us turn, now, to some of the symbols, laden with age-old meanings and yet newborn, that people the tales Reb Nahman told. The typology that follows is an attempt to reconsider three collective images in Hebrew literary tradition. All three have become quasi-cultural symbols within the Jewish world. Through untold transformations, much of their original numinosity still shimmers within them,[147] and in the tales they are innocently planted as moments of eternal truth.

The first element I would like to explore is *water*. As the Bible recounts, the world itself was created by the momentous separation of the upper and lower waters; rain, the sign of God's mercy upon His seedling world, manifests for all the generations of man the connection between human needs and divine responsiveness. The search for understanding, for enlightenment, empowers us like the deer's longing to drink from cool springs. In the dry land of the Bible (and not only there), water sources represent magnetic fields of truth. In many ways, they are places of meeting: places where separate destinies intersect (Isaac and Rebecca; Jacob and Rachel; Moses and Zipporah), where prophets hear the word of God, or the embodiment of a dynamic principle ("And a river went out of Eden to water the garden" [Gen. 2:10]; "All rivers flow to the sea" [Eccl. 1:7]). Such compelling imagery becomes a vital element in rabbinic literature as well, and it comes as no surprise that Reb Nahman's tales both perpetuate that symbolic system and reflect the romantic fascination, in his own day, with the watery element of nature.[148] From the river of wine *(Lost Princess)*, the ocean of milk *(Master of Prayer)*, the heartrending spring *(Seven Beggars)*, the stormy seas *(King and Kaiser)*, and the unleashed floods *(The Cripple)*, to the seven enigmatic places of water *(Burgher and Poor Man)*, we realize that this polymorphous symbol carries great significance—perhaps subconscious as well as conscious—in his worldview. Let us turn to this last, composite symbol, the "seven places of water" that mark the secret path traced and retraced by the protagonists of *Burgher and Poor Man*.

The poor man's wife, kidnapped by an evil general, is rescued thanks to the mad daring of the burgher. As the two flee, they are forced to conceal themselves from pursuers in a well filled with rainwater. In that dark, close space, overcome with gratitude, the pious woman swears to her rescuer, in reward for his heroism, that any gift fortune sends her will be his. Such an oath, however, must of course be confirmed by a witness. Alone together, the only witness to be found is the well itself, and so it bears witness to her portentous promise. The man and woman continue their escape, hiding in six more places of water—after the well, in a *mikveh*, a pond, a spring, a stream, a river, and finally the sea, which brings them back home again at last. Their chastity throughout the precarious escape is recompensed; the childless burgher and his wife are blessed with a son, while the barren woman and her husband are given a beautiful daughter. Loyal to the indisputable laws of a fairy-tale world, the two children must be destined for each other; the rest of the story proves the force of that oath, which ultimately conquers all human wiles to circumvent it. In the comments that follow, I would like to consider some textual associations aroused by this story and try to understand Reb Nahman's transformation of this prevalent symbol—water in general and the seven places of water in particular.

We recall, from early aggadic descriptions, the implicit sexual valence perceived in the places where water gathers: "The floods of rain that fall to the earth—they are masculine waters, and the underground caches that emerge from the depths—they are feminine waters, and the two join with each other."[149] Thus by their very genesis, our lakes, springs, and seas, formed of waters from the heavens and the earth's abyss, have a certain intimacy, offering a natural and highly charged meeting place for man and woman. The fateful oath uttered by the poor man's wife and its curious damp witness lead us back to a kindred folk tradition, recounted by Rashi:

> Once there was a girl who wished to go to her father's house; on the way was a well and she fell into it. A boy came along and said to her, If I take you out of it, will you marry me? She answered, Yes, and they swore to each other that he would not marry another woman, nor she another man. And they said, Who will bear witness between us? Just then, a rat walked by the well and the two said, The well and the rat will be our witnesses. And each went his way. Well, she kept her promise but he married another woman, who bore a son. A rat came and bit him, and he died.

> She bore a second son, but he fell into a well and died too. His wife said to him, Why has all this befallen us, us and no one else? Then he remembered his oath, and told his wife the whole story. When he finished she said to him, Go back and take her. He wrote his wife a bill of divorce, and went and married the maiden. Thence it is said, "Believe in the well and the rat, for they bore witness."[150]

As we see in Reb Nahman's tale, the seven places of water testify to an identical pact between the children of the poor man's wife and the burgher. Each of the daughter's suitors can hope to convince her of his true identity as her promised one only by recharting the legendary path that led to their birth. Neither the hellish pirate nor the sea's high waters can keep the oath from being fulfilled.

The number 7 in this story remains allusively significant. Beyond the *mikveh*, the other places are only listed one after another like the words of a secret charm, or alluded to as "the seven places" (*SW*, pp. 112, 121, 131, 133). Yet the effect in the tale of their combined presence, the map of interconnected loci of truth, cannot be ignored. The boundless source of water in the heavens, the rain's descent to the earth, its gathering and flowing imperceptibly, inevitably, to the great seas—this image of continual movement illustrates, of course, the classic kabbalistic concept of emanation, from *Hokhmah* down to the six lower *sefirot* in their earthly form.[151] Although the image never becomes explicit in the tale itself, it guides the narrator's listener unfailingly to the esoteric reaches beyond itself.

The events of *Burgher and Poor Man* are modeled by one additional motif as well: the seven bodies of water mark both a moral test and a path of purification. The beautiful heroine rejects each false beloved with the words "But the waters have not passed over you" (*SM*, p. 121)—You have not endured a trial of faith.[152] The seven places of water, then, become a constellation of secret signs; lost, forgotten, searched for, discovered, they guide the tale to its messianic end.

The second element I would like to consider whirls through many of the stories. It serves each time as a pivot on which the plot turns drastically, yet remains mutely referential in every case. That element is the storm wind. The story *King and Kaiser* begins as a storm wind seemingly possessed, like the wind in the prophet Jonah's story, with a will of its own carries the heroine out to sea. In *Burgher and Poor*

Man, the course of the protagonists' lives is altered over and over again by storm winds: the hero is shipwrecked (*SM*, p. 118); he is shocked from lethargy on his desert island when a storm wind rips through the woods, uprooting the tree where he has hidden the map that promises him his betrothed (*SM*, p. 122). Meanwhile, the heroine, in the clutches of the evil eunuch, is cast by a storm wind upon the shores of the same island (*SM*, p. 133), where the paths of the two eventually cross once again. It is a storm wind, similarly, that drives the blind beggar's fellows to take refuge in their tower *(Seven Beggars)*. In all of these cases, the storm wind is a narrative element that furthers the plot of the story and clearly reflects biblical imagery. The sight of waves raging in a stormy sea reveals God's awe-inspiring might (Ps. 107:25). Yet from the Bible we learn a basic lesson about divine providence concealed in nature: although the storm wind wreaks havoc, like all of creation, it is subservient to His will (Ps. 148:8). In the *Zohar*, the storm wind becomes personified through a linguistic play between storm *(saʿar)* and Esau *(seʿir)*, the epitome of evil in the non-Jewish world. Reb Nahman, guided by the colorful imagery there, declares that the "tempest-tossed" nation of Israel (Is. 54:11), caught in the whirlwind of Esau's impurity, will nevertheless not remain there forever. In the end, a life-giving wind will revive it, driving away the tumult of the storm.[153]

But most telling of all is the story of *The Master of Prayer*; there, the legendary kingdom is thrown into chaos by a storm wind that changes the surface of the world itself, rendering it unrecognizable. Diabolically, the storm wind enters the king's very own house and snatches the queen's infant from her arms (*SM*, p. 196). This tragic event, which catalyzes the entire story, illuminates an additional aspect of this recurring symbol's power. The midrash recounts what happened on the fatal Ninth of Av, the day the Temple in Jerusalem was destroyed twice over. On that very day a baby, Menahem ben Hezkiyah, was born, and the same day of the disaster, his tearful mother relates, "a stormy wind came and snatched him out of my hands and carried him away."[154] The infant, of course, is the Messiah; his loss causes his people to search for him with the pathos they would have searching for a stolen son, transparently represented as the infant of *The Master of Prayer*. Thus, the storm wind evokes both a sense of helplessness before God's wrath and a realization that disregard for Him (in the age of the Temple's destruction) invited the forces of chaos to be unleashed upon unsuspecting souls.

The third, and perhaps most gripping, image in Reb Nahman's oeuvre is that of *hands*. In chapter 2 we spoke of the human palm as one of the main symbolic texts scattered through his world. Here, if you will, our subject is whole hands, their movements and the understanding they point to, far beyond their own physical presence.

Indeed, the term "referent," so popular in the jargon of literary criticism, reflects the quintessentially *handlike* nature of symbols: extended before our faces, they direct our attention elsewhere, toward more abstruse correlatives. In an image in *Likkutei Moharan*, which will serve to introduce our theme, Reb Nahman describes the vital importance of hands in keeping one afloat in the "sea of wisdom."[155] The boundlessness of the sea, its impenetrable mystery, and the vulnerability of a human being paddling weakly in its midst initiates the comparison (not Reb Nahman's invention) with infinite divine wisdom. Each day, within the four walls of the *beit midrash*, all who learn Torah plunge themselves into that endless sea. The rebbe, a spiritual guide and source of buoyancy, can convey his most profound understanding only through suggestion: "The hands that are in the sea of wisdom—those are allusions. For when a wise man, at times, reveals his wisdom, he utters a word that hints certain hints to his students, things he cannot say explicitly." The signs the rebbe relays—we can understand them as nothing other than the gestures he makes with his hands. Those physical movements, which accompany his speech, add a vital dimension to the truth he wishes to impart. This lively picture of the gesticulating *hasid*, however contemporary it may seem, is in fact inspired by a classic mystical exegesis on the Hebrew letter *aleph*: the diagonal stroke is like a human body, and the two "arms" (which the scribe forms by writing two inverted *yods*) evoke the outstretched hands *(yodayim)* of the excited speaker.[156]

Yet hands, for Reb Nahman, do much more than merely accompany speech. Perhaps the most widespread anthropomorphic symbol of the Bible, hands are evoked in myriad expressions to describe the nature of God Himself and His involvement in the world. Reb Nahman resists the philosophical reductionism of, most prominently, Maimonides, who holds that "the hand of God" must be understood as no more than a symbol of divine influence, as in describing the phenomenon of prophecy. For Reb Nahman, hands are actual containers of spiritual power; they are the essence of being itself, as well as the source of revelation.[157]

Indeed, hands may be mute indicators. Yet they are also the epitome of *action*, of bringing into being. Folded hands, it would follow, are the sign of inaction, of stasis. This principle leads Reb Nahman to the fundamental kabbalistic notion of the right and left hands of God, their corresponding attributes of potentiality and actuality, and their necessary combined action in God's engendering the world. In the beginning, "His two hands, so to speak, were still held together. That is, they had not yet spread and separated . . . there was yet no distinction between right and left. This, then, was before the Creation, before potentiality had been actualized. Until 'My hand laid the foundation of the earth, and my right hand spanned the heavens' (Is. 48:13)."[158] God, in this image, stands poised like a noble conductor, his arms clasped behind Him, in a hall shrouded in silence. Slowly He raises His hands; the lights rise. And all of a sudden His hands break into movement, the orchestra is there, and the music begins.[159]

The orchestra master calls the concert into being. But what about the musicians themselves—who sit, their instruments in their hands, and, by breathing life into cold brass and silver, by drawing a bow across mute strings, give them voice and song? The figure of the musician, the minstrel, the prophet, is perceived, from the earliest phase of Western culture, as invested with a spirit not his own, which enables him to express, in poetry or in music, truths unknown to other men.[160] In his oeuvre, Reb Nahman spins an intricate web of connections between the vital action of the artist's hands with his gift of divine inspiration, the meeting between this "holy spirit" *[ru'ah ha-kodesh]* and the musician's own breath *(ru'ah)*, and the ultimate importance of the dexterous, inspired prophet-musician, in both a spiritual and eschatological sense. The focus of the following discussion will be the character of the handless beggar, the final guest to appear at the wedding of the orphan children and tell his story, the most complex story of all. The hands he seems to lack and their truly fortuitous power provide the link between this beggar and two monumental figures of Jewish tradition, Moses and David. Moreover, those hands point to a resolution of the multiplied symbol, the rose of concentric tens evoked in the last pages of his story.[161]

The handless beggar prefaces his narrative with the pronouncement: "Really, my lack of hands is no flaw, in fact I have great power; it's just that I don't use the strength of my hands in this world, for I need that strength elsewhere. The fortress that is called 'the palace of water' can confirm all this" (*SM,* p. 275). He then proceeds, like the beggars before him, to tell of a competition: a number of individuals, one after another, boast of the strength of their hands and the wondrous things they can do. Our hero responds to each one that his talent is ridiculously partial: the first can return a poisoned arrow after it has been shot, but there are nine other kinds of arrows and nine other kinds of poison; another can confer his own knowledge to a worthy few by a laying on of his hands, but there are ten measures of knowledge; another can capture and calm a storm wind, but there are ten sorts of wind, and so forth. The final blow the handless beggar deals each competitor is the cryptic rebuke: "But you cannot heal the princess . . . of ten arrows, you can return only one; of ten pulses you can take only one; and you know only one of the ten melodies that will restore her." Finally, stymied, they challenge him: "What, then, can *you* do?" And so the handless hero is persuaded to tell the story of the princess in distress. Forced to flee from a jealous and enamored king who seeks her ruin, she has found refuge in an enchanted castle, surrounded by waves and walls of water. There the princess waits, fainting with weariness. The handless beggar masters all the talents the others profess; he alone can return all the king's poisoned arrows, can penetrate the watery barriers without drowning, can revive her by sensing her pulse and, finally, save her life with his ten-voiced melody (*SM,* pp. 277–81). A composite figure, he is at once musician, doctor, warrior, seer. In order to understand his raison d'être, we must turn first to *Likkutei Moharan* and then to the roots of Reb Nahman's thought in rabbinic and mystical tradition.

The crucial link between divine inspiration and the movement of hands lies in Reb Nahman's literal understanding, set out in *Likkutei Moharan,*[162] of biblical accounts of prophecy. Hoshea (12:11) relays God's declaration: "I have also spoken by the prophets, and I have multiplied visions, and used similes *by the hand* of the prophets."

Intermediaries conveying the words of God, the prophets must be aroused to receive their message, and here the vital role of hands is made explicit: Elisha the prophet calls for a minstrel, "and as the musician played, God's hand came upon him" (2 Kings 3:15). Reb Nahman explains: "When the prophet hears that melody played by the wise bard, he is given the spirit of prophecy from his hand. . . ." That hand, though, is not simply an open palm, spread to receive its gift from above. Rather, it must be a distinguishing hand, "able to gather together the good from amidst the evil." Here, then, we glimpse the true nature of the prophet's greatness: he is blessed with the spirit of God because he strives to make his own spirit pure; his song is born by the breath of his mouth and the work of ready hands. The connection, of course, turns on the polysemous Hebrew word *ru'ah*, which may designate at once spirit, inspiration, breath, and wind, as well as sadness, evil, depression. The musician's own breath makes his instrument come alive, but it is his hands that, finally, transform sound into melody. Music, then, emerges only when pure air is winnowed from the winds of impurity. "To play on a musical instrument means to gather up good wind from base wind, from sadness. Indeed, music of holiness is truly sublime; when the good is separated from the evil, melodies and song are born."[163] The music of the prophet-bards was no mere source of entertainment in the lives of the biblical kings. When King Saul was overwhelmed with spirits of evil, "David took a lyre and played with his hand: so Saul was refreshed, and was well, and the evil spirit departed from him" (1 Sam. 16:23). The young musician is Saul's fleeting salvation; the power of music alone can rescue him from the grip of melancholy. David's wisdom, then, is in his triumph over the forces of evil, in his ability to build a melody, "rising and descending on the instrument he plays, establishing happiness in all its fullness."[164] Once again, hands are the essential element in this enterprise, for it is they that contain and direct all spirit/winds.[165]

This conception of the inspired musician-prophet composed from portraits that fill the Bible is transplanted, in Reb Nahman's worldview, to the soil of nineteenth-century Ukraine and reincarnated in the zaddik, the spiritual leader of the Hasidic community. It is this identification that offers the first hint of the meaning of the handless beggar's healing powers.

Music and the joy it arouses, perhaps the most well-known element of Bratslav Hasidism, became, in the hands of the zaddik, a potent weapon against the social and economic hardships that weighed on his community. But the adjuration to "be happy," far from being a platitude, actually mandates a fierce battle against sadness. This striving to reach a higher state from which evil is banished reflects a fundamental conviction, voiced in the Talmud, that God's presence dwells in this world only where happiness reigns: "The Shekhinah does not abide in places of laziness, nor of sadness, nor of ridicule nor foolishness nor vanity, but only in happiness. . . ." But how can that so essential, yet so elusive, precondition be attained? The answer is found in the already-familiar prooftext the Talmud offers: "Now bring me a musician, and when the musician played, God's hand came upon him" (2 Kings 3:15).[166] R. Nathan speaks directly of the effect of music in engendering spiritual growth: "Turning despair and gloom to happiness, that is the essence of refining the spirit of good from evil . . . for the voices of song have the power to break man's heart and help him rise, to pull him ever closer to God. . . ."[167] Through this image of the zaddik and his melodies, we reach the first explanation of the handless beggar's powers. He masters all ten types of song, the ten modes in which King David was inspired to compose the book of Psalms. The arsenal of these ten modes alone, mystical tradition teaches, can defeat all the forces of evil.[168] And so the handless beggar, a humble *hasid*, sits before the princess and plays her a *niggun*, and it is that simple tune and the gladness it brings that will draw her out of her despair, out of her watery prison.

The sweet singer of Israel, David the shepherd king with his ten-stringed harp provides a rich model, throughout Jewish tradition, of God's impassioned servant. The sages remark on the effortlessness of his inspiration: "R. Simeon Hasida said, David's harp was hung above his bed, and when midnight came, a northern breeze would blow through it, and it would play by itself."[169] The utter freedom of that melody, unencumbered by any musician's ego, roused by the world's winds themselves is a captivating symbol of poetic inspiration in its most ideal form. In the romantic mind, this image becomes an aspiration. Shelley in his "Ode to the West Wind" implores:

> Make me thy lyre, even as the forest is:
> What if my leaves are falling like its own!
> The tumult of thy mighty harmonies

Will take from both a deep, autumnal tone,
Sweet though in sadness. Be thou, Spirit fierce,
My spirit! Be thou me, impetuous one!

Drive my dead thoughts over the universe
Like withered leaves. . . .

The European romantics of the nineteenth century are drawn to a pantheistic fusion between the "spirit of nature," artistic creativity, and the "divine Spirit." Reb Nahman's romanticism, tempered by the tenets of Judaism, leads him to combine—without merging—cosmic pneumatics, human respiration, and God's animating power in a brilliant mosaic, held together by language and the chords it conceals.

R. Simeon Hasida's comment suggests a fundamental metonymy between David's harp and the prophet himself. The Baʿal Shem Tov sharpens the association in his warning that only when one aspires to transmit God's truth without distracting self-consciousness, without flaunting one's own voice, as the instrument itself sings, will one be worthy of divine inspiration.[170] The human spirit and the spirit of God thus meet, uniting in the body of the instrument, of the player himself. And the fruit of this union is words of prayer, of praise, of insight. The correspondence, far from accidental, between the two "spirits" is verified over and over in myriad contexts. One of the most illuminating in terms of the handless beggar's story is found in *Tikkunei Zohar*, where the relationship is set out in detail: "The north wind blew through David's harp. And that wind struck the five strings, which are the five laps of the lungs, and the voice passes from the heart through the windpipe."[171] Magically, man's body becomes simultaneously a stringed instrument and a wind instrument, composed of tubes and cords enabling the generation of his song, that is, his life. In this image, the musician's hands are conspicuously absent, perhaps because they have nothing to refine. An unsettling thought though it may seem, hands become obsolete in a utopian world of holiness. Thus, the nightmarish dream told in the Talmud of one's hands having been cut off is interpreted as a promising portent: "You will no longer need the work of your hands."[172] As for the handless beggar, he is as spiritually innocent as a selfless instrument. Uncontaminated by evil, the pure wind of inspiration that fills him is exclusively good; thus the beggar's whole being may sing in harmony, of its own accord.

As we learn from Onkelos's interpretation of the biblical Creation story, man's very ability to express himself verbally is by grace of God's own spirit within him. "And the Lord God formed man of the dust of the ground, and breathed into his nostrils the breath of life; and man became a living soul" (Gen. 2:7). Onkelos translates into Aramaic the last words of the verse: "And man became a *speaking* spirit." Speech, then, is an integral aspect of man's humanness; the moment he begins to breathe he cannot be silent: as the Talmud attests, he immediately breaks into a soliloquy of praise and thanks.[173]

Man is *animated*—both brought to life and invested with his anima—by receiving within his earthly form the breath of God Himself. Yet the human spirit remains, nonetheless, as volatile as alcoholic spirits, as diffusive as the wind, as evanescent as the very air we breathe. The verbal correspondence of breath *(neshimah)* and soul *(neshamah)*, transparently evident in Hebrew, is an eternal reminder of the genetic connection between the two. It recalls both man's haunting mortality (without his soul, he returns to dust) and his immortal essence (the soul that will leave him at death as a bird flies from its cage). Browning avers this incommensurability: "But the soul is not the body, and the breath is not the flute."[174] The two, though, remain somehow interdependent: without the north wind, David's harp would hang silent, yet, if not for the harp, the wind could blow and blow and never turn into melody.

Who, the, is the princess in the watery castle; what is her part in this web of pneumatic symbolism? R. Nathan reminds us of what we may have forgotten, that "the queen's daughter alludes to the *Shekhinah*, the Assembly of Israel, the assembled souls of all Jews. . . . Only he [the handless beggar] can breach the ten walls of water and come to the place where she has lain, unconscious, for hundreds and hundreds of years."[175] A sleeping beauty, cut off from the world, suspended in timeless waiting, she yearns for her Prince Charming. But centuries before Perrault's fairy tale, *Tikkunei Zohar* has already told the beggar's story, that is, the legend of Sleeping Beauty.[176]

The seeds of the tale are sown in the Song of Songs. Languishing in loneliness, the heroine's voice rises: "I charge you, O daughters of Jerusalem, if you find my beloved, that you tell him I am sick with love" (5:8). The author of *Tikkunei Zohar* describes the Shekhinah in her exile as near to death; she has no strength left, her breathing has grown shallow, her pulse is weak. Many wise men (forefathers of the handless beggar's competitors) come to revive her with spices, pomegranates, nuts, and roses, "Yet her pulse is not restored, until the faithful shepherd comes. He brings with him an apple; she breathes its fragrance and her spirit is restored to her." His merciful resuscitation is what brings the dis-spirited Shekhinah back to life, enabling her, at last, to respire. To emerge from the narrow, airless distress of exile, to breathe freely once again—this possibility is the harbinger of redemption, for "the breath of our nostrils [is] the anointed of the Lord" (Lam. 4:20).

Lest we suppose all this is but a fairy tale, Reb Nahman brings the apocalyptic vision home to his followers: "Know, that in each and every generation there is such a shepherd, and he is an aspect of Moses, the Faithful Shepherd." Every generation has its zaddik, "gifted to make melodies by gathering the bits of good that exist in each and every Jew."[177] The handless beggar is an embodiment of that zaddik. And the princess—she is the collective soul of Israel as well—enchained with each Jew in his own spiritual estrangement from God. We return to *Tikkunei Zohar* and the exegesis there of the Song of Songs. "'Hark, my beloved is knocking' (5:2). The soul comes and knocks upon the gates of the heart . . . and implores, 'Open to me, my sister, my love, my dove, my undefiled' (5:2)." The pounding upon a locked door—this, the author of *Tikkunei Zohar* says, is the sound of the shofar, signaling to the princess, in the traditional code of ten notes, how long her exile will endure.[178] But the shofar, from year to year, plays an urgent role in the religious life of each individual as well. Between Rosh ha-Shanah and Yom Kippur, its call sounds repeatedly, entreating hardened hearts to open, shaking awake those sleeping the enchanted sleep of sin.[179] R. Nathan comments that during those ten days of awe, the ten voices of the shofar evoke ten sorts of melody; when people open themselves to their Maker, draw near Him once again, their imprisoning alienation is transformed to happiness.[180]

The being of the handless beggar, in Reb Nahman's eyes, is epitomized in the verse of Proverbs (30:4) which seems (!) to speak of God: "Who has ascended up to heaven and come down again? Who has gathered the wind in his fists? Who has bound the waters in a garment? Who has established all the ends of the earth?" It is the inspired musician, Reb Nahman teaches, who rises and descends with his melody, collecting amorphous wind into harmonious breath; the "winds" he gathers in his fists are spirits as well—as a spiritual leader, he guides and unites the souls of his community.[181] That community is the embodiment of the Assembly of Israel, the daughter of the queen, whose spirit he alone is able to redeem and restore by his masterful handless playing.

The symbols we have chosen to discuss—hands, the storm wind, and water—are but three examples among many, for Reb Nahman's stories are peopled with such multifaceted signs. Their dual nature—seemingly innocent elements, yet concealing wells of ingathered allusion—grants them tremendous power. Symbols, in other words, number among the disguises so vital in the play of the fantastic.

Metaphor

In the contest for the title of champion metaphorist, the hunchbacked beggar nearly meets his match in the final competitor, who boasts that, despite his diminutive stature, he has the vital role of leading an immense being, poor yet filled with light *(sagi nahor)*. Instinctively, our perceptive beggar recognizes the helpless giant: "He means that he leads the moon, who is blind, for he has no light of his own . . . yet the world's very existence depends on him, for the world needs the moon" (*SM*, p. 271). How did Reb Nahman come to invent this bizarre figure? Implanted in no larger fictional context, he seems to float freely in the fantastic atmosphere of *The Seven Beggars*, as anomalous as the other creatures with strange powers that people this story. The "poor, blind giant," I would suggest, is a personification of *metaphor* itself. A monumental figure charged with hidden resonances, his identity is a nexus of linguistic manipulations. Metaphors employed in biblical, talmudic, and aggadic sources to describe the moon and its attributes become, in the *sagi nahor*, a literal reality.

Let us begin with his strange name. The poverty-stricken, sightless giant is called by the euphemism used in rabbinic literature to speak of people bankrupt or blind—*sagi nahor* (full of light).[182] In truth, the moon is poor; it has no light of its own, and all its white gleam is but an illusion. Both the moon and a blind man's eyes know nothing but darkness; the man's only light is from his name, the moon's is reflected from the sun. Reb Nahman adopts the euphemism used by the rabbis to speak of human blindness and poverty and transfers it to speak of the moon's nonluminary nature. Yet the euphemism also conceals a paradox with vital historical implications. For the midrash recounts that, in actuality, the moon itself was ignominiously impoverished soon after God brought it into being. In an attempt to contend with the contradiction implicit in the verse "And God made the two great lights; the greater light to rule the day and the lesser light to rule the night" (Gen. 1:16), R. Simeon ben Pazi explains that, although originally created as the sun's equal ("the two great lights"), it was the moon's tragic hubris that brought it to ruin. "The moon came before God and protested, Lord of the Universe, can two kings wear a single crown? He responded, Go and diminish yourself!"[183] Thus, because it desired exclusive reign over the world, the moon was chastised by becoming "the lesser light."

Like all the figures in the hunchbacked beggar's tale, however, the blind giant also illustrates the principle of "the little that contains a lot," and this attribute contains the secret of the moon's destiny. The question, then, is: in what sense is the moon, or the poor, blind giant "manifold"? The small man who leads him claims that the world owes its very existence to the moon; this suggestion also originates in the source quoted above.[184] After its embarrassing demotion, the moon is partly consoled by God's urging: "Go then, and the people of Israel will measure the days and years by you, and you will be a sign, fixing the festivals. . . ." Indeed, Jewish religious life is guided by the moon's orbit. Were it to disappear, the monthly and yearly cycle could not be calculated; following a fantastic logical extrapolation, time would cease to exist, the Jewish nation would crumble. Thus the moon's responsibility toward the people of Israel is momentous. But what is more, the boundless sunlight the blind giant contains intimates the inward truth of the euphemism: the moon's affliction will not endure forever; full light will one day become its own; glory will return, crowning the true king with honor. That once and future king, of course, is the Messiah in the person of King David.[185] We see, then, that from the most ancient midrashic sources, the moon's transformation—its perpetual rebirth as a faint and vulnerable sliver, gradual waxing to round and perfect shining signifying redemption—this cycle speaks of the promised restoration of the Jewish nation. Just as God gives light to the blind, so the moon will, once again, regain its original luminary power. In the beggar's tale, metaphorical descriptions of blindness, of diminution and poverty, and of the moon itself, gleaned from many sources, are gathered together in the person of the sightless giant "full of light."

Reb Nahman's art of literalizing such metaphors is what serves to create the fantastic personages of his stories. Yet this technique is, in fact, not at all original. On the contrary, it perpetuates a well-established tradition of scriptural exegesis. The insights of Dan Ben Amos, though his own theme is the talmudic genre he calls "tall tales," may shed much light on Reb Nahman's tales as well. He speaks of the "rhetorical mode of distancing" that such talmudic anecdotes employ. An example of a tale of that genre appears in B.T. *Ketubbot:*

> Rami bar Ezekiel once paid a visit to Benei Berak where he saw goats grazing under fig trees, while honey was flowing from the figs and milk ran from them, and these mingled with each other. He exclaimed, This is indeed "A land flowing with milk and honey"![186]

In this scene, the verse "a land flowing with milk and honey" is understood, not as a poetic image conjuring a *sense* of ease and plenty, but as reality. The metaphor becomes a concrete "statement of truth, a denotative, factual description rather than a connotative, symbolic expression." The distancing characteristic of talmudic "tall tales" occurs in linguistic terms, as biblical verses are removed from their original position in the language and transplanted to another, tropic mode of language use.[187] Todorov recognizes, similarly, that the supernatural world of fantasy is created in the moment "when we shift from the words to the things those words are supposed to designate."[188]

In Reb Nahman's oeuvre, we find a classic case of such concretization of biblical as well as rabbinic metaphor in the tale told by the first beggar. In a cryptic phrase, he hints at the double paradox of his infant agedness and mysterious blindness, and at its inner meaning. "I am not really blind at all, it's just that all the time of this world is no more to me than the blink of an eye" (*SM*, p. 243). What he seems to suggest is that temporal perception as well as vision are absolutely relative matters. With his superhuman stature, he indeed does not see the vanities of this world, but the underlying suggestion is that it is his audience who is truly blind to the monumental movement of history and of cosmic change—all this we are too shortsighted to grasp. The juxtaposition between realms of time seen from human perspective, or conversely from divine perspective, is exposed in Ps. 90:4—"For a thousand years in Your sight are but like yesterday when it is past, and like a watch in the night." The metaphor the beggar chooses to describe his blindness, though, has a past all its own. Literally, the expression "the blink of an eye" speaks of the momentary state, repeated every few instants, in which the eyelid closes, blocking the physical world from the seeing eye. Figuratively, it means an infinitesimal, fleeting period of time. We meet this expression in the Talmud in R. Yose's attempt to define that illusive moment of twilight "between the luminaries"—after the sun has set and before the moon and stars are visible. That evanescent between-time, he says, "is like the blink of an eye—the one goes in and the other comes out, and it is impossible to witness it."[189]

Reflections on the elusive passage of time combine with meditations on mortality in the *Zohar*, where the same phrase serves as a metaphor of human experience itself. R. Yohanan sets the tone with a verse from the Song of Songs: "Before the day cools and the shadows flee away, turn, my beloved, and be like a gazelle or a young hart" (2:17). Those moments when the day is about to pass away, he teaches, remind man that "all his life, as long as he is in the world, is but the blink of an eye. See, it is written: 'For though he live a thousand years two times told . . . does all not go to one place?' (Eccl. 6:6). On his dying day, all that had been is, for him, as a single day."[190] As the shadows flee into the darkness, so a life as it ends slips into the night. We disregard the instants of blindness (when we blink) that fill our days; yet the whole of existence is, in effect, just as insignificant, a negligible moment in the universe of aeons. In the figure of the beggar, literal sense shifts to metaphorical: he *lives* the blink of the eye—in this world his eyes are as if unseeing. This life, relative to the vast time expanse he has experienced, is but a moment of darkness between two ages of light. Thus, his blindness has no substance at all. After his moment of sightless being, his eyes will open once again, and that past moment will, for him, be as naught.

Interestingly, though metaphors begin by distancing, we see that in a fantastic setting they come full circle. The moon truly is filled with light; that light is not yet its own but, in an age to come, it *will be*. Mortal life—not only *like* the blink of an eye—really *is* that fleeting moment. The blind beggar, through his very person, impresses his listeners with the full truth of his paradox.

Allegory

We turn, now, to the third form of figurative language outlined at the beginning of this part: allegory. Italo Calvino's brilliant and labyrinthine tale, *The Castle of Crossed Destinies,* is founded on what he calls "a fantastic iconology." The novel unfolds as the characters, one by one, mutely tell the story of their own lives by pointing to a series of cards of the Tarot spread out on a great oak table before them. It seems to me that Reb Nahman's oeuvre is, as well, a "fantastic iconology"; the images for his inspiration, rather than the mysterious Tarot, are the great portraits of the Bible, the visions of the prophets, the parabolic landscape of that world. As in *The Castle of Crossed Destinies,* he contemplates those images, and the stories that emerge are—at once—autobiography, imaginary narrative, and interpretation.[191]

The question of allegory is a slippery one. A text is present, phrased in certain language—but are its words a disguise, a parable veiling some existential meaning, or do those words embody the body itself, to be embraced in its simple, naked truth? For the rabbis, to recognize allegory as the simple meaning is mandated as a tenet of faith—witness the adjuration that the Song of Songs is not to be made a love song.[192] Thus, in midrashic as well as medieval commentary, allegory becomes a primary exegetical tool, playing a much more prominent role than the *pshat* or "simple" meaning. As we will see, Reb Nahman continues this hermeneutical tradition within his tales and theoretical works.

The diametrically opposed view to that of the sages is expressed in postromantic criticism. Here, all veils are torn away—the naked body, such reading contends, is all that matters. Northrop Frye, for example, holds that "the normal structure of allegory . . . does not fit the Bible, [which is] concerned with actual people and events."[193]

But it is the Kabbalists, of course, who voice a radical third alternative: what transfixes their gaze is neither the disguise nor the breathing form beneath it. In their eyes, all is transfigured: the body *itself* is a veil, a shadow—all its limbs reflect sublime, spiritual entities, and these entities are their true essence.[194] According to a mystical reading, therefore, the Torah actually speaks not only of a particular historical reality of defined moral attributes, nor of historical process, but of a divine order far beyond human understanding. The allegories that emerge in kabbalistic and Hasidic sources link these various levels in unending connections, and this mode of reading, in addition to the midrashic mode, is an essential model that guides Reb Nahman in creating and recreating his fantastic world.

Allegory and allegorical interpretation, in his oeuvre, appear in a number of forms: as the animation of a biblical pre-text expressed in poetic language; as the dramatization of a relationship between biblical personalities; as the arrangement of cultural symbols in a fantastic topology that becomes the setting for the tale's events. We must never forget that the images Reb Nahman sees before him, though originating in the Bible, are indelibly marked by generations of Jewish hermeneutical tradition. In the following pages, I hope to show Reb Nahman's simultaneous integration and transformation of existing allegories to invest the stories he told with their imaginative force. As we mentioned at the outset of this section, Reb Nahman's tales have, in turn, been subjected to allegorical interpretation, most perceptibly throughout the generations of Bratslav Hasidism. I have excluded these comments from the following discussion, certainly not because I question their value, but because they are not relevant to the matter at hand. The comments on the stories in *Likkutei Halakhot*, *Hayyei Moharan*, and *Sihot Haran* represent the second, removed degree of self-consciously generated allegory outlined above, in which the fantastic dimension cannot survive. The hesitation between modes of perception we described as inherent in that dimension is resolved in these texts, and the strangeness and anomalies are rationally explained as allusions to other texts and ideas. In the tales themselves, on the other hand, the presence of allegory remains implicit, and this is the core of their emotive and spiritual effect. Nonetheless, the references Reb Nahman's students provide are an invaluable aid in discovering the pre-texts that inspired their master in his own creative process.

The scaffolding of a number of the tales is an autonomous biblical passage. The events of the story, one after another, actualize the evocative verses of the text by giving life to its metaphors, by investing them with a connotative, literal meaning. In *The Cripple*, for example, Psalm 1 is animated—the protagonist can neither walk nor stand, and after the attack of bandits cannot even sit in his carriage. Throughout his trials, his overwhelming concern remains that the tree left by his father may be watered and flourish. The wicked, the chaff in the wind, the mockers, the paths that crisscross this psalm—all reappear in new guise, woven into the tale. Other examples of this perhaps most straightforward type of allegory through animation appear in *The Seven Beggars* in the tale of the third beggar, based on Psalm 61 (to be examined more closely below); in *Master of Prayer*, animating the chapter of Isaiah 31; and in *Fly and Spider* and its pre-text, Psalm 3.

In other tales, dramas that marked the lives of biblical figures are reenacted. This restaging of portentous scenes serves to evoke both a sense of uncanny familiarity with events in the unfolding tale and heightened expectation of the new, fantastic turns the drama may take. Key words often suggest the referential nature of the tale, alerting astute listeners to its allegorical aspect. Examples include the power struggle in *The Sons Who Were Reversed*, the king's true son playing the role of Jacob and the slave's true son that of Esau. When the pretender-king sells his birthright for a morsel of bread, the parallel finds overt expression. Similarly, in *Burgher and Poor Man*, the secret "signs" linking the hero to the heroine reflect the three "signs" that implicate Judah in his intrigue with Tamar, and the story of their tragic misplacement recounted in aggadic sources.[195]

Thirdly, the fantastic topology in which all the tales unfold is an amalgam of symbols, the legacy of midrashic and kabbalistic tradition, which combine freely to form a sort of allegory through mere association. The most striking instance of this third allegorical variation is the wondrous garden where *The Two Sons Who Were Reversed* climaxes. Motionless objects, enchanted as spellbound symbols, fill the silent, walled-in space. The petrified human figure, the mighty chair surrounded by wooden animals, the triumvirate of bed-table-lamp, the golden lion, the many-petaled rose—all these famous props will be awakened from their suspended animation by the hero, who can interpret and understand them with the aid of his magic box.[196]

In the examples above, allegory is the infrastructure for the building, the tale itself. Yet through his tales, we witness Reb Nahman's conviction that allegory is much more than a potent narrative tool; it is an inherent component of reality itself. In *Fly and Spider*, for example, the protagonist himself is led to discover the allegorical nature, first of his waking experiences, then of his dreams, and is finally led to a revelation concerning the mystery of his historical role in the world. Three times in the course of the tale, the king sees himself from without, as an actor in a parabolic scene. It is this triple encounter with allegory that gradually induces the king to assume his true destiny. The initial scene between the spider and the fly plants in the king's heart the suspicion that what he witnesses is no accidental event, but that it has been, somehow, placed in his path. The king's hypersensitivity to the symbolic valence of this scene illustrates what, in Reb Nahman's eyes, is a fundamental truth. All of nature is guided by God's hidden providence. Thus the king's compulsion to seek the meaning of what he sees expresses the most natural desire to decipher the divine message sent directly to him, and acted out by the two subhuman agents.[197] This first encounter with implicit allegory is followed by the king's second experience, his dream. Yet the meaning of the drama that enthralls him also remains beyond his grasp. Only when he reaches the ancient sage is he granted understanding of all that has befallen him—conscious and subconscious—by way of a third allegory, a waking vision in a cloud of incense. This final experience opens his eyes at last to the cosmic vista in which his soul actually moves, to his messianic responsibility in foiling the satanic foe.

A closer look at that strange priest with his mysterious alchemy, by the way, reveals another flash of inspiration in the mode of allegory that serves to conjure up the tale's fantastic atmosphere. After a trying search, fraught with foreboding, the king at last comes upon this sage, confides his dream, and requests an interpretation. The sage rejoins that he himself cannot explain it, but only on a certain day of a certain month does he compound the incense that can induce, in the dreamer himself, a superconscious vision. These few cryptic details, which envelop the sage himself in a cloud of mystery, point to the talmudic pretext from which he is born. R. Joshua ben Levi recounts that when Moses ascended on high, the ministering angels were up in arms. "Master of the Universe," they said, "what is a mortal, born of woman, doing in our midst?" God answers, "He has come to receive the Torah." They protest Moses' utter unsuitability for such an honor: the Torah, hidden away 974 generations before the world's creation—how could it be given to a creature of flesh and blood? God insists that Moses must answer in his own defense; Moses argues that the commandments are relevant to the conditions of human life alone, not to angelic existence. The angels are inspired by his logic, and surge forward to offer him gifts of good will. All this is to stage the enigmatic verse: "You have ascended on high, you have led captivity captive; you have received gifts from men . . ." (Ps. 68:19). Even the angel of death gave him something, R. Joshua ben Levi continues—and here we find the link to Reb Nahman's tale. As it is said of Aaron, "He put the incense [on the fire] and made atonement for the people. And he stood between the dead and the living" (Num.17:12–13). The gift bestowed by the angel of death, Rashi explains, is the secret of the incense; that compound has the power to halt the spread of plague by signaling the people's repentance for their sins.[198] Thus, the aggadic figure of Aaron and the cultic wisdom he possesses are transplanted into Reb Nahman's tale. The nameless sage makes good use of this invaluable gift in his Virgilian role of guiding the king through endless underworlds, spiraling beyond the throes of death and earthly life.

The Tale of Heart and Spring

As we saw in chapter 3, the romantic spirit that pervades Reb Nahman's worldview inspires him to speak of what can only be called, in the phrase of the English romantics, "the indwelling soul of nature." The lyric anthropomorphism born of his contemplation takes form in countless nature motifs throughout Reb Nahman's tales and *Likkutei Moharan*. Perhaps the most beautiful of these motifs, with far-reaching philosophical, theological, and ethical implications in his oeuvre, is presented, as an allegorical tale, in the third, mute beggar's gift in *Seven Beggars*. He begins:

> There is a mountain. On this mountain is a rock, and a spring flows from it. And the world, like every thing, has a heart; . . . well, the mountain, rock, and spring are at one end of the world while the heart of the world is at the other. That heart is turned toward the spring, and yearns and longs ceaselessly to come to the spring; filled with great desire, it even cries out to the spring. And the spring, too, pines for the heart. . . . But if the heart desires so ardently, why can he not go to the spring? Ah, because the moment he wishes to draw closer to the mountain, he can no longer see the incline of the mountain, and he loses sight of the spring. And if he cannot gaze upon the spring, his soul would go out of him, for he draws his very being from the spring. . . . So he can never reach the spring, but only long for it from afar. . . . (*SM*, pp. 257–59)

This consuming, unrequitable love, with all its emotional intensity, describes an archetypical relationship. The distance and existential longing endured by heart and spring echoes and reechoes in Reb Nahman's thought—in the quest of the *hasid* to approach his rebbe, in every Jew's desire to draw closer to God, even in the romance pulling the solid letters of the Hebrew alphabet to union with their soul, the vocal points. This multiple resonance is the most audible indication of the fundamentally allegorical nature of the beggar's words. Our exploration of his tale must follow two paths: one, to search out the preexisting sources on which Reb Nahman drew, and the other, to consider the variations on this theme, and the message they bring, elsewhere in his oeuvre. But before we begin, we must let the beggar end his tale. He introduces a countertheme:

> That spring—he is timeless, he is wholly beyond time. The only time the spring has is given him as a gift, day by day, from the heart. For when each day draws to its end, the spring's time would be used up, and [if not for the heart] it would perish, heaven forbid, and with it, the heart as well, and all the world would become nothingness. So, near the day's end, the two begin to take leave of one another, to "bid farewell," and they begin to speak secrets and wondrous songs to each other. . . . Then the merciful man of truth gives a day to the heart, and the heart gives that day to the spring, and once again time is his. . . . (*SM*, pp. 258–59)

The wrenching tension between heart and spring, we realize, engenders not a sense of futility or frustration, but rather a vital—indeed, essential—benefit, for it alone holds the power to perpetuate the world's existence.

The counterpoint of love and longing, of timeless being and temporal becoming, creates, in this tale, a polyphonic harmony. We hear certain themes from the same fugue, once again, in Reb Nahman's teaching concerning the ontology of language. The radically opposite essence of these letters and vowels, and their dynamic combination to form words, reenacts, on a molecular phonetic level, the love story of heart and spring. As Reb Nahman writes, "The vowel points must be drawn to the letters. For without the vowels, it would be impossible to say anything at all, as we know from our own experience. And when the vowel-points are drawn to the consonants, true speech can emerge; what was potential becomes actual."[199] In another, parallel passage, the interrelationship between vowels and consonants is portrayed yet more anthropomorphically. "The union and combination of the letters is effected by the vowel-points, for the vowels are the letters' vitality and mobility. Without the vowels, the consonants are a golem, totally bereft of movement."[200] In both passages, Reb Nahman subsequently reveals the secret of how these Pinocchio letters are imbued with a soul. "The vowel points and the consonants are drawn together by their desire and longing . . . that is the meaning of the verse in the Song of Songs (1:11), 'We will make you necklets of gold, studded with silver'" (lit. "points of silver," read alternately as "points of desire" based on the double meaning of the Hebrew root *KSF*). The second passage, likewise, continues, "The vowel points are love and longing, and that longing is the soul, for 'My soul longs, it fails for You' (Ps. 84:3)."

The romance of the phonemes, glimpsed in these two texts, is retold on a macroscopic level in man's relationship to God. The union of consonants and vowels, Reb Nahman explains, indeed gives birth to words, possessed of a soul. Yet, as long as these words remain *unspoken*, they lie dormant; they are animated only in the moment they are pronounced. And it is desire, once again, that stimulates this process as well. Every act of speech, Reb Nahman declares, must be preceded by a need to speak, must evolve from within, first as an embryonic thought.[201] Thought comes to realize itself, slowly growing to maturity in the secret places of the soul. Just as Romeo cannot gaze silently at Juliet's balcony but breaks into an impassioned soliloquy, so

> It is not enough for a person to yearn for God in his heart alone. He must express his longing with his own life, and so prayers are formed. The yearning of the heart engenders the soul with the vowels, but that soul remains in potentiality. Only when man externalizes his desire verbally—then *his own* soul becomes actualized.[202]

The proof, offered by Reb Nahman, that the soul can leave the body, not in death but in an act of *birth*, carried in human speech, is in a reverse reading of the verse "My soul went out with his words" (Song of Songs 5:6).

Yet, can we really imagine that the intrigue between the letters could result in such easy consummation, in their simple union and actualization? In a third text from *Likkutei Moharan*, the fugal song of heart and spring is sung once again, but here the paradox of timelessness in time is audible as well in the counterpoint to that first melody. The romance, in this case, is played out between the word, already formed, and the soul:

> When a person stands to pray, and says the words of his prayer, he is gathering blossoms and pleasant roses. Just as one walks through a field, picking flowers and joining them to make a single bouquet . . . so in prayer he goes from letter to letter until a number of letters are connected, and a word is formed. And these completed words are joined, one to another, and then he gathers more until he has finished a whole blessing.[203]

This would be the impossibly happy end of one person's idyll in the fair field of phonemes. But, Reb Nahman continues, the words are a desperate lover; they know the soul cannot rest silent, but must continue to speak, to wander, seeking other letters, words, and phrases to bring into being.

> And so the words begin to plead and beg the soul not to leave them. . . . "For how can you separate yourself from me? The intimacy and love between us is so very great. You have seen my beauty, my brilliance, my splendor and glory—how can you cut yourself off from me and abandon me? It is true, you must go on, must gather other treasures and precious things, but could you leave me, could you forget me? Whatever happens, wherever you go, never forget me, you must never forget me."

Reb Nahman's sympathy is with the words; indeed, the soul must be loyal to every letter it has spoken; not one must fade from his mind. That, he declares, is the highest form of prayer. "In every word a person utters, *all* the words of his prayers, from beginning to end, must be contained. When he has reached the last word, the first word must still be present. In that way, he can complete all his prayers without parting from even the first letter he utters."[204] Here, as in the story of heart and spring, continuity is juxtaposed with motionlessness in a logical paradox. A person speaks, gathering the scattered fragments of speech, and reaches the final words of his prayer, and yet he has not moved; after all the phrases he has pronounced, he still stands at the very first letter. And the spring—symbol of atemporal, continuous becoming, Heraclitus's endless stream of flowing moments—is still somehow kept alive only by the heart's gift of love *within time*, sung to it evening by evening.

When we turn to the most obvious allegorical sense of the tale, we realize that here, on the theosophical level as well, Reb Nahman's great sensitivity to human emotion has guided his imaginative vision. The experience lived by the heart, in the tale, is the unremitting dynamic between the relative and the absolute: man's distance from God, his desire to draw near, and yet the impossibility of any union in life.[205] André Neher, in his enlightening work, *The Exile of the Word*, speaks of "horizon silence." The boundary of the horizon is, for him, "a perpetual coincidence of bestowal and refusal"; like the place of the mountain and the spring, "the horizon is at the same time the thing most clearly seen by man and a thing he can never attain; it is the boundary, but the boundary of his true being."[206] Yet, this ambivalence of attraction and existential separateness, which pervades man's relationship with God, is, indeed, an intrinsic element; it cannot be annulled. Reb Nahman addresses the problem directly in *Likkutei Moharan:*

> For the Holy One, blessed be He, there must be both revealing and concealing: one must cleave to God, always approaching Him as if God were revealed and approachable. But the closer he draws to God, the more he must draw away. That is, though he nears God, he must know that he is very far from Him. For whoever thinks, even imagines to himself, that he has already come closer to God, and knows Him intimately, that is a sign he knows nothing at all. If he had even the smallest understanding of God, he would know how truly distant he is. . . .[207]

The heart of the world stands at the vantage point where the source of life is revealed in its (His) entirety. But the moment the heart attempts to move closer, terror and panic overtake it; "You hide your face and I am lost" (Ps. 30:8)—the features of His unknown countenance are suddenly gone. Desire leads to yet more terrible distance. Thus, it is the dialectic, born of separateness, of I and thou alone, "the tangible aspect of His unseizability," in Neher's words, that provides man the only possibility of maintaining any relationship at all with the transcendent, elusive mystery of God.

Having followed the path of the allegory of heart and spring through Reb Nahman's teachings in *Likkutei Moharan*, let us turn to its second branch, which leads through the leafy forest of his literary heritage. In his presentation of the characters in his allegory, Reb Nahman comments that "everything has a heart, and the heart of the world has a full stature, with face, hands, legs, etc." (*SM*, p. 257). In light of the heart's role in the tale that unfolds, we look to other stages on which the heart has played in its theatrical career. The concept of the heart of the cosmos, which finds close parallels in the Kabbalah and in the medieval philosophy of the *Kuzari* is expressed in this parable. All the nations of the world are like the organs of a body and Israel is the heart of the entire organism; like the heart, the chosen nation must fulfill essential functions through the course of history. R. Judah ha-Levi adds, "Our relationship to the Divine Influence is the same as that of the heart to the soul."[208] The spring, in turn, "without time" as God is beyond time, reflects the dynamic image of the fountain spoken of in the *Zohar*. The fountain springs from the depths of the mystical Nothing, or from a mystical Eden. All blessings flow from this fountain; divine life takes its course from it and streams through the emanation of all the *sefirot*, through all hidden reality.[209] Thus the two principal actors of the blind beggar's allegory clearly personify preeminent images of kabbalistic tradition.

In other details of his tale, as well, Reb Nahman makes use of images gleaned from earlier sources, creating a mosaic of inlaid allegory. He describes, for example, the pathos of the heart's predicament in this way: "The heart has two weaknesses. First, the sun persecutes him with its burning heat." Second, when his longing for the spring has brought him to exhaustion "and he must rest and catch his breath, a great bird comes and spreads its wings over him and shelters him from the sun" (*SM*, p. 258). It is the metaphorical conception of the *Zohar*, once again, that introduces the precursors of these two images planted in Reb Nahman's tale. The prophet Isaiah's theophany with the six-winged angels (Is. 6:1ff.) engenders a double allegory: the heart of Jewish faith, the Torah, is like the body of the angel, while the two wings that envelop its face are like the holy ark; just as the ark projects the precious Torah, so, in man's body, the "wings" of the lungs envelop the human heart. What is more, if not for the cooling breath of the lungs, the heart's burning heat would ignite the body and consume it utterly.[210]

The striking similarity between the allegory in *Tikkunei Zohar* and the image in the beggar's tale must be more than coincidence, and reflects, if nothing else, the effect such figures had on Reb Nahman's imagination.

But the most ancient pre-text for the beggar's allegorical tale is, undoubtedly, Psalm 61. Sung by King David, "the heart of Israel,"[211] the biblical text evokes the fugue of distance, love and timelessness echoed by the mute beggar's tale. "From the end of the earth I will call unto You, when my heart faints; lead me to a rock that is too high for me" (61:3). The fainting heart, searching for a path to ascend, declares, "I will trust in the covert of your wings" (61:5)—the compassionate shade of the "great bird." And in the same way the praying voice requests days and years of long life for the king, the prize of the heart's *lider* is also time. He promises to "sing praise to Your name for ever, as I perform my vows day by day" (61:9); the heart, as well, gives voice to its song dusk by dusk. And the spring's timeless answer of farewell, like the painted sky of evening, is a trust, a promise—that the world will endure another day.[212]

The allegorical mode allows an author the possibility of joining familiar, recognized elements in unexpected permutations. This makes allegory an ideal medium for the creation of a fantasy whose every word speaks on multiple levels. We have seen how the tale of heart and spring resonates through Reb Nahman's oeuvre—to the extent that each appearance of the allegory is made richer by its echoes in other contexts. I would like to consider one additional allegory central to Reb Nahman's thought—indeed, perhaps the most fundamental allegory in the Jewish worldview crystallized after the Second Temple's destruction. My interest in the following discussion is to realize the extent to which Reb Nahman integrates the *emotive* content of his pretexts in his tale. The wholly fantastic result: the transparently recognizable figures of his fiction are animated, and the potential expressed in their metaphorical essence is actualized. The story of the two birds lost to each other, told by the fourth, crooked-necked beggar, dramatizes the pathos of exile—as a personal, historical, and cosmic experience. Yet, like all his compatriots, the tale this beggar has lived not only speaks of the past but points, with a secret smile, toward a future of repair, of reunion that can be reached by his listeners themselves, if only they will understand. This is the core of Reb Nahman's innovation: on one hand, it is the reiterated words of pre-texts that invest his tale with its depth and power and, on the other, those texts are extrapolated, projecting the original drama they contain to a fantastic end point. The vision of that eschatological end suggested in the tale can, ironically, be reached only beyond the confines of the story itself.

> There are two birds, male and female; they are unique in all the world. And the female was lost, and he goes in search of her, and she searches for him, and they sought each other greatly, until they wandered so far that they saw the other was nowhere to be found, and they stayed where they were and built, each one, a nest. . . . And when night comes, the pair of birds begins to cry, each for the other in a terrible wailing voice. (*SM*, pp. 263–64)

The heartbreaking pain of their calls is unbearable to hear; across a thousand parasangs it rends the night, troubling people from their sleep. The separated winged lovers, consumed with loneliness for each other, are prefigured in the metaphor of Prov. 27:8, "As a bird wanders from its nest, so a man wanders from his place." The most elementary sense of exile and helplessness evoked by the image of the homeless bird makes it a ready metaphor for the exile of the Shekhinah, driven to wander through the wide world after the Temple is laid waste. The bird's plaintive call haunts the night, and not only in the beggar's tale. R. Yose heard her lamentation as well—his memory of it is preserved in the Talmud. Once he entered a ruined building in Jerusalem to pray. As he finished, he found himself face to face with Elijah the prophet. Elijah inquired what he heard as he stood amidst the ruins, and R. Yose answered: "I heard a voice *[bat kol]* moan like a dove, saying, 'Woe to my sons—for their sins I have destroyed my house, burned my sanctuary, and banished them among the nations.'"[213] This feminine voice, overheard by R. Yose in the lonely hours before dawn, is but the echo of a male voice that sounds, as R. Isaac bar Samuel declares in the name of Rav, through the night watches. "The Holy One, blessed be He, sits and roars like a lion, saying, 'Woe to my sons. . . .'" The notion of God's own remorse for what has happened to His people comes, as R. Eliezer says, from the verse in Jer. 25:30—"The Lord shall roar from on high, and utter His voice from His holy habitation; he shall roar mightily because of His sanctuary. . . ."[214] Reb Nahman's tale, interestingly, magnifies this suggestion that the anguish of the exile is shared by the exiler Himself. The Assembly of Israel, driven from their native home, dream of returning. Yet God, for His part, bewails their departure as well; the longing of the male bird for the female is as all-encompassing as her longing for him.

These talmudic descriptions of nights alive with disembodied voices join allusive forces in the crooked-necked beggar's tale with other verses that speak, equally, of distance and estrangement. "A voice is heard on high, lamentation, a bitter weeping: Rachel weeping for her children; she refuses to be comforted for her children, because they are not" (Jer. 31:14); and "To God I will cry aloud—Aloud to God. O, hear Me / My hand is stretched out in the night and rests not, my soul refuses to be comforted...I call to remembrance my soul in the night, I speak with my heart, and my spirit searches" (Ps. 77:1–7). To the personification of the Shekhinah in the figure of Rachel, and the Everyman of this psalm present in Reb Nahman's tale, R. Nathan adds a third dimension, interpreting the crooked-necked beggar's allegory. The two birds, he suggests, play out the fate of another primeval winged pair. While the Temple stood, he reminds us, the two *keruvim* (cherubs) stood above the holy ark, face gazing into face. With its destruction, they are lost to each other, turned back to back. We grasp the full significance of this alienation when we recall that the original charged space between the two countenances was the locus of divine revelation. "And when Moses was gone into the Tent of Meeting to speak with Him, then he heard the voice speaking to him from off the covering that was upon the ark of Testimony, from between the two *keruvim*, and it spoke to him" (Num. 7:89). This holy space between the faces is violated, and prophecy is no more. Thus, in exile, once direct knowledge of God becomes impossible, there remains an inconsolable longing for that connection.[215]

The crooked-necked beggar's intent, though, in portraying the separation of the two lonely birds goes far beyond an allegory of the Jewish nation's plight through history. Indeed, the gift he bestows on the bride and groom—the heart of his message—is hinted at in the tale he tells. With his wondrous voice and ventriloquist skill, he alone, of all musicians, is able to draw the lost and wandering birds back together. Moreover, like the reflection of a reflection, this somewhat disjointed tale conceals, almost tongue in cheek, a testimony of Reb Nahman's own ways in his world. Allusively, his tale implies that the orphan boy and girl are one aspect of the two birds; the beggar's eloquent song unites separate entities—from the simple souls of bride and groom to the most sublime level—the Holy One, blessed be He, and His Shekhinah.

The allusion is founded on an idea from the *Zohar*, ingeniously reworked and expounded in *Likkutei Moharan*: "The essence of melody comes from the tribe of Levi"—in the Temple, they were the chosen musicians and singers. Indeed, the third son born to Leah, named Levi, embodied the neglected wife's hope that through him "my husband will be rejoined to me" (Gen. 29:34). Reb Nahman makes the link between these two elements: "The birth of Levi, who represents the aspect of melody, is thus a force of attraction, drawing [Jacob] to her. . . ."[216] And elsewhere: "It was Levi who introduced the essence of music and instruments to the world, . . . with his birth, melody and musical instruments were born. . . . For the union of two things occurs through playing on instruments of song—understand. That is the secret of the musical instruments played at a wedding."[217] Reb Nahman's words suddenly become contemporary in the aside that follows; all at once, we see that the crooked-necked beggar is but an alter ego of Reb Nahman himself. "Once," R. Nathan recalls, "we were standing near him while there was a wedding in the town, and that was when he said all this. For that was his way in holy matters—he would teach of things as they occurred before us. . . ."[218] We come, then, full circle. The crooked-necked beggar, with his voice, can draw together the two wandering birds; through this tale of music and its powers of union, he returns his listeners to the framework story, their own reality. Their union in marriage, empowered by the *klezmer* who play, realizes the longed-for reunion between God and His lost Shekhinah.

As we conclude our exploration of figurative language and its metamorphoses in the creation of the fantastic dimension, let us consider a vital chapter in *Likkutei Moharan* in which Reb Nahman expressly reveals his own semiotic theory. The core of this teaching is suggested at the end of *The Humble King*, where the connection is drawn between the near homonyms *zion* and *ziun*—Zion, the metaphysical center of the Jewish world, is the place where the "signs," the vital symptoms of all the nations, gather together. Pursuing the traces of this double entendre, we come to a passage in *Likkutei Moharan* where it appears once again, inspiring a new reading of the verse "May He send you help from the sanctuary, and strengthen you out of Zion" (Ps. 20:3).

Coupled with the bivalent meaning of Zion/sign, Reb Nahman understands the root *Sa'AD* (strength) as referring, instead, to *se'udah* (making a meal). This twofold transformation leads him to declare: "Your repast, that is, eating and drinking and all such pleasures, should be a *sign* and symbol pointing to the letters that designate every thing. For taste and smell and image, all are but signs, symbolizing the letters contained in that thing."[219] Reb Nahman's overt subject here is an esoteric phenomenology of the Hebrew alphabet, yet I believe his comments speak, as well, of the play between signifier and signified, between words themselves and the objects, or concepts, they signify. The tropes that inform his tales, whether symbols, metaphors, or allegory, draw us to them as we are drawn to food by its taste, aroma, or appearance. It is these attributes that entice us to eat, that compel us to read or to listen. Yet, though attractive, what nourishes us in the end is not the sweetness of the food, nor its color, nor its scent, but the substance of the food itself. In the same way, our imagination internalizes the tale's forms, yet the strength and insight we gain from this repast comes, ultimately, not from these signs. Rather, we are sustained by something beyond them, by the truths to which the figures refer.

God commands the prophet Ezekiel to eat the scroll, the words He has given him, and go and speak to the house of Israel. He begins and, miraculously, "it became as sweet as honey in my mouth" (Ezek. 3:1–4). In his tales, likewise, Reb Nahman transfigures the almost indigestibly vast wisdom of Jewish tradition: by his compelling use of literary trope, we are drawn to listen, and the divinely inspired sources on which they are founded may, in that way, become an integral part of our being.

5. THE EFFECT OF THE DIMENSION OF THE FANTASTIC ON THE LISTENER/READER

In a psychologically incisive treatise, also found in *Likkutei Moharan,* Reb Nahman describes the spiritual dormancy in which most people are imprisoned, miserably living out their days in a state of heavy half-consciousness. His depiction of this common plight—indifference, existential poverty, and helplessness—prefaces a declaration of seminal importance in our understanding of Reb Nahman's stories. For, following his diagnosis of this all-too-human malady, he presents what, in his eyes, is the only possible, though precarious, remedy. Clearly, "the sleeper must be awakened. But he must wake up by his own power; the process must be incited from below. . . . And the moment he awakens, he must be 'faced' with favor, the face lost to him during his sleep must be restored. . . . When he is to be awakened, his face must be clothed—with [fantastic] tales."[220] This revolutionary notion, that the process of spiritual enlightenment is necessarily effected, not by philosophical arguments, but by fictions born of imagination—this notion is the foundation stone of Reb Nahman's entire oeuvre. The subsequent comments uncover his guiding convictions. He continues, explaining that when a person is awakened, tremendous care must be taken. Enchained in a subhuman slumber, the sleeper was as if blind. Indeed, the eyes of a blind person, if they are to be healed, must be protected so that he does not see the light too suddenly: the light must be partially blocked out if his sudden vision is not to harm him. In the same way, one who has slept in existential darkness for a long time must be shielded from the shock of sudden light. The bandages mercifully covering the patient's eyes—they are the fictions, woven of allegory, metaphor, and symbolism, that conceal the brilliance of divine truth. In the first, vulnerable time of consciousness, Reb Nahman's listener is healed by the tales he hears; the fantastic world they speak of envelops him, allowing him to awaken to the understanding they embody. Yet, Reb Nahman concludes this fundamental teaching with a startling contention: as the patient's psyche gains strength, *all* that was hidden to him is hidden no longer. "The clothing [of the face]"—that state of potential, yet concealed vision—yields to radically deeper insight that was unimaginable in his previous state. "Your master shall withdraw himself no longer [lit., "hide his face beneath his wings"]; rather, your eyes shall see your master."[221] In these words, the dialectic inherent in the tales comes to light. By the force of his narrative, Reb Nahman draws his listeners out of faithless oblivion; their own eyes, heavy-lidded for so long, will come to see. At the very same moment, meeting their newborn gaze is the face of the concealed one Himself. As we conclude this chapter, I would like to discuss two separate motifs, each of them a distinctive, pervasive characteristic of Reb Nahman's tales, which presage or induce this sense of revelation.

The first motif, to adopt the language of Ernst Cassirer, is the recognition of "*concrescence* or coincidence." This "law of mystical thinking" perceives the equivalence of the parts with the whole—"The whole is the part, in the sense that it enters into it with its whole mythical-substantial essence, somehow sensuously and materially 'in' it. The whole man is contained in his hair, nail-cuttings, clothes, footprints."[222] We find this principle expressed over and over in Reb Nahman's tales: his evocation of enchanted places, of points of time, of instances where *being* is intensely concentrated. The song of the mute beggar that "contains all wisdom," the voice of the crooked-necked beggar that "contains all the world's voices"; the garden of the deaf beggar, where fruits grow "with all the tastes in the world"—all these present one all-inclusive, archetypal essence, beyond all partial and worldly manifestation. Likewise, the iconlike hand in *The Master of Prayer*, which depicts all the history of the cosmos from creation to the eschatological end (*SM,* p. 190), and the country, in *The Humble King*, encompassing all countries, the city within that contains all cities, and the house there, representing all houses, down to the individual who epitomizes all the clowning of his scornful land (*SM,* p. 61). In each of these instances, Reb Nahman presents a sort of DNA model, an imaginatively conceived microcosm in which an absolute, macrocosmic world order is coded.

In some tales, the fantastic microcosm is evoked as a long-for sanctuary of wholeness, where the broken imperfection of this world is unknown or has been triumphantly overcome. Other tales unfold in an equally fantastic context, yet their microcosm is engendered by pursuing a diametrically opposed vector. In this second possibility, the microcosm is conceived, not through nostalgia, but rather through the technique of satire. Here, instead of following a path of abstraction, leading *away* from the failings of this world—the flawed melodies, the misplaced roses, the imperfect candelabras—Reb Nahman strikes at the very heart of those deficiencies, driving them *ad absurdum*, beyond the pale of realism. A relentless attack against society is launched in *The Master of Prayer*: each cult metonymically embodies the most intolerable moral sin of its members—greed, lust, pride, etc. *The Humble King*, similarly, takes place in a land that is the epitome of falsehood, in which lies become the omnipresent quality penetrating every corner of the kingdom. In analyzing this tale, the comments added by Reb Nahman's commentators guide us to some important insights regarding the true nature of this apparent satire. The tale's setting betrays no overtly "Jewish" landmarks, yet, in the notes concluding it, two verses are evoked, suggesting the wordplay between Zion and *ziun* (sign) mentioned above: "The ways of Zion do mourn . . ." (Lam. 1:4) and "The rangers that pass through the land, when any sees a human bone, then shall he set us a *sign* by it . . ." (Ezek. 39:15). This intimation of a connection between Zion, the metaphysical and religious nexus of the Jewish world, and its inherent referential essence is pursued in *Likkutei Moharan* and further clarified by Reb Nahman's students. These sources, in turn, lead us to an understanding of the concept of microcosm as a fundament of Jewish thought, integrated into Reb Nahman's own oeuvre.

Somewhat surprisingly, perhaps, R. Nahman of Tcherin, author of the commentary *Rimzei Maʿasiyot*, identifies the "kingdom of lies" with no hesitation: "The country that contains all countries . . . is the Land of Israel; the city in it that encompasses all cities is Zion, or Jerusalem; the house that comprises all houses is the Temple. . . ." Surprising—that the nadir of negativity, a realm of falsehood, should be associated with the most holy center of Jewish faith. But this identification actually proves the supreme value, beyond good and evil, contained in the notion of microcosm. Zion, in the eyes of the rabbis, is a primordial point from which the world was created.[223] Zion is a mystical root, a pillar of holiness timelessly standing.[224] In *Likkutei Moharan*, Reb Nahman recognizes the "zaddik of the generation" as a metaphorical foundation stone; just as pilgrimages were made to Zion, so the yearly journey must be undertaken to that human axis of the *hasid*'s spiritual world.[225] It is, thus, the concept of Zion as a sign, a symbolic microcosm, that Reb Nahman enlists in his tale. We find prototypical models for Reb Nahman's fantastic microcosms throughout rabbinic texts. The Song of Songs, for instance, divinely inspired, "contains the praises of the entire Torah"; it comprises the whole story of Creation, the lives of the patriarchs, the labyrinthine history of the Israelite nation, past, present, and future, until the Seventh Day.[226] But undoubtedly the most profound linguistic microcosm recognized by the rabbis is the first verse of Genesis, "In the beginning God created. . . ." Unlike the other nine utterances by which the world came into being, this first speech act is not preceded by the words "And God said." From this verbal void thus springs a *maʾamar satum* (hermetically closed utterance, incomprehensible utterance) "which contains everything, for all ten utterances are comprised in this primordial *maʾamar satum*."[227]

We see, then, that the fantastic realm in which so many of Reb

Nahman's tales take place is conceived through a logical process of abstraction, which follows a most innovative tendency in rabbinic tradition. The seemingly surreal context of the stories in fact reflects, of course, none other than the reality their author himself confronts. Whether perceived through the rosy glass of idealization or through the crooked mirror of ironical satire, the microcosm those stories describe is presented as a higher truth, a truth beyond all the illusions posed by the dispersive, contradictory world of everyday life.

The second motif, integrated in Reb Nahman's stories, that accompanies and heightens a sense of revelation is that of all-encompassing happiness. To a superficial reader, the sixfold refrain in *The Seven Beggars*—"And there was great happiness and very great joy"—seems but a platitude; the pure gladness of the simple son *(Clever Son and Simple Son)* at every turn of his destiny is laughable; the pleasure that the forest song arouses in the hearts of the sons who were reversed appears exaggerated. Yet deeper contemplation of Reb Nahman's worldview helps us realize that these expressions of happiness are, on the contrary, a trust, an intimation of the messianic future. The juxtaposition of music and overflowing happiness that appears in so many tales, and becomes a fundament of Bratslav Hasidism springs, perhaps, from an idea expressed in the Talmud: "Prophecy does not dwell in sadness, nor in idleness, but only in great joy." Maimonides extends the same notion: "Thus the sons of prophets always had a lyre, drum, flute and harp before them when they sought to prophesy. . . ."[228] And Reb Nahman, in turn, in one of his most famous teachings, exclaimed, "It is a great *mizvah* to be forever happy, to overcome sadness and melancholy, to distance oneself from them with all one's strength. . . . All the illnesses that beset us originate in melancholy and sadness, and happiness is the great healer. . . ."[229] In future days, happiness will even increase; as the sages said, "The Holy One, blessed be He, will lead the dance of the zaddikim in times to come." This only imaginable reality, in which happiness reigns victorious, is realized vicariously in the fantastic world of Reb Nahman's tales. Their author's personal spiritual striving is lived out by his characters. Though his own life may have been weighed down—like many of ours—with uncertainty, melancholy, and sorrow, at least in his tales Reb Nahman could *tell* of worlds filled with singing, dancing, music, and happiness. And through the telling, the tales, indeed, come true.

NOTES

Chapter I. The Poet's Self and the Poem

1. *Hayyei Moharan*, Sippurim Hadashim, 23b:19. On the archetypical king and palace he built, see *Genesis Rabbah* 1.1.

2. Many scholars have probed this sense of mission and its pervasive effect on Reb Nahman's life. Mendel Piekarz, for instance, sketches the following scenario: The daring and innovative nature of many of Reb Nahman's teachings, combined with paradoxical behavior, aroused tremendous suspicion in Hasidic leaders of his time. As his following increased, and his own self-consciousness and messianic aspirations grew stronger, the tension gave way to persecution. This forced him to restraint and caution in expressing his ideas and in promulgating them—either through hiding away or destroying secret and antinomian writings, or through self-censorship of writings published in his life or prepared strictly for publication. Mendel Piekarz, *Hasidut Braslav* (Jerusalem, 1972), pp. 10–11. While awareness of biographical events and conditions influencing Reb Nahman's actions and self-image is essential to a complete understanding of his writings, full exploration of them lies beyond the scope of our discussion. Important studies of connections between biography and oeuvre include: Arthur Green, *Tormented Master: A Life of Rabbi Nahman of Bratslav* (New York, 1981); Piekarz, *Hasidut Braslav;* and Joseph Weiss, *Mehkarim be-Hasidut Braslav* (Jerusalem, 1984), esp. pp. 150–71.

3. Weiss, *Mehkarim*, p. 50.

4. *Shivhei Moharan*, Maʿalat Torato, 16b:50.

5. *Sihot Haran* 205, and see Weiss's discussion in *Mekharim*, pp. 244–48. Reb Nahman's scathing reminder that *all* his teachings are but faint shadows of their divine counterparts is voiced in *Shivhei Moharan*, Maʿalat Torato, 14a:20. The contention is reiterated in other places as well.

6. Joseph Dan and Isaiah Tishby set out the historical background behind this idea. They observe that belief in divine immanence gives Hasidism the possibility of raising sinners and repairing their souls *(tikkun),* for despite their sins, all people have a holy essence *(yesod);* recovering that unchanging essence enables the zaddik to aid in *tikkun*. Man can also achieve *tikkun* of his own thoughts, as their roots are divine as well. See that discussion (in Hebrew) in Tishby and Dan, *Ha-Encyclopedia ha-ʿIvrit* (Jerusalem and Tel Aviv, 1964), 17:775, s.v. "Hasidut." Compare the treatment of the zaddik in Weiss, *Mekharim,* pp. 99–108 and Piekarz, *Hasidut Braslav,* pp. 112–13. On the famous *tikkun ha-kelali* and its role both on the escatological level (redemption of the Shekhinah from exile) and on the individual level, see Yehudah Liebes, "Ha-Tikkun ha-Kelali shel R. Nahman me-Bratslav ve-Yahaso le-Shabbta'ut,"

Zion 45 (1980): 198–217. An English translation of this important essay may be found in *Studies in Jewish Myth and Jewish Messianism,* trans. Batya Stein (Albany, 1993), pp. 115–50. On the concept of the zaddik in Kabbalistic tradition, see Gershom Scholem, *Pirkei Yesod be-Havanat ha-Kabbalah u-Semaleha* (Jerusalem, 1956), pp. 213–58; and idem, *The Messianic Idea in Judaism* (New York, 1960), pp. 251–56.

7. *Shivhei Moharan* 4a:11. Some of Reb Nahman's most perceptive psychological comments concern a dialectic the zaddik must master in order truly to benefit those loyal to him. To people proud and confident in their knowledge, he reveals how lowly and distant they really are from understanding a transcendent God; and to the humble, tormented by their alienation, he shows how immanent God really is, "For the whole world is full of His glory" (Is. 6:3). See *Likkutei Moharan,* pt. 2, 91.

8. Reb Nahman ben Simhah of Bratslav, *Sippurei Ma'asiyot* (1811; reprint, Jerusalem, 1985), p. 175. This edition is henceforth abbreviated in the text as *SM,* followed by the page number(s).

9. *Likkutei Moharan,* pt. 2, 91.

10. *Likkutei Moharan* 64.3. Green points out that it was R. Jacob Joseph of Polonnoye, among early Hasidic thinkers, whose conception of the zaddik and his social role particularly influenced Reb Nahman. Cf. *Tormented Master,* p. 214 n. 1. On the Sabbatian aspect of the notion of the true zaddik's descent into the abyss to redeem the souls of others, cf. Weiss, "Reishit Zemihata shel ha-Derekh ha-Hasidit," *Zion* 16 (1951).

11. *Likkutei Moharan,* pt. 2, 68. In a parallel text, *Likkutei Moharan,* pt. 2, 7, Reb Nahman recognizes both figures—biological father and spiritual father—as engaging in a single task: the commandment of populating the world with human beings. And the woeful existential plight of a man who fails in this task is portrayed, in mystical tradition, in no uncertain terms: "Whoever has no children in this world—it is as if he had never been created and had never been; he is called forlorn (*'ariri*) in this world and the world to come." *Zohar Hadash,* Ki teze, fol. 97a (Midrash ha-Ne'elam). See also *Zohar* 1.90b; 130b; *Zohar* 3.56a.

12. *Likkutei Moharan* 4.8.

13. *Hayyei Moharan,* Sippurim Hadashim 23b:21. On the relationship between the *hasid* and his rebbe as a central phenomenon in developing Hasidic tradition, see S. A. Horodezky, *Ha-Hasidut ve-Torata* (Tel Aviv, 1944), pp. 86-90; Piekarz, *Hasidut Braslav,* pp. 87, 128–32; J. Hasdai, "Reshit Darkam shel ha-Hasidim ve-ha-Mitnaggdim le-Or Sifrut ha-Drush" (diss., Hebrew University, 1984), pp. 261–69.

14. *Likkutei Moharan* 66.

15. Tishby and Dan, *Ha-Encyclopedia ha-'Ivrit,* 17:811.

16. The parallelism Reb Nahman perceived between the zaddik and God, a trenchant component of his philosophy, as Weiss remarks (*Mehkarim,* p.112), is most evident on this point. In *Likkutei Moharan* 8.2, Reb Nahman asks rhetorically, "But how can the breath of life be received?" He continues: "Know,

that the true breath of life comes from the zaddik and rebbe of the generation, for the essence of that life-breath is in the Torah, as it is written, 'The spirit of God hovered over the surface of the waters' [Gen. 1:2]. And because the zaddikim cleave to the Torah, this essential life-spirit is with them. . . . Indeed, the zaddik inspires the breath of life in each and every person, bringing him to fullness."

17. *Likkutei Halakhot*, Yore De'ah 2, Nedarim 4.25. The identification of the zaddik with the shofar is explicit in *Zohar* 3.18b. As R. Hamnuna Sava used to say, "The prayer and voice of the shofar that emerge from the zaddik, from his spirit and his soul, those voices ascend on high. . . . Happy is the lot of those zaddikim who know how to find favor before their Lord, and who know how to repair the world on that day through the voice of the shofar."

18. *Likkutei Halakhot*, Yore De'ah 2, Nedarim 4.36.

19. On the historical development of this phenomenon, see A. Wertheim, *Halakhot ve-Halikhot be Hasidut* (Jerusalem, 1960), pp. 156–60. Reb Nahman capitalizes on the urgent necessity of such a personal encounter between rebbe and *hasid* in *Likkutei Moharan* 19. The metaphors of mirroring eloquently suggest the profound interaction possible when rebbe and *hasid* see themselves reflected in each other's countenance.

20. See *Likkutei Moharan* 19.

21. *Shivhei Moharan*, 5a:9. The tremendous effect of Reb Nahman's physical presence compels his students to insist that only in their live telling was the power of the tales fully revealed. Like every true fabulator, R. Nathan notes, Reb Nahman's fictions were created by the movements of his hands (First Introduction to *SM*, p. 6). In the image of God Himself, Reb Nahman declares, "The true zaddik builds and destroys worlds" (*Likkutei Moharan*, pt. 2, 91). His seminal creative act—the narration of his tales—is effected almost magically by his very hands, "which are instruments of action; they hold the essence of revelation, the breath of life" (*Likkutei Moharan* 56.2). In a final statement ringing with the notion of parallelism between the zaddik and the Creator, Reb Nahman suggests that the zaddik is able "to renew the act of Creation through the miracles he performs in the world" (*Likkutei Moharan* 49.7). When we recall the superhuman powers of the seven beggars/storytellers, we realize that those figures embody their human creator's own self-image. See also below, chapter 2, n. 71.

22. *Likkutei Moharan* 164. In *Hayyei Moharan*, Ma'alat Torato ve-Sippurav ha-Keddoshim, 16b:51, a similar tale is related in Reb Nahman's name, this one concerning a king whose son is desperately ill. As a last resort, the father consults a wonder doctor. He suggests a cure, but tries to discourage the father because of its difficulty and expense. The father, though, is willing to do anything to restore his son. The moral, Reb Nahman explains, is: this "Because we are all brought low by this sickness of our hearts, the zaddik, faithful doctor, must heal us with expensive and terrible potions. Although all hope seems almost lost (heaven forbid) . . . after many days, perhaps we may merit catching one precious, marvelous drop in our mouths. . . . Then we could hope

for a complete healing. . . ." On the notion of healing the body through the soul, see *Shivhei ha-Ba'al Shem Tov* (1814–15; reprint, Tel Aviv, 1947), p. 113.

23. *Zohar Hadash*, Shir ha-Shirim, fol. 40b. A more detailed version of the same allegory is found in *Tikkunei Zohar*, Tikkun 25. See my discussion of that text in chapter 4.

24. *Likkutei Moharan*, pt. 2, 24.

25. See B.T. *Pesahim* 113a and *Tikkunei Zohar*, Tikkun 69, 105a, as well as Reb Nahman's presentation of *ha-tikkun ha-kelali* in *Likkutei Moharan* 25. On the controversial history of the *tikkun ha-kelali* and its role in Bratslav tradition, see Yehudah Liebes's important article, "Ha-Tikkun ha-Kelali" (above, n. 6). Response to Liebes's contentions was vociferous. See, for example, Yehoshu'a Mondshine, "'Al 'Ha-Tikkun ha-Kelali' . . . ," *Zion* 47 (1982): 198–223 and Ada Rapoport-Albert, "He'arot le-Ma'amaro shel Yehudah Liebes," *Zion* 46 (1981): 346–51. Liebes responded to Mondshine in *Zion* 47 (1982): 224–31 and to Rapoport-Albert in *Zion* 46 (1981): 352–55.

26. *Likkutei Moharan* 54.3. Reb Nahman clinches the identity between the "zaddik of the generation" and the figure of the shepherd in his declaration: "Know, that each and every one of the zaddikim of the generation is a shepherd, for each one of them shares an aspect of Moses" (*Likkutei Moharan* 185). On the traditional Seven Shepherds, see *Zohar* 3.42a. On the number seven and its importance in Jewish tradition, see Avidov Lipsker, "Ha-Kallah ve-Shiv'at ha-Kabbzanim—Le-She'elat Mekorotav shel Sippur-ha-Misgeret shel *Ma'aseh me-Shiv'at ha-Bettlers,*" *Jerusalem Studies in Jewish Folklore* 13–14 (1991–92): 248–95. The role of the shepherd/musician in the romantic worldview is discussed in greater detail in chapter 3.

27. *Likkutei 'Ezot*, Zaddik 90, cited in *Rimzei Ma'asiyot,* p. 23.

28. *Zohar* 2.166b.

29. *Likkutei Moharan* 65.

30. *Likkutei Moharan* 65.1. In chapter 4, we discuss the continuation of this teaching, where Reb Nahman speaks of the prayers uttered by this whispering field of souls and the role of the zaddik in uniting those wisps of words, binding them into a community, and bringing them before God.

31. Cf. René Wellek, "The Concept of Romanticism in Literary History" (1949), in *Romanticism: Points of View*, ed. R. F. Gleckner and G. E. Enscoe, 2d ed. (Detroit, 1975). And consider the words of Gotthelf Heinrich Schubter quoted by Paul Wolfgang Wuhrl in *E. T. A Hoffmann, Der goldene Topf: Erlauterungen und Dokumente* (Stuttgart, 1982), p. 94. On the motif of the garden as a central place in the romantic outlook, see chapter 3, below.

32. Refer to chapter 4 for an extensive consideration of the third beggar and his story.

33. *Likkutei Moharan,* pt. 2, 63, based on Rashi's interpretation of *zimrat ha'arez* in that verse (Gen. 43:11), literally translated as "the choice fruits of the land." In this teaching, Reb Nahman proceeds to draw the link between the shepherd's life and musical instruments. (Gen. 4:21) To discern the symphony of nature is the unique gift of the prophet; as Isaiah exalts, "From the

wings [ends] of the earth we heard melodies" (Is. 24:16). All the patriarchs, Reb Nahman asserts there, tended flocks; all of them shared this romantic bond to nature.

34. *Likkutei Moharan* 64.5 My thanks to R. Daniel Epstein for sharing his insights concerning Reb Nahman's place in the context of Western philosophy. In kabbalistic terms, *Hokhmah* is the second of the *sefirot; Keter,* the highest, is humanly inconceivable because it is superrational. (Like the crowns of the letters, lit. *ketarim*, built on the letters and the understanding they convey, music soars beyond the notes that symbolize it.) In fact, that oneness is primordial and eternal; the partial melodies of all cognitive systems originate in, and are drawn from, the sublime music of that highest sphere.

35. Ibid.

36. Ibid. Moses' was a universal soul; his empathy for all compelled the rabbis to declare, "Moses was equal to sixty thousand people" (Song of Songs Rabbah 1:64). And Reb Nahman, in the footsteps of the *Zohar* (1.25b, 27a), declares that every individual must direct his prayers to joining himself with the zaddikim of the generation. "For each zaddik of his generation is an aspect of Moses. . . . And Moses is an aspect of the Messiah" (*Likkutei Moharan* 2.6). See also *Song of Songs Rabbah* 1.15.

37. B.T. *Sanhedrin* 91b.

38. *Sihot Haran* 202. Compare the view of R. Yehudah Loew ben Bezalel of Prague (Maharal). He censures those who would decry the technique of *asmakhta* (i.e., use of biblical references to back up rabbinical enactments) as a merely artificial exegetical device, used only to fabricate a textual link where none really exists. For the Maharal, *asmakhta* is a divine allowance for scriptural supplementation on the part of the sages, and by no means a synthetic and deceptive excuse for textual embellishment. (See *Gur Aryeh* on Ex. 19:16.) Quoted by David Weiss Halivni, "On Man's Role in Revelation," in vol. 2 of *From Ancient Israel to Modern Judaism: Essays in Honor of Marvin Fox,* ed. Jacob Neusner et al., Brown Judaic Studies (Atlanta, 1973), p. 43.

39. Gershom Scholem, *Major Trends in Jewish Mysticism* (New York, 1941), p. 9. The potential conflict between innovation and tradition comes to the fore in *Likkutei Moharan* 54.7. There Reb Nahman explains the rabbinic statement (B.T. *Pesahim* 66a; *Niddah* 19b): "One may not infer a ruling on one's own that is derived from inference [*gezerah shavah*]" through an ingenious play on words: "For it may be the work of his imagination [*ko'ah ha-medammeh*], i.e., that he imagines connections between one word and another [*medammeh milta le-milta*]."

40. *Likkutei Moharan*, pt. 2, 91. Here Reb Nahman recalls the talmudic anecdote (B.T. *Megillah*, 9a) of the Egyptian king Talmei, who isolated seventy-two elders from one another and commanded each of them to reproduce the words of their Torah. "And the Most High inspired each of their hearts to make new combinations"; each of them wrote "God created in the beginning" (instead of "In the beginning, God created") to silence all doctrines of dualism. In this teaching, Reb Nahman's sympathy and interest in the artistic license of

the seventy-two elders and its divine source are clear. Many are his admonitions, however, that the modest garb veiling his words conceals understanding too vast and profound for his own generation. This sense that the eternal truth of his words can be revealed only in generations to come, or in the world to come, or that the Messiah alone will interpret them vehemently attests to his belief in their divine inspiration. See *Sihot Haran* 195 and 208; *Hayyei Moharan*, Nesiʿato le-Lemberg, 37a:5; *Shivhei Moharan*, Maʿalat Torato, 16a:49. And cf. Green's comment that Reb "Nahman's novellae are seen by him as a sort of inner revelation, rather than as a creation of his own mind" (*Tormented Master*, p. 91 n. 66).

41. See Isaiah Tishby, *The Wisdom of the Zohar*, trans. David Goldstein (Oxford, 1989), 3:1364–65 and his references to *Zohar* 1.59b, 1.216a, 2.203a. See also *Wisdom of the Zohar*, 3:1413–14. And cf. Idel's discussion in *Hasidism: Between Ecstasy and Magic* (New York, 1995), pp.189–209.

42. The sociological dynamics of this role are treated in many studies. Consider Rachel Elior's discussion, "Between *Yesh* and *Ayin:* The Doctrine of the *Zaddik* in the Works of Jacob Isaac, the Seer of Lublin," in *Jewish History*, ed. Ada Rapoport-Albert and Steven Zipperstein (London, 1988), pp. 430ff. concerning the connection to the figure of Joseph.

43. *Likkutei Moharan* 19.4. On the importance of dreams in Reb Nahman's teaching, see my discussion in chapter 4.

44. The vast range of works concerning the theme of language and thought is beyond my cartographic abilities even to outline. Please refer to chapter 4 for more complete discussion of this subject in Reb Nahman's conception of his tales.

45. B.T. *Taʿanit* 23a.

46. *Likkutei Moharan* 60.9. An additional testimony to Reb Nahman's identification with Honi ha-Maʿagel is found in *Hayyei Moharan*, Nesiʿato le-Lemberg, 37b:13. See also Reb Nahman's interest in Honi as a dreamer, discussed in chapter 4.

47. *Shivhei Moharan*, Gedulat Hasagato, 7b:39. Perhaps the spirit of this belief may be traced to the words of R. Hayyim Vital, who states in his introduction to *ʿEz Hayyim* (1782; reprint, Jerusalem, 1988) that mystical tradition is always transmitted personally—the deceased master revealing himself to his living pupil (p. 28). He recognizes a chain of supernatural inspiration, guided by Elijah the Prophet and spanning centuries, from R. Simeon bar Yohai, R. Abraham ben David, and R. Moses ben Nahmanides, to his own rabbi and teacher, R. Isaac Luria. As an aside, we remark R. Vital's characterization there of his master's vast wisdom, including knowledge of "the language of birds, of palms, trees, plants, even stones" and recall the third, mute beggar, who mastered all the songs voiced in all the orders of nature.

48. *Hayyei Moharan*, Sihot ha-Shayyakhim le-Torot, 4b:5.

49. *Shivhei Moharan*, Gedulat Hasagato, 5a:7. On the apologetics of Bratslav Hasidim regarding this declaration, see *Hayyei Moharan*, Hashmatot 46a:1 and Liebes, "Ha-Tikkun ha-Kelali," p. 201 n. 2.

50. *Likkutei Moharan* 64.4.

51. Mishnah *Avot* 1.8.

52. Reference, of course, is to the Lurianic doctrine of *zimzum*. On the role of this teaching in Reb Nahman's creation of the dimension of the fantastic, see chapters 2 and 4. Green sees the idea of *zimzum* as "a central focus of the mystic's speculations" (*Tormented Master*, p. 295).

53. One controversy among scholars centers on the authenticity of a critical paragraph in *Iggeret ha-Ba'al Shem Tov*. From that famous document, penned to his brother-in-law R. Gershon of Kotov in 5513 or 5514 (1753–54), and published by R. Jacob Joseph of Polonnoye at the end of his book *Ben Porat Yosef* (Koretz, 1781), certain historians (Dinur, Horodezki) understand that "in the year 5507, the Ba'al Shem Tov learned, from the Messiah himself, the Hasidic doctrine of redemption, and took upon himself the messianic-prophetic task to ready his generation for the Messiah's advent through propagation of Hasidic teaching." B. Dinur, *Reishita shel ha-Hasidut* (Jerusalem, 1943-45), pp. 181-184, cited by Isaiah Tishby, "Ha-Ra'ayon ha-Meshihi," *Zion* 32 (1967): 29. According to Tishby, two major assumptions emerge from Dinur's analysis: "1. The Ba'al Shem Tov saw himself as an aspect of Moses (Messiah) or Elijah (messenger announcing his advent), and so was he seen in his Hasidic community, and 2. Hasidic leaders after the Ba'al Shem Tov—R. Jacob Joseph of Polonnoye, the Maggid of Mezherich, his students, and the other *'zaddikim,'* early and late—testify to the messianic essence of Hasidic teaching." Gershom Scholem disagrees with these conclusions, arguing that Dinur's claims are based on scant evidence in Hasidic writings. See *Messianic Idea in Judaism*, p. 183. Tishby, for his part, weighs the possibility that the letter was penned by someone else or that the original text was altered. His conclusion: "The issue of messianism in modern Hasidic teaching, i.e., in views and institutions concerning service of God and lifestyle, remains an open question; to solve it, we must turn from the letter to Hasidic literature itself" ("Ha-Ra'ayon ha-Meshihi," p. 31). Contributions to the debate on messianism and Bratslav Hasidism are many. Undeniably, Reb Nahman saw himself as continuing the tradition of redeemers and revealers of esoteric mysteries; cf. *Shivhei Moharan*, Gedulat Hasagato, s. 36. The conviction that the soul of the Messiah transmigrates from generation to generation was instrumental, both in Reb Nahman's own self-consciousnes and in informing the image of leaders before him, who were believed to bear that monumental soul as well—among them, R. Simeon bar Yohai, R. Isaac Luria, and the Ba'al Shem Tov. On the kinship between Reb Nahman and R. Simeon bar Yohai, see Piekarz, *Hasidut Braslav*, pp. 13–15; Liebes, "Ha-Tikkun ha-Kelali," p. 203; and Green, *Tormented Master*, p. 186.

54. Such an intent is, of course, dominant in many sources. See Liebes, "Ha-Tikkun ha-Kelali," esp. pp. 201, 202, 213; Green, *Tormented Master*, pp. 182–211; Piekarz, *Hasidut Braslav*, pp. 59ff.; Weiss, *Mehkarim*, pp. 189–213. Also consider testimony in *Shivhei Moharan* 3b:7; 6b:26.

55. B.T. *Sanhedrin* 98a.

56. On the identity between the Messiah, son of David, and the *sefirah* of

Malkhut, with its humble status, see *Zohar* 1.238a. And cf. Yehudah Liebes, *Studies in the Zohar,* trans. A. Schwartz, S. Makache, and P. Peli (New York, 1993), p. 3.

57. On this image of redemption through the suffering of the redeemer, see *Likkutei Moharan* 118. The subject is raised by Liebes, "Ha-Tikkun ha-Kelali," n. 81, pp. 223–24; and Weiss, *Mehkarim,* pp. 49, 248. See Mondshine's refutation of Liebes's claim that this teaching originates in Sabbatianism: "ʿAl Ha-Tikkun," p. 221 n. 87. Mondshine counters that the idea appears in the Talmud and the *Zohar* and offers additional references.

58. *Rimzei Maʿasiyot* 10. In the "Hashmatot" at the end of the Bratslav edition of the tales, this notion is developed further: "The soul of the Messiah, as well, is captured in exile and held by the *kelippot* [evil husks] in a desert waste where no man travels. . . ." (p. 30).

59. The three represent the gradual refinement of a single theme; each is an intrigue of concealed identity, leading eventually to recognition and its far-reaching implications. Lot is completely oblivious to his daughters' deeds (Gen. 19); Judah mistakes his daughter-in-law Tamar for a harlot (Gen. 38); Boaz finds Ruth in the darkness of the threshing-floor. The messianic thread weaving together the three narratives is revealed in the genealogy concluding the book of Ruth: the lines of descent running from Moav, son of Lot, and from Perez, son of Tamar and Judah, converge in the union of Ruth the Moabite and Boaz, of the family of Perez—leading to the birth of King David, the messianic king.

60. See *Genesis Rabbah* 85.1 and B.T. *Sotah* 10b. Also Targum Neofiti to Gen. 38:25 for variations on this event.

61. *Rimzei Maʿasiyot,* p. 30. Green cites a precedent for this "tragedy" in "the well-known claims of the Safed Kabbalists that both Isaac Luria and Hayyim Vital were incarnations of Messiah ben Joseph, but that the sins of their unworthy generations had caused them to pass away without effecting the great and final *tiqqun*" (*Tormented Master,* p. 191).

62. See R. Ashlag's commentary to *Zohar* 1.25b, 1:203–4, s. 234. And cf. Green's explanation and speculations regarding Reb Nahman: "The Biblical Joseph was a prior, perhaps the first, incarnation of Messiah ben Joseph. Moses, who prefigures Messiah ben David, has to take Joseph's bones with him in order to bring about the redemption. The relationship of Joseph to Messiah is thus a prototype of the relationship between the two messiahs; Ben David's coming requires the deaths of Nahman and the others, all of whom here are seen to be participants in the Josephite Messiah's soul" (*Tormented Master,* p. 192).

63. *Hayyei Moharan,* Shayyakh le-Sippurei Maʿasiyot, 15b–16a:2. On the "chamber of transformations" in Lurianic mysticism, see below, chapter 4 n. 101.

64. *Likkutei Halakhot,* Oreh Hayyim, Berakhot ha-Shahar, 3.4. See also 3.31.

65. The allusion is to 1 Sam. 16:18 and the description of David: "I have seen a son of Yishay the Bethlehemite, who knows how to play, and a fine

warrior, and a man of war, and *wise in speech*, and a comely person, and the Lord is with him." Rashi, on Ex. 31:3, describes this ability as the gift also granted Bezalel, the divinely inspired artist. See B.T. *Hagigah* 14a and *Sanhedrin* 93b for further associations clinging to this phrase.

66. "For something may be called in one way, and elsewhere, something else . . . sometimes a character has one name, and sometimes another, and so it is with everything" (*SM*, p. 171).

67. *Hayyei Moharan*, Ma'alat Torato, 13a:7.

68. *Likkutei Moharan,* pt. 2, 61.

69. *Likkutei Halakhot*, Oreh Hayyim, Tefillin 5.15 The web of connections spun in the *Zohar* between King David, the baby's seven golden hairs, the Messiah and the transcendence of time promised with his advent is set out in *Rimzei Ma'asiyot*, p. 31. Additional reference is made there to *Tikkunei Zohar*, Tikkun 70 (fol. 222b) and to *Zohar* 1.73b.

70. *Shivhei Moharan* 7a:32.

71. Cited by R. Daniel Epstein.

72. On the last example, see B.T. *Sanhedrin* 98a. His mysterious presence and absence throughout the history of the Jewish people, vitally involved and yet distant, is described in *Seder 'Olam Rabbah* 17: "And in the second year of the reign of Ahaziyah, Elijah was hidden away and did not appear again until the Messiah King; then he appeared and was hidden away a second time and will not reappear until Gog and Magog. Now he records the deeds of all the generations—'And so he died according to the word of the Lord which Elijah had spoken (2 Kings 1:17). . . .'" On the figure of Elijah in Jewish tradition, see Gedaliyah Nigal, *Ha-Sippur ha-Hasidi* (Jerusalem, 1981), pp. 264–79.

73. B.T. *Shabbat* 33b.

74. B.T. *Ta'anit* 22a. R. Broka, at the market with Elijah, asks him who there will merit the world to come. Elijah points to a man wearing black shoes and no *zizit* (ritual fringes worn by observant Jews). Amazed, R. Broka asks the (apparently impious) man about his deeds. He answers that he is a guard in a prison and devotes himself to protecting the virginity of Jewish girls. Deliberately, he wears no outward signs of his religion, preferring to act incognito. On Elijah's appearance as a non-Jew in rabbinic literature, see T.B. *Berakhot* 6b; *Midrash Ruth Zuta* 1.20 and other sources cited by Nigal, *Ha-Sippur ha-Hasidi,* p. 269 n. 19.

75. An aggadah in B.T. *Sanhedrin* 63b describes the interchange between Elijah and an abject idolator: the prophet's attempt to open his eyes, offering him new life, and the child's stubborn clinging to his icon, even as death tightens its grip. The linguistic parallels between this text and *The Master of Prayer* are clearly more than accidental. Cf. "He pulled his icon from his breast and hugged it and kissed it" and "Each one had such icons, and they would hug them and kiss them, for that was their way of worshipping . . ." (*SM,* p. 181).

76. This, according to a popular tradition, expressed in the folk etymology of the word *teiku*, is an anagram of "the Tishbite [Elijah] will solve all difficulties and problems." Cf. *Encyclopedia Judaica*, s.v. "Elijah."

77. According to Adin Steinsaltz, Reb Nahman perceived the Ba'al Shem Tov as "the most perfect image of the true zaddik," and he wished to emulate him. *Shishah me-Sippurei ha-Ma'asiyot shel R. Nahman me-Bratslav* (Jerusalem, 1981), p. 133.

78. J.T. *Shekalim* 3.3.

79. *Likkutei Moharan* 61.

80. *Likkutei Moharan,* pt. 2, 1.12. See my discussion of this understanding in chapter 4.

81. The direct parallels between events in Reb Nahman's private life and the events shaping the tales have been analyzed extensively by many scholars, such as Green, Sade, Weiss, and Kaplan, with various attitudes regarding their subject. Pinhas Sade's criticism that Weiss treats Reb Nahman as a "psychiatric patient" rather than a "religious genius" (*Tikkun ha-Lev* [Jerusalem, 1982], p. 261) alerts us to the fact that the subject must be approached with great care. In the present context, we are less concerned with specific causes—Reb Nahman's contacts with *maskilim* (non-observant figures of the Jewish Enlightenment), the animosity between himself and *"ha-zaken"* (R. Aryeh Leib of Shpola [1725–1812], also known as the Shpoler Zeide), his journey to Erez Israel, etc.—and their correspondence to the tales' plots than in the emotional experience accompanying them. Statements in *Likkutei Moharan* and *Hayyei Moharan* provide much information in this respect, and raise the discussion from the biographical to the typological level. In his critique of Green's *Tormented Master* ("Zaddik le-Benei ha-'Olam ha-Hadash?!" *Tarbiz* 51 [1982]: 154–57), Piekarz holds that Weiss goes too far in claiming every line of the stories speaks of Reb Nahman's life and mission. Turning to Green, Piekarz charges that although Green pays lip service to the possibility that Weiss exaggerates, his entire book is based (erroneously, in Piekarz's view) on Weiss's methodology. Cf. "Zaddik," p. 157. While such a sweeping statement as Weiss's is certainly problematic, and the mind of any great thinker forever remains a mystery, I do believe the tales may yet reveal much regarding their author.

82. Weiss, *Mehkarim*, p.152. And cf. pp. 157–59,. where Weiss discusses the "split personality" of the author as portrayed in the heroes of the tale *Clever and Simple Son* and in the tale *The Two Sons Who Were Reversed.*

83. This approach, of course, already appears in the commentaries of R. Nathan and R. Nahman of Tcherin, and is adopted by modern scholars as well, such as Weiss, Piekarz, Dan, Band, Steinsaltz, Elstein, Haidenberg, and Oron. Consider, for example, Dan's comments in his preface to the translation of the tales published by Arnold Band: *Nahman of Bratslav: The Tales* (New York, 1978), p. xvii: "[W]e do find major Kabbalistic elements, especially the Lurianic concepts of mythological cosmic history and mystical redemption, serving as major motifs within the tales. But there is a basic difference between 'using' Kabbalistic ideas and 'expressing' them in the tales: those elements which are present in the tales ceased to be building blocks of a mystical theology and became chapters in the mystical biography of Rabbi Nahman's soul." And "this unity between the author and the work of fiction, involving the complete

transformation of every external element into a personal, intense biographical element, is both a basic requirement and the sign of success of every major literary work."

84. Cited by Marie-Louise von Franz in *Problems of the Feminine in Fairy Tales* (Dallas, 1972), p. 6.

85. *Shivhei Moharan,* Gedulat Hasagato, 4a:1. This paradox of appearances versus reality finds cogent expression in *Likkutei Moharan* 243: "Know that there is a zaddik of such greatness that the world cannot bear his holiness—thus he is unassuming, and shows no excessive holiness or separateness." The comparison Reb Nahman makes in the lines that follow is between that zaddik and the Song of Songs, called "holy of holies" though it contains no overt mention of purity, holiness, or even God's name. Cf. Piekarz, "Zaddik," p. 156.

86. *Hayyei Moharan,* Nesi'ato le-Erez Israel, 33:19. See also *Likkutei 'Ezot* 92b. For a different view of the figure of the beggar, his role in Jewish and world folklore, and negative reactions to his appearance, see Lipsker's analysis in "Ha-Kallah ve-Shiv'at ha-Kabbzanim." On the radical change in Reb Nahman's evaluation of the faculty of imagination between his early teachings and those after Rosh ha-Shanah 1809, see Green, *Tormented Master,* p. 341.

87. *Likkutei Moharan* 23.1. In another teaching, formulated as his physical illness grew more severe, Reb Nahman spoke of these conditions with great pathos: "Only through happiness can one conduct one's thoughts in accordance with His will and find peace of mind. For happiness is the world of freedom . . . enabling one to leave one's exile" (*Likkutei Moharan,* pt. 2, 10). For more on the dialectical meaning of happiness emerging from despair, see *Likkutei Moharan,* pt. 2, 78 and Liebes, "Ha-Tikkun ha-Kelali," pp. 207ff., 237.

88. *Likkutei Moharan,* pt. 2, 12

89. Weiss, *Mehkarim,* pp. 127–28.

90. *Likkutei Moharan* 64.6 For more detailed discussion of this teaching concerning the role of distortion in the creation of the fantastic dimension, see chap. 4. In *Zohar* 1.148b, the imitative, grotesque nature of the ape *(kof)* is drawn from the Hebrew letter *kof.* In its graphic form, that letter resembles the perfectly formed letter *heh,* but for its leg that is hopelessly too long.

91. King Saul's nightmarish degeneration from prophet to madman is clearly a precedent for this crucial dialectic (1 Samuel). According to Weiss (*Mehkarim,* p.144) understanding gained in madness is in fact a premonition of a new era: "The messianic age will bring about a fundamental change in the world: what now appears as *kushiya* [a problem, argument] will become, in those days, a *teruz* [resolution], its meaning clearly understood. In that sense, we could say that the madman's fleeting glimpses of the *teruz* are a personal premonition of things to come, a private anticipation of future harmony." Reb Nahman himself states in *Likkutei Moharan,* pt. 2, 64 that madness is an intrinsic quality shared by all prophets. And in *Likkutei Moharan,* pt. 2, 8.15 Reb Nahman contends that one must actually appear to be mad in order truly

to fulfill divine will; such behavior grants a person insight into wisdom that transcends the rational mind. See Liebes's remarks on madness and inspiration in "Ha-Tikkun ha-Kelali," pp. 212–33. Two stories from the later Bratslav tradition in which madness is central are discussed by Piekarz, "Zaddik," pp. 154–55 and Weiss, *Mehkarim*, p. 169. In Piekarz's view, it is highly doubtful the two are Reb Nahman's invention.

92. *Hayyei Moharan*, Maʿalat Torato, 14a:21. Compare the reflections attributed to the Baʿal Shem Tov on the mechanism of divine inspiration versus that of madness: "At times, when the sparks of the Shekhinah in the soul of the zaddik emerge and disperse, when she speaks the words in his mouth, it seems that he himself is not talking, rather that the words leave his mouth of their own accord. This is a very high level. And we see the opposite in madmen" (*Keter Shem Tov* 28b:217). See the sources cited by Green on this experience of being the mouthpiece of the Shekhinah, as it were, in Jewish tradition: *Tormented Master*, p. 92 n. 68.

Chapter II. Telling Tales; or, The Physics and Metaphysics of Fiction

1. My paraphrase of the tale recounted by G. Scholem as he heard it told by S. Y. Agnon (Scholem, *Major Trends in Jewish Mysticism*, pp. 349–50) The core of the story may be found in *Kenneseth Israel* (Warsaw 1906), fol. 12b. The midrashic prototype of the tale seems to be *Lamentations Rabbah*, Petichta 30, concerning four generations of kings and each one's declining strength compared to the activity of his predecessor. A parallel is found in *Yalkut Shimʿoni*, 2 Sam. s. 160. In Hasidic tradition, the story appears in *Toledot Yaʿakov Yosef*, Shemot. As Yoel Elstein observes, the structural similarity between the two texts—with the replacement of the fourth king's quietism with the fourth zaddik's storytelling—highlights the Hasidic narrator's novel conception. In his eyes, the midrash speaks, not of degeneration and even more paralyzing passivity, but rather of a preference for intuitive involvement guided by self-conscious forces over aggressive activity. See Elstein, *Maʿaseh Hoshev* (Ramat Gan, 1983), pp. 54–57. Moshe Idel offers another interpretation of the story, with important differences in the version analyzed. See Idel, *Hasidism*, pp.185–86.

2. Tishby and Dan, *Ha-Encyclopedia ha-ʿIvrit*, 17:816, s.v. "Hasidut." These *drushim* are preserved in two forms: those written by the author himself, such as the teachings of R. Jacob Joseph of Polonnoye, and those transmitted orally by the rebbe and recorded by his pupils, such as the teachings of the Maggid of Mezherich. Cf. Nigal, *Ha-Sippur ha-Hasidi*, pp. 13ff. and pp. 81ff. for a more detailed discussion of the Hasidic tale and its history. Nigal indicates the similarity between Hasidic tales and the traditional hagiographical literature. Reb Nahman's tales, of course, are an anomaly even within the genre of Hasidic tales.

3. Tishby and Dan, *Ha-Encyclopedia ha-ʿIvrit*, 17:817, s.v. "Hasidut."

Most of his non-narrative teachings are found in the two parts of *Likkutei Moharan*, though many of those in part 2 are fragments of more complete formulations that, as the authors explain, Bratslav Hasidim apparently hesitated to publish intact for fear of reactions to the extremism of their ideas.

4. S. A. Horodezski, *Ha-Hasidut ve-ha-Hasidim* (Tel Aviv, 1951), 3:54.

5. Shmeruk, *Sifrut Yiddish: Perakim be-Toledoteha* (Tel Aviv, 1978), pp. 221–22; Piekarz, *Hasidut Braslav*, pp. 151–89, and esp. p. 157 on the question of the language in which the stories were told. Important discussions of the tale in Hasidic tradition include Dan, *Ha-Sippur ha-Hasidi*, pp. 3–63 on Hasidic tradition in general and pp. 132–88 on the tales of Reb Nahman of Bratslav; and Elstein, *Paʿamei Bat Melekh* (Ramat Gan, 1984), pp. 76–107.

6. End of Second Introduction.

7. Jacob Elbaum, "Tavni'ot Mishtarsharot ve-Nishbarot," *Jerusalem Studies in Hebrew Literature* 4 (1984): 60 n. 4.

8. *Sihot Haran* 151. In other contexts, we find the conviction that, in effect, the tales Reb Nahman told bear within them an immortal soul: they metamorphose through the ages in accordance with the needs and conditions of their time. Some, as Reb Nahman says, were told only once before the First Temple, yet even the prophets did not comprehend their mystery. The same tales appear centuries later, in utterly new guise, yet trailed by "clouds of glory." See *Hayyei Moharan* 10b.

9. *Likkutei Moharan* 60.6–9. A parallel passage is found in *Sihot Haran* 138. On the distinction between the two categories of tales, see Elstein, *Maʿaseh Hoshev*, p.158. And cf. Arnold Band's observations in *Nahman ben Simhah of Bratslav: The Tales* (New York, 1978), p. 33. Among those who have perceived themselves, in one way or another, as Reb Nahman's literary sons are Yiddish storytellers such as I. L. Peretz, Der Nister, and I. B. Singer, as well as S. Y. Agnon, Elie Wiesel, Aharon Appelfeld, and Pinhas Sade. The vital role Reb Nahman's tales played in the creative development of the first three figures is examined in David R. Roskies's study, *A Bridge of Longing: The Lost Art of Yiddish Storytelling* (Cambridge, 1995). The question of Reb Nahman's influence on other Jewish writers—a fascinating and important subject—lies beyond the bounds of our discussion.

10. In Freudian terms, the patient is led to recall the traumas of his past, and through his own verbalization of those events, he can come to terms with them. Joseph, cast into Pharaoh's dungeon in Egypt, understands this mechanism intuitively. He can help the butler and baker understand their dreams—the inchoate expression of their fears. Like a true analyst, he says "Tell me them, I pray you" (Gen. 40:8)—*you* yourselves, through your narration, will reveal their meaning. And paradoxically, we know that the retelling is, many times, much more real for us than the original experience. Often, it is only through our own narration that we succeed in consciously living the events we ourselves have gone through. We recall the midrash, quoted by Rashi on Ex. 38:8 concerning the mirrors Jewish women donated to line the laver placed before the Tabernacle. Moses' first reaction was to reject their offering, tainted,

in his eyes, by coquetry and pride. Yet he is reprimanded by God Himself: by grace of those mirrors, he is told, these brave women managed to preserve the Jewish nation through dreadful days. How? Pharaoh sentenced their husbands to backbreaking labor in the fields of Egypt, in the attempt to exhaust them and stifle the urge to procreate. The wives, though, stole to the fields, brought their men food and drink, and aroused their desire by an ingenious alienation device. Each of them would show her husband his reflection together with her own in her mirror and say, "I am more beautiful than you." . . . Though dehumanized by their enslavement, the men were restored by a story of their former selves, by the sight of their wife's and their own *image* in her silvered glass.

11. My thanks to Avivah Gottlieb Zornberg for the insight she shared on this subject in her provocative discussion of "Hayyei Sarah" in January 1992. Very relevant to this theme are, of course, the first words opening *Sefer Yezirah*, in which the three roots of reality are named as "number," "book," and "story" *(sfar, sefer, sippur)*. R. Saʿadia Gaon's commentary to that work, describing these alternate means of representation and conceptualization, suggests many of the ideas set forth above.

12. Among them, interpretations by Steinsaltz, *Shishah me-Sippurei ha-Maʿasiyot* and *The Tales of Rabbi Nachman of Bratslav* (Northvane, 1993) and Aryeh Kaplan, *Rabbi Nahman's Stories* (New York, 1983).

13. *Likkutei Halakhot*, Oreh Hayyim, Tefillah 4.2.

14. See Steinsaltz, *Shishah me-Sippurei ha-Maʿasiyot*, p. 153; compare Kaplan's variant schema, *Rabbi Nahman's Stories*, pp. 324–53. On a characterization of the individual *sefirot*, see Tishby, *Torat ha-Rʿa ve-ha-Kelippah be-Kabbalat ha-ARI* (Jerusalem, 1964), esp. pp. 31–32.

15. See *Be'ur ha-Likkutim*, p. 60, s. 17, cited by Kaplan, *Rabbi Nahman's Stories*, p. 34.

16. *Zohar* 1.138a. And see *Midrash Tehillim* 92 (ed. Buber, p. 404 and his notes).

17. *Zohar* 1.123a. The evening prayer is represented by the bed; the morning prayer, with the sacrifices offered upon the altar, is represented by the table; the *Shemʿa*, uttered while seated, is represented by the chair, while the communal *kedushah* is represented by the lamp. Based on the biblical story of the Shunammite, the pious woman who provided an attic room—and in it a bed, table, chair, and lamp—for Elisha, the man of God, on his journeys (2 Kg. 4:10), the *Zohar* teaches that every individual must create such a spiritual room in his own life; through his prayers, God Himself, so to speak, may come to rest with him there day by day (1.123a).

18. The notion that all human action and thought cannot escape the fundamental truth of this paradigm is expressed in *Keter Shem Tov* (fol. 13b:99). A more extensive consideration of the subject, the existential reflection of Lurianic myths in the tales, appears below in part 2 of chapter 3. For a discussion of the stages of the Lurianic paradigm in the development of folk tales, see Dan, *Ha-Sippur ha-Hasidi,* pp.46–52 and part 2 of this chapter.

19. Wendy D. O'Flaherty, *Dreams, Illusions and Other Realities* (New

Haven and London, 1988), p. 304. See also *Likkutei Moharan*, pt. 2, 91. The dialectic of revealing and concealing is indeed an ineluctable aspect of all esoteric teaching. Consider R. Nathan's warning voiced in *Likkutei Halakhot*, Yore De'ah, Behemah ve-Hayyah Tehorah 4.32: "Now the truth must necessarily be concealed, for if it is wholly revealed, falsehood may even gain the upper hand. . . . True sages, therefore, must be exceedingly cautious in their speech, concealing their meaning in many layers, that falsehood not overcome the truth, heaven forbid." On the centrality of this dialectic in Reb Nahman's teaching, see Weiss, *Mehkarim*, pp. 181–248 and Piekarz, *Hasidut Braslav*, pp. 10–16. And see Liebes's comments regarding what he considers the internal censorship of Reb Nahman's teachings within the circle of Bratslav Hasidism, evident in the widespread use of "etc." *(ve-khule)* in sensitive areas of certain texts. Cf. "Megammot be-Heker Hasidut Bratslav," *Zion* 46 (1982): 225.

20. B.T. *Yoma* 72b.

21. *Shivhei Moharan*, Gedulat Hasagato 7b:40. The statement turns on a wordplay, or a double reading of the unvocalized word *rk:* it may be read as *rek* (empty, meaningless) or as *rak* (only).

22. Quoted by Dan, *Ha-Sippur ha-Hasidi*, p. 50. The idea of "uniting disparate entities" *[le-yahed yihudim]* originates, of course, in Lurianic teaching, in which the fulfillment of each commandment must ideally be done with the mystical intention of "reuniting the Holy One, blessed be He, and His Shekhinah." See also n. 51 below.

23. Dan, *Ha-Sippur ha-Hasidi*, p. 50.

24. *Likkutei Halakhot*, Yoreh De'ah 2, Nedarim 4.25.

25. Henie G. Haidenberg and Michal Oron, *Me-'Olamo ha-Mysti shel R. Nahman mi-Bratslav* (Tel Aviv, 1986), p. 15. See also Piekarz, *Hasidut Braslav*, pp. 20, 80–86; Elstein, *Ma'aseh Hoshev*, pp. 173–89; Green, *Tormented Master*, pp. 212, 223. In his critique of Green, Piekarz stresses, however, that Reb Nahman's tales are not to be read as a messianic document, "planned and deliberately composed." Instead, he contends, "They stem, first and foremost, from artistic impulses from within; though expressed in his teachings, *sihot* and parables before 1806, they found most cogent artistic expression in 1806, when he was at the height of his spiritual prowess" ("Zaddik," p. 163; my translation). Indeed, Piekarz's view seems to me more reasonable than Green's.

26. *Sihot Haran* 52.

27. *Likkutei Moharan* 33.2. See also Tishby and Dan's discussion (*Ha-Encyclopedia ha-'Ivrit*, 17:758, s.v. "Hasidut" concerning the doubleness of this divine vitality—as a positive presence in all of creation and as a negative absence, a situation of deracination and imprisonment. In their view, the tragic nuances of the Lurianic paradigm are mitigated in the Hasidic conception: the fall of the holy sparks, their imprisonment in matter, is seen not as a fatal disaster but as a condition of necessary *presence* of the divine in the physical world. This approach, in turn, became the basis of the teaching of *'avodah begashmi'ut*—service of God through interaction with the material world.

28. M. M. Bakhtin "The Forms of Time and the Chronotopos in the Novel:

From the Greek Novel to Modern Fiction," *PTL: A Journal for Descriptive Poetics and Theory of Literature* 3 (1978): 516.

29. To cite Bakhtin once again: "The meeting is one of the most ancient plot-forming events of the epic and particularly of the novel" (ibid, p. 504).

30. B.T. *Sotah* 21a, quoted in *Likkutei Moharan* 4.8.

31. On other folk motifs in Reb Nahman's tales and their sources, see S. Petrushka, "Makor Polani le-Sippurei Ma'asiyot shel Reb Nahman me-Bratslav," *Ketuvim* 2, no. 42 (12 July 1928); A. Schoenfeld, "Ma'asiyat Shiv'at ha-Kabbzanim shel Reb Nahman me-Bratslav," *Yed'a 'Am* 11, no. 30 (1956); Shmeruk, *Sifrut Yiddish*, pp. 224, 227–29; Piekarz, *Hasidut Braslav*, pp. 106–7; Dan, *Ha-Sippur ha-Hasidi*, pp. 136–37, 154–55; Band, *Nahman of Bratslav*, pp. 36, 39, 45. Among them: barrenness and deliverance, lovers' promises, nature as witness, and the kidnapped princess. Liebes points to the similarity in motifs between Reb Nahman's tales and those appearing in *Sefer Divrei ha-Adon* by Jacob Frank. Cf. "Ha-Tikkun," p. 229 n. 99.

32. Italo Calvino, *Six Memos for the Next Millennium* (Cambridge, 1988), pp. 45–46.

33. P. Maranda, in *Soviet Structural Folkloristics* (The Hague, 1974), p.75, points out the differentiation between the classical fairy tale (the subject of Propp's structural study) and myth, remarking that "the mythological world view is translated into one of fantastic *dramatis personae* and objects which, to a certain extent, superseded mythic heroes in assuming the lost values (object, status, etc.), re-establishing justice, etc." In chapter 4 we discuss the relationship between Reb Nahman's tales and the "mythic" tradition from the Bible to Lurianic kabbalistic teaching. Clearly, Maranda's differentiation applies here as well; the cast of Reb Nahman's tales are the fantastic embodiment of the "mythic heroes" every learned person knows intimately. Their transformation to fantastic dramatis personae, though, makes the most esoteric concepts of Jewish tradition accessible and relevant to all manner of listeners.

A second, noncognitive value of tales, recognized by Bruno Bettelheim, concerns their therapeutic effect, which is furthered, as well, by their unrealistic nature and their peculiar style of narration. Dialogues, riddles, and problems demanding resolution draw the listener to active involvement in the tales. Fantastic figures and events are an important device, in that they "make obvious that fairy tales concern, not information about the external world but the inner processes taking place in an individual." In Bettelheim's words, the patient contemplates "what the story seems to imply about him and his inner conflicts at this moment in his life. The content usually has nothing to do with the patient's external life but much to do with his inner problems, which seem incomprehensible and . . . insolvable." Bruno Bettelheim, *The Uses of Enchantment: The Meaning and Importance of Fairy Tales* (New York, 1977), p.25. Yet another stylistic detail, pointed out by Elbaum, concerns the use of repetitive utterances, actions, and situations. The effect of this compositional instrument, he comments, is that what originally appeared strange becomes familiar, and what is familiar becomes logical. See "Tavni'ot Mishtarsharot," p. 63.

34. B.T. *Baba Batra* 72–75.

35. *Likkutei Moharan* 2–22.

36. In chapter 4, though, we will consider some aspects of mythopoesis in rabbinic thought and its possible effect on Reb Nahman's thought.

37. A. Karlin, "Sippurei Pela'ot shel Rabba bar bar Hannah," *Sinai* 20 (1947): 56. For other interpretative approaches to these tales, see *Eiyn Ya'akov*, vol. 4, *Baba Batra* 73a in the name of Ritba. In Green's view, Reb Nahman's "early attraction to the most fantastic legendary passages in the Talmud and his later turn to storytelling as a means of instruction bear further witness to his struggle with the somewhat confining medium of traditional homiletics" (*Tormented Master*, p. 287).

38. B.T. *Sanhedrin* 91a. Piekarz contends, as well, that not all parables Reb Nahman told, or were heard in his name, are, in fact, his own invention at all; e.g., The Parable of the King and the Palace He Built and its possible origin in *Sefer ha-'Akedah* by R. Isaac 'Aramah. See Piekarz, *Hasidut Braslav*, p. 154 and n. 19.

39. These three biblical examples number among the ten visions listed in the midrash as descriptions of the new reality that will materialize in the end of days. See *Exodus Rabbah* 15.21.

40. For more on the presence of rabbinic literature in Reb Nahman's oeuvre, see Elstein, *Pa'amei Bat Melekh*, pp. 161–222.

41. *Midrash Tehillim,* Psalm 3.2. Quoted by Scholem, *On the Kabbalah and its Symbolism* (New York, 1975) p. 37.

42. Scholem, *On the Kabbalah*, p. 69. The symbolism of the two trees already appears in rabbinic literature. See B.T. *Ta'anit* 7a; *Pesahim* 112a; *'Avodah Zarah* 7b. The notion of the first tablets as presenting an infinitely polysemous text is made vivid in Nahmanides' interpretation of an ancient mystical image: "The entire Torah is composed of the names of God. . . . It seems that in the case of the Torah written in black fire upon white fire [J.T. *Sotah* 8.3 (fol. 37a)], as we have said, the writing was contiguous, with no separation between words; it could be read either as names, or as the teaching and commandments. It was given to Moses our teacher as an account of the commandments and transmitted to him in its reading as names" (introduction to his commentary on the Pentateuch). See Tishby's comments on Nahmanides in *Wisdom of the Zohar,* 1:283. See also *Sefer ha-Mefo'ar* by R. Solomon Molkho (Amsterdam, 1709), fols. 7b, 12a. There, we find a description of the metaphysical nature of these first tablets, never contemplated by human eyes, and lost to humanity through the treachery in Eden: "Were it not for Adam's sin, the Torah would have been given in complete and unblemished state, without chapters, words, vowels and cantillations; man could have read it in various combinations, and with them he would have had the power to grasp, conceive and rule both upper and lower spheres, to build worlds and destroy them. Yet in the wake of the Primal Sin, he was given but the interpretation related to the vowels. Only in the world to come, new meanings will be revealed, meanings more precious than gold." This dual identity—on one hand a configuration of

chapters, verses, and words and, on the other, in Scholem's words, a "living incarnation of the divine wisdom which eternally sends out new rays of light," the Torah thus represents much more than the historical law of the Chosen People; it is, rather, "the cosmic law of the universe as God's wisdom conceived it" (*Major Trends*, p. 14). In yet a third study, Scholem mentions the daring interpretation, suggested as early as the thirteenth century and referred to in Hasidic texts as well, that in reality the white fire is the true text of the Torah, while the text of black is merely the mystical Oral Law. It is then concluded that the true Written Law has become entirely invisible to human perception and is concealed now in the white parchment of the scroll; the black letters are no more than a commentary on this vanished text. In the messianic age, it is the meaning of this 'white Torah' that will be revealed. Gershom Scholem, *Kabbalah* (Jerusalem, 1974), p. 174. The problematics of interpretation and innovation so central in Reb Nahman's thought clearly reflect his sympathy with this view.

43. *Shivhei Moharan,* Gedulat Hasagato 7b:40. The eyes of the mystic, open to receive such knowledge, can read not only modern history but also events that have not yet come to pass. Bratslav tradition has it that "those who learn Torah should rightly know what the future will bring, as it is written, 'Concerning your testimonies, I have known of old that You have founded them forever' [Ps. 119:151]. 'Known of old'—that I knew previously what will be and whence; 'from your testimony'—i.e., from the Torah" (*Nahal Noveʿa*, p. 211).

44. In *Likkutei Moharan* 56.4 Reb Nahman recognizes the symbolic nature of the sacred text as a result of the disparity between the sublime realm and our "lower" world. The true meaning of the Torah is hidden, clothed in the form we see so that the *kelippot* (forces of impurity and evil) cannot draw strength from above. And in *Hayyei Moharan* this symbolism is expressed yet more graphically—there, "the Holy One blessed be He necessarily disguised *Himself*, so to speak, in all that happened in Egypt until, afterwards, He began to be recognized, so to speak, to make His greatness more and more evident . . . but in the beginning the only possible way to draw near to He was through disguise— those events in Egypt" (*Hayyei Moharan,* Nesiʿato ve-Yeshivato be-Uman, 41a–b:4).

45. *Genesis Rabbah* 1.5. This idea recurs in many variations in rabbinical sources: In *Genesis Rabbah* 1.4, "Six things that preceded Creation" are named, among them Torah; in B.T. *Pesahim* 54a, "Seven things were created before the world . . . Torah and repentence . . ."; in *Midrash Tehillim* 90.12, the Torah existed two thousand years before God created the world, etc. In Mishnah *Avot* 5.6, a related idea is set out: "Ten things were created at twilight on the eve of the Sabbath—the mouth of the earth [that swallowed up Korah's sons], the mouth of [Miriam's] well, the mouth of [Bilʿam's] ass, the rainbow, the manna, [Moses'] staff, the *shamir* [a legendary worm or stone used to hew certain jewels and the building stones of the Temple], the *ketav*, the *mikhtav*, and the tablets." This text evokes much inquiry into the nature of the last three mentioned. Maimonides understands the *ketav*, or "writing," as "the Torah

written before Him, and its nature is unknown. And the *mikhtav*, or 'script' is the marks on the tablets." (Cf. his commentary on *Avot* 5.6.) Rashi explains otherwise: he vocalizes the second element as *makhtev*, and recognizes it as an inscribing instrument used to carve the tablets (B.T. *Pesahim* 54a). And in *'Arukh ha-Shalem*, the *ketav* is seen as the shape of the letters while the *mikhtav* is their combination, forming words. These three interpretations are quoted by Lipiner, *Hazon ha-Otiot* (Jerusalem, 1989), p. 31 n. 2.

46. Elstein, *Ma'aseh Hoshev*, p. 132. See Green's discussion of this concept in *Tormented Master*, pp. 346–47.

47. *Likkutim Yekarim* 105b.

48. *Degel Mahanei Efraim*, fol. 6a. Quoted by Elstein, *Ma'aseh Hoshev*, p. 130. The latter posits that the Bible was perceived by many Hasidic thinkers as a historical model for future generations. He cites *Toledot Ya'akov Yosef* (1780) as an early expression of this view: "'And Sarah died in Kiryat-Arb'a. . . . Then Abraham again took a wife and her name was Keturah . . .' (Gen. 23:1–25:1). These verses speak of the fact that the principle of two women, Sarah and Keturah, exists *in every individual*, in every age, for if it were not so, why would such a matter be recounted in the Torah, as it is eternal?" (Hayyei Sarah, fol. 18a). In this astonishingly modern reading, R. Jacob Joseph of Polonnoye thus interprets this biblical narrative as the externalization or projection of the human psyche. His words remind us of the critical approach of thinkers such as Bruno Bettelheim to the psychological commentary they perceive at the core of all fairy tales. In this context, consider but one instance of the admonition often made in the *Zohar:* "If a man says that a story in the Torah is there simply for the sake of the story, may his spirit depart! For if it were so, it would not be a supernal Torah, a Torah of truth . . . and every single word is there to demonstrate supernal matters" (*Zohar* 3.149a–b; translated by D. Goldstein in Tishby, *Wisdom of the Zohar,* 3:1124–25).

49. Cited in Scholem, *Major Trends*, p. 141.

50. See B.T. *Eruvin* 21b; *Menachot* 29a and Benjamin Ze'ev Bacher, *Aggadot ha-Tannaim* (trans. from German), vol.1, pt. 2 (Jaffa, 1922), p. 51.

51. *Shivhei Moharan* 13a:9. Consider also *Hayyei Moharan*, introduction, fol. 2b: "But in truth, all the excurses *[sihot]* and stories written here [in this volume] are meaningful . . . even his simplest statements must be recorded, for each and every one of his excurses contains deep intentions. . . ." The frequent use of the word *kavvanot* (mystical intent) emphasizes the contention, mentioned above, that for the Hasidic masters, telling tales accomplishes what prayer cannot do; thus, the *kavvanot* so central in Lurianic teaching, for example, "to reunite the Holy One blessed be He with His Shekhinah" through meditation are transfigured. What appears in the kabbalistic context as the demand to take up the task of projecting one's will beyond the mundane concerns of earthly life reappears here; the same acceptance of responsibility is expressed, but now the means is the narration of a tale rather than introspective spirituality.

52. Compare classical medieval Jewish commentary on the double account

of Man's creation in Gen. 1:27ff. with Gen. 2:7ff. Or see Ex. 17:1–4 and Abravanel's commentary on those verses, with Num. 20:8.

53. Consider the words of R. Nahman of Tcherin, author of the commentary *Rimzei Ma'asiyot*. On *King and Kaiser*: "The secret meaning of this tale has not yet been understood, so what have we to say about it? Especially since we have no knowledge of hidden matters." On *The Cripple*: "It is clear to all that the contents of this tale are so sublime and so profound that no one is able to unlock their meaning." R. Nathan of Nemirov, in his afterword comments on *Master of Prayer*: "And still these matters are enigmatic and sealed, for the secret meaning of the tale has not been revealed at all . . . ," etc.

54. *Zohar* 3.152a; translated in Tishby, *Wisdom of the Zohar*, 3:1126.

55. *Keter Shem Tov* 11a:84. The notion of Light hidden away for time to come originates in *Genesis Rabbah* 3.6.

56. See Elstein's comments, *Ma'aseh Hoshev*, p.133. This thesis is at the root of the allegorical mode of interpretation. The same lexicon (the system of the *sefirot*, the thesaurus of Lurianic Kabbalah, etc.) that is the mainstay of esoteric exegesis is applied freely by Reb Nahman's followers to probe the depths of their master's tales.

57. Examples of this phenomenon: Deut. 8:10 reads literally, "And you ate, and were satisfied, and you blessed God," with the clear meaning of an injunction: "You shall eat and be satisfied, and then you will bless God. . . ." See Elbaum's discussion of biblical patterns in Reb Nahman's tales: "Tavniot Mishtarsharot," esp. pp. 61–62. On the matter of *"kol 'va-yehi' hu zara"* in the following comments, see *Genesis Rabbah* 42.3.

58. Leviticus Rabbah 11.7.

59. An entrenched mode of exegesis, such interpretations are termed *al tikre*—"do not read x, but y." This image of the letters as a golem without movement appears also in *Likkutei Moharan* 31.9. Moshe Idel traces the belief in plurality of significance based on the absence of vocalization in the text of the Torah to R. Jacob ben Sheshet, and names other Kabbalists who shared it. See *Kabbalah: New Perspectives* (New Haven, 1988), pp. 213–14 and notes on pp. 379–80.

60. B.T. *'Eruvin* 54a. See also *Exodus Rabbah* 41.9 for interpretations based on the same alternate reading of *herut*: "R. Yehudah said, Free from exile; R. Nehemiah said, Free from the angel of death; the rabbis said, Free from suffering. . . ."

61. Mishnah *Avot* 6.2.

62. *Likkutei Moharan* 66.4 In chapter 4 we will see how this principle is illustrated in *The Seven Beggars*, in the story of desire told by the mute beggar.

63. *Likkutei Moharan* 64.3.

64. Based on J.T. *Shekalim* 6.1 (fol. 49b). See above, n. 42.

65. *Sihot Haran* 203. In *Likkutei Moharan* 19.6, Reb Nahman outlines the ideology behind this declaration. An additional, celebrated technique through which the power of the letters themselves may be released is the phenomenon of

translation. This technique, he says, actually serves to make complete the divine language in which the world was created; through translation, the strength of the letters, which contain all that exists in the world, arises and grows, and ultimately makes the Holy Tongue itself more whole. An interesting discussion of talmudic interpretation and the challenge of designification undertaken by Reb Nahman is presented by Marc-Alain Ouaknin in *The Burnt Book* (Princeton, 1995).

66. Green names at least three senses in which the "technical term," as he calls it, of *behinah* is used, and sees it as "a key to fathoming [Reb Nahman's] associative processes." At times, he says, *behinah* "should be translated as 'aspect'; in other places it reflects analogy or comparison; still elsewhere it will denote some other form of relationship between two terms or ideas" (*Tormented Master*, p. 286).

67. *Likkutei Moharan* 38.2.

68. This continual tendency to designification, perhaps the most idiosyncratic quality in Reb Nahman's oeuvre, is present in his tales as well, albeit in simpler, less compressed, less labyrinthine form.

69. *Likkutei Moharan* 64.

70. Hakdamah, 5a.

71. *Likkutei Moharan,* pt. 2, 91. The phrase "builds and destroys worlds" is transplanted from the midrash *Genesis Rabbah* 3.7, where it is used to describe God's deeds before He came to create our own universe. Compare chapter 1, n. 21, above.

72. See chapter 1 and Ouaknin's discussion in *The Burnt Book*, p. 295.

73. Tzvetan Todorov, *Mikhail Bakhtin: The Dialogical Principle,* trans. Wlod Godzich (Minneapolis, 1984), p. 110.

74. *Nahal Nove'a,* p. 200 (chap. 34).

75. *Likkutei Moharan* 281. The combination of letters, particularly of the Divine Name, as a "mystical technique" was endorsed by many Kabbalists, from R. Eleazar of Worms, Spanish Kabbalists, and R. Abraham Abulafia to R. Joseph ben Shalom Ashkenazi and R. David ben Yehudah ha-Hasid. See Idel, *Kabbalah*, pp. 97–103.

76. E.g., in the afterword of *The Seven Beggars*, *The Master of Prayer*, *The Cripple*, etc. See above, n. 53.

77. See Tanhuma, Pikkudei 3; *Tikkunei Zohar*, Tikkun 69, fol. 100b; ibn Ezra on Gen. 1:26; R. Meir ibn Gabbai, *Derekh Emunah*, chap. 1, response 1. The rabbis, rereading the biblical Hannah's exclamation, "There is no rock *[zur]* like our God" (1 Sam. 2:2) declare "there is no artist *[zayyar]* like our God" (B.T. *Megillah* 14a). This recognition of divine craftsmanship leads R. Isaac Huttner, author of *Pahad Yizhak,* to state that in fact, all of Creation, the Torah commandments, the Sabbath, and man himself are indeed "miniatures" of the world, i.e., *ziyyurim*, symbolic entities that stand as shadows relative to "the things themselves." All of those "microcosms" are time-bound in the present of human experience, while the entities they signify are enrooted in the future, in worlds beyond our own. R. Isaac Huttner, "Shabbat," in *Pahad*

Yizhak (Brooklyn, 1986), pp. 101–12. R. Huttner comments that although Bezalel's inspired artistry fashioned the Tabernacle, it is Moses alone who can present and dedicate the finished work. For Bezalel's vision is confined to the *signifier*, the details of the "microcosm" itself; to Moses, in contrast, the *signified* was revealed on Mount Sinai; he alone of all human beings has glimpsed the cosmos to which this miniature refers. If we may extend the analogy, we may say that Reb Nahman, by weaving "microcosms" into his stories, implies that though his listeners and characters remain enthralled with the hand, the map, and the portrait, the author himself gazes beyond them, his own eyes set on the sublime truths they confer.

78. *'Ez Hayyim*, 'Iggulim ve-Yosher 2.3; *Zohar* 3.135a (Idra Rabba), quoted by Idel, *Kabbalah*, p. 107. See also R. Moses de Leon, *Sefer ha-Nefesh ha-Hakhamah*, col. C, 2, 3–4; a parallel view may be found in *Zohar* 2.259a (Cf. Idel, *Kabbalah*, p. 119 n. 54).

79. R. Yehudah Loew ben Bezalel of Prague (Maharal); *Tiferet Israel*, chap. 12.

80. *Zohar* 2.73b, and see Idel, *Kabbalah*, p. 107. Max Picard, in his moving work, *The Human Face*, trans. Guy Endore (London, 1931) explores the idea of the human countenance as "a reflex of God's own beingness," "the presentation of God's being in human guise," "an inventory of the world." Interestingly, the very term chosen as the modern Hebrew equivalent to the Latin "microcosm" is *ze'ir anpin*, literally "small face."

81. *Zohar* 2.74b. The laserlike line of light described here in the *Zohar* that fills space after the contraction of God's endless light joins with the powers of stern judgment *(din)* then revealed. In the words of the *Zohar*, "It strikes the hand of man as he sleeps and leaves marks and lines in his palm. According to his deeds, so is it inscribed." The light leaves signs there in the form of letters. The peculiar notion of letters on the king's hand image in Reb Nahman's *Master of Prayer* seems to reflect this ancient kabbalistic idea.

82. Two microcosms central in *Likkutei Moharan* but less explicitly present in the tales are that of the human face (cf. *Likkutei Moharan* 3, 19.9, 21.1, 31.9, 57.6, 60.6, 63, 66.3, 67.2, 74, etc.) and of language (refer to my discussion in chapter 4).

83. In the genre of folktales, and more dramatically in European romantic literature, the natural world often serves as a metaphor to depict internal spiritual states. The deserts of despair through which the king's servant trudges *(The Lost Princess)*, the seas of moral depravity on which the kaiser's daughter sails *(King and Kaiser)*, the winds of chaos *(Burgher and Poor Man)*, the dawn of enlightenment *(The Two Sons Who Were Reversed)*, and bifurcating paths of faith *(The Cripple)* are a few examples of this function. For more on this notion, see chapter 3.

84. *Likkutei Moharan* 10.

85. *Pirkei de Rabbi Eliezer*, 48. See also Steinsaltz, *Shishah me-Sippurei ha-Ma'asiyot*, pp.135–38 on this symbol.

86. *Genesis Rabbah* 1.1; *Zohar* 1.134a.

87. *Zohar* 1.20b. R. Daniel Epstein connects the moral teaching of *Master of Prayer* to this hand imagery. In the spirit of Deut. 30:12 that "the Torah is not in heaven, nor beyond the seas . . . but very, very close to you, in your mouth and in your heart that you may enact it," he emphasizes the immediacy of that divine truth: it is in your own hand. Look into yourself and find the paths that will allow you to draw closer to God. As we ask of Him, "Open your hand and satisfy all living things with your favor" (Ps. 145:16)—so should our hands be open in giving and receiving—not like the closed fists, the grabbing fingers, of the lonely people in the land of wealth.

88. *Likkutei Halakhot*, Oreh Hayyim, Tefillah 4.20. See also *Likkutei Moharan* 54. Reb Nahman points out the correspondence between the letter *yod* representing the numeral ten and the Hebrew word for hand, *yod*—an affirmation that the system of ten *sefirot*, the upper and lower worlds, is revealed through God's handiwork.

89. See my discussion of this story in detail in chapter 4. In the *Cripple*, portraits are used as photographs—a simple way of identifying individuals (*SM*, p. 43).

90. *Genesis Rabbah* 54.4; *Zohar* 2.138a.

91. *Tanhuma,* Vayeshev 4. My gratitude, once again, to Dr. Avivah Gottlieb Zornberg for her discussion of this text in December 1990. See also chapter 4 following n. 43 and n. 45.

92. This verse (Ps. 95:7) is the prophet Elijah's interpretation (in B.T. *Sanhedrin* 98a) of the response to the question of when the Messiah will enter history. What the sages teach through this exchange is that his advent, potential and predetermined, is continually on the verge of actualization. Yet it is the free human agent who catalyzes that realization by his complete and loyal acceptance of God's commandments.

Chapter III. The Romantic Drama

1. MS British Museum 768, fol. 14a; MS Oxford 1856, fol. 7a. These manuscripts were cited by Moshe Idel in a lecture in November 1988. See also Moshe Hallamish, *Perush le-Parashat Bereshit le-R. Yosef ben Shalom Ashkenazi* (Jerusalem, 1985), pp. 132–33. In B.T. *Berakhot* 61a (parallel text in *'Eruvin* 18a), R. Jeremiah ben Eleazar is quoted as saying, "The Holy One, blessed be He created Adam as a double countenance, as it is written: 'You have formed me behind and before, and laid Your hand upon me' (Ps. 139:4)." The medieval author extends this ancient allegory to reveal the bivalence that is, in fact, a fundamental principle of Creation: "The same is so of the true servants whose acts are true [an allusion to the sun and the moon, universal symbols of masculine and feminine forces; in midrashic tradition, created as luminous equals]—the matter of 'countenance' [*parzuf*] signifies two things. First, it is known that two opposites were emanated: complete *din* [strict judgment] and its counterpart, complete *rahamim* [tender mercy]. Had they not been emanated double-

faced, each would act autonomously, as two separate and unrelated forces. But because they were created double-faced all their action is unified. . . ." Clearly, the ultimate oneness of these polar attributes is, for the author, a theological necessity; their apparent disconnection in our earthly world but mirrors the temporary fission between the sexual valences in the primeval human soul. The parallel concept in Hellenic mythology is set out in Plato's *Symposium* 190.

2. Tishby explains this "divine union" in kabbalistic terms as the dynamic between the *sefirah* of *Tiferet* (male) and that of *Malkhut* (female). See *Wisdom of the Zohar,* 3:1372 n. 7, 1:278.

3. *Zohar* 1.85b.

4. *Likkutei Moharan* 31.9. The teaching is based on the polysemous verse, central in Reb Nahman's worldview, from the Song of Songs 1:11: "We will make thee necklets of gold studded with silver" (the root of "silver" being *ksf*, alternately read as "desire"). Reb Nahman draws the analogy to "the longing of the Jew for God." By manipulating the verse (Ps. 84:3), "My soul longs, indeed it faints for the courts of the Lord," he concludes, "The very fact of my longing for the Lord, from that effort itself my soul comes into being." See *Likkutei Moharan* 31. On the "romance of the phonemes" in greater detail, see below.

5. In the Second Introduction to the standard Bratslav edition of Reb Nahman's tales, R. Nathan of Nemirov affirms the omnipresence of this motif in sweeping terms: "All of the Song of Songs, the most sacred of sacred [books] . . . is founded on that mystery; all the writings of the holy ARI [R. Isaac Luria] and the books of the *Zohar* are filled with it. . . . And [the prayer] we say before Psalms, that 'the wife of His youth be joined to her beloved' and the 'Unification' spoken before binding on *tefillin*, 'the bridegroom [shall embrace his bride].' . . . Anyone who glances though the holy R. Luria's teaching will see that the entire foundation of Kabbalah/tradition concerns the union of the aspects of bridegroom and bride, male and female; all the [divine] names, the *sefirot*, the emanation of the worlds, are described in the image of the 'countenances of man and female' . . . the notions of meeting and conjoining, conception and birth, nursing and growth from infancy to maturity. . . . All of our sages, may their memory be for a blessing, spoke of the fundamental union of all the worlds in terms of the union of bridegroom and bride, for 'God created mankind in His own image, in the image of God He created him, male and female He created them' (Gen. 1:27). . . ." We will return throughout this chapter to a more extensive topological comparison of the tales to elements in earlier sources.

6. This last stage is recognized by René Wellek in "Romanticism Reexamined," in *Romanticism Reconsidered*, ed. N. Frye (New York, 1963) p.118. He is citing Eudo C. Mason, *Deutsche und englishe Romantik* (Göttingen, 1959).

7. In the first edition of his *Vorschule der Aesthetik*, published in 1804, J. P. Richter modified terms set out by Novalis in his notes, published two years earlier in 1802 by F. Schlegel and L. Tieck. Quoted by Raymond Immerwahr,

"The Word 'Romantisch' and its History," in *The Romantic Period in Germany,* ed. Siegbert Prawer (New York, 1970), p. 49. Immerwahr points out that "the literature which gave rise to the adjective and eventually to the noun 'die Romantik' was the extravagantly imaginative narrative fiction of the Middle Ages and the first centuries of printing." In the third and fourth quarters of the eighteenth century, he remarks, there developed "a growing interest in and affirmation of the historical era most intimately associated with romance: the age of feudalism, knighthood and the Crusades." In part 2 below, we will consider such "romantic" epic motifs as journey, search, rescue, and chivalric love and union in the context of Reb Nahman's tales.

8. Quoted by Immerwahr, "The Word 'Romantisch,'" pp. 52–53. As early as 1762, Gerstenberg unequivocably championed the romantic poetry of Spenser, Ariosto, and Tasso as "different in kind but equal in merit to the 'classical' beauties of Homer" and attributed the quality 'romantisch' (i.e., fictitiously imaginative) to Ariosto and Homer equally. *Deutsche Literaturdenkmale,* vol. 29/30 (Stuttgart, 1890), pp. 18ff. See Immerwahr, "The Word 'Romantisch,'" p. 34.

9. Among them: the attention "to 'nature', or innate capacity in the orator and poet . . . ; the tendency to conceive of the invention, disposition, and expression of material as mental powers and processes, and not only as the overt manipulation of words; and the common assumption that irrational or inexplicable occurrences such as inspiration, divine madness or lucky graces are indispensible conditions of the greatest utterance. Particularly noteworthy . . . — the stress that rhetoricians had always put on the role of emotions in the art of persuasion." M. H. Abrams, *The Mirror and the Lamp: Romantic Theory and the Critical Tradition* (New York, 1958), p. 70. In the course of this chapter, we will see how these and other "romantic" qualities correspond to Reb Nahman's thought.

10. The latter argument is presented by Ronald Taylor in his essay "Romantic Music," in Prawer, ed., *Romantic Period in Germany*, pp. 287–88. Reb Nahman's encounter with representatives of the Haskalah has been treated by Weiss, *Mehkarim*, pp. 61–65; Piekarz, *Hasidut Braslav*, pp. 21–55; and Green, *Tormented Master*, pp. 238–74.

11. Novalis, *Schriften*, ed. Kluckhohn-Samuel, 2d ed. (Stuttgart, 1977), 3:545. Cited by Immerwahr, who adds that, essentially, Novalis saw the *Romantiker* as "a person whose business it was to experience life poetically, as romance, and to create a literary expression of this experience. Being a 'romanticist' . . . was nothing less than the craft of poetry viewed as a mystic vocation" ("The Word 'Romantisch,'" pp. 47–48).

12. Abrams, *Mirror and the Lamp,* p. 296. A. A. Avni, in his study of the susceptibility of German romantic theory and practice of writing to the influence of the "Old Testament," links the figurative language inherent in biblical verse to the symbolism manifest in all romantic poetry. "In looking for suggestive objects and legendary characters to read the heiroglyphs of Nature, as Novalis refers to them, the German romantic is certainly apt to use biblical

allusions and reinterpret them symbolically, as he does to different mythologies." A. A. Avni, *The Bible and Romanticism: The Old Testament in German and French Romantic Poetry* (The Hague, 1969). p. 25. Please refer to chapter 4, part 3, below and my discussion of trope connecting Reb Nahman's tales to Jewish poetic tradition.

13. *Deutsche Literaturdenkmale des 18 und 19 Jahrhunderts* (Stuttgart, 1890), 17:91–95; cited by Abrams, *Mirror and the Lamp,* p. 90.

14. Northrop Frye, "The Drunken Boat: The Revolutionary Element in Romanticism," in *Romanticism: Points of View*, ed. R. F. Gleckner and G. E. Enscoe (Detroit, 1975), p. 304.

15. See Abrams, *Mirror and the Lamp,* p. 240. In the romantic age, medieval hermeneutics are thus plied to generate secular literary works; surely it is more than coincidence that Reb Nahman's tales, as well, are born from a transformation of classic kabbalistic interpretative techniques (whose influence on the Christian poets Dante and Petrarch and on Pico della Mirandola's hermeneutics have been documented). Cf. Idel, *Kabbalah*, p. 214. Also compare chapter 2, part 3, above and chapter 4, part 3, below.

16. Schleiermacher, *Monologen*, ed. R. M. Schiele (Leipzig, n.d.), p. 22; Herder, "Vom Erkennen and Empfinden" (1778), in *Sämtliche Werke,* (Munich, 1984), 8:208. Both poets are quoted by Abrams, *Mirror and the Lamp,* p. 227. Clearly, chapter 1 of the present work, concerning the self-referentiality of Reb Nahman's tales, reflects, in part, such a "romantic" reading. Far from anachronistic, Reb Nahman himself, throughout *Likkutei Moharan*, indirectly affirms the relevance of that mode of understanding, and his students and followers continue unquestioningly in his wake, perhaps unaware of the "romantic" nature of their interpretation.

17. Cf. J. F. von Schiller, *Sämtliche Werke* (Munich, 1960), 2:234f., 265f. Cited by Immerwahr, "The Word 'Romantisch,'" p. 41.

18. He describes the unconscious as "an instinct which eternally has a presentiment of and demands its objects without regard to time, because these dwell beyond the reaches of time." Cf. Richter, *Vorschule der Aesthetik*, 11:50–51, 47 n, cited by Abrams, *Mirror and the Lamp,* pp. 211–12. In chapter 4, part 2, below, the dream paradigm seminal in Reb Nahman's conception is discussed.

19. See James Trainer's informative essay "The Märchen," in Prawer, ed., *Romantic Period in Germany*, pp.98, 99, 118. Shelley is quoted by Wellek, "The Concept of Romanticism in Literary History," p. 195. Ludwig Tieck, following his observations of Shakespearean method ("Shakespeares Behandlung des Wunderbaren" [1793, pub. 1796]), constructs his own *Märchenwelt* which, in Trainer's eyes, "denies the subjective distinction between the real and the marvellous in favor of a world in which every object possesses its own animate existence and where all external appearances exist but to disguise inner reality" ("The Märchen," p. 101). The romantic poets' choice of the *Kunstmärchen* as a medium for presenting their new worldview, and the parallel phenomenon of the Hasidic movement's adoption of folktales as a genre for

transmitting their teaching, is discussed in chapter 4, part 1, below and in chapter 2, part 2.

20. August Schlegel, "Vorlesungen über schöne Literatur und Kunst" (1801–4), in *Deutsche Literaturdenkmale* (Stuttgart, 1884), 17:94–98. Quoted by Abrams, *Mirror and the Lamp,* p. 281.

21. Cf. Abrams, *Mirror and the Lamp,* p. 272. On the historical development of this view from the late fifteenth century through English eighteenth-century criticism, particularly that of Sydney, to the critics of 1740, Breitinger and Bodmer, and down to Schlegel himself, see Abram's discussion, pp. 272–85.

22. Friedrich Schelling, "System des transcendentalen Idealismus," in *Sämtliche Werke* (Stuttgart and Augsburg, 1858), p. 617, quoted by Abrams, *Mirror and the Lamp,* pp. 209–10. The latter points out that, similarly, J. G. Salzer (*Allgemeine Theorie der schönen Kuenste,* 1771–74) propounds the "psychological 'mystery' that certain conceptions clarify and develop independently of the intention or attention of the artist." Salzer reaches this conclusion in his discussion entitled "Invention," which he begins by expounding Leibniz's theory that "no ideas are absolutely new, but all are latently present in the mind, until, in correlation with external circumstance, one of them becomes clear enough to emerge into consciousness." Cf. Abrams, *Mirror and the Lamp,* p. 203. Regarding Reb Nahman, the fascinating problem of innovation and the perpetuation of tradition, and the image of the zaddik-storyteller as creator, is raised in chapter 1, part 1 and chapter 2, part 1 of the present work.

23. Shelley, *Essays on Christianity* (1815), quoted by Abrams, *Mirror and the Lamp,* p. 61. In his "Ode to the West Wind" Shelley entreats: "Make me thy lyre, even as the forest is. . . ." Wordsworth also describes his sympathy with the moods of nature: "In a kindred sense of passion [I] was obedient as a lute That waits upon the touches of the wind." As a result, "I had a world about me; 'twas my own, I made it" (*Prelude* [1805], bk. 3, lines 136ff.). Indeed, as early as 1795 Coleridge suggested the harp as an analogue for the thinking mind:

> And what if all of animated nature
> Be but organic harps diversely fram'd,
> That tremble into thought as o'er them sweeps,
> Plastic and vast, one intellectual breeze
> At once the soul of each and God of all?

("The Eolian Harp," stanza 2, lines 44–48.) The motif of David's harp as a metaphor of divine inspiration, widespread in the Talmud and midrashic literature, and transplanted by Reb Nahman to his own works (especially *Likkutei Moharan* 8.2 and 54.6) is discussed in chapter 4, part 3.

24. *Prelude* (1850), bk. 6, lines 743–45. The obvious comparison, in this case, is the image of the heart of the world and the stream, evoked by the blind beggar *(Seven Beggars).* Yet the metaphor itself, as we see in chapter 4, is a

dramatization of the allegorical scene described in Psalm 61, portraying the individual (specifically King David) in his prayer to God. Clearly, this "romantic" perception of the natural world as verbal—singing praises to God, speaking its inmost thoughts, communicating to the human beings in its midst—has its inception in lyrical biblical imagery. This figurative language is developed and evoked in manifold forms throughout the ages of Hebrew literature.

25. "A heart full of harmony is called to glory near a throne; on rugged steps the poet ascends and becomes the king's son." The parallels to Reb Nahman's *Two Sons Who Were Reversed* are nearly self-evident; that tale, as we suggested in chapter 1, part 3, has been considered by Reb Nahman's students and other critics as one of the most transparently autobiographical. A variation on the theme is brillantly presented by E. T. A. Hoffmann in his *Der goldene Topf.*

26. Needless to say, treatment of this vast subject is beyond the parameters of this work. See Idel's comprehensive discussion on symbolism and kabbalistic hermeneutics in Idel, *Kabbalah*, pp. 200–249. For a general index of kabbalistic sources, see relevant sections in Tishby, *Wisdom of the Zohar*; the collection edited by Horodetzski, *Torat ha-Kabbala shel R. Yitzhak Ashkenazi ve-R. Hayyim Vital* (Tel Aviv, 1947); and Elias Lipiner, *Hazon ha-Otiot* (Jerusalem, 1989). In Hasidic teaching, many such esoteric concepts were retranslated, once again, and roles shifted: the male figure becomes the human individual, or the Assembly of Israel in search of the beloved, in the figure of the Shekhinah, God's female manifestation. R. Nathan cites the omnipresence of the hermeneutic code of mystical teaching: "It is clear that in all the books of the *Zohar* and the *Tikkunim*, and in all the writings of the ARI *zal,* that the king's daughter is another name for the *Shekhinah* and the Assembly of Israel" in order to justify his rebbe's use of the same cast of characters in his own teachings (Second Introduction to *SM*, p. 9).

27. Song of Songs Rabbah 3.1.

28. Tishby, *Wisdom of the Zohar,* 1:376 on *Zohar* 1.12b.

29. *Zohar* 1.36a. Concerning the verse from Ps. 39:3, "I was dumb with silence, yet held my peace. I had no comfort and my pain was stirred up," the author of the *Zohar* writes: "—this verse is spoken in exile by the Assembly of Israel. For what reason? Because the voice *[Tiferet]* governs speech, and when she is in exile, the voice is separated from her and no word is heard. . . . Silent she remains, silenced and mute" (translated in Tishby, *Wisdom of the Zohar,* 1:384). In Reb Nahman's oeuvre, this concept becomes central. See, for example, *Likkutei Moharan* 66.4 and below in this chapter.

30. Song of Songs Rabbah 5.1. See chapter 4 for additional uses of this allegory, and their links to Reb Nahman's tale of *The Seven Beggars*. Compare *Likkutei Moharan* 8.9.

31. Consider, for example, the examples presented by Tishby in *Wisdom of the Zohar,* 1:376–79. Some of these texts and their relationship to Reb Nahman's portrayal of women are treated in the last section of this chapter.

32. *SM*, p. 219. See chapter 4 for detailed discussion of the theme in this

story. Green comments that "the motif of unfulfilled longing is a thread that runs through almost all of Nahman's tales" (*Tormented Master*, p. 300).

33. *Likkutei Moharan* 66.4. Reb Nahman uses a familiar and touching scene to illustrate his point—"As for example when a small child is shown something he likes, and then it is snatched from him and hidden away—then the child chases after the adult and begs and pleads for that thing. Indeed, his desire is so great because it was snatched and hidden from him." It seems to me that the same rule guides Reb Nahman in his teachings themselves: readers of Reb Nahman may feel that his allusions, his meaning, are recognizable. Yet still, somehow, something of them evades us—what we have almost understood dodges into abstraction; we realize we have understood nothing at all. This veiling of true meaning, the enticing form that cannot be fully gazed upon, does have a certain magnetism; its role in Reb Nahman's oeuvre must not be ignored. Compare Green's discussion of the motif of "obstacles" in *Tormented Master*, p. 83.

34. *Likkutei Moharan,* pt. 2, 12. Reb Nahman's student, R. Nahman of Tcherin employs a similar principle in his interpretation of the tale *Burgher and Poor Man.* Hero and heroine are brought together again at last, yet their true identity is concealed. In the same way "God causes holiness to be very close to man, even right next to him. Only they do not recognize one another. Even after she restored the signs [of their betrothal] to him, even then despair and disregard overcame him—wherever should he search for holiness, for she, too, [i.e., the Shekhinah] has endured what she has endured. Where is she now? Then holiness herself reassures man, and asks him to come with her. Until both return to their first home, to the source and root of their holiness, and then they join together, and union and happiness become complete" (*Rimzei Maʿasiyot,* p. 15).

35. Scholem comments that this "mystical function"—to lead the Shekhinah back to her master and unite her with Him—lends human action a special dignity. See *Major Trends in Jewish Mysticism* (New York, 1941) p. 275. On the "motif of spiritual quest" in Reb Nahman's tales, see Green, *Tormented Master*, pp. 346, 366.

36. *Likkutei Moharan,* pt. 2, 12.

37. *Rimzei Maʿasiyot*, pp.14–15.

38. In the words of Avni, *Bible and Romanticism*, p. 24.

39. *Likkutei Moharan* 4.4.

40. *Tiferet* being masculine; *Din* feminine. See my discussion in the first pages of this chapter and end of part 4. Interestingly, a Freudian interpretation of fairy tales points to the same principle in psychoanalytic terms. As Bruno Bettelheim explains, "The permanent union of . . . prince and princess symbolizes the integration of the disparate aspects of the personality—psychoanalytically speaking—the id, ego and superego. . . . Separation anxiety is transcended when the ideal partner has been found" (*Uses of Enchantment*, p.146).

41. *Zohar Hadash*, Shir ha-Shirim, fol. 62b. See also the description, attributed to the Baʿal Shem Tov, of the cosmic effects of mystical devotion in

prayer and action: "All the worlds unite in one—great happiness and pleasure without measure—like the happiness of groom and bride in the lower, material world; all the more so on the most sublime level" (*Keter Shem Tov* 2a:1).

42. *Zohar* 2.10a–11b. As Tishby notes in his commentary, the hind of the dawn is a symbol of the Shekhinah, who conjoins with *Tiferet,* called "Day." She then leaves him. Tishby, *Wisdom of the Zohar,* 2:671.

43. Abrams, *Mirror and the Lamp,* p. 204. Or as Wordsworth writes in the *Preludes*:

> To every natural form, rocks, fruits, or flower
> Even the loose stones that cover the highway
> I gave a mortal life: I saw them feel,
> Or linked them to some feeling: the great mass
> Lay bedded in a quickening soul, and all
> That I beheld respired with inward meaning.

Hillel Zeitlin characterizes Reb Nahman as a visionary with a total sense of oneness with nature: "His was the perspective of a man who knew no distinction between 'self' and 'other,' a man who is drawn into all that he sees and feels in full and complete admiration . . . merging the beauty of every thing with the aspirations of his own soul, in his own moral attributes, with the holiness and purity of his soul." Hillel Zeitlin, *'Al Gevul Shenei 'Olamot, Ketavim* (Tel Aviv, 1976), 2:304 (my translation).

44. *Zohar Hadash*, Yetro, fol. 31b; see also *Zohar* 1.42a–b; quoted by Lipiner, *Hazon ha-Otiot*, p. 101. Both in the *Zohar* and in Lurianic mysticism, anthropomorphism is a primary conceptual element. Cf. Horodezki, *Torat ha-Kabbalah*, p. 138.

45. Tieck, "Der Blonde Eckbert"; Brentano, "Traume der Wüste." Personification of nature, though, is frequent in the books of the *Zohar* as well. The Shekhinah, for example, in the form of a doe, searches for food, venturing deep into the "mountains of darkness," symbolizing the dwelling place of the *kelippot.* See *Zohar* 3.249a–b; Tishby, *Wisdom of the Zohar,* 1:395. In Jewish sources, a classic (though clearly less "pathetic") means of describing the experience of revelation is by portraying the responsiveness of nature to man's heightened awareness. Thus, when R. Eleazar ben Arakh begins to speak with his master, R. Yohanan ben Zakkai, of the mysteries of the Heavenly Chariot, fire falls from the sky and surrounds all the trees of the fields—whereupon they break into song, proclaiming, "Praise God from the earth, O monsters and all the deeps, fire and hail; snows and vapors; stormy wind fulfilling His word: mountains and all hills, fruitful trees and all cedars . . ." (Ps. 148:9). Cf. B.T. *Hagigah* 14b.

46. This, indeed, is the most basic principle of kabbalistic symbolism: nature is seen as the 'garment' or guise in which God manifests Himself. See *Zohar* 3.152a and chapter 4 below concerning the motif of disguises in roman-

tic literature and the renaissance of the fantastic. Consider also, in part 3, below, the notion of music's power to "make a garment."

47. *Tikkunei Zohar*, Tikkun 57, fol. 91b.

48. *Zohar* 2.15b–16a. In the same context, the author affirms that even "every growing plant, with their appointed ministers in heaven, each and every one contains its own secret, in the image of its sublime form. . . . As it is written: 'He calls them all by [His] names' (Is. 40:26). All that exists in the world is a mystery unto itself. . . ." According to talmudic legend, although the Fall rendered the language of nature incomprehensible to humankind, a few sages still possessed that secret original knowledge. R. Elisha owed his life to the advice of a dove (B.T. *Gittin* 45a); R. Yohanan ben Zakkai conversed with palm trees and ghosts, not to mention angels (B.T. *Sukkah* 28a).

49. *SM*, pp. 121–22.

50. *Likkutei Moharan* 65.1.

51. *Likkutei Moharan* 65.1–2.

52. *Likkutei Moharan* 65.4.

53. *Shivhei Moharan*, Maʿalat ha-Mitkarvim Elav, 10a:77.

54. *Likkutei Moharan* 163. See also *Likkutei Moharan* 25 concerning the practice of *hitboddedut*, or solitary wandering for the purpose of communing with God. As a tradition, it has won extensive attention by Reb Nahman's followers; the animation of the natural world is assumed unquestioningly, leading to such developments: "Winter is like a time of pregnancy; all the herbs and plants seem dead because their strength has waned. But as summer comes, it is like a birth; all of them awaken to new life. Then it is good to walk [*lasuʾah*, also meaning "to converse"] in the fields; to speak words of prayer and pleas, desire and longing to God. And then all the plants [*siʾah*] of the field begin to live and to flourish, all of them surging forth to join in his words and his prayer." *Likkutei ʿEzot*, Hitboddedut 4. Cf. n. 138 below.

55. *Likkutei ʿEzot*, Hitboddedut 4.

56. *Likkutei Moharan* 8.7. The image is clearly born from the *Zohar*'s reading of the biblical myth of Creation. Beginning with the verse "And no plant of the field was yet in the earth, and no herb of the field had yet grown: for the Lord God had not caused it to rain upon the earth, and there was not a man to till the ground" (Gen. 2:5), the author of the *Zohar* comments that "the People of Israel are the plants and the trees"; the seeds of vegetable life waiting unborn within the soil are the souls of the Messiah, or of the zaddikim of every generation, or of the single "true zaddik," Moses himself. See *Zohar* 1.25b.

57. In another text (*Likkutei Moharan,* pt. 2, 8.1), we find a development of the idea that prayer, or "voice" flows out like the "river that emerged from Eden to water the garden" (Gen. 2:10). Here the futuristic song is an invocation of the ineffable holy names of God in their seventy-two-letter combination. The sages detect, in the words prefacing the Song of the Sea, a premonition of the "new song" of final redemption to be sung in days to come: "Then

Moses and the Children of Israel sang [lit. "will sing"] . . ." (B.T. *Sanhedrin* 91b). See also *Midrash Tehillim* on Psalm 98; cf. the verse "Sing to the Lord a new song" and my discussion later in this chapter.

58. *Zohar* 1.12b–13a; see Tishby, *Wisdom of the Zohar,* 3:1382–84. Reb Nahman's use of water as a recurrent motif in his tales is examined in chapter 4, part 3.

59. The spell cast on Reb Nahman's listeners by this enchanted garden is made more potent through his allusive language. For example, its dangerous seduction is compared to the "Pardes" evoked in B.T. Hagigah 14b, from which only R. Akiva, like the king's son, could "enter and exit and remain whole" (*SM,* p.166). In the *Zohar Hadash*, Shir ha-Shirim, fol. 1b, the Garden of Eden "bursts into song" on the day King Solomon's Temple is complete, in words strongly reminiscent of Reb Nahman's own. See also *Zohar* 2.133b where the effect of prayers uttered by the People of Israel in pure devotion is also described as an enchanted garden's crescendo of praise. In *Zohar* 1.77b, the nightly entrance of the Holy One, blessed be He, into the Garden of Eden is met by choruses of singing trees; in *Zohar* 3.144a, Jacob's arrival there arouses a similar reaction. The motif also appears in *Zohar* 2.195b–196a, 3.25b; *Zohar Hadash* Bereshit, fols. 13a–b, 17b–18a.

60. E. T. A. Hoffmann, "Die Automate," in *Sämtliche Werke,* ed. E. Griseback (1900), 7:96. Quoted by Taylor, "Romantic Music," p. 294.

61. E. T. A. Hoffmann, "Alte und neue Kirchmusik," in *Sämtliche Werke,* 1:37–39, quoted by Taylor, "Romantic Music, p. 285.

62. I.e., the third beggar's tale in chap. 4; the fourth beggar's tale in chap. 4; the sixth beggar's tale in chap. 4; images of the shepherd-musician in chap. 1 and chap. 3; images of prophet-musicians in chap. 4; the motif of David's harp in chap. 4; of Moses' song in chap 3; the music of holiness in chap. 4, etc.

63. "Alte und neue Kirchmusik," p. 37. Blake, similarly, speaks of poetry, painting and music as the three forms of conversing with paradise which the flood did not sweep away. Cf. Northrop Frye, *Creation and Recreation,* (Toronto, 1980), p. 57. Or, as Georg Brandes said, "The ideal of German Romanticism is not a figure but a melody, not definite form but infinite aspiration. Is it obligated to name the object of its longing?" Brandes, *Major Currents in Nineteenth Century Literature* (New York, 1923), 2:3. Quoted by Barbara Fass, *La Belle Dame sans Merci and the Aesthetics of Romanticism* (Detroit, 1974), p. 93.

64. "Phantasien ueber die Kunst" (1799) in *Deutsche National-Literatur* CXCV, 71. Cited by M.H. Abrams, p.93.

65. *Die Welt als Wille und Vorstellung*, in *Sämtliche Werke* (Leipzig, 1891), 1:346; quoted by Taylor, "Romantic Music," p. 285.

66. *Likkutei Moharan* 64.5. See also *Likkutei Moharan* 49.7, where Reb Nahman explains the graphic form of the letter *heh*, composed in effect of the letters *dalet* and *yod*: "*Dalet* [= 4] is an aspect of the four corners of the earth, i.e., 'From the corners of the earth . . .' [Is. 24:16]. And *yod* [= 10] is an aspect of the ten kinds of playing, i.e., '...we heard melodies.'"

67. See the sources cited in n. 75 below.

68. *Likkutei Moharan* 54. R. Nathan Sternharz, a formative influence in the development of Bratslav Hasidism, celebrates music as the most important element of spiritual life. "The essence of *devekut* and conjoining with God in this so lowly, humble world is through melody and song" (*Likkutei Halakhot*, Oreh Hayyim, Nesi'at Kappayim, 5); "The essential way to draw forth the spirit of a life of holiness is through music and song to the Lord" (*Likkutei Halakhot*, Hoshen Mishpat, ʿOseh Shali'ah Ligbot Hov, 3.24; "'All of Israel has a portion in the world to come' [Mishnah *Sanhedrin* 1.11], and the essence of enjoyment in the world to come is the voice of music and song that will one day be awakened" (*Likkutei Halakhot*, Hoshen Mishpat, Avedah u-Mezi'ah, 3.14).

69. *Likkutei Moharan* 282; see also *Likkutei Moharan* 54.

70. B.T. *Menahot* 29b.

71. *Likkutei Moharan* 64.3. Compare my discussion in chapter 4.

72. *Likkutei Moharan* 64.5. Reb Nahman substantiates this idea, once again, with the famous rabbinic teaching that Moses is destined to raise the dead (B.T. *Sanhedrin* 91a), alluded to in the Song of the Sea: "And so Moses sang [lit. 'will sing'] (Ex.15:1). See above, n. 57.

73. See, for example, *Likkutei Moharan* 42. From the verse (Ps. 106:44) "He regarded their affliction when he heard their cry/song," Reb Nahman teaches: "By grace of music, harsh judgment is sweetened." The Kabbalists' practice of rising in the dark of night to pray and sing thanks to God has the identical effect—see *Likkutei Moharan* 149. Indeed, the archetypical Kabbalist and musician is none other than King David himself, author of Psalms: his metonymic lyre played of its own accord as the north wind blew upon it at midnight (B.T. *Shabbat* 30b; B.T. *Pesahim* 117a; *Lamentations Rabbah* 2.22; *Midrash Tehillim* 57.4). For development of the concept in esoteric sources, see *Zohar* 1.180b; 217b; *Tikkunei Zohar*, Tikkun 11, fol. 26b; Tikkun 13, fol. 28b; Tikkun 69, fol. 119a. R. Moses Cordovero attributed to the cantillation of the Torah the power "to cancel harsh judgments and sweeten them" (*Shiʿur Komah*, fol. 88a), as Lipiner notes in *Hazon ha-Otiot*, p. 386. See my discussion below of *Likkutei Moharan* 42 in greater detail.

74. *Likkutei Halakhot*, Oreh Hayyim, Berakhot ha-Shahar 3.2, commenting on the tale. As we saw in chapter 1, the "chamber of transformations" is the mechanism causing this schism between identity and referent. For R. Nathan, it is most evident in the inescapable disparity between the orthographic representation of God's name YHVH and its vocal evocation.

75. This according to *Zohar* 2.130a, 2.162b; see Tishby, *Wisdom of the Zohar*, 2:524–25. The two sons express their awareness, as well, that the night forest is a place where evil spirits roam in their talk of it as *makom ha-yeduʿim* (*SM*, p. 153).

76. In the continuation of that allegory, the day brings the light of redemption. See *Zohar* 2.138a. Alternately, night is this, our dark world, while "day," bearing endless mercy in its wings, is the "world to come." See B.T. *Hagigah* 12b.

77. This idea, recorded in *Zohar* 1.34a is recalled in *Likkutei Moharan* 65 with variations.

78. The image of the candle flame, suggested by Reb Nahman himself in his afterword to *The Two Sons Who Were Reversed* finds poetic expression in B.T. *Hullin* 60b, as well as in *Zohar* 2.130b, 2.166b. On the identification between the moon and the Jewish people in greater detail, see my discussion in chapter 4, esp. n. 185.

79. B.T. *Hullin* 60b.

80. *Zohar* 2.130b.

81. This text—*Zohar* 3.216a—is clearly a major source of inspiration for Reb Nahman's thought.

82. The core of prayer (halakhically defined) is the nineteen blessings called the *ʿamidah*. In its opening words, the patriarchs' names are recalled. The content of the first blessing concerns *hesed* (Abraham's attribute); the second *gevurah* (Isaac) and the third *kedushah* (corresponding with Jacob). Cf. *Zohar* 3.216b, which speaks of the zaddik whose merits and deeds permit him to "illumine the Queen [*matronita*, i.e., the *sefirah* of *Malkhut*], to strip her of the blackened garments of simple reading and adorn her with the luminous garments of esoteric secrets." A few pages later, this symbiotic relationship becomes metonymy: "[T]he zaddik *himself* is called 'bow' [*keshet*] . . ." (*Zohar* 3.230b).

83. *Likkutei Moharan* 42. My three citations of this teaching are continuous, without ellipses, and preserve Reb Nahman's text in its original order.

84. See R. Ashlag's commentary on *Zohar* 2.216a. The last words of *Likkutei Moharan* 42 gesture toward yet another manifestation of the triad: the three sounds of the shofar—*teKiya*, *Shevarim*, *Teru'ah*—hinted in the word and acronym *KeSHeT* parallel the patriarchs as well.

85. *Tikkunei Zohar,* Tikkun 5, fol. 20b. In his commentary, R. Ashlag reminds us that "prayer" represents the *sefirah* of *Malkhut,* as it is the archetypical act of speech *(dibbur)*. Indeed, the only link still missing is the logical connection hinted in *Tikkunei Zohar* and in *Likkutei Moharan* 42 as self-evident, joining the concept of the Shekhinah with the act of speech, or the words or letters of prayer. The statement that "the Shekhinah is prayer" seems to be founded on the complex in kabbalistic teaching of "thought-voice-speech." In this schema (based, of course, on the human mechanism of verbality), presented, among other contexts, in *Zohar* 1.246b, each step in the process parallels cosmic entities. The details of this schema and its reinterpretation in Reb Nahman's teachings are beyond the bounds of our discussion; their relevance, though, to the subject at hand should not be ignored.

86. On the importance of trope in the creation of the fantastic dimension, see chapter 4.

87. *Likkutei Halakhot*, Oreh Hayyim, Berakhot ha-Shahar 3.11. In loyalty to his polemic message, it must be pointed out that R. Nathan is concerned, in this context, with the distinction between "true zaddikim" (i.e., Reb Nahman, his master, among others) and "false zaddikim," obscurantists (op-

ponents to Reb Nahman in his own day yet existing in every age) who lead innocent Jews astray from true faith.

88. *Zohar* 2.52b. In a variety of biblical contexts, the event of salvation is accompanied by the donning of new robes. Cf. Is. 52:1, "Awake, awake, put on your strength, O Zion; put on your beautiful garments, O Jerusalem"; and Gen. 41:42, "And Pharaoh arrayed [Joseph] in garments of fine linen. . . ." See also midrash *Tanhuma,* Vayigash 11 and *Midrash Alpha Beta* 14 concerning this coincidence.

89. B.T. *Pesahim* 68a.

90. *Zohar* 2.138a.

91. *Likkutei Halakhot*, Oreh Hayyim, Berakhot ha-Shahar 3.39.

92. B.T. *Sukkah* 29a.

93. *Likkutei Halakhot*, Oreh Hayyim, Berakhot ha-Shahar 3.41 His reference is to the Lurianic doctrine of *zimzum* and *shevirah*. See chapter 4 on this concept and its influence in Reb Nahman's worldview.

94. *Likkutei Halakhot*, Oreh Hayyim, Netillat Yadayim 2.1, 2.4.

95. *Likkutei Moharan,* pt. 2, 8.10. Notably, in his conception, this "new song" is intimately connected to the phenomenology of the Divine Name. See *Likkutei Moharan,* pt. 2, 200.10 and Reb Nahman's discussion of the "single, double, triple and quadruple" song and its correspondence to the Tetragrammaton. The permutations of the letters, in esoteric thought, correspond to the enigmatic notion of the melody's "multiplication." Refer also to R. Nathan's further development of this concept in *Likkutei Halakhot*, Oreh Hayyim, Keriyat ha-Torah 6.5 and Netillat Yadayim 2.16.

96. Based on an alternate reading of the verse "And the cows walked straight on / sang [*yisharna*, from the root *ShIR,* song]. . . ." See B.T. *ʿAvodah Zarah* 24b; *Zohar* 2.137b–38a.

97. *Zohar* 1.20b. Here, as well, the tension of this temporal polarity is resolved through a conceptualization of essence and its names. The author proceeds to evoke the prophet's avowal that, in the end of days, "God will be one and His Name shall be one." R. Ashlag expands the statement, i.e., "The Holy One, blessed be He, who is *zeʿir anpin*, the greater luminary, will be one with His Name—*nukba*, or femininity, the lesser luminary."

98. Cf. *Zohar* 2.207b, 2.137b, and my discussion in this chapter, part 2, on the Lurianic teaching of the unification of the Holy Only, blessed be He, and His Shekhinah.

99. *Zohar* 1.132b. See also Tishby, *Wisdom of the Zohar,* 3:1357. Cf. *Daily Prayer Book*, ed. P. Birnbaum (New York, 1977), p. 81 for the context in the liturgy.

100. B.T. *Berakhot* 9b.

101. Man, of course, as a universal—albeit androcentric—euphemism for "human." I apply it throughout with impunity, and point only here to the literal significance of the term. Examples of his technique: comparing the human relationship to God to the individual's relationship to his rebbe or his

parents (*Likkutei Moharan* 60.4); describing the seductions of external wisdom to those of a prostitute; making abstract existential trials tangible in the form of journeys, wandering, physical distress, etc.

102. Although Reb Nahman's tales, like any literary work, are open to feminist interpretation, to the best of my knowledge no such research has yet been made. Athalya Brenner, in *A Feminist Companion to the Song of Songs* (Sheffield, 1993), introduction, p.13, states that "being a feminist woman, or womanly reader, means that every issue is a feminist issue, and there is a feminist perspective on every subject." My approach is not so univocal; I aspire to no "comprehensive world view" (ibid., p. 15). But it does seem to me that some perspectives articulated by critics interested in women's issues might focus our understanding of Hasidic texts in general and Reb Nahman's in particular. Justifiably, among traditional Jewish sources, the Bible has received the lion's share of attention from feminist scholars. One serious study applying Jungian archetypes to reading the Bible is Joan Chamberlain Engelsman, *The Feminine Dimension of the Divine* (Philadelphia, 1979). Other theological discussions of feminist issues in the Bible include: Judith Plaskow, "Jewish Theology in Feminist Perspective," in *Feminist Perspectives in Jewish Studies*, ed. L. Davidman and S. Tenenbaum (New Haven, 1994), pp. 62–81; Virginia Ramey-Mollenkott, *The Divine Feminine: The Biblical Imagery of God as Female* (New York, 1989); and R. F. Ellis, *The Feminine Principle in Biblical, Theological, and Psychological Perspective* (Ann Arbor: University Microfilms, 1985).

103. Versus Susannah Heschel's contention that God as "Father, King" and woman as "the Other" is a "basic theological supposition in Judaism." Susannah Heschel, ed., *On Being a Jewish Feminist* (New York, 1983), p. xxii. Her perspective is shared by R. Gross, who claims "the lack of Jewish female imagery of God." Rita Gross, "Steps Toward Feminine Imagery of the Deity in Jewish Thought," *Judaism* 30 (1981), 190. She asks, "How can God be a parent but not a Mother? How can the Creator and Caretaker of the world be devoid of femaleness?" (ibid., p. 191).

104. See, for example, Green's discussion , where he states, "There is in the tradition of the rabbis a great love of feminine imagery. Again and again the most poignant passages to be found in rabbinic literature will involve a female voice or image." Arthur Green, "Bride, Spouse, Daughter: Images of the Feminine in Classical Jewish Sources," in Heschel, ed., *On Being a Jewish Feminist*, p. 254. Green lists some of the female hypostases of the Shekhinah in Kabbalah—daughter, bride, mother, moon, sea, faith, wisdom, speech—and comments, "The *Shekhinah* is the chief object of both the divine and human search for wholeness and perfection" (ibid., p. 255). This, of course, does not address a fundamental concern of feminist criticism: the problem of predominantly male authorship of these texts and consequent filtering or masking through male perspective of whatever authentic women's voices may have been heard. Cf. Brenner, *Feminist Companion,* p. 22.

105. This suspiciously Freudian view of the man's multifaceted relationships to woman appears in a variety of sources. See, for instance, *Exodus Rabbah*

52.5, *Numbers Rabbah* 12.8, *Song of Songs Rabbah* 3.25, and Rashi's commentary on Song of Songs 3:11. Consider also Jung's analysis of the four stages in the development of the female anima: *Man and his Symbols* (New York, 1968), pp. 195ff. And see Engelsman's comments (*Feminine Dimension,* p. 21) on the "transformational mode," the second characteristic of the "Great Mother"—the figure Jung and Erich Neumann identify with the anima, the characteristically feminine part of a man's psyche.

106. The extensive presence of these concepts in the *Sefer Bahir*, one of the earliest kabbalistic sources, is documented by Scholem in *Origins of the Kabbalah* (Princeton, 1987), pp. 163–68ff. In the *Zohar* (1.132b) the passivity of femaleness *(nukba)* or the *sefirah* of *Malkhut,* is portrayed through the interrelationship between the last two letters of the Tetragrammaton. The dependence of the final *heh* upon the *vav* that preceeds it mirrors, in the author's view, the relationship of moon to sun, night to day, the zaddikim to their Creator. In fact, the structure of the sefirotic system as a whole bespeaks the complex of interpersonal relationships at the core of Creation. See *Zohar* 3.77b and Tishby, *Wisdom of the Zohar,* 1:299. For a feminist critique of moon symbolism, see Arthur I. Waskow, "Feminist Judaism: Restoration of the Moon," in Heschel, ed., *On Being a Jewish Feminist.*

107. See Steinsaltz, *Shishah me-Sippurei ha-Ma*ʿ*asiyot*, pp. 22–23, 30–31 for parallels to the classic description of that *sefirah.*

108. A central tenet of Simone de Beauvoir's seminal feminist critique, *The Second Sex* (1949) was that women are seen, in the still-patriarchal Western world, as the second, inferior sex while men are the first and authentic sex. Although other issues have been added to the agenda of feminist criticism, "the feminist struggle with the inherited dualistic categories of Western thought" continues. Cf. Tamar Frankiel, *The Voice of Sarah: Feminist Spirituality and Traditional Judaism* (San Francisco, 1990), p. 109. For some examples, see *Feminist Aesthetics*, ed. Gisela Ecker (Boston, 1985). Another view, though, voiced by Susan Griffin (*Woman and Nature*, [New York, 1978]) and others is that a profound connection between the feminine, "nature," and "immanence" does indeed exist, as de Beauvoir held, but "this is not negative: embodiment is part of our deeply feminine mode of being" (Frankiel, *Voice of Sarah,* p. 110). It seems to me that in the case of Reb Nahman, a much more complex approach is in order. In his worldview (inherited and innovated), "masculine" and "feminine" do not designate qualities that belong, respectively, to men and women but rather are ontological valences simultaneously inherent in all of reality—from the world of the *sefirot* to human beings and even to "inanimate" things.

109. B.T. *Sanhedrin* 100a. My thanks to R. Daniel Epstein for his discussion of this subject in June 1992, which guides me in all I write.

110. *Likkutei Moharan* 60.6–9.

111. *Likkutei Moharan* 60.9. This teaching is also discussed in chapter 2 and chapter 4. See *Zohar Hadash* Shir ha-Shirim, fol. 61a–b as well, in which the violent pain of birthing is evoked to speak of the divine process of creation

itself. And cf. chap. 5 of *Sha'arei Orah*, ed. Ben-Shelomo [Jerusalem, 1981], p. 230): "In the time of Abraham, the Shekhinah was called Sarah. In the time of Isaac, she was called Rebecca. In the time of Jacob she was called Rachel." On these themes in feminist reading of the Bible, see for example, Phyllis Trible, *God and the Rhetoric of Sexuality* (London, 1978), pp. 61, 69.

112. *Likkutei Moharan*, pt. 2, 4.2. In a series of double entendres, the author of the *Zohar* interprets this verse from the Song of Songs (5:2) with the same anatomical/spiritual imagery—"'I am asleep yet my heart wakes, The voice of my beloved knocks: Open for me . . .': 'Open for me'—for the way to come into me is in you. . . . If you do not open your opening, I will be closed, and no one will be able to find me . . ." (*Zohar* 3.95a). The text returns us to the discussion earlier in this chapter. Clearly, only with human 'openness' to divine mercy, Torah, abundance can any mystical union with God take place; the presence of the erotic imagery so widespread in the *Zohar* indeed seems manifest in Reb Nahman's own thought.

113. See B.T. *'Eruvin* 18b where a woman's body is described as a granary [*ozar*]—narrow at the top and wide at the bottom, it holds a fetus like a storehouse holds the harvest. The author of the *Zohar* expands the same imagery, naming the Shekhinah as the "mother of all souls," the "container of all seed" (*Zohar* 1.125b; *Tikkunei Zohar*, Tikkun 43, fol. 82b; *Tikkunei Zohar*, Tikkun 21, fol. 60a). Finally, the notion that souls beyond number, unborn and reborn, have a single home and a single source is presented by Reb Nahman in a fascinating chain of associations. From the talmudic story in B.T. *Hagigah* 15b of Moses who was nearly chased out of Heaven by a troop of envious angels, he learns an important moral. Moses was saved by clinging to the divine throne, for the roots of all souls are quarried from beneath that supernal seat, an aspect of the "Mother of all living" (Gen. 3:21) What God counseled Moses to do, in his eyes, was to grasp the roots of souls of great Jews, to give himself to them with all his faith and power (*Likkutei Moharan*, pt. 2, 1.1–3). The motif of clinging to the chair for protection is transferred, of course, to *The Two Sons Who Were Reversed*. See *SM*, p.166.

114. This according to R. Moses Cordovero, *Pardes Rimmonim*, Sha'ar ha-Otiot, chap. 8. Quoted by Lipiner, *Hazon ha-Otiot*, p. 437. On the symbolism of *Malkhut* (personified in the letter *heh*), or the Shekhinah in her role as nurturer, see above. Cf. *Zohar* 3.249b.

115. *Zohar* 3.217b. Cf. Rashi on Gen. 2:4, referring to B.T. *Menahot* 29b and *Genesis Rabbah* 12.9. This interpretation of Gen. 2:4 is reiterated in *Zohar* 1.25a; 46b; *Zohar* 3.34b; 298a, etc. On the *heh* as a sign of fertility in the lives of the patriarchs, see also *Zohar* 1.90b and the summary of kabbalistic sources in Lipiner, *Hazon ha-Otiot*, p. 434.

116. B.T. *Sanhedrin* 68b.

117. *Likkutei Moharan* 53.

118. *Likkutei Moharan* 53. This is the role acted out by the master of prayer, who is able to answer the questions each individual asks, thus helping him,

through cognition, to greater spiritual growth. In two other texts, Reb Nahman attributes the sage *(hakham)* with additional midwifely powers as well: the most worthy of them can "draw down" new souls from heaven through the Torah they teach (*Likkutei Moharan* 13.6). As the student hears his rabbi, he is like a newborn; his innovations are intimately connected with the coming into being of new souls and their renewal, reanimated in infant bodies. See *Likkutei Moharan* 192.

119. *Likkutei Moharan* 36.1. The waiting period of pregnancy, its hiddenness as a time of secret growth, serves Reb Nahman in a very personal way: he compares (obliquely) his own path, or the preparations of any leader, readying himself to appear in the world, to the situation of pregnancy—seen, though, from the perspective of the unborn baby. Such a future leader bides his time in secrecy, "like a fetus in its mother's womb," until he reaches spiritual maturity; ideally, only then does he emerge. The sad possibility of a miscarried appearance is weighed as well; disputes might induce him to emerge too early, and the damage may be fatal. See *Likkutei Moharan*, pt. 2, 20.

120. *Likkutei Moharan* 36.5.

121. In the *Zohar*, this exile is described as occurring, in parallel, first of all on the cosmic level, severing the lower levels of the sefirotic system from the Shekhinah. See *Zohar* 2.17a–b (translated and annotated in Tishby, *Wisdom of the Zohar,* 1:410); *Zohar* 3.290b, 3.291a.

122. B.T. *Megillah* 29a.

123. *Zohar* 2.217b.

124. See *Zohar* 2.216b and Tishby, *Wisdom of the Zohar,* 1:383. In Lurianic teaching, mother's milk is the product of divine light that rises from lower *sefirot* in the form of blood to fill the mother's breasts in more perfect form. Cf. *'Ez Hayyim* 4.3.5. The idea that blood transforms to milk after the birth of a child already appears in the Talmud; cf. B.T. *Berakhot* 6b.

125. Cf. Tishby, *Wisdom of the Zohar,* 1:382–85, 406–11 for translation of passages from the *Zohar* on this subject.

126. Tishby, *Wisdom of the Zohar,* 1:377. Tishby cites *Zohar* 2.219b.

127. In both these tales, a second and critical allegorical element is present as well: it concerns the idea, expressed in the *Zohar* and developed greatly in Lurianic teaching, that a woman may be forced to endure relationships with the *wrong* partner and his premature death while she awaits her true husband. The latter, in turn, must undergo two or more reincarnations, rising gradually in spiritual purity until he is worthy of union with his promised bride. See Zohar 3:283b and Tishby, *Wisdom of the Zohar,* 3:1356.

128. Scholem, *On the Kabbalah and its Symbolism* (New York, 1965), p. 106; Tishby, *Wisdom of the Zohar,* 1:377. Cf. the Jungian view of the dual nature of the anima, personified in its negative aspect by the Gorgon or Medea, terrifying and pitiless. Chamberlain, *Feminine Dimension of the Divine*, p. 20.

129. Tishby, *Wisdom of the Zohar,* 1:375–79. The powers of evil swarm like flies to her; in Lurianic teaching, "the *sitra ahra* wishes to grasp only the

female; all his desire and lust is to draw her from her source, for there he finds her abundance and holiness." *'Ez Hayyim*, Sha'ar 22, fol. 104c, quoted by Tishby, *Torat ha-R'a*, p. 75.

130. "Know truly, my dear brother, that the letter *heh*, in its form and structure . . . forever alludes to the quality of *nukba*, femininity, and the attribute of *din*." R. Jacob Kapil of Mezherich, *Sha'arei Gan 'Eden* (Lemberg, 1864), fol. 68a; quoted in Lipiner, *Hazon ha-Otiot*, p. 440 n. 29. Interestingly, the femme fatale of folklore really does make a comeback in the romantic age. Beautiful and imperious, she is "the unattainable temptress who keeps her admirer in a perpetual state of longing." The actions of the heroine in *King and Kaiser* are a striking dramatization of this figure of ancient lore. See Barbara Fass's discussion in *La Belle Dame sans Merci*, pp. 20ff.

131. See *Zohar* 2.50b–51a, translated in Tishby, *Wisdom of the Zohar*, 1:398–99.

132. Sigrid Weigel, *Feminist Aesthetics*, ed. G. Ecker (Boston, 1985), p. 61.

133. The author of the *Zohar* applies this metaphor of mirror as well to describe the intrinsically female model of divine revelation in our lower world. Based on a wordplay between *mareh* (vision, one level of prophecy, cf. Gen. 46:2) and *marah* (mirror), God's presence is made visible through the act of reflection off a polished glass surface. In this text, the supposedly derogatory act of reflecting another person's image (implying self-effacingness, lack of unique identity, colorlessness) becomes the highest value, for it is these qualities alone that grant humankind a glimpse of their Creator. See *Zohar* 1.149b.

134. *Zohar* 1.228b. The figure of the Shekhinah is discussed in many scholarly works. Most prominent among them: Scholem, *Pirkei Yesod le-Havanat ha-Kabbalah u-Semaleha*, in the chapter entitled "Ha-Shekhinah"; Tishby, *Wisdom of the Zohar*, 1:371–421, 3:1355–1406.

135. Cf. *Zohar* 1.36a, cited in n. 29, above. Tishby comments, "This is the mystical explanation for the cessation of prophecy in exile: the divine speech is dumb." In the state of exile, as Tishby explains, the unity of the four-letter Name is destroyed, for the last letter, *heh*, symbol of the Shekhinah, is cut off from the rest of the letters. He refers the reader to *Zohar* 2.25b-26b as well, and to *Zohar* 3.77b.

136. Cf. *Zohar* 1.181a–b, translated in Tishby, *Wisdom of the Zohar*, 1:403–4. Reb Nahman incorporates this motif in numerous contexts: most literally in the forest dawn of *The Two Sons Who Were Reversed*, but also in every tale of reconciliation—*King and Kaiser*, *Burgher and Poor Man*, *Seven Beggars* (the two birds, the heart and spring), *The Lost Princess*. See also *Likkutei Moharan* 78. Reb Nahman points out that not only the moon but the sun as well suffers an eclipse of his full brightness; he too is dulled by his present state (*Likkutei Moharan* 31.9).

137. *Likkutei Moharan* 65.4 In another context concerning the nature of the night and morning and their effects on human beings, Reb Nahman links the story of Ruth to that longed-for instant of the moon's redemption. Boaz entreats Ruth, "Lie here [in the granary with me] until the morning" (Ruth

3:13); Reb Nahman comments: "For at that time [dawn] all the opponents who rule over speech are defeated, and then speech bursts forth in song and praise, glorifying the Holy One blessed be He. The outburst of mercy, shining forth as the brightest sun, is what restores voice to the speechless, redeeming all from their mute estrangement" (*Likkutei Moharan* 38.4).

138. Cf. *Likkutei Moharan* 78. The linguistic connection linking the Messiah *(meshiʾah)* and the act of speech *(siʿah)* widens into a romantic triangle in *Likkutei Moharan* 1.11–12, where Reb Nahman suggests, on the basis of Gen. 24:63, that it is the plants *(siʾah)* of the field that converse with the individual who walks among them, conveying to him their wisdom and strength.

139. My thanks to Galit Hasan-Rokem for her comments in January 1990 concerning female voice and this tale.

140. *Midrash Tehillim* 73.4. The object of this homily, as the text proceeds to explain, concerns an analogous relationship: in this world the Holy One, blessed be He courts Israel, that they may return in repentance and do His will, but in time to come, Israel will pursue God, entreating Him to do their will, as it is written, "And I will put my spirit within You" (Ezek. 36:27).

141. *ʿEz Hayyim*, Shaʿar ha-Gilgulim, Hakdamah 20, p. 54.

142. Refer to B.T. *Sanhedrin* 22b, and the metaphysics of the letter *heh* discussed above, n. 106 and following n. 113. And compare Erich Neumann, *The Great Mother: An Analysis of the Archetype,* trans. R. Mannheim (New York, 1955), p. 39: "Woman as body-vessel is the natural expression of the human experience of woman bearing the child 'within' her and of man entering 'into' her. . . ."

143. *Likkutei Moharan* 64.1.

144. S. Trigano, *Le recit de la disparue* (Paris, 1978), p. 25, quoted by Ouaknin, *Burnt Book*, p. 273. On the root *RHM* as "a major metaphor for biblical faith" in the feminist commentary of Trible, see *God and the Rhetoric of Sexuality*, pp. 33, 38, 50, 56.

145. *Likkutei Moharan* 73.

146. Despite the apparent resemblance of this idea to contentions voiced in the camp of Jewish feminists, I do not mean to echo their missions of political, social, religious, or liturgical reform.

Chapter IV. The Dimension of the Fantastic

1. The notion of theophany is based on the use of the word *ha-makom* (the Place) to signify omnipresence, thus designating God. On interpretations of the word *ha-makom* in rabbinical sources, see Urbach, *Sages,* 1:66–79. Cf. my discussion below in this chapter, following n. 119.

2. Ernst Cassirer speaks of the sense, toward which myth strives, of a "unity of the world"; in such a view, objects come to be regarded in a new light: multiplicity is replaced with a substantial unity. As a result, the outward appearance of an object "constitutes only a kind of veil, a mask," and reality

acquires some magical interest. Cassirer's presentation of the spiritual aspect of myth has much in common with the mystical view of revelation expressed in Hasidism. See *The Philosophy of Symbolic Forms,* vol. 2, *Mythical Thought,* trans. R. Mannheim (New Haven, 1955), pp. 62–63.

3. In *Tormented Master,* Green comments that "the most pervasive struggle in Reb Nahman's life [was] over issues of fantasy and reality" (p. 342) and suggests that "in the tales . . . Nahman began to propose a liberation within fantasy . . ." (p. 343). Note, though, that Green's definition of fantasy concerns psychological rather than literary aspects of Reb Nahman's thought and does not directly address the matter at hand.

4. Tzvetan Todorov, *The Fantastic: A Structural Approach to a Literary Genre,* trans. R. Howard (Ithaca, 1970). For other views of the fantastic in literature, see: Diana Waggoner, *The Hills of Faraway: A Guide to Fantasy* (New York, 1978); and Eric S. Rabkin, *The Fantastic in Literature* (Princeton, 1976). Liebes, similarly, speaks of the "mythopoetic inclinations" of the author of the *Zohar* and states: "It is its creation of myths that sets the *Zohar* apart in Jewish literature. The author of the *Zohar* was well aware that he was not describing an existing mythical world but creating one out of his own literary imagination and homiletic talents. This . . . though, did not detract . . . from the ontological status of the mythical world he had created, for in his understanding, the inner world of man's imagination took precedence over the external world. The latter owed its very existence to the external projection of thought by means of words" (*Studies in the Zohar*, pp. 55–56).

5. Todorov, *Fantastic,* p. 25.

6. Cf. Rabkin, *Fantastic in Literature,* p. 33. Rabkin suggests that one may, hypothetically, look for a fantasy among fairy tales, as "they are clearly more fantastic than even such fantastic satires . . . but the fairy tale has a whole set of perspectives that exist in another world altogether." He quotes Tolkien's naming of this land "Faerie," his definition of the fairy tale being "one which touches on or uses Faerie." Thus, for Tolkien, a fairy tale is not a true fantasy, though it may contain what he calls fantasy, "an aspect of imaginative subcreation present in all art."

7. Todorov, *Fantastic,* p. 33. Pinchas Sade voices this conviction in adamant protest against the abstract interpretations of Reb Nahman's tales proposed by "intellectuals," those mortal beings who inflict their own finitude upon the ethereal images of the tales (*Tikkun ha-Lev,* p. 248).

8. Todorov, *Fantastic,* p. 60.

9. Ibid., pp. 63-64.

10. Ortsion Bartana, *Ha-Fantasia be-Sifrut Dor ha-Medinah, 1960–1989* (Tel Aviv, 1989), p. 36.

11. Todorov, *Fantastic,* p. 107.

12. Rabkin, *Fantastic in Literature,* p. 223.

13. Todorov, *Fantastic,* p. 92.

14. Northrop Frye, *Creation and Recreation,* p. 6.

15. Consideration of mythic and primitive modes of thought is a forma-

tive influence in the works of Walter Benjamin, Northrop Frye, and many other thinkers.

16. Rudolf Otto, *The Idea of the Holy,* trans. J. D. Harvey (1923; reprint, London, 1950), pp. 25–40.

17. Ibid., p. 40. This notion of degeneration, however, is opposed by a view emphasizing the opposite trend. In this view, folktales are premythological; or, at the very least, folktales and myth exerted an influence on one another. Scholars of myth and folklore supporting this view include M. Eliade, G. Campbell, and M. Gaster.

18. Michael Fishbane observes that the category of myth is relevant in discussion not only of the Bible and rabbinic literature, but of Kabbalah as well: "[Its] theosophical hermeneutics are a dramatization of hypostatic realities of the boldest mythic sort" ("The Holy One Sits and Roars," p. 16).

19. See, for example, Vladimir Propp, *Morphology of the Folktale* (Austin and London, 1975); Stith Thompson "Myth and Folktales," in *Myth: A Symposium,* ed. Thomas A. Sebeok (Bloomington and London, 1965); and Geza Roheim, "Myth and Folktale," in *Myth and Literature,* ed. John B. Vickery (Lincoln, 1966).

20. For an extensive discussion of the prehistory of the folktale as a narrative form, with reference to modern anthropological criticism, see Max Luethi, *The European Folk Tale: Form and Nature,* trans. John D. Niles (Philadelphia, 1982), esp. pp. 66–125

21. Cf. Gonthier-Louis Fink, "Volk und Volkesdichtung in der ersten Berliner Romantik," in *Romantik in Deutschland: Sonderband der Deutschen Vierteljahrsschrift für Literaturwissenschaft und Geistesgeschichte* (Stuttgart, 1978), pp. 543, 545.

22. *Anmerkung zu den Kinder und Hausmärchen der Brüder Grimm* (Hildesheim, 1956); quoted by Luethi, *Märchen,* p. 62, with no page citation.

23. Ernst Ribbat, *Ludwig Tieck: Studien zum Konzeption und Praxis romantischer Poesie* (Kronberg: Athenaeum, 1978), p. 120. Interestingly, the Ba'al Shem Tov and Reb Nahman use the same terminology of garments *(Gewand; levushim)* in expressing their desire to reformulate folktales seemingly bereft of "religious" or Jewish content. See my discussion of disguises in part 2 below.

24. Vladimir Propp, "The Functions of Dramatis Personae," in *Morphology of the Folktale,* pp. 25–65. This comparison could be pursued beyond the incident outlined above, following Tieck's story through Propp's list of thirty-one basic functions. The entire story is loyal to the universal paradigm outlined by Propp.

25. Joseph Dan outlines the chronology of the former development, noting its shadowy beginnings during the life of the Ba'al Shem Tov (d. 1760), marking the narration of Reb Nahman's tales (told between 1806 and 1811) and the publication of *Shivhei ha-Ba'al Shem Tov,* at last, in 1815. Cf. Dan, *Ha-Sippur ha-Hasidi* (Jerusalem, 1975), pp. 34–35. The time frame suggested by Manfred Grätz designates the milestone publication by Johann Carl Musäus,

Volkmärchen der Deutschen (1782–87), and the collection by Benedikte Naubert (1786–89). The manifold works of E. T. A. Hoffman, one of the most prolific romantic writers, were published between 1827 and 1828. See Grätz, *Das Märchen in der deutschen Aufklärung* (Stuttgart, 1988), pp. 233-72, 378–79.

26. Cf. Campbell's comment that the passage of the mythological hero is fundamentally inward—"into depths where obscure resistances are overcome, and long lost, forgotten powers are revived, to be made available for the transfiguration of the world." Joseph Campbell, *Hero with a Thousand Faces* (New York, 1956), p. 29.

27. Sigmund Freud, "The Uncanny," *Imago* 5, nos. 5–6 (1925). We must note that this idea of strangeness and familiarity contained in a single element was no discovery of Freud's. It was anticipated by Novalis in his recognition that "the art of alienating in an agreeable way, of making something strange and still familiar—that is Romantic poetics." Quoted by Luethi, *Märchen,* p. 78.

28. Jung describes, using that term, the composite symbol the Greek god Hermes came to be. As a psychopomp, literally "soul guide," his function was to guide the dead to the underworld (Jung, *Man and His Symbols,* p. 155). Italo Calvino remarks on the aptness of the Olympian god Hermes-Mercury as the patron of literature: "[U]nder the name of Thoth he was the inventor of writing, and according to C. G. Jung in his studies on alchemical symbolism . . . represents the *principium individuationis.* Mercury with his winged feet, light and airborne, astute, agile, adaptable, free and easy, established the relationships of the gods among themselves and those between the gods and men, between universal laws and individual destinies, between the forces of nature and the forms of culture, between the objects of the world and all thinking subjects." Italo Calvino, *Six Memos for the Next Millennium* (Cambridge, 1988), p. 45.

29. It shows, as well, Reb Nahman's transparent allusion to the parable in the *Zohar* 1.199a. The *nesher* (eagle) assumes the role of the archangel Metatron. See my discussion of this source later in this chapter, following n. 52.

30. Jung, *Man and His Symbols,* p. 155.

31. B.T. *Berakhot* 18b.

32. It is not my intent here to discuss any kind of search in practice for a connection with a reality beyond earthly reality, such as visits to the graves of zaddikim, among them that of Reb Nahman of Bratslav in Uman.

33. Dan Ben Amos raises this question of setting in relation to rabbinic literature. Cf. "Talmudic Tall Tales," in *Folklore in Context* (New Delhi, 1982), p. 97. As for Reb Nahman, Green suggests (*Tormented Master,* pp. 343–44) that his tales themselves may be described as "myth," and Reb Nahman as a "mythmaker." Green, though, defines myth as an atemporal phenomenon—"a myth is a tale that bespeaks an inner truth portrayed as an ancient truth" (ibid.); my conception, in contrast, concerns a process of mythic transformation, in which exegesis of received traditions plays a major part.

34. R. Yaʿakov Leiner divides the world into the existentially distinct realms

of ocean, desert, and settlement *(yishuv)*, and evokes the term *yishuv ha-da'at* to speak of the solidity offered by urban life. See *Beit Ya'akov*, Bereshit 2, fol. 1 lb.

35. Mishnah *Avot* 3.4.

36. *Hitbodedut*, in general terms, includes solitary meditation and spontaneous, earnest conversing with God. Originating in kabbalistic thought, the concept became a cornerstone of Bratslav teaching. See Green, *Tormented Master*, pp. 145–48. On the roots of the practice in earlier kabbalistic thought, see M. Idel, *Ha-Havayyah ha-Mystit ezel Avraham Abulafia* (Jerusalem, 1988), in his index under *hitbodedut*. The seeds of the notion of *hitbodedut* were sown already in the Middle Ages. See, for example, Idel's discussion in ibid., pp. 38–39, 48, 55, 56–75, and, on the question of the prophetic experience and *hitbodedut*, p. 119. Regarding the development of the concept in Reb Nahman's thought, see *Likkutei Moharan* 52, 108, 156, 258; *Likkutei Moharan* pt. 2, 2, 25, 93, 95, 96, 97, 98, 99, 100, 101.

37. *Likkutei Moharan* 52

38. Cf. Scholem, *Major Trends*, pp. 235–39, 256–65; Tishby, *Torat ha-R'a*, pp. 62–90. See also Tishby, *Wisdom of the Zohar*, 2:447–545.

39. *Likkutei Moharan* 64.1.

40. The concept will be discussed at length in part 2 of this chapter.

41. In Aramaic, *leit atar panui minei*. Cf. *Tikkunei Zohar*, Tikkun 57, fol. 91a.

42. *Likkutei Moharan* 64.2. See Weiss's discussion on faith in Reb Nahman's teachings in *Mekharim*, pp. 96–108, and Green's excursus, "Faith, Doubt and Reason," in *Tormented Master*, pp. 285–336.

43. *'Ez Hayyim* 1.3, fol. 13a. See also *'Ez Hayyim*, Mevo Sha'arim, Sha'ar ha-Kelippah 1.

44. Namely, *Likkutei Moharan* 64.1.

45. I borrow this idea of the double meaning inherent in *plot* (both in Hebrew and English) from Avivah Gottlieb Zornberg. In December 1990, encouraged by Thomas Mann's *Joseph and His Brothers*, she discussed the biblical story of Joseph in Egypt, and broached the charged theological question of God's "stratagems" in arranging human history. Cf. Avivah Gottlieb Zornberg, *Genesis: The Beginning of Desire* (Philadelphia, 1995), pp. 254–57, 263–66. And see above, the end of chapter 2.

46. *Likkutei Moharan* 64.6 on Ex. 10:2. See Green's comments on this teaching in *Tormented Master*, p. 324 n.64.

47. *Likkutei Moharan* 64.6.

48. *Zohar* 1.121b. See R. Yehudah Leib Ashlag in his commentary on the *Zohar*, *Sefer ha-Zohar* (Jerusalem, 1985), 7:75 n. 238. On the nature of the Tree of Life/Tree of Knowledge in the *Zohar*, see Tishby, *Wisdom of the Zohar*, 1:356–59.

49. Frye, *Creation and Recreation*, p. 53.

50. Cf. P. Maranda, ed., *Soviet Structural Folkloristics* (The Hague, 1974), p. 25.

51. Ernst Cassirer recognizes time as the basic power of history itself, and charts the mythical vision of time in the following way: (1) "time before time"—the world is already luminous but not yet perceptible; it exists only spiritually; (2) a "primordial age"; (3) an "era of battle" in which the history of mankind on earth begins (this stage is perhaps the narrative present); and (4) the "end of the end"—a world of eternity in which evil is overpowered. See *Philosophy of Symbolic Forms,* 2:115.

52. The self-referential aspects of the figure of the blind beggar cannot be ignored; in *Likkutei Moharan,* pt. 2, 7.6, Reb Nahman draws a clear connection between what he calls the "wise man" and "spiritual leader of his generation" and the figure of the blind beggar. In the continual dynamic he describes, in which the rabbi, or teacher, imbues his students with metaphysical knowledge, thus making room in his own mind for new understanding of ever-higher truths, it is the zaddik of the generation whose own insight approaches the unconceivable. Reb Nahman portrays this insight as a realm of still unattained knowledge *(mekkifim),* a sort of halo of amorphous wisdom that envelops the rabbi or zaddik. Existing only a hairsbreadth beyond his grasp, this sea of thought yet unconceived belongs to the "world to come." And as Reb Nahman reminds his reader, that world is described in the Talmud as "a day of endless length," "beyond time" (B.T. *Kiddushin* 39b; B.T. *Hullin* 142). The implication, then, is that the privilege of learning from the wise man of one's generation is what grants one access to infinity. I would suggest the unspoken relationship between the beggars and children reflects the essential dialogue—a leitmotif threaded throughout *Likkutei Moharan*—that Reb Nahman believed must exist between student and teacher.

53. *Zohar* 2.199a.

54. An interesting parallel to such a contest is found in J.T. *Ketubbot* 5, in which illustrious sages vie with one another regarding their earliest memory. R. Joshua ben Levi recalls the *mohel* who circumcised him, R. Yohanan recalls the women present at his birth, and Samuel claims he remembers the midwife who delivered him. This anecdote may have been a model for the scene told by the first beggar, although the memories of these sages date only from the moment of birth, while the recollections in the tale are prenatal.

55. In *Likkutei Halakhot,* Oreh Hayyim, Tefillin 5.26, R. Nathan expands the imagery suggested in this tale and links the state of being beyond time with the highest *sefirah* in the kabbalistic system, *Keter.* The divine name associated with Keter, the first, primordial *sefirah,* is EHYH (I will be). It is a level compared to pregnancy, a state of becoming; one cannot yet say "I am" but only "I will be." It is this sense of perpetual and dynamic potential, then, that unites the blind beggar's essence with *Keter.*

56. *Ozar Yisrael,* s.v. "nesher," cited by Dan Pagis, "'Of ha-ʿAlmavvet: Motif ha-Phoenix be Sifrut ha-Midrash ve-ha-Aggadah," in *Jubilee Volume of the Hebrew Gymnasium* (Jerusalem 1962), p. 76. On the moral demands implicit in this connection in the eyes of R. Nathan, see *Likkutei Halakhot,* Oreh Hayyim, Tefillin 5.5, and Tefillat Minhah 7.93.

57. *Genesis Rabbah* 19.5; *Tanhuma* introduction (ed. Buber, p. 155); and *Midrash Shmuel,* 12.2. See Pagis's discussion, "ʿOf ha-ʿAlmavvet," esp. pp. 76–77.

58. B.T. *Yebamot* 17b; J.T. *Yebamot* 1.6 (fol. 6b), 1.7 (fol. 17a); *Genesis Rabbah* 69.6; *Zohar* 1.95b, 143a.

59. R. Nathan continues the allegory presented in the *Zohar;* in *Likkutei Halakhot,* Oreh Hayyim, Tefillin 5.18, the Zoharic parable is made more graphic as it is applied to the details of Reb Nahman's story.

60. T. S. Eliot, "Little Gidding," in *Four Quartets,* stanza 5, lines 1–3.

61. See *Likkutei Moharan,* pt. 2, 61 concerning the relativity of human time versus divine time. Compare this concept with my discussion in chapter 2 of the Messiah as *yanuka,* an infant or child, in Reb Nahman's stories and earlier sources.

62. The metaphorical significance of the beggar's blindness is discussed later in this chapter following note 187.

63. Alex Preminger, ed., *Encyclopaedia of Poetry and Poetics,* (Princeton, 1965), p. 270.

64. Waggoner, *Hills of Faraway,* p. 3.

65. Quoted by Frye, *Creation and Recreation,* p. 10.

66. B.T. *Pesahim* 50a; B.T. *Baba Batra* 10b.

67. *Genesis Rabbah* 44.17.

68. This idea of Jacob's precipitous slumber is based on Rashi's comment on Gen. 28:11. He remarks the uncustomary formulation of the verb *ba* in past rather than future tense— "because the sun was set"—and explains it as a sign the sun set suddenly, before the normal time of sunset, in order to cause Jacob to spend the night there. See also *Leviticus Rabbah* 29.2 and parallels.

69. B.T. *Berakhot* 55a. See also *Genesis Rabbah* 68.12, 89; *Lamentations Rabbah* 1.19; *Ecclesiastes Rabbah* 5.4. Jung recognizes this stance as a basic universal religious phenomenon, i.e., the belief that the voice that speaks in our dreams is not our own but comes from a source transcending us. He states, "Man is never helped by what he thinks for himself, but by revelations of wisdom greater than his own." C. G. Jung, *Psychology and Religion* (New Haven, 1938), p. 45. On the nature of dreams and approaches to their interpretation in the Hellenic period, see Isaac Afik, "Tefisat ha-Halom ezel Hazal" (Ph.D. thesis, Bar Ilan University, 1990).

70. B.T. *Berakhot* 55b.

71. This recognition of the vital role of interpretation as the actualization of dreams becomes central in Lurianic teaching. In *Shaʿar ha-Pesukim* (Vayeshev 39) sleep is described as a lower state of consciousness; dreams, therefore, are a kind of obscured, partial vision. The interpretation, on the other hand, reveals and illuminates the hidden messages inchoate in the dream. The interpreter literally unties *(poter)* the truth bound up in it, setting its meaning free and allowing the light it contains to expand into the lower worlds. Thus, the interpretation actually verifies the dream, brings it from potentiality to realization by causing it to *mean.* We cannot ignore the resonance between this classic

kabbalistic view and modern literary hermeneutics. Dream interpretation parallels textual exegesis: the basic tenet of structuralism, of course, is that the text has no meaning in and of itself; it is the reader alone who, inevitably, invests the text with his own subjective meaning.

72. B.T. *Berakhot* 55b; see also Isaac Levin and Abraham Peleg, *'Olam ha-Sheinah ve-ha-Halomot* (Tel Aviv, 1981), p. 101.

73. B.T. *Berakhot* 55a.

74. Maimonides, *Moreh Nevukhim,* 2.47. He draws a sharp distinction, though, between the style of the later prophets and that of Moses, stressing that while all the prophets were sent visions in an unconscious state, Moses, the greatest of the prophets, spoke with God face to face (e.g., Ex. 33:11), rather than through the veil of dreams, indirectly through an angel, or masked in enigmatic language. Clear, distinct, unalterable, Moses' communication with God was free of the precarious task of interpretation; it was pure revelation. Compare *Mishneh Torah,* Yesodei ha-Torah 7.4, 7.6.

75. *Zohar* 1.82b.

76. *Zohar Hadash,* Vayezeh, fol. 47b *(Midrash ha-Ne'elam).* On sleep and dreams in the *Zohar*, see Tishby, *Wisdom of the Zohar,* 2:809–27.

77. *Likkutei Moharan,* pt. 2, 7.6.

78. In Freud's view, any element in a dream can be interpreted in four basic ways: (1) in a negative or positive sense (a contrast relationship); (2) historically (as a memory); (3) as symbolic; (4) its valuation based upon its wording. Cf. *The Interpretation of Dreams*, trans. A. Brill (New York, 1950), p. 230. Interestingly, the extensive discussion of dreams in B.T. *Berakhot*, beginning on fol. 55a, incorporates all these possibilities.

79. This relativistic stance was eloquently expressed by the Chinese philosopher who said: "Once I dreamt I was a butterfly fluttering from flower to flower. I awoke and discovered I am a man and not a butterfly. But what am I really—a butterfly dreaming it is a man, or a man who dreams he is a butterfly?" Quoted by Levin and Peleg, *'Olam ha-Sheinah ve-ha-Halomot,* p. 101.

80. See n. 75, above.

81. *Zohar* 1.83a. Cf. Yoram Bilu, "Sigmund Freud and R. Yehuda—On a Mystical Tradition of 'Psychoanalytic' Dream Interpretation," *Journal of Psychological Anthropology* 2 (Fall 1979): 446. In many instances, the Talmud conjectures the demonic sources of dreams. The view, for example, that supernatural powers (evil spirits, demons, returning dead, wandering souls) are the source of dreams is suggested in B.T. *Shabbat* 152b, *Hagigah* 5b, and *Berakhot* 55b. A discussion of whether dreams contain truth is found in *Horayot* 13b. The belief that one may sleep on a grave to receive a message from the dead in a dream appears in *Berakhot* 18b and *Sanhedrin* 65b. In *Shabbat* 30b it is said that bad dreams are caused by demons who torture the sleeper, and the belief that demons cause erotic dreams, either in goatlike form (like a Roman faun) or as Lilith is voiced in *Shabbat* 141a, *Gittin* 68a, and *Pesahim* 11b. For complete discussion of these and other references, see Sandor Lorand, "Dream

Interpretation in the Talmud," *International Journal of Psychoanalysis* 38 (1957): 92–97. And see Afik, "Tefisat ha-Halom ezel Hazal."

82. The day world, Fromm writes, is as unconscious in our sleep experience as the night world in our waking experience. The stuff of dreams, he adds, is not subject to the laws of reality but is controlled, rather, by other logical rules. In sleep, we are free from the task of defending the order familiar to us and attacking all that threatens it, free from watching and mastering reality. Erich Fromm, *The Forgotten Language* (New York, 1951), p. 27.

83. Aeschylus used the phrase "a dream that wanders in the daylight" to describe the old men, helpless and weak, left behind in time of war: "The overold, in the parching of the leafage, walks its three-footed way, no better than a child; it wanders, a dream in the daylight" (*Agamemnon* 1.82). Quoted by W. O'Flaherty, *Dreams, Illusions, and Other Realities* (Chicago, 1984), p. 304.

84. Maimonides, *Moreh Nevukhim,* 2.47. On the four levels of prophecy distinguished by Maimonides, see ibid., 2.41.

85. *Pirkei de Rabbi Eliezer* 6.7. See also J.T. *Rosh ha-Shanah* 2.3 (fol. 58a); *Exodus Rabbah* 15.22.

86. *Sefer ha-Likkutim,* Shaʿar ha-Pesukim 84.

87. Phylacteries *(tefillin)* are bound on the arm and head with leather straps; both the fabric of the prayer shawl *(tallit)* and its fringes *(zizit)* are spun from wool. A very probable pre-text for this motif is J.T. *ʿAvodah Zarah* 2.1 (fol. 9a): "R. Hiyyah bar Luliani said in the name of R. Hoshʿiyah: All the commandments will one day be accepted by the sons of Noah [i.e., non-Jews], for this is the meaning of '. . . all the earth shall be devoured with the fire of my jealousy. For then I will convert the peoples to a purer language, that they may call upon the name of the Lord, to serve him with one consent' (Zeph. 3:8–9). In the end they will regret what they have done, saying 'Let us break their bonds asunder, and cast away their cords from us' (Ps. 2:3)—that is the commandment of *tefillin* and of *zizit.*"

88. *Aggadat Bereshit* 66.7.

89. Pinchas Sade, in the afterword to his anthology of Reb Nahman's writings, *Tikkun ha-Lev,* speaks of the dreams related in *Hayyei Moharan* as a bridge linking the narrative and the excurses *(sihot)* and remarks the prominence of the "dream element" in the tales (p. 245). His interest in the autobiographical aspect of one of Reb Nahman's most revealing dreams, the Circle Dream discussed below, led to the analysis published in the Israeli newspaper *Davar* on 13 April (20 Nissan) 1983. That discussion was refuted by Micah Ankori in *Davar,* 8 October (21 Tishrei) 1983.

90. *Hayyei Moharan,* Sippurim Hadashim, 18b:3.

91. Classic prophetic visions, punctuated by the authenticating verb "and I saw" include: Moses (Gen. 32:31, 33:10; Ex. 33:33); Ezekiel (37:8, 41:8); Daniel (10:7, 12:5). This formulation is employed in talmudic texts as well. The medieval Spanish Talmudist, R. Yom Tov ben Abraham Ishbili (Ritba),

writes that the phrase "I myself saw" is recognized by the *geonim* as signaling dream visions inspired by natural wonders seen during sea voyages. See *Eiyn Ya'akov,* vol. 4, Baba Batra 73a.

92. For full translation of this dream and one interpretation, see Green, *Tormented Master,* pp. 199ff., 218 n. 36 on its last episode.

93. Harold Fisch writes of the "free flow of images and the shifting kaleidoscope of a dream" in the Song of Songs. See *Poetry with a Purpose: Biblical Poetics and Interpretation* (Bloomington, 1988), p. 89.

94. Erich Fromm defines symbol as "a pictoral image or words standing for an idea, feeling or thought." In symbolic rituals, further, an action rather than a word or image represents some inward experience (*Forgotten Language,* p. 41). Although Fromm's concern there is symbolic language in general, dreams are obviously the ideal hunting grounds for such symbolic transference. Piekarz observes that the tale *Fly and Spider* was told in the summer of 1807, during a period when Reb Nahman felt greatly persecuted by the "Sava" (R. Yehudah Leib of Shpola) and holds that such an experience is clearly apparent in the tale. Cf. *Hasidut Braslav,* pp. 60–67.

95. On the process of displacement that Freud recognized as fundamental to dreams, see his analysis in *The Interpretation of Dreams,* p. 229. Jung discusses the "unconscious aspect of words and images, produced in the form of dreams" in the first pages of *Man and His Symbols.*

96. This analogy may, at first glance, appear a bit anachronistic. Yet I believe it is Reb Nahman who is precocious. The interaction between rabbi and pupil, or between the zaddik and his followers described extensively in *Likkutei Moharan* (cf. 4.9; pt. 2, 2.4, 7.4, 91) is the identical dynamic so essential to psychotherapy. The story *The Master of Prayer* in fact dramatizes that same relationship. For this insight into the connection between theories of modern psychology and Reb Nahman's conception, I am indebted to R. Daniel Epstein. In chapter 1, we discussed the ways in which this relationship—so unique to Hasidism and highly developed in Reb Nahman's teaching—is transferred to the narrative act itself.

97. In a number of Reb Nahman's stories, dreams serve to awaken the characters to their true destiny, inspiring them to change their lives. Consider, for example, the tale *The Two Sons Who Were Reversed,* where the dreams of both sons catalyze their decision to leave their home; in *Burgher and Poor Man* the disquieting and simultaneous dreams of both protagonists presage the events of the story; and in *Rabbi and Only Son* the father's dream admonishes him, tragically late, for his misperception of the zaddik.

98. *Hayyei Moharan,* Makom Yeshivato ve-Nesi'otav, 30b:25. I refer to this account, as well as the following text, because of the nuances they add to the discussion. Clearly, though, *Hayyei Moharan* is not a canonical work as the tales are; its accuracy as a historical text is open to question. Nonetheless, it is regarded by Reb Nahman's followers as the loyal biography of their rebbe, and—questions of authenticity aside—does offer an additional perspective. Yet another illustration in this biography of Reb Nahman's fascination with mir-

ror images is found in the story of a king who instigates a competition between two artists to determine which is more gifted. He challenges them to draw a likeness of his new and beautiful palace. The first artist labors until he has mastered all the secrets of his art, finally reproducing an incredible living likeness of his half of the palace. The second does nothing, waits until the last possible moment, then paints his half of the palace black and gleaming like a mirror. He hangs a curtain before it. When the king comes to judge the two reproductions, he admires the first, then turns to the second. The lazy artist unveils his handiwork and in a flash of sunlight his black half reflects the other's drawing. "All that the king saw in the first half he saw in the second half as well." And not only that, "everything the king *could wish* to put in the first half of his palace *appeared* in the second half" (*Hayyei Moharan,* Sippurim Hadashim 23a:18). Perhaps we could read this parable as an allegory of the narrative art. One can tell a story of reality that suddenly (when revealed) seems more real that the original—it evokes more wonder precisely because it is an imitation of reality. Art, then, is even more capable of reflecting, of relaying the king's will than reality itself. Alternately, the parable speaks of the various planes of reality we have discussed above. The palace is that intangible domain called "life"; the first artist creates a dream of life. The second artist creates a *story* about that dream, and though further removed, it somehow pleases the king with its uncanny realism.

99. *Likkutei Moharan,* pt. 2, 119.

100. Perhaps we may even say that each beggar is doubly disguised: not only does their physical defect conceal their true attributes, but their very existence as characters, as actors in a fiction, conceals their true identity as a partial embodiment of Reb Nahman himself. On the autobiographical aspect of this story, see chapter 1; on the motif of the "poor man who comes to a wedding" and its metamorphoses, see Lipsker, "Ha-Kallah ve-Shivʿat ha-Kabbzanim," pp. 229–48.

101. Cf. *Rimzei Maʿasiyot,* p. 16 and *Likkutei Halakhot,* Oreh Hayyim, Berakhot ha-Shahar 3.3 and 3.41. The same model of justice perverted and destined to be set aright underlies the story *The Burgher and the Poor Man.* A prevalent motif in folktales, it is perhaps best known in classic form in Mark Twain's *The Prince and the Pauper,* vol. 21 of *The Complete Works of Mark Twain* (New York, 1881).

102. *Zohar* 3.204b. Cf. Michael Fishbane's *The Garments of Torah: Essays in Biblical Hermeneutics* (Bloomington, 1989), esp. chap. 3, pp. 33–46. There he discusses the kabbalistic image "that the Torah is cloaked in several garments of concealment, an image used to express the vision of the primordial processes of divinity originating in supernal realms as only progressively exteriorized into less spiritual forms until finally coming to symbolic expression in the Torah which we have on this earth" (p. 42).

103. *Zohar* 2.42b; *ʿEz Hayyim,* ʿIggulim ve-Yosher 5 (p. 43).

104. Compare my discussion in chapter 1 of the messianic figures clothed in numerous disguises that people Reb Nahman's tales. On the dynamics in the

Zohar of self-concealment and disclosure as a psychological dilemma experienced by R. Simeon bar Yohai, see Liebes, "Studies in the *Zohar*," pp. 28–30. Another recent study of the concept of *levushim* is Dorit Cohen-Alloro's *Sod ha-Levush ve-Mareh ha-Malakh be-Sefer ha-Zohar*, Research Projects of the Institute of Jewish Studies, Hebrew University, Monograph Series 13 (Jerusalem, 1987).

105. In a fascinating innovation presented in *Likkutei Moharan* 64.6, Reb Nahman interprets the verse "Tomorrow I will bring the locusts into your borders . . ." (Ex. 10:4) as speaking of the limitation inherent in appearances. He cites the locust as a creature devoid of contradiction between its internal and external aspect (based on *Genesis Rabbah* 21.5 and "all the books of the Kabbalah" in the parenthetical comments accompanying the text). Hence, it symbolizes a vision of "tomorrow," of a future of greater completeness in which there will no longer be a distinction between the "covering" *(levush)* and the essence, between appearances and the reality they conceal.

106. B.T. *Sanhedrin* 98a.

107. The dramatic tension created by such scenes makes them a centerpiece of tragedy. Consider the classic scene in book 19 of the *Odyssey,* in which the old housekeeper Euryclea recognizes her long-lost master by his scar, and must conceal her discovery from the crowd. See Erich Auerbach's treatment in *Mimesis: The Representation of Reality in Western Literature* (Princeton, 1953), pp. 3–23. And compare the story of the two sons of Zaddok that appears in *Lamentations Rabbah* 1:46, and the discussion of the motif by Galit Hasan-Rokem in "Ha-Messer ha-Ideologi ve-ha-Messer ha-Psychologi be-Maʿaseh be-Shenei Benei Zaddok ha-Cohen," *Jerusalem Studies in Hebrew Literature* 3 (1983): 122–39.

108. The enigmatic figure of the forest man in *The Two Sons Who Were Reversed* may well be inspired by an aggadah recounted in the *Zohar*. (*Zohar* Hakdamah, 5a–7a). Central to this story, too, is the question of recognition. R. Eleazar and R. Abba, stymied by a theological argument, encounter a lowly mule driver, who offers to help them on their way. The profound esoteric wisdom he gradually reveals astounds the sages, until they are moved to wonder at his unlikely profession and his true identity. Yet he answers only, "Do not ask who I am, but let us go together and study Torah." They walk on, until the sages ask once more his name and his dwelling place. And he replies, "The place where I live is fine and exalted for me. It is a tower, flying in the air, great and beautiful. . . . ." Cf. Tishby, *Wisdom of the Zohar*, 1:169–77.

109. *Likkutei Moharan* 33.2, 33.5. For a moving and perceptive discussion of "God's hidden face" and muteness in the Bible and rabbinic literature, see André Neher, *The Exile of the Word: From the Silence of the Bible to the Silence of Auschwitz,* trans. D. Maisel (Philadelphia, 1981), pp. 45ff.

110. *Likkutei Moharan* 64.3 and cf. Weiss, *Mehkarim,* pp. 137, 140, 148. Compare my discussion in chapter 3.

111. Mordechai Rotenberg, *Dialogue with Deviance: The Hasidic Ethic*

and the Theory of Social Contraction (Philadelphia, 1983), p. 183. Cf. *Likkutei Moharan,* pt. 2, 52.

112. Ouaknin, *Burnt Book,* p. 275.

113. Weiss, *Mehkarim,* p. 121. Cf. pp. 109–50.

114. Green, *Tormented Master,* p. 330. Cf. pp. 285–336.

115. Rotenberg, *Dialogue with Deviance,* p. 183.

116. Weiss, *Mehkarim,* p. 183. Cf. *Likkutei Moharan,* pt. 2, 8.7. In *Likkutei Moharan,* pt. 2, 52, even more audaciously, Reb Nahman recognizes this situation of paradox as the most authentic interaction with the divine: "It should be so that *kushiyot* are posed to God; He takes great pleasure in them. For his greatness and majesty . . . make it impossible for us to understand all His ways . . . if we could, that would mean our understanding equalled His understanding . . . Heaven forbid."

117. Green does include parts of three tales in his excurses (cf. *Tormented Master,* pp. 290–91, 292, 301–2) but uses all of them to illustrate the complex "relationship between simple and dialectical faith" (p. 302) at the heart of his discussion.

118. *Likkutei Moharan* 64.6. Green claims that the three protagonists of this tale—the wise man, the simple man, and the messenger—"are all aspects of Nahman's own tortured and conflicted mind" (*Tormented Master,* p. 291) and uses the tale as a paradigm illustrating the dialectical "paradox of faith" in Reb Nahman's theology. Such an approach seems to me unnecessarily restrictive in understanding this or other tales Reb Nahman told. My attempt is to read the tales not solely as a "fantastic biography" of their author.

119. See *Likkutei Moharan* 4.9. In this teaching, Reb Nahman discusses the paradox around which *The Humble King* is built with the addition of its kabbalistic dimensions.

120. *Genesis Rabbah* 68.9.

121. The teaching of divine immanence, heritage of the Lurianic conception, became central to the founders of Hasidism, and is central in Reb Nahman's worldview, as well. See, for instance, *Likkutei Moharan* 14, 54, 62.2, and esp. 64. See also note 1 above.

122. An innovation on the biblical verse Deut. 32:47. This statement was doubtless influenced by *Genesis Rabbah* 22.2: R. Ishmael asked R. Akiva, saying, "Since you have served Nahum of Gamzu for twenty-two years [and he taught], Every *akh* [save that] and *rak* [except] are limitations, while every *et* and *gam* [also] are extensions, tell me what is the purpose of the *et* written here? . . . Thereupon he quoted to him: 'For it is no empty thing for you' (Deut. 32:47) and if it seems empty, it is so on your account, because you do not know how to interpret it." See *Shivhei Moharan,* Gedulat Hasagato, 7b:40.

123. *Likkutei Moharan,* pt. 2, 12.

124. Quoted by K. W. Stace, *Mysticism and Philosophy* (London, 1960), p. 269. Cf. Stace's discussion in the chapter "Mysticism and Logic," pp. 251–76, and in "Mysticism and Language," pp. 277–306. We recall Scholem's remark

that "the religious world of the mystic can be expressed in terms applicable to rational knowledge only with the help of paradox" (*Major Trends,* p. 4).

125. A brilliant example of such a paradox in classical mystical literature is found in the *Zohar*'s discussion of Eccl. 1:1. (*Zohar* 2.10a). Here the discovery of the paradox expressed in the first verse of Ecclesiastes—"Vanity of vanities, says Kohelet, Vanity of vanities; all is vanity"—is the clearest sign of its ultimate truth. The kabbalistic teaching that the world is built of the seven lower *sefirot* can be learned from many sources. But to learn that such a truth is the very implication of this particular verse is truly shocking. "R. Eleazar said: King Solomon composed this book and founded it upon the seven breaths *[havalim]* on which the world stands, that is, the seven pillars that form the foundation of this world." The number 7 is reached by counting each repetition of the word *hevel*—literally, futile, empty breath; moralistically, "vanity"—with the plural form counted as two "breaths." He continues, "Just as the human body cannot exist without breath, so the world cannot exist if not for that wasted air of which King Solomon spoke." My thanks to R. Daniel Epstein, who called my attention both to this psychological-exegetical technique and to the prooftext quoted above.

126. These two quotations are cited in *Likkutei Moharan,* pt. 2, 7.7. See also *Likkutei Moharan* 69.

127. *Likkutei Moharan,* pt. 2, 7.7.

128. *Likkutei Halakhot,* Even ha-ʿEzer, Periʾah u-Reviʾah, 33.

129. *Likkutei Moharan,* pt. 2, 7.6–7.

130. The dialogical relationship, a central issue in Martin Buber's work *I and Thou,* also finds expression in his reflections on Hasidism. Cf. *Tales of the Hasidim* (New York, 1947), p. 3. Emmanuel Levinas's concept of discourse, the Other, and infinity may shed much light on the subject as well. Cf. *Totality and Infinity* (1961; reprint, Pittsburgh, 1969).

131. *Likkutei Moharan* 277. The analogy of the relationship between father and son to that of God and man is a mainstay in the teaching of the Maggid of Mezherich. See, for example, *Maggid Devarav le-Yaʿakov* s. 7 and s. 122, ed. R. Schatz-Uffenheimer (Jerusalem 1976), pp. 21, 201. The phenomenon of *zimzum* is explained there through this motif and the notion of *shaʿashuʿim.* As Schatz notes (ibid., p. 201), in the teachings of the Maggid this connection between *zimzum* and *shaʿashuʿim* is a classic formula of Lurianic mysticism according to R. Israel Sarug. *Maggid Devarav le-Yaʾakov* was originally published in 1784, and Reb Nahman quite likely was familiar with the teachings of the Maggid, as well as the Lurianic doctrine that inspired him.

132. *Likkutei Moharan,* pt. 2, 7.6. See Green's more comprehensive discussion of *mekkifin* in *Tormented Master,* p. 292ff.

133. B.T. *Berakhot* 31b.

134. Cf. *Moreh Nevukhim* 1.26; *Midrash Tehillim* 1.4; Buber's comment in *Midrash Tehillim,* n. 48.

135. Isaiah Tishby, *Netivei Emmunah ve-Minut* (Ramat Gan, 1964), pp. 12–14. In effect, Tishby explains, symbols may be used to express concepts in

one of two opposing ways: either to reveal or to conceal meaning. See also Tishby, *Wisdom of the Zohar,* 1:283ff. For an extensive discussion of kabbalistic hermeneutics, see Idel, *Kabbalah,* pp. 200–249, esp. "The Flowering of the Kabbalah," pp. 210–18.

136. This is Cassirer's famous definition of man, whose ability to conceive the world symbolically is what distinguishes him from other living creatures. See *Essay on Man* (1944; reprint, New Haven, 1974), p. 41 and cf. *Philosophy of Symbolic Forms,* 1:88. The following etymologies are drawn from the *Oxford English Dictionary.*

137. R. H. Hook, ed., *Fantasy and Symbol: Studies in Anthropological Interpretation* (London, 1979), p. 274. Freud suggests, similarly, the ultimately genetic nature of symbolic relationships: "What is today symbolically connected was probably united, in primitive times, by conceptual and linguistic identity. The symbolic relationship seems to be a residue and reminder of a former identity" (*Interpretation of Dreams,* p. 240).

138. The first reference to the Tree of Life is, of course, in Gen. 2:9; for later biblical appearances, see Ezek. 37:7, Psalm l, and Dan. 4:7ff. *Midrash Tehillim* comments on why it is called the "Tree of Life." "Because it is beloved of all living things; just as the Tree of Life was presented before all creatures in the Garden of Eden, so the Torah spreads out a lifetime long and leads to life in the world to come" (on Psalm l; see also *Midrash Tehillim* on Psalm 19). The relevant sections in *Sefer ha-Bahir* are 3, 4, 78, 84, and 45, quoted by Scholem in *Origins of the Kabbalah,* pp. 74–81. On the Tree of Life in mystical thought, see Tishby, *Wisdom of the Zohar,* 1:356–58. R. Nathan speaks of the Tree of Life as "beyond space"; the soul rises, by way of it, to delight in the Lord and "behold His beauty" (Ps. 27:4); see *Likkutei Halakhot,* Oreh Hayyim, Sefer Torah 3.2.

139. For Reb Nathan's allegorical exegesis of this story, see *Likkutei Halakhot,* Oreh Hayyim, Sefer Torah 3.7. The expression "the little that contains a lot" has a rich history in rabbinic literature. The notion of the infinite volume secreted in linguistic signs finds fascinating expression in the talmudic tradition that "the Holy One, blessed be He, sits and connects 'crowns' to the letters. And Akiva ben Joseph is the name of the man who will one day interpret them, drawing from each and every crown mountainous reams of laws" (B.T. *Menahot* 29b). The phenomenon of language in mystical thought, though, reaches beyond its penetration by the human mind: the letters are recognized as prime agents in the genesis of the universe itself: "R. Yehudah bar R. ʿIllaʿi expounded: 'These are the two worlds God created—one with the letter *heh* [this world] and the other with the letter *yod* [the world to come]. As it is written, "These are the generation of the heavens and the earth when they were created" (Gen. 2:4)—do not read 'when they were created' but 'they were created with [the letter] *heh*'" (ibid.). The term "the little that contains a lot" is applied, as well, to express a profound understanding of the concept of holiness: in the Talmud, the distinguishing character of holy places is their nonspaciality, for they are the locus of *metaphysical* content. Thus, "R. Levi,

and some say R. Yohanan, said, It is a belief passed from father to son that the place of the Holy Ark and the *keruvim* [cherubim] is immeasurable. . . . The ark that Moses made is ten cubits wide on each side. The *keruvim,* R. Samuel said in the name of Ravnai, therefore stand miraculously, for 'five cubits was one wing of the *keruv,* and five cubits the other wing of the *keruv:* from the uttermost part of the one wing to the uttermost part of the other were ten cubits' (1 Kg. 6:24)." As we know, the entire breadth of the Holy of Holies was twenty cubits. Yet if the ark had ten cubits on either side of it, room for the outspread *keruvim,* there would be no place for the ark itself. This architectural impossibility can be solved only by a miracle, and that is the phenomenon of "the little that contains a lot"—the holiness contained in the ark imbues it with spacial insubstantiality (B.T. *Baba Batra* 99a). The term reappears, throughout the Talmud, in the concentric geographical circles of holiness: in the Temple courtyard, "people stand pressed together and bow down to God with room aplenty. . . . In Jerusalem no person ever said to another, I haven't enough space" (Mishnah *Avot* 5.5; B.T. *Yoma* 21a). And the Land of Israel itself is described as "a beautiful country" (Ezek. 25:9)—literally "a deerlike land" because, like a deerskin, its borders expand from within to contain whatever number of inhabitants come to live in it (B.T. *Gittin* 57a). For other examples in midrashic literature of "the little that contains a lot" see *Genesis Rabbah* 5.7 and *Leviticus Rabbah* 10.9.

140. See, for example, *Tikkunei Zohar*, Tikkun 15, fol. 30b; and cf. Tishby, *Wisdom of the Zohar,* 1:287–88.

141. *Shivhei Moharan,* Maʿalot Torato ve-Sippurav ha-Keddoshim 15a:33.

142. Schatz-Uffenheimer, ed., *Maggid Devarav le-Yaʿakov,* s. 193 (p. 307). The expression *ʿolam katan* already appears in midrash *Tanhuma,* Pekkudei 3. See my discussion in chapter 2 on the notion of microcosms as variegated 'texts' and their symbolic meaning.

143. *Zohar* 1.103b, translated in Tishby, *Wisdom of the Zohar* 1:400. See also *Zohar* 3.141a–b.

144. Quoted by Todorov in *Mikhail Bakhtin: The Dialogical Principle*, pp. 48–50.

145. My awareness of this vital aspect of mystical linguistic theory was aroused by Walter Benjamin's essay "On Language as Such and the Language of Man" and nurtured by the insights of Prof. Stéphane Mosès. Gershom Scholem, of course, discusses the subject extensively; see, for example, *Major Trends,* p. 24.

146. Todorov, *Fantastic,* p. 60.

147. This idea of collective cultural representation is the major thesis of Jung's monumental study, *Man and His Symbols;* see especially pp. 41, 83.

148. Water in its various forms serves to illustrate a host of theological teachings in talmudic and midrashic sources. Cf. B.T. *Berakhot* 56b; *Yoma* 78a; *Taʿanit* 7a; *Hagigah* 12a, 14a; 15a; *Baba Kamma* 17a; J.T. *Hagigah* 2.2 (fol. 77b); *Genesis Rabbah* 2, 4, 5, 13; *Exodus Rabbah* 16; *Deuteronomy*

Rabbah 3; *Song of Songs Rabbah* 1.3; *Tanhuma* Tavo 3; *Midrash Tehillim* 1; *Zohar* 1.66, 128, 256; *Zohar* 3.219, 233; *Tikkunei Zohar*, Tikkun 5, fol. 19b.

149. *Pirkei de-Rabbi Eliezer* 23.

150. Rashi and Tosefot, B.T. *Ta'anit* 8a.

151. See *Zohar* 1.3b translated in Tishby, *Wisdom of the Zohar*, 1:328.

152. On the importance of ritual immersion for reaching spiritual purity, see Reb Nahman's teachings in *Likkutei Moharan* 14.5, 17.8, 56.7, and esp. 21.7, in which the connection is drawn between a life of holiness, water, and the seven voices with which King David appealed to God. See also the historical analysis of Hasidic *kavvanot,* or mystical intentions, related to the *mikveh* presented by A. Wertheim, *Halakhot ve-Halikhot be-Hasidut* (Jerusalem, 1960), pp. 66–68.

153. See *Likkutei Moharan* 8.3, 38.2. A note in *Likkutei Moharan* refers the reader to *Tikkunei Zohar,* Tikkun 18 fol. 35b and the whole of Tikkun 69.

154. *Lamentations Rabbah* 1. Compare J.T. *Berakhot* 2 (fol. 5a).

155. *Likkutei Moharan,* pt. 2, 7.10.

156. Reb Nahman suggests this comparison in *Likkutei Moharan* 66.2; the concept of the letter *aleph* is found in Tikkunei *Zohar*, Hakdamah, fol. 7b; *Peri 'Ez Hayyim,* Sha'ar ha-Zemirot 5.

157. See *Likkutei Moharan* 66.2.

158. Ibid. And cf. B.T. *Hagigah* 12a; *Ketubbot* 5a; *Menahot* 36b; *Genesis Rabbah* 1.15; *Leviticus Rabbah* 36.1; *Tanhuma,* Bereshit 5; *Pirkei de-Rabbi Eliezer* 18. See also Avivah Gottlieb Zornberg's discussion of "the hands of God" in *Genesis,* pp. 17–20.

159. My gratitude to R. Daniel Epstein for remarking on this apt metaphor. The music truly seems to wait, abstractly potential, in the hands of the conductor; the sight of such a figure commanding his orchestra inspires the sense it is his will alone that magically draws the music from potentiality to actuality the moment the performance begins. Other details of this metaphor link it to *The Seven Beggars:* the conductor's mastery over rhythm (the pulse of the king's daughter); the role of the biblical conductor *(menaze'ah)* in the Temple service.

160. The blind bards of antiquity, dearest to the Muses, spent their lives singing such truths to the world. Thus Homer's *Odyssey* is punctuated by such descriptions: "[T]he minstrel stirred, murmuring to the god, and soon clear notes came one by one, a vision . . ." (8.99–100). *The Odyssey,* trans. Robert Fitzgerald (New York, 1961).

161. On the significance of the number 10, its presence in the Talmud, and its development in the *Zohar* and *Tikkunei Zohar,* and in Bratslav Hasidic thought, see Liebes, "Ha-Tikkun ha-Kelali," pp. 234–35 and his references.

162. *Likkutei Moharan* 54.6.

163. *Likkutei Moharan* 282.

164. *Likkutei Moharan* 54.6.

165. Ibid. Reb Nahman's prooftext for this contention is a daring transfer

of two biblical verses that speak of God's mastery over the human spirit to the prophet's formation of his human song: "Into your hand I commit my spirit" (Ps. 31:6) and "In whose hand is the soul of every living thing and the spirit of all mankind" (Job 12:10).

166. B.T. *Pesahim* 117a; *Shabbat* 30b.

167. *Likkutei Halakhot, Even ha-ʿEzer, Periʾah u-Reviʾah* 3.1.

168. The original statement is in B.T. *Pesahim* 117a and *Zohar* 3.101a: "R. Joshua ben Levi said, The book of Psalms was uttered in ten expressions of praise. . . ." The subject is laconically suggested in *Likkutei Moharan* 205 and *Likkutei Moharan,* pt. 2, 92 in reference to Reb Nahman's famous *tikkun ha-kelali.*

169. B.T. *Berakhot* 3b.

170. Quoted by Martin Buber, *Or ha-Gannuz* (Jerusalem, 1969), pp. 73–74. The original source is R. Uziel Meislisch, *ʿEz ha-Daʿat Tov* (Warsaw, 1863).

171. *Tikkunei Zohar,* Tikkun 13.

172. B.T. *Berakhot* 56b. See also *Beit Yaʿakov,* Bereshit 2 (fol. lb) concerning the futuristic orientation of this dream.

173. B. T. *Rosh ha-Shanah* 31a.

174. "La Saiziaz," line 37 in *The Poems and Plays of Robert Browning* (New York, 1934). *Tikkunei Zohar*, Tikkun 13, like B.T. *Berakhot* 10a, emphasizes the kinship between man's eternally living soul and God Himself through a series of parallels: "Just as the Holy One, blessed be He, nourishes all the worlds, so the soul nourishes all the body. Just as He sees and is not seen, so the soul sees yet remains invisible. Just as He dwells in remote chambers, so the soul dwells secretly remote; just as He fills the world, so the soul fills the body. . . ." Indeed, our soundless spirit first becomes audible when it is breathed through a musical instrument; then "the breath of life" *(neshimah, neshamah)* is suddenly perceptible. Music, in that sense, is the voice of the soul itself.

175. *Likkutei Halakhot,* Even ha-ʿEzer, Periʾah u-Reviʾah 3.10. We discussed extensively in chapter 3 the seminal concept of the exile/imprisonment of the Shekhinah as it appears in Reb Nahman's oeuvre.

176. The following discussion is based on the exegesis found in *Tikkunei Zohar*, Tikkun 25, fols. 70a–71a. I make no attempt to explicate the kabbalistic symbolism in the text, but only to draw parallels between it and Reb Nahman's tale, following the most simple and literal reading. The translation and paraphrase are my own, guided in part by the commentary by the Gaon of Vilna on those pages.

177. *Likkutei Moharan,* pt. 2, 282.

178. The pattern in which the shofar is sounded: *tekiʿah—shevarim—teruʿah—tekiʿah * tekiʿah—shevarim—tekiʿah * tekiʿah—teruʿah—tekiʿah.* This series consists of long and short tones, as the Gaon of Vilna explains—the long tones foretell a time of mercy; the short ones, trials of stern judgment yet to come. See his comments on *Tikkunei Zohar*, Tikkun 25, fol. 70a–b.

179. Maimonides distinctly hears the message the shofar calls: "Wake up,

you sleepers, from your slumber! And you dormant ones from your drowsiness! Search your acts and return in repentance: remember your Creator!" *Mishneh Torah,* Hilkhot Teshuvah 3.4.

180. *Likkutei Halakhot,* Even ha-ʿEzer, Periʾah u-Reviʾah 3.10.

181. *Likkutei Moharan* 54.6. The conclusion of this teaching alludes to the ultimate victory—accomplished by the seventh beggar, without legs, whose appearance is not told—over the delusions that mask the material world. The "ends of the earth" signify a furthermost extremity—"legs of holiness," the most recondite, unseen traces of God's presence on our human earth. These footprints must be discovered. But that, as Reb Nahman's uncompleted tale would suggest, is an accomplishment stored away for a brave new world of the future.

182. In B.T. *Berakhot* 58a, Rav Sheshet is mentioned as being blind, *sagi nahor.* In J.T. *Peah* 8.9 (fol. 21a) and in *Leviticus Rabbah* 34.13, two attributes of the moon, poor and blind, describe those who have lost their wealth. The relevance of this second detail will presently become apparent. The *Zohar* 1.249b is the source of the Aramaic phrase inserted in the tale, "he has nothing of his own" (*SM,* p. 271).

183. B.T. *Hullin* 60b.

184. Ibid.

185. One talmudic source suggesting the identity between King David and the moon is B.T. *Rosh ha-Shanah* 25a: "Rabbi said to R. Hiyya, Go to En Tob and sanctify the moon, and send me the watchword: 'David, King of Israel is alive and vigorous,'" and Rashi there: "David, King of Israel is compared to the moon, about which it is said (Ps. 89:37) 'His seed shall endure forever, and his throne shall be like the sun before me. It shall be established forever like the moon, and the witness in the sky is sure.'" See also B.T. *Pesahim* 68b; *Sukkah* 29a; and *Exodus Rabbah* 15.6. In the *Zohar* the link between the messianic king and the poor moon whose source of light is the sun becomes explicit. See *Zohar* 1.138a. The story of the moon's diminution becomes a paradigm in Reb Nahman's oeuvre; it is incorporated in other stories as well, notably *Rabbi and Only Son* and *The Two Sons Who Were Reversed.* The connection, in the second, between the "new song" of the moon and the restoration of the Israelite nation likewise has its inception in the *Zohar* (1.123a–b). The absence of King David's name in the opening of Ps. 98:1, "Sing to the Lord a new song," points to its futuristic orientation. As it says in the *Zohar,* the "'Holy Spirit' will sing this song when God raises Israel from the dust . . . such a song has not been uttered since the day the world came into being. . . . The new song—it is the moon's, for then the moon will be renewed under the sun."

186. B.T. *Ketubbot* 111b.

187. Ben Amos, 'Talmudic Tall Tales," p. 100.

188. Todorov, *Fantastic,* p. 119.

189. B.T. *Berakhot* 2b and *Shabbat* 34b.

190. *Zohar* 1.99b (Midrash ha-Neʿelam). Quoted and annotated by Tishby, *Wisdom of the Zohar,* 2:837.

191. Italo Calvino, *The Castle of Crossed Destinies,* trans. William Weaver (London, 1978). Calvino's comments in another context on the literary imagination ring true in the case of Reb Nahman as well. Among the various elements that concur in forming its visual aspect, he numbers direct observation of the real world, phantasmic and oneiric transfiguration, the figurative world as it is transmitted by culture at its various levels, and a process of abstraction, condensation, and interiorization of sense experience, a matter of prime importance to both the verbalization and visualization of thought. In our own discussion, we have seen the vital role of dreams in Reb Nahman's stories, and we realize throughout that acute consciousness of sensory experience pervades the stories as well—the beggars, for example, are abstractions of all five senses. See *Six Memos for the Next Millennium,* p. 94.

192. B.T. *Sanhedrin* 101a. Other prominent instances of allegorical interpretation, i.e., detecting and magnifying the moral teaching or historical information the text presents, include personification in the verse "Sin lurks at the door" (Gen. 4:7) and in the statement by R. Simeon bar Lakish, "He [sin] is Satan, he is the Evil Urge, he is the Angel of Death" (B.T. *Baba Batra* 16a); and drawing the analogy between man and trees, as in this explication of Ezek. 17:22: "'And all the trees of the field will know . . .'—that is society—'that I the Lord have brought down a high tree'—that is ʿAmalek—'and exalted a low tree'—that is Abraham—'I have dried up a green tree'—those are the wives of Elimelekh—'and made a dry tree to flourish'—that is Sarah" (*Genesis Rabbah* 53.1). Cf. Isaac Heinemann, *Darkhei ha-Aggadah* (Jerusalem, 1950), pp. 150–161.

193. Frye, *Creation and Recreation,* p. 59.

194. As Tishby explains, the Torah itself, for the Kabbalists, is inherently and necessarily phrased in figurative language (*Wisdom of the Zohar*, 1:283); see also Scholem, *On the Kabbalah and its Symbolism,* pp. 32–86.

195. The connection between this story and aggadic sources was first brought to my attention by R. Adin Steinsaltz in a lecture he gave in Jerusalem in 1989. See the discussion in chapter 1.

196. Even before their interpretation, the referential valence of the objects is evident: the mighty chair is "the throne of glory" with its retinue of supernatural creatures envisioned by the prophet Ezekiel; the bed-table-lamp suggest the room prepared by the Shunammite woman for Elisha the prophet (2 Kg. 4:10ff.); the rose, with its kabbalistic overtones, speaks for itself. See Tishby, *Wisdom of the Zohar,* 1:391–92 (translation and commentary on *Zohar* 1.1a and 1.221a). See also passages in *Zohar* 2.20a–b, 3.133a–b, 286b; *Tikkunei Zohar*, Tikkun 68, fol. 78b; *Zohar Hadash*, Yetro, fol. 39a.

197. In *Likkutei Moharan,* pt. 2, 17 Reb Nahman declares the conviction that "nature" and providence *(hashgahah)* are indistinguishable: "In truth, we are unable to understand what nature and providence are, because nature is actually His providence. Man cannot grasp that these two matters are one, that nature truly is identical with divine providence."

198. B.T. *Shabbat* 88b–89a.

199. *Likkutei Moharan* 66.4. What Reb Nahman means, of course, is the impossibility of pronouncing any consonant, whether labial, guttural, etc., without the help of vowels. Vowel sounds combine breath (i.e., "spirit," *ru'ah*) with body (lips, tongue, teeth, etc.) to give birth to words. To be sure, the Hebrew language itself has always been a focal point for mystical thought. Cf. Lipiner, *Hazon ha-Otiot.*

200. *Likkutei Moharan* 31.9. We cannot ignore the overtones of Reb Nahman's terms. The "union" he describes between consonants and letter, between corporeal form and spirit is the "union" *(zivvug)* of man and woman as well.

201. *Likkutei Moharan* 55.1. Here, as in *Likkutei Moharan* 66.4, the Aristotelian paradigm of potentiality and actuality comes into play, manifest this time in the progression leading from thought to speech, and from speech to action.

202. *Likkutei Moharan* 31.7.

203. *Likkutei Moharan* 65.2. Reb Nahman's language in this, and especially the dialogue in the following quotation, is astonishing. Though my translation may sound like a take-off on Romain Rolland, it is faithful to the Hebrew text.

204. Ibid.

205. Green remarks that the "symbol of the heart of the world . . . may be said at once to represent the Shekhinah, the true *zaddik* (who is the heart of his generation), and the soul of every individual who longs for God" (*Tormented Master,* p. 302).

206. Neher, *Exile of the Word,* p. 176.

207. *Likkutei Moharan* 63.1. Compare *Sihot Haran,* s. 24a and *Hayyei Moharan,* Sihot ʿAvodat ha-Shem, 4.

208. *The Kuzari (Kitab Al Kharizi),* translated from Arabic by H. Hirschfield (New York, 1984), Parable of the Heart, 2:36–44. See also *Sefer ha-Bahir* s. 67 and Scholem's discussion of the theme in Origins of the Kabbalah, p. 78.

209. *Zohar* 1.15b. Cf. Scholem, *Major Trends,* p. 219.

210. *Tikkunei Zohar*, Tikkun 25, fol. 77a, and see the comments by the Gaon of Vilna there.

211. *Zohar* 2.108a.

212. In *Likkutei ʿEzot,* Tefillah 25, the allegory of the mute beggar's tale becomes a metaphor describing appropriate human conduct on which the world depends. "When day draws to an end, man must arouse himself and remember how the heart of the world and the spring, who are the essence of the world's existence, begin to bid each other farewell with great love. . . . And he, too, must join in with them and arouse himself to a powerful longing and yearning for God, and pray with great devotion."

213. B.T. *Berakhot* 3a.

214. Ibid. In *Tikkunei Zohar*, the verse quoted above, "As a bird wanders from its nest, so a man wanders from his place" is read as a reference to the mutual lostness of the Shekhinah and God. See Tikkun 6, fol. 21b. On this

image in the "Jewish theological imagination," see Fishbane, "The Holy One Sits and Roars," pp. 1–21.

215. *Likkutei Halakhot,* Yoreh De'ah, Nedarim 4.36. On the connection between prophecy and the *keruvim,* see *Zohar* 2.53b and *Likkutei 'Ezot* B, Zaddik, s. 93.

216. *Likkutei Moharan* 226, based on *Zohar* 2.19a.

217. *Likkutei Moharan* 237.

218. Ibid.

219. *Likkutei Moharan* 19.8.

220. *Likkutei Moharan* 60.6. This teaching alludes to the mystical conviction, adopted in Hasidism, of the dialectic between human spiritual awareness (*it'aruta diletata,* awakening in the lower realm) and the response this heightened state arouses in the divine realm *(it'aruta dele'ela).* And consider the statement recorded in *Hayyei Moharan,* 5a:23: "People say that tales are for going to sleep to, but I say that, through tales, people can be shaken from their sleep."

221. *Likkutei Moharan* 60.9, based on Is. 30:20. Cf. Green's comment: 'We must recall that Nahman always saw himself as a spiritual guide and teacher, rather than as an abstract thinker. . . . As a teacher, Nahman had to be aware of the process of growth which he sought in his disciples, only not in its end result. The stages of increasing awareness are important to him . . ." (*Tormented Master,* p. 323).

222. Cassirer, *Philosophy of Symbolic Forms,* 2:64.

223. B.T. *Yoma* 54b.

224. *Rimzei Ma'asiot,* p. 7.

225. *Likkutei Moharan* 61.7

226. *Song of Songs Rabbah* 1.7.

227. R. Nathan makes the link between this most esoteric teaching, drawn from B.T. *Rosh ha-Shanah* 32b, and Reb Nahman's tale *The Seven Beggars.* See *Likkutei Halakhot,* Oreh Hayyim, Rosh ha-Shanah 6.12.

228. B.T. *Shabbat* 30b; *Mishneh Torah,* Hilkhot Yesodei ha-Torah 7.8. Though a compelling subject, consideration of the vital role of music, dance, and happiness in Bratslav tradition lies beyond the scope of the present discussion. Comments on this subject appear in *Shivhei Moharan,* 12a:1.

229. *Likkutei Moharan,* pt. 2, 24.

BIBLIOGRAPHY

Primary Sources

The following list includes works attributed to Reb Nahman and his followers cited in the course of our discussion. The Bible, rabbinic sources (Talmud and midrashim) and pre-Hasidic texts are not cited here.

The list is in alphabetical order by title. A brief description follows the most central works. A comprehensive bibliography of works by Bratslav Hasidim and other Hasidic sources may be found in Arthur Green's *Tormented Master,* pp. 381–84, and one of criticism on the tales in Yoav Elstein's "Structuralism in Literary Criticism: A Method and Application in Two Representative Hasidic Tales" (in Hebrew) (diss., University of California at Los Angeles, 1974), pp. 448ff; available through University Microfilms of Ann Arbor, Michegan.

Be'ur ha-Likkutim. By R. Abraham ben R. Nahman ha-Levi Hazan. 1908. Reprint, Jerusalem, 1935.

Hayyei Moharan. By R. Nathan ben Naftali Sternharz of Nemirov. 1840. Reprint, Lemberg, 1875. Part 1 is *Hayyei Moharan;* Part 2 is *Shivhei Moharan* and *Sihot Moharan.* Documents principal events in Reb Nahman's biography and comments on diverse subjects; includes noncanonical tales and records dreams attributed to Reb Nahman.

Keter Shem Tov. 1799. Reprint, Brooklyn, 1987. Contains teachings attributed to the Ba'al Shem Tov.

Likkutei Halakhot. By R. Nathan ben Naftali Sternharz of Nemirov. 1861–90. Reprint, Jerusalem, 1950–63. Presents, develops, and extends Reb Nahman's basic teachings. Structured after the *Shulkhan 'Arukh,* the authoritative codification of Jewish law, it is in effect a ramified commentary both on the teachings recorded in *Likkutei Moharan* and on the thirteen canonical tales, rich in original thought. Commentary on the tales is interspersed throughout the numerous volumes of *Likkutei Halakhot.*

Likkutei Moharan. By R. Nahman ben Simhah of Bratslav. Edited by R. Nathan Sternharz of Nemirov. Pt. 1, 1808. Pt. 2, 1811. Reprint, Jerusalem, 1969. Collected teachings formulated over the course of Reb Nahman's life, some written by himself and others transcribed by his disciples.

Maggid Devarav le-Ya'akov. By R. Dov Baer of Mezherich. 1784. Reprint, Jerusalem, 1976.

Nahal Nove'a. By A. Weizhendler. Jerusalem, 1961.

Rimzei Ma'asiyot. By R. Nahman of Tcherin. 1902. Reprint, Jerusalem, 1985.

Interprets each of the tales individually; is included at the end of *Sippurei Ma'asiyot* (Jerusalem, 1985), the standard Bratslav edition of the tales.

Shivhei ha-Ba'al Shem Tov. 1814–15. Reprint, Tel Aviv, 1947.

Shivhei Haran and *Sihot Haran*. By disciples of the Ba'al Shem Tov. Edited by R. Nathan ben Naftali Sternharz of Nemirov. 1840 (?). Reprint, Benei Berak, 1944.

Sippurei Ma'asiyot. By Reb Nahman ben Ṣimhah of Bratslav. 1811. Reprint, Jerusalem, 1985. Collection of thirteen canonical tales told orally; edited and published with First Introduction and Second Introduction by R. Nathan Sternharz of Nemirov.

Toledot Ya'akov Yosef. By Jacob Joseph of Polonnoye. Korets, 1780.

Yemei Moharant. By R. Nathan ben Naftali Sternharz of Nemirov. Part 1, 1876; part 2, 1905. Reprint, Benei Berak, 1957. Contains biographical and exegetical material.

Zimrat ha-Arez. By R Nahman of Tcherin. Lemberg, 1876.

Secondary Sources

Only works cited more than once in the course of our discussion have been listed.

Abrams M. H. *The Mirror and the Lamp: Romantic Theory and the Critical Tradition*. New York, 1958.

Afik, Isaac. "Tefisat ha-Halom ezel Hazal." Diss. Bar Ilan University, 1990.

Apter, T. E. *Fantasy Literature: An Approach to Reality*. London, 1982.

Armin, Geise. *Der Phantasie bei Ludwig Tieck: Ihre Bedeutung für den Menschen und sein Werk*. Hamburg, 1973.

Ashlag, Yehudah Leib. *Sefer ha-Zohar*. 24 vols. Jerusalem, 1985.

Avni, Abraham Albert. *The Bible and Romanticism: The Old Testament in German and French Romantic Poetry*. The Hague, 1969.

Bakhtin, Mikhail. 'The Forms of Time and the Chronotopos in the Novel: From the Greek Novel to Modern Fiction." *PTL: A Journal for Descriptive Poetics and Theory of Literature* 3 (1978): 493–528.

Band, Arnold. *Nahman ben Simhah of Bratslav: The Tales*. New York, 1978.

Bartana, Orsion. *Ha-Fantasia be-Sifrut Dor ha-Medinah*. Tel Aviv, 1989.

Ben Amos, Dan. *Folklore in Context*. New Delhi, 1982.

Bettelheim, Bruno. *Freud and Man's Soul*. New York, 1983.

——— *The Uses of Enchantment: The Meaning and Importance of Fairy Tales*. New York, 1977.

Bilu, Yoram. "Sigmund Freud and R. Yehuda: On a Mystical Tradition of 'Psychoanalytic' Dream Interpretation." *Journal of Psychological Anthropology* 2 (fall 1979): 443–63.

Bottigheimer, Ruth. *Grimm's Bad Girls and Bold Boys: The Moral and Social*

Vision of the Tales. New Haven, 1987.

Brenner, Athalya. "On Reading the Bible as a Feminist Woman." In *A Feminist Companion to the Song of Songs*. Sheffield, 1993.

Calvino, Italo. *Six Memos for the Next Millennium*. Cambridge, 1988.

Cassirer, Ernst. *Essay on Man*. 1944. Reprint, New Haven, 1974.

———. *The Philosophy of Symbolic Forms*. 1929. Translated by Ralph Mannheim. New Haven, 1955.

Dan, Joseph. *Ha-Sippur ha-Hasidi*. Jerusalem 1975.

Dinur, Ben-Zion. *Reishita shel ha-Hasidut ve-Yesodoteha ha-Soziali'im ve-ha-Meshihi'im be-Mafne ha-Dorot*. Jerusalem, 1943–45.

Echer, Gisela, ed. *Feminist Aesthetics*. Boston, 1985.

Elbaum, Jacob. "Tavniot Mishtarsharot ve-Nishbarot be-Ma'aseh be-Burgher ve-'Ani le-R. Nahman me-Bratslav." *Jerusalem Studies in Hebrew Literature* 4 (1984): 59–85.

Eliade, Mircea. *The Myth of the Eternal Return*. Translated by W. Trash. New York, 1954.

Elior, Rachel. "Between *Yesh* and *Ayin*: The Doctrine of the Zaddik in the Works of Jacob Isaac, the Seer of Lublin." In *Jewish History*, edited by Ada Rapoport-Albert and Steven Zipperstein. London, 1988.

Elstein, Yoav. *Ma'aseh Hoshev*. Ramat Gan, 1973.

———. *Pa'amei Bat Melekh*. Ramat Gat, 1984.

Engelsman, Joan Chamberlain. *The Feminine Dimension of the Divine*. Philadelphia, 1979.

Fass, Barbara. *La Belle Dame sans Merci and the Aesthetics of Romanticism*. Detroit, 1974.

Fink, Gonther-Louis. "Volk und Volksdichtung in der ersten Berliner Romantik." In *Romantik in Deutschland: Sonderband der Deutschen Vierteljahrsschrift für Literaturwissenschaft und Geistesgeschichte*, edited by R. Brinkmann. Stuttgart, 1978.

Fishbane, Michael. *The Garments of Torah*. Bloomington, 1989.

———. "The Holy One Sits and Roars: Mythopoesis and the Midrashic Imagination". *Journal of Jewish Thought and Philosophy* 1 (1991): 1–21.

Frankiel, Tamar. *The Voice of Sarah: Feminine Spirituality and Traditional Judaism*. San Francisco, 1990.

Frazer, James George. *The Golden Bough*. New York, 1929.

Freud, Sigmund. *The Interpretation of Dreams*. 1900. Translated by A. Brill. New York, 1950.

——— 'The Uncanny." *Imago* 5, nos. 5-6 (1925): 297–324.

Fromm, Erich. *The Forgotten Language*. New York, 1951.

Frye, Northrop. *Creation and Recreation*. Toronto, 1980.

Green, Arthur. "Bride, Spouse, Daughter: Images of the Feminine in Classical Jewish Sources." In On Being a Jewish Feminist, edited by S. Heschel, pp. 248–60. New York, 1983.

———. *Tormented Master*. New York, 1981.

Gross, Rita. "Steps Toward Feminine Imagery of the Deity in Jewish Theology." *Judaism* 30 (1981): 183–92.

Halivni, David Weiss. "On Man's Role in Revelation." In vol. 2 of *From Ancient Israel to Modern Judaism: Essays in Honor of Marvin Fox,* edited by Jacob Neusner et al., pp. 29–52. Brown Judaic Studies. Atlanta, 1973.

Hartman, Geoffrey. "Romanticism and Anti-selfconsciousness." In *Romanticism: Points of View*, edited by R. F. Gleckner and G. E. Enscoe. Detroit, 1975.

Heinemann, Isaac. *Darkhei ha-Aggadah*. Jerusalem, 1970.

Heschel, Susannah, ed. *On Being a Jewish Feminist*. New York, 1983.

Hook, R. H., ed. *Fantasy and Symbol: Studies in Anthropological Interpretation*. London, 1979.

Horodezki, S. A., ed. *Torat ha-Kabbalah shel R. Yizhak Ashkenazi ve-R. Hayyim Vital*. Tel Aviv, 1947.

Huttner, Isaac. *Pahad Yizhak*. New York, 1987.

Idel, Moshe. *Hasidism: Between Ecstasy and Magic*. New York, 1995.

———. *Kabbalah: New Perspectives*. New Haven, 1988.

Immerwahr, Raymond. "The Word 'Romantisch' and its History." In *The Romantic Period in Germany,* edited by Siegbert Prawer, 34–69. New York, 1970.

Jung, Carl. *Man and His Symbols*. New York, 1968.

Kaplan, Aryeh. *Rabbi Nahman's Stories*. Jerusalem, 1983.

Karlin, A. "Sippurei Pela'ot shel Rabba bar bar Hanna." *Sinai* 20 (1947).

Levin, Isaac, and Abraham Peleg. *'Olam ha-Shenah ve-ha-Halomot*. Tel Aviv, 1981.

Liebes, Yehudah. "Ha-Tikkun ha-Kelali shel R. Nahman me-Bratslav ve-Yahaso le-Shabbta'ut." *Zion* 45 (1980): 201–45. Translated by Batya Stein in *Studies in Jewish Myth and Jewish Messianism* (New York, 1993), 115-50.

———. "Megammot be-Heker Hasidut Bratslav: Le-Bikkorto shel Y. Mondshine." *Zion* 47 (1982): 224–31.

———. *Studies in the Zohar*. Translated by Arnold Schwartz et. al. New York, 1993.

———. "Teguvot le-He'aroteha shel A. Rapoport-Albert." *Zion* 46 (1981): 352–55.

Lipiner, Elias. *Hazon ha-Otiot*. Jerusalem, 1989.

Lipsker, Avidav. "Ha-Kallah ve-Shivat ha-Kabbzanim: She'elat Mekorotav shel Sippur ha-Misgeret shel 'Ma'aseh me-Shiv'at ha-Bettlers.'" *Jerusalem Studies in Jewish Folklore* 13-14 (1991–92): 248–99.

Luethi Max. *The European Folktale: Form and Nature*. Philadelphia 1982.

———. *Märchen*. Stuttgart, 1962.

Maranda, P., ed. *Soviet Structural Folkloristics*. The Hague, 1974.

Mondshine, Yehoshu'a. "'Al 'Ha-Tikkun ha-Kelali . . .' me-et Yehudah Liebes." *Zion* 47 (1982): 198–223.

Neher, André. *The Exile of the Word: From the Silence of the Bible to the Silence of Auschwitz*. Translated by David Maisel. Philadelphia, 1981.

Nigal, Gedaliah. *Ha-Sipporet ha-Hasidit.* Jerusalem, 1981.

O'Flaherty, Wendy. *Dreams, Illusions, and Other Realities.* Chicago, 1984.

Ostriker, Alicia Suskin. *Feminist Revision and the Bible.* Cambridge, 1993.

Otto, Rudolf. *The Idea of the Holy.* 1923. Translated by J. D. Harvey. London, 1950.

Ouaknin, Marc-Alain. *The Burnt Book: Reading the Talmud.* Translated by Llewellyn Brown. Princeton, 1995.

Pagis, Dan. "ʿOf ha-Almavvet: Motif ha-Phoenix be-Sifrut ha-Midrash ve-ha-Aggadah." In *Sefer ha-Yovel shel ha-Gymnasia ha-ʿIvrit,* 74–90. Jerusalem, 1962.

Peckham, Morse. *The Birth of Romanticism, 1790–1815.* Greenwood, Conn., 1986.

———. "Toward a Theory of Romanticism." In *Romanticism: Points of View,* edited by R. F. Gleckner and G. E. Enscoe. Detroit, 1975.

Petrushka, S. "Mekor Polani le-Sippurei Maʿasiyot shel R. Nahman me-Bratslav." *Ketuvim* (Tel Aviv weekly) 42 (12 July 1928).

Picard, Max. *Die Welt des Schweigens.* Zurich, 1948.

———. *The Human Face.* Translated by Guy Endore. London, 1931.

Piekarz, Mendel. *Hasidut Braslav.* Jerusalem, 1972.

———. "Zaddik le-Benei ha-ʿOlam ha-Hadash!?" *Tarbiz* 51 (1982): 154–57.

Plaskow, Judith. "Jewish Theology in Feminist Perspective." In *Feminist Perspectives on Jewish Studies,* edited by L. Davidman and S. Tenenbaum, 62–81. New Haven, 1994.

Preminger, Alex, ed. *Encyclopaedia of Poetry and Poetics.* Princeton, 1965.

Propp, Vladimir Iakovlevich. *Morphology of the Folktale.* Austin, 1968.

Rabkin, Eric. *The Fantastic in Literature.* Princeton, 1976.

Ramey Mollenkott, Virginia. *The Divine Feminine: The Biblical Imagery of God as Female.* New York, 1989. Originally published in German in 1983.

Rapoport-Albert, Ada. "Heʿarot le-Maʾamaro shel Y. Liebes." *Zion* 46 (1981): 346–51.

Ribbat, Ernst. *Ludwig Tieck: Studien zur Konzeption und Praxis romantischen Poesie.* Kronberg, 1978.

Roskies, David R. *A Bridge of Longing: The Lost Art of Yiddish Storytelling.* Cambridge, 1995.

Rotenberg, Mordechai. *Dialogue with Deviance: The Hasidic Ethic and the Theory of Social Contraction.* Philadelphia, 1973.

Sander, Lorand. "Dream Interpretation in the Talmud." *International Journal of Psychoanalysis* 38 (1957): 92–97.

Sade, Pinhas, ed. *Tikkun ha-Lev.* Jerusalem, 1982.

Schatz-Uffenheimer, Rivka. *Ha-Hasidut ke-Mystika.* Jerusalem, 1968.

———, ed. *Maggid Devarav le-Yaʿakov.* Jerusalem, 1976.

Schoenfeld, Elishevʿa. "Maʿasiyat Shivʿat ha-Kabbzanim shel R. Nahman me-Bratslav." *Yedʿa ʿAm* 11, no. 30 (1956).

Scholem, Gershom. *Kabbalah.* Jerusalem, 1974.

———. *Major Trends in Jewish Mysticism.* 1941. Reprint, New York, 1954.

———. *The Messianic Idea in Judaism*. New York, 1960.
———. *On the Kabbalah and its Symbolism*. New York, 1965.
———. *The Origins of the Kabbalah*. 1962. Reprint, Princeton, 1987. Originally published in German in 1960.
———. *Pirkei Yesod be-Havanat ha-Kabbalah u-Semaleha*. Jerusalem, 1976.
Schweikle, Gunther, and Irmgard Schweikle. *Metzlern Literatur Lexikon*. Stuttgart, 1984.
Shmeruk, Chone. *Sifrut Yiddish: Perakim be-Toledoteha*. Tel Aviv, 1978.
Stace, W. T. *Mysticism and Philosophy*. London, 1961.
Steinsaltz, Adin. *The Tales of Rabbi Nachman of Bratslav*. Translated by Yehuda Hanegbi et al. Northvane and London, 1993.
———. *Shishah me-Sippurei ha-Maʿasiyot shel R. Nahman me-Bratslav*. Jerusalem, 1981.
Taylor, Ronald. "Romantic Music." In *The Romantic Period in Germany,* edited by S. Prawer, 282–304. New York, 1970.
Tishby, Isaiah. "Ha-Raʿayon ha-Meshihi ve-ha-Megammot ha-Meshihiot be-Zemihat ha-Hasidut." *Zion* 32 (1967): 1–45.
———. *Netivei Emmunah ve-Minut*. Ramat Gan, 1964.
———. *Torat ha-Rʿa ve-ha-Kelippah be-Kabbalat ha-ARI*. Jerusalem, 1984.
———. *The Wisdom of the Zohar.* Translated by David Goldstein. 3 vols. Oxford, 1989.
Tishby, Isaiah, and Joseph Dan. "Hasidut." In *Ha-Encyclopedia ha-ʿIvrit,* 17:755–821. Jerusalem and Tel Aviv, 1964.
Todorov, Tzvetan. *The Fantastic: A Structural Approach to a Literary Genre*. Translated by R. Howard. Ithaca, 1970.
———. *Introduction à la litterature fantastique*. Paris, 1970.
———. *Mikhail Bakhtin: The Dialogical Principle*. Translated by Wlod Godzich. Minneapolis, 1984.
Trainer, James. "The Märchen." In *The Romantic Period in Germany,* edited by S. Prawer, pp. 97–121. New York, 1970.
Trible, Phyllis. *God and the Rhetoric of Sexuality*. London, 1978.
von Franz, Marie-Louise. *The Problem of the Feminine in Fairy Tales*. Dallas, 1972.
Urbach, Elimelekh Efraim. *The Sages: Their Concepts and Beliefs*. Translated by Israel Abrahams. Jerusalem, 1975.
Waggoner, Diana. *The Hills of Faraway: A Guide to Fantasy*. New York, 1978.
Waskow, Arthur. "Feminist Judaism: Restoration of the Moon." In *On Being a Jewish Feminist,* ed. S. Heschel, 261–72. New York, 1983.
Weiss, Joseph. *Mehkarim be-Hasidut Bratslav*. Jerusalem, 1974.
Wellek, René. "The Concept of Romanticism in Literary History." In *Romanticism: Points of View,* edited by R. F. Gleckner and G. E. Enscoe. Detroit, 1975.
Wertheim, Aaron. *Halakhot ve-Halikhot be-Hasidut*. Jerusalem, 1960.

Whurl, Paul Wolfgang. *E. T. A. Hoffmann, Der goldene Topf: Erlauterungen und Dokumente.* Stuttgart, 1982.
Zeitlin, Hillel. *'Al Gevul Shenei 'Olamot.* Tel Aviv, 1976.
Zornberg, Avivah Gottlieb. *Genesis: The Beginning of Desire.* Philadelphia, 1995.

INDEX OF SUBJECTS

Index prepared by Mr. David Kirschen, to whom the author here expresses her gratitude. [O.W.]

INDEX OF SOURCES

Rabbinic Sources

Mystical Sources

Hasidic Sources

Bratslav Sources